THE ESSENTIAL KROPOTKIN

THE ESSENTIAL KROPOTKIN

Edited by

EMILE CAPOUYA AND KEITHA TOMPKINS

LIVERIGHT NEW YORK

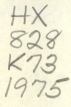

Copyright © 1975 by Emile Capouya and Keitha Tompkins

FIRST EDITION

Library of Congress Cataloging in Publication Data
Kropotkin, Petr Alekseevich, kni̇az', 1842–1921.
    The essential Kropotkin.

    1. Anarchism and anarchists. 2. Socialism.
3. Social history—20th century. I. Capouya, Emile,
ed. II. Tompkins, Keitha, ed. III. Title.
HX828.K73   1975   320.5′7   74–28041
ISBN 0–87140–591–1
ISBN 0–87140–096–0 pbk.

Published simultaneously in Canada
by George J. McLeod Limited, Toronto

PRINTED IN THE UNITED STATES OF AMERICA

1 2 3 4 5 6 7 8 9 0

Contents

Introduction

The emancipation of the human race from social and industrial servitude was the common aim of revolutionaries in the socialist tradition from 1848 to 1917. Of those revolutionaries, only the Marxians, and their spiritual heirs in the middle years of the twentieth century, had great success in accomplishing political revolution; the Soviet Union and its allies in Eastern Europe and the People's Republic of China are monuments to the practical efficacy of the theory that the state is a proper instrument for bringing about social change.

As for the anarchist strain of the socialist tradition, that movement flourished up to 1917, giving serious promise of achieving fundamental change by means of its own organizations and in keeping with its own conception of the nature of human nature. But the Russian Revolution, which in its early stages was as much a ratification of anarchist theory—or none—as of Marxist doctrine, was soon taken in hand by the Bolsheviks and directed with inspired political and military skill to its eventual triumph. At that point the attraction of the Leninist idea of the revolutionary state proved irresistible to the greatest number on the left. That, coupled with the forcible suppression, by imprisonment, judicial murder, assassination, or summary execution of the anarchists themselves— first in the Soviet Union, then in the United States, and finally in Spain—put an end to anarchism as an organized political force. And with that quietus came an almost universal effacement, in the imagination of the Left, of the long record of thought and struggle of the libertarian socialists. The bequest of a number of theoreticians of genius, and of a host of devoted militants, lived on only in the minds of a few sectaries, benevolent Odd Fellows niched inconspicuously in the interstices of the more or less totalitarian industrialized societies—capitalist or communist—that rule the modern age.

And yet, in 1974 a specter haunts—not Europe merely, as in Marx's famous phrase—but the world. The specter of the libertarian creed, exorcized again and again with legal sanctions or rites of blood, has risen once more, evoked by the social pressures within industrialized nations. Groping adumbrations of anarchist ideas appear again and again among persons cut off from all connection with the anarchist tradition, who painfully reinvent in response to the force of circumstance the principles developed over a century and a half of the history of a great social movement. In the age of totalitarianism, anarchist themes are once more on the order of the day—not, in the main, as advanced by living anarchists, but thrown up among human beings of the most diverse circumstances, temperament, and opinion who feel in their soul the intimation of the end of the human experiment—by war, by the despoiling of the whole earth, by the progressive enslavement of mankind to the machine in the name of rationalization of industry and of ever-expanding physical production. It is as if the theories of a Godwin, a Proudhon, a Bakunin, a Kropotkin, were too profound and too far seeing to find the requisite points of leverage in the immature forms of industrial organization that those thinkers had before their eyes. Only in our own time are the human contradictions of the system, under their capitalist and communist forms alike, sufficiently developed to answer fully to the critical analysis proposed by anarchism. It is at this moment that a mere listing of the problems universally acknowledged to be the most fateful, corresponding point by point with the strictures and solutions advanced by anarchism, amounts to a clear political and social agenda.

First, a number of issues directly connected with the size of human populations in relation to the limits of available natural resources: Is the formula of Malthus—that the food supply expands arithmetically while population grows by geometric progression—a general and absolute rule or one of limited applicability? The detailed answer given by Peter Kropotkin amounts to a demonstration that the Malthusian doctrine describes the demographic profile of capitalist society in particular, reflecting, among other factors, the consequences of the international division of labor brought about by economic forces which are more or less peculiar to capitalism, and to which finance capital and industrial capital are peculiarly responsive.

Again, is the minute subdivision of the labor process within the boundaries of each nation, and within industries and trades, and indeed within the soul of the individual workman, an inevitable feature of advanced industrial societies? The response of anarchist theory is that the reduction of the worker to no more than a source of undifferentiated labor power (here Bakunin and Kropotkin followed Marx implicitly, and if they did so without acknowledgment it may have been as much because they regarded his doctrine as being self-evident as that they were moved by political partisanship) is the essential feature of one historically specific mode of production—the capitalist mode. (It seems scarcely necessary to remark that the capitalist mode of production has been adopted by those advanced industrial nations that call themselves communist or socialist.) The ends achieved by the system are an astounding proliferation of certain classes of goods, a concentration of political and economic power in fewer and fewer hands, and a relative impoverishment—despite so-called high standards of living—of the working population. That last effect, quite palpable to the worker but generally beyond the ken of middle-class sociologists, operates in two unexpected ways: first, through the degradation of the processes of work, so that a worker cannot aspire to a minimum of creativity in his daily task; then, through the intensification of the work so degraded, to the point that it degrades the worker's character, stultifies him with the hebetude of endlessly repetitive activity, cutting him off from the possibility of self-cultivation, and from the possibility of self-respect and political initiative in his quality of man and citizen. And that helotization of the worker is an immediate function of his role in the process of production, quite without reference to the formal aspect of his impoverishment—that is, the terms of trade that he is powerless to alter, the terms on which he sells his labor in the market and buys his sustenance in the market.

On this general issue, the starting point for the anarchist thinkers was the paradox resumed by Henry George at the turn of the century in the formula, "Progress and Poverty"; the seeming contradiction that Franklin Delano Roosevelt alluded to several generations later in reminding us that one-third of the nation, in the richest country in the world, was ill-fed, ill-clothed, and ill-housed; the anomaly rediscovered at the very height of the Great American Celebration by Michael Harrington, and set down in his book, *The Other America*—that poverty and the ghetto were keeping pace with the long bull market and the affluent suburb, that the American economic system appeared to deal out with the impartiality of physical laws consistent proportions of want and obloquy on the one hand and of luxury and uneasy privilege on the other.

To the demoralization, stultification, and relative penury that are the lot of the worker in the industrialized nations, Kropotkin opposed what he regarded as a perfectly attainable ideal. He began by tracing the effects of carrying on industrial production and commercial exchange in the manner developed under capitalism, and he demonstrated that, for the great majority, the activity was necessarily self-defeating. For instance, it was generally accepted—and still is—that simply on the material level it "did not pay" for England to produce her own foodstuffs; it did pay for her to export manufactured goods (or even pedigreed cattle, for breeding purposes) and buy foodstuffs abroad. But an odd result of the policy was that the average Englishman was nourished on bread and dripping. That fact sets the concept of profitability in a new light. Some Englishmen, indeed, were lavishly rewarded by the system, and could afford to feed their children so that they grew to be taller by a head than other people's children. But most of their fellows contributed their labor and their lives of deprivation to procure meat, vegetables, and fruit for the favored few; the small stature and poor teeth of *their* children were a measure of how imperfectly adjusted to their needs was the system of international production and exchange that assured Britain's "favorable balance of trade."

Views and arguments related to many aspects of Kropotkin's social thought, expressed in books and pamphlets separated by as much as four decades, coalesce here to suggest a full solution to the problem posed by Malthus, showing again that his premises were not absolute but contingent. If the arable land of England, and those portions once arable but long ago converted to pasture and woodland (the process was well under way, of course, before the passage of the Enclosure Acts which gave it formal sanction), were seized, expropriated by the people of England, one basis of the profitability of exporting manufactured goods and importing food would be destroyed. And if the expropriated lands were cultivated in accordance with modern principles, they could support with their product many times the present population.

Now, by "modern principles" Kropotkin did not mean the kind of intensive agriculture dependent on chemical fertilizer, whose immediate advantage in raising gross productivity had set the pattern for advanced agriculture everywhere—a pattern of progressive destruction of the soil and progressive degradation of the quality of the crop. The economic cost of chemical fertilizer, its bad effects upon soil, even the use of natural deposits like nitrates in the form of guano, which made agriculture dependent on a species of mining that was bound in the foreseeable future to exhaust such resources completely—all these objections Kropotkin advanced against the practice of farming with chemicals some fifty years before there was a body of respectable opinion on his side of the question; indeed, the chemical fertilizer industry is still in our own day endowing chairs in universities and granting funds for experiments whose intended effect is to sustain the demand for their product. But Kropotkin was an early convert to what is now called organic farming and gardening. He had seen that the market gardeners in the suburbs of Paris made their own soil from manure—so that, as Kropotkin observed, they could, if they wished, commence operations upon an asphalt pavement—and raised crops of vegetables and fruits of the first quality in astounding abundance, with no expenditure for artificial fertilizer, in the space of a few square yards, feeding Paris and exporting the surplus to England.

In *Fields, Factories, and Workshops,* he gives the statistics of the productivity of the French gardeners and suggests how their techniques could be adapted to grain crops; he also tabulates the yearly decline in the acreage that England had allotted to wheat in the last decades of the nineteenth century, till the point was reached at which the country became a regular importer of wheat on a large scale. And all this time the price of grain was rising in Britain. It is in terms of that Q.E.D. that we are to understand his prescribing the expropriation by the people of the arable land of England, and the development of an agriculture that would be truly modern because it would be richly productive without injury to the capital that is the common patrimony, the soil that supports us.

Kropotkin was acutely aware that the practice of an agriculture that had come more and more to resemble an extractive industry had two kinds of unfortunate consequences. The first, as we have come to know feelingly in our own time, was the desecration of the environment. The second was the rise of extensive monocultures, which by their nature contribute greatly to the impoverishment of the soil, but also breed a rural proletariat whose status and fortunes are particularly depressed, the manpower necessary to run what Carey McWilliams' classic phrase describes as "factories in the fields." The decentralization of agriculture and the development of a mixed agriculture were Kropotkin's ideal solutions to both these problems, the environmental and the social; and those solutions were a feature of his larger conception of a mixed economy, as much agricultural as industrial, whose smaller, decentralized units would be favorable to personal development in that they would substitute individual initiative for regimentation—immediately, in the planning and carrying out of the processes of work, and in the long run on a larger field of human activity because of the influence of the kind of political organization with which they would be most compatible. Battalions of machine operatives and field hands sort well with the modern totalitarian systems—those of a relatively amiable cast and those that are naked tyrannies—which almost without exception derive their authority, in theory, from the consent of the governed. In practice, of course, the regimes in question have substituted for the consent of the governed the principle of "virtual representation" that Parliament invented for the benefit of the American colonies. The irony is that the Americans, who made a revolution in order to do away with the sham of virtual representation, live under just such a system to this day, and it is better luck than management—the result of a blessed historical accident—that gives them a milder government to resent than that which the peoples of the Soviet Union are called upon to endure.

Kropotkin did not care for virtual representation because he did not care for class rule, whether on the part of industrial and commercial oligarchies or of a vanguard revolutionary party. He could not but have been familiar with Bakunin's prophetic objection to the Marxist theory of revolution: that the party would soon substitute itself for the people, the central committee for the party, and a smaller cabal or an individual tyrant for the central committee. Leon Trotsky took up the identical formulation during the period of his differences with Lenin before 1917—and after 1917 contributed with all the power of his military and political genius to the fulfillment of the prophecy, which included his own eventual discomfiture and brought calamitous misfortune to the citizens of the Soviet Union.

Why was Kropotkin, almost alone among the committed revolutionaries in the socialist tradition, so penetrated with the intimate connections among the organization of industry and agriculture, the consequences for the land and for the personal fate of the workers, and the nature of the political administration that would lend formality and sanction to those effects? Or rather, why did the Marxians, with the advantage they enjoyed of following the supernal political and social intelligence of modern times—Marx himself— fail to recognize as Kropotkin did that if men and women were ever to come into their full humanity, it must be by virtue of a different kind of social order than the one envisaged by the majority faction within the International Workingmen's Association?

The reasons are complex, but they can be summarized without undue distortion. To begin with, Marxism itself was imbued with the religion of progress, cast in nineteenth-century terms, and departing from them only in that it meant to extend to every human being the privileged existence made possible by the Industrial Revolution—in essence, freedom from want. This creed, we may remark at once, is at bottom the merest good sense of social hygiene, near kin to the ideal of human dignity that effected the American Revolution, the French Revolution, the Russian Revolution, and the Chinese Revolution. But the fact that Marxism was very much in the spirit of the nineteenth century, to the point of sharing the assumptions of persons and institutions far removed from any inclination toward deliberate social revolution, ensured that it would represent in many respects a kind of postgraduate capitalism, and exalt, in the name of the rationalization of industry, the idea of salvation by the machine. The spirit of quantification, the monetization of all values, the quasi-sacred status of expanded material production—these, in the short run of politics, were for Marx, that genuine humanist and master ironist, as much "the Law and the Prophets" as they were for the capitalist entrepreneurs whose idolatrous devotions he contemned and ridiculed.

In contrast, the anarchist strain of socialism was a form of romantic reaction, the necessary antithesis to the religion of mechanical progress. Marxism was fully in accord with what appeared to the nineteenth century to be the wave of the future, and in the twentieth century it has been in accord with the consequences of the systematic regimentation of human beings in the name of increased production—so much so that a large manufacturing plant in the Soviet Union (save for some edulcorations or exacerbations like organized cultural pursuits or mandatory political activities) is indistinguishable in its operations from one in Western Europe or the United States. Perhaps because of the social origins of the persons most influential in the anarchist movement during its classic period, Russian aristocrats and Western European craftsmen, neither of which orders of men feels much natural sympathy with the mechanization of the economy, the social order, and personal life, anarchism's retrograde impulse very early took on the aspect of a romantic protest against the *deus ex machina* of the age. In so doing it assured its peculiar relevance for the latter half of the twentieth century, which, pinched by its special predicament, has brought persons unacquainted with the anarchist tradition to improvise, piecemeal and helter-skelter, the reforms proposed with magisterial scope by Peter Kropotkin.

For the anarchist theorist, moreover, the mixed economy had a particular role to play in the nurture and culture of human beings. Even as the effects of the present division of labor are represented on the international, the national, the regional, and ultimately the personal scale, it was Kropotkin's ideal to exchange specialization of function for a more liberal and liberating activity, whose consequences would revolutionize the lives of individuals and relations among the countries of the world. On the individual level, he hoped for a system of production in which every citizen might contribute to the work of agriculture and industry alike, uniting in his own person planning and execution, theory and practice. The consequences for organizing formal education are obvious, and Kropotkin drew those consequences. He proposed that the acquisition of manual skill, and developing the ability to do physically demanding work be as much a concern of the school curriculum as the acquisition of theoretical knowledge. He also proposed that the processes by which men secure food, clothing, and shelter should be made familiar to every citizen in their connections with the intellectual systems of mathematics, physics, and chemistry, so that useful work might be illuminated with understanding, be better done, and make better men of the doers.

Contrast that with our current educational practice, in which some favored young persons among the poor attend trade schools

where they learn, mostly by rote, the operations required of workers in industries that are expressly organized to minimize the necessity for intelligence or initiative on the part of the workers; in
which favored young persons in the middle class learn, mostly by
rote, the theoretical knowledge that is supposed to equip them for
carrying on one or another profession; in which the rich are exposed to literary classics and to the arts and sciences as a preparation for finance, politics, or mere ownership—and left in salutary
ignorance about the social cost of their own maintenance; in which
the great majority is fitted—by years of custodial discipline and
systematic indoctrination rather than by anything that might properly be called education—for the tasks of clerkship, the service
jobs, the thousand and one debasing forms of alienated labor that
are required by our industrial and commercial system; in which a
substantial number are prepared, formally and informally, for lives
of destitution, lives on the margin of the industrial and commercial
system, spent in urban and rural slums, the armed forces, and the
jails.

The education of the mind, the senses, the muscles, familiarity
with science as with physical labor, the cultivation of the sympathies, of the humane imagination—these things Kroptokin expected,
not unreasonably, to have their effect first upon the individual
personality, then upon the character of communities and regions,
ultimately upon a world governed by an ideal of the physical,
intellectual, and moral well-being of its inhabitants.

A Utopian vision? Undoubtedly. But scarcely dismissable on that
account. Firstly, there is in it no hint of an ignoble or simply
unworthy appeal, no suggestion that work can or should be rendered superfluous by the efficient organization of computers and
servomechanisms, no sordid arrangements to purchase a meaningless leisure for a race that is to be progressively divorced from an
intelligent concern with the sources and processes of its own material sustenance. Again, the clear egalitarian bias that suggests that
every person is best employed when his work requires him to use
mind and body alike, outdoors and within doors, as planner and
executor, does not deal in the secret flattery of doctrines that advance the desirability of hierarchies. Kropotkin's vision is demanding, athletic. In his Utopia, distinction is available to everyone—
that is, for everyone it must be and can be earned.

Then, Kropotkin shows a psychological acuity most often lack-
ing in apologists for the way we live now, and in reformers, too. He
understands that the patterns of human nature that most thinkers
accept as given, once and for all, are as much social artifacts as
they are the result of physical structure and instinct. The defeated,
the incurious, the bellicose, the spiteful character appear to him to

be examples of social pathology. He had experienced at firsthand some of the conditions and institutions that are the nurseries of such pathology—prisons, slums, armies, invidious class distinction, want, demeaning toil. He is not so foolish as to imagine that such things have no effect upon the hearts and minds of the human beings who are exposed to them, nor that those exposed to them have by statistical coincidence and inherited talent a special predisposition toward degradation that is denied to persons more fortunately situated in the social order. He assumes that a man or woman not already spiritually crippled by a lifetime of abuse is likely to respond positively to a pattern of living that demands the exercise and expansion of the most manlike faculties—will hunger for just such exercise and seek it fervently. Those who are in the happy position of being able to entertain argument on this subject (most are too overwhelmed by the effects of their social disabilities to do so) are sure to make that very assumption about themselves, that is that they themselves respond to stimulating occupation, to the possibility of using their imagination and initiative. But they are not so sure to extend the principle to their fellow human beings. What is suspect about every form of argument for the genetic inferiority of this or that class or race of mankind is that it is always put forward about other people, never about ourselves. In this instance, too, Kropotkin's plain style is the expression of a most sophisticated spirit: he understands that the favorable view that each of us takes of his own character and actions is not the end of the matter but, in ethics at least, the beginning, requiring to be extended to a reasonably benevolent view of the rest of the species. And he appears not to have struck any compelling reason for supposing that bad morals may be good science.

In his *Memoirs of a Revolutionist,* and again in the essays collected under the title *In Russian and French Prisons,* Kropotkin gave an account of an experience which had been shared by generations of political radicals, including a great many adherents of socialism—the experience of arrest, conviction, and incarceration. Here again he is very nearly alone in having understood the social import of imprisonment in terms that are consistent with the humane passion which is the emotional driving force of socialism. His observations and conclusions, arrived at by the turn of the century, are far in advance of what now goes by the name of modern penology. Having noticed that the great majority of prisoners comes from one social class, and that their number can be accurately predicted from year to year, it was clear to him that the existence of that class was the true ground of antisocial actions—not the bad bloodlines dear to the sociology of the day, carrying the psychic deformations categorized by Max Nordau and Lombroso, and appealed to as a matter of course by Zola. What scientific prejudice looked upon as natural and inevitable, the concentration of bad bloodlines in the poorest class, Kropotkin saw as a comforting illusion. The conditions of life to which that class was subjected would amply explain the incidence of crime within it; there was no reason to appeal to the role of heredity, which in any case had been reduced in Nordau's popular system to a single effect, "degeneration."

Given want, ignorance, and spiritual deprivation, only exceptional individuals among the poor could hope to secure themselves against the fate of their class, whose natural condition was sporadic employment as the "reserve army of industry." The means of life were in the hands of banks, landowners, and industrialists—and their deputies, shopkeepers and the owners of rented dwellings. In a money economy that rationed out grossly inadequate sums to a large portion of the working class, the demands for cash that shopkeepers and landlords made of all would-be purchasers and tenants left a substantial number with insufficient food, poor clothing, and miserable shelter. The consequences for that large group were general desperation, a high disease and mortality rate, prostitution on a scale scarcely conceivable in these more affluent times (mainly because industry has now found profitable uses for female labor), a large number of crimes against property, as with unconscious wit we are accustomed to call them, and a much smaller but still appalling number of crimes against persons—in those days as in ours almost uniformly crimes of the poor against the poor.

By a kind of shorthand, Kropotkin represented as a single quality the psychological traits that might possibly help a poor man or woman to escape the statistical catastrophe connected with membership in the lowest class. That is, singular intelligence, application, ruthlessness, and so forth he resumed under the term "will"— the exercise of a steady determination to perdure in the midst of misery while avoiding its almost unavoidable consequences. The discipline of the prison—of all prisons everywhere—Kropotkin rightly understood as designed specifically to crush the will of the prisoner. Insofar as the process was effective, and over the long run it is very generally effective, its final result is a prisoner trained to abandon forethought, initiative, self-reliance, and all the other qualities implicit in the concept of will. Accordingly, the sure fruits of the prison system are recidivism—a statistically predictable number of continual offenders and offenses—and the existence of a special criminal culture. That culture is indeed socially heritable, whereas the supposedly heritable "criminal tendency" is biological nonsense. (The Y chromosome, that triumph of contemporary scientific sociology, had not been invented in Kropotkin's time, which saved him

the labor of exploding it as a significant factor in promoting criminality. *Plus ça change. . . .*)

Kropotkin's conception of crime and its origins identified two
contributing causes. The first was the social order, which depended
absolutely on the maldistribution of socially created wealth; that is,
the property system, which concentrated the ownership of the
means of life within a small group and gave its members power
over their social inferiors. The laws that reflected this state of affairs
were designed to protect and perpetuate it, and Kropotkin regarded
the transgressing of those laws as an inevitable consequence of the
instincts for self-defense, self-enlargement, and self-realization. His
formulation of this aspect of the question argues that the law is
literally the origin of crime; it defines all crimes, inventing new
categories from time to time and dropping others—for the most
part in the interest of the ruling class—and is the point of contact
and conflict between the people and the state. The complexity of
the law, and, humanly speaking, its arbitrary character, make crime
a by-product of the normal functioning of society. The cure for the
kind of crime that is a perennial feature of the social order and the
legal system that defends it is simply the abolition of that social
order and that legal system. If there is no invidious affluence, if
there is no implacable economic pressure, most of the actions classified as crimes will not occur.

Clearly, Kropotkin did not believe in the Fall of Man—perhaps
because in practice only the poor seemed to have inherited Adam's
curse. And if the solution proposed by Kropotkin strikes the reader
as too sweeping and simpleminded, a panacea rather than a specific, let him call to mind the part of our experience that nevertheless confirms it. The law itself, as we all know perfectly well, makes
one large class of crime happen simply by defining it as crime:
when the production and sale of alcohol were declared unlawful in
the United States, two crimes were created *ipso facto* and on a
grand scale, moonshining and bootlegging. And we know very well
that social inequities are the absolutely essential conditions for
other varieties of offenses: rich women do not become prostitutes,
poor women do; rich men do not engage in mugging or burglary,
poor men do. And on the other hand, stock fraud, defalcation, or
price-fixing are not offenses that are within the reach of most of us.
These practices are restricted to persons who have an appreciable
share of economic power already and are in a position to take
advantage of their fellows in good fortune. These facts, of course,
are so plain and so universally understood as to be omitted from
most discussions of the subject, so that it is worth remarking on
them in the most naïve way. Kropotkin's naïveté is a good part of
his genius.

The second cause of crime in Kropotkin's view is an indirect result of social arrangements adopted for the benefit of the ruling class. That is the moral degradation entailed upon the working class not by hard conditions merely but by hard conditions that are mostly man-made and which their victims are nevertheless powerless to change. The habit and the expectation of failure are the most negative aspect of what it is now fashionable to call the culture of poverty. That culture no doubt compares favorably at some points with the culture of invidious affluence—it is hard for the disadvantaged to be as selfishly obtuse about the living conditions of the majority of their fellows because they experience those conditions themselves—but on the whole the moral and esthetic advantage lies with the comfortable classes, just as one would expect. What did we imagine was being mass-produced in the slums, sweetness and light? We knew better than that, but were accustomed to look on such things as being inevitable and therefore not our business. Kropotkin regards the demoralization of the poor as perhaps the worst social evil, the more so in that it is enforced by the common modes of social discipline. Among that class, crimes of violence occur in a much higher proportion than in any other, even when entirely divorced from the prospect of material gain, as in robbery or extortion. Murder (as a matter of statistics the victim is most often a relative or friend of the murderer), assault, rape— these are crimes that testify in Kropotkin's terms to mental and moral sickness, the greater part of which he attributes to the living conditions of the working class. It is a matter for wonder that social theorists should prefer to this reasonable supposition one or another variety of the theory that the poor—meaning most people —are a vast pool of unfavorable genes, a theory, incidentally, that libels the grandparents of most of the theorists in question.

It is striking that Kropotkin's method of social analysis was also, and designedly, a method of social therapy. His inveterate habit was to deal with social problems as if they were necessarily susceptible of solution. That would in any case seem to be the part of wisdom, since social phenomena do not generally appear to us to constitute problems until we reach a stage in our evolution that suggests the possibility of making improvements. But, especially in this era of problem-solving, when for two centuries authors have busied themselves with the uniquely modern preoccupation of offering solutions in every department of human affairs, it is easy to overlook a peculiar virtue of Kropotkin's social therapy, and that is its radical, its transcendental character.

Let us consider a familiar case of problem-solving, the concern of that useful class of books whose titles start with the words, "How to." *How to Win Friends and Influence People, How to Get and Keep the Job You Want, How to Make Money in Commodi-*

ties, or even *How to Avoid Probate*. One thing is understood about any book that honorably lives up to a title of this kind: it takes the world and mankind as given, and suggests how the reader can profit by what is given, turning to his personal advantage the unchanging structure of the social universe. The instinct exhibited here is prudential. At its best it can be a form of wisdom—not simply laudable but indispensable to the progress of the human race. Indeed, it is probably the impulse to which we owe the fact that at some point our species came down from the trees and began to devise a more ample culture. The instinct in question takes one step at a time, and over periods measurable on the scale contemplated by geology, accomplishes, in terms of civilization, a work as striking as the raising of a mountain range or the carving of the Grand Canyon. But when mankind has achieved a measure of civilization—some power over natural forces and a degree of self-awareness—the indispensable prudential instinct working through long centuries is no longer adequate. With self-awareness, men's dissatisfactions have grown acute. Intimations of moral possibility not vouchsafed to societies in the savage state exacerbate our present discontents, making them next thing to unbearable.

In the case of our own civilization specifically, another force, and a sinister one, is also at work to intensify the urgency we feel. That is the spiritual underemployment which ravages human beings in industrialized countries, the disease of the will that affects men and women for whom there is no fulfilling occupation, no fulfilling leisure, but only mechanical work and mechanical distractions. Societies so afflicted are more than a little mad, more than a little drawn to self-destruction, as the history of this century must suggest. At such a time the prudential instinct devises atomic weapons and gas chambers, or, with equal innocence and insouciance, data banks and microwave ovens.

In this regard, the prudential instinct seems to pose the question of life in some such terms as these: How to do more cheaply, more efficiently, more effectively, what we are already doing. If we trust blindly to that impulse, two inconveniences are likely to arise in any world that is, like ours, a conditional one. First, the prudential instinct is at war with the ideal of the examined life, whose central question is, how are we to live? That is, not simply, what means shall we adopt, but what means to what end? If our innovations and adaptations are not made in that spirit, then it is a mere accident if to persevere in what we are already doing is not simply to compound a social, political, ethical mistake. Then, it is a matter of experience, especially in an exploitive system directed by the desire for profit, that in innumerable cases practices and products are altered for the worse in the attempt to procure their benefits more cheaply and efficiently in terms of a narrow calculus of money costs. As cheap and efficient methods replace forever the methods and materials adapted to more desirable ends, our standards of what is in fact desirable sink. We forget what is desirable and make do with what is procurable—even developing a refined connoisseurship of the inferior. If we seek a monument, let us bethink ourselves what kind of food affluent Americans have accustomed themselves to find acceptable during the last twenty-five years. Or, if that example appear too trivial, what about the history of the socialist movement during this century of its practical triumph and moral decline? What horrors have socialists not learned to accept, little by little, in the name of socialism?

Peter Kropotkin's attitude appears to be naturally a philosophic one, concentrated upon this central issue. His habit of framing all practical measures in terms of ultimate goals—the habit of a moralist, asking, what is the aim we seek? Is it consistent with our other aims, with our best insights?—is the habit that underlies his method of social criticism and his program of social construction. Not only does that characteristic bent liberate his thought from the hopeless karma entailed upon mere prudential instinct, but it also frees him in an unexpected way for the work of self-analysis that is the beginning of any useful analysis of society.

C. Wright Mills suggested that the task of political sociology was to find the connections between private troubles and public issues; in doing so, the great political theorists always start, like the great poets, from the same point, their sense of the meaning of their own experience. It is that kind of insight that often permits Kropotkin to transcend, like a genuine poet, philosopher, prophet, the habits and interests of his social class, the limitations of his own experience. Kropotkin remarked about the socialist movement in general—of which movement he was, as an anarchist, a conscious, ardent adherent—that its imaginative scope was limited by the social experience of its leaders and doctrinaires, middle class and upper class almost to a man, and imbued with an uncritical faith in theories and social modalities already developed under capitalism.

An argument of the nineteenth century, almost unintelligible today, so far have we lost the genuine impetus toward the reconstruction of society, is that the revolution must not be political only, but social. *La sociale,* the radical Left in France called that needful revolution, omitting the substantive, too well understood as the ground of a thousand debates. *La Sociale* implied, among other things, the abolition of the wage system, for unless the working class were in possession of the means of life, and not simply accorded rations at the discretion of leaders, no fundamental change in the condition of that class could be achieved by whatever revolu-

tion. And the wage system is an integral feature of capitalist organization, but no more so than representative institutions, which are
historically dependent upon so-called free labor—that is, the existence of a proletariat, defined as a class that has nothing but its
labor to sell, and must sell its labor in order to live. In his essay,
"Anarchist Communism", Kropotkin draws the moral, one completely at odds with Marxian socialism:

> Representative government has accomplished its historical
> mission; it has given a mortal blow to court-rule; and by its de-
> bates it has awakened public interest in public questions. But to
> see in it the government of the future socialist society is to com-
> mit a gross error. Each economic phase of life implies its own
> political phase; and it is impossible to touch the very basis of the
> present economic life—private property—without a correspond-
> ing change in the very basis of the political organization. Life al-
> ready shows in which direction the change will be made. Not in
> increasing the powers of the State, but in resorting to free organ-
> ization and free federation in all those branches which are now
> considered as attributes of the State.

And in *Modern Science and Anarchism*, he repeats the argument:

> Socialism, we have said—whatever form it may take in its evo-
> lution towards communism—must find *its own form* of politi-
> cal organization. Serfdom and absolute monarchy have always
> marched hand in hand. The one rendered the other a necessity.
> The same is true of capitalist rule, whose political form is repre-
> sentative government, either in a republic or in a monarchy. This
> is why socialism *cannot* utilize representative government as a
> weapon for liberating labor, just as it cannot utilize the church
> and its theory of divine right, or imperialism and Caesarism, with
> its theory of hierarchy of functionaries, for the same purpose.
> A new form of political organization has to be worked out the
> moment that socialist principles shall enter into our life. And it
> is self-evident that this new form will have to be *more popular,
> more decentralized, and nearer to the folk-mote self-government*
> than representative government can ever be.

Because history, in the capitalist and socialist world alike, has
taken a very different path than that suggested by Kropotkin, the
power of the ruling classes everywhere has grown in our own day
in proportion with the increase in material wealth. That power is
now most dramatically represented by the ability of three governments—swollen and turgid with the wealth produced by their
enormous populations—to destroy the prospects for civilization and
perhaps render the planet uninhabitable in a quarter of an hour.

We are sleepwalkers approaching a precipice, and our judgment of the outcome is clouded both by fear and by the habit of living with the possibility of universal destruction. But so far as it is given to us to see the future, the end of the human experiment may well be at hand. The time accorded us before we are extinguished by the folly of the governments of the world may simply prove too short to allow the social inventiveness of mankind to devise the means of salvation.

But if the sentence is not carried out swiftly, there are strong forces at work that may revoke it. To put the matter plainly, those forces will revoke the sentence by destroying the state, whose ultimate expression is atomic bombs. For modern governments are not only more powerful than governments have ever been, with a more absolute grip on the life of every human being, but they are also more unstable and more vulnerable to revolution. That vulnerability is not confined to the advanced industrial countries of the West; the advances in communications have spread a common consciousness around the world in the last half century—that is the meaning of the most striking political phenomenon of our time, the entry upon the stage of history of brown, black, and yellow men armed with automatic weapons. In our time the government of China is as vulnerable as that of France, or Russia, or the United States. Inflation, industrial depression, pollution of the environment, war, depletion and destruction of natural resources—not only are governments helpless to prevent the social catastrophes that take those varied and closely related forms, but it has become quite clear that the coercive state is itself the origin and instrument of those plagues. Society is indeed the human condition, but the state as an expression of society is no longer viable in the proper sense of the word; it will die. Its death flurries are more and more alarming, and may overwhelm the peoples of the world. Or the peoples of the world may dispatch the moribund state before the atomic arsenals are breached.

History presses upon the modern age as it could not do in any former time, when the state had not yet amassed the totalitarian power that is supported by industrialization. If we are not now in a supreme crisis, mankind has never known any. And it is precisely in this era of forced and sharpened choices that the wisdom and humanity of Kropotkin's vision of man commends itself to us. If we do not look upon ourselves as creatures worth saving—and our sense of worth as individuals and as nations has suffered enormously from the unfulfilled promises of the democratic revolutions —then Kropotkin will appeal to us as no more than a figure of a happier time, when hope was permissible, when men knew no better than to hope. But if we have any remnant of virtue as men and women, then Kropotkin will not serve our nostalgia for a golden time. Instead, his social vision will encourage our self-respect, and his social expedients suggest how we may set about making a society that actively encourages the exercise of generosity, dignity, and honor.

EMILE CAPOUYA
KEITHA TOMPKINS

Part I

Part I

The Spirit of Revolt

There are periods in the life of human society when revolution becomes an imperative necessity, when it proclaims itself as inevitable. New ideas germinate everywhere, seeking to force their way into the light, to find an application in life; everywhere they are opposed by the inertia of those whose interest it is to maintain the old order; they suffocate in the stifling atmosphere of prejudice and traditions. The accepted ideas of the constitution of the State, of the laws of social equilibrium, of the political and economic inter-relations of citzens, can hold out no longer against the implacable criticism which is daily undermining them whenever occasion arises,—in drawing room as in cabaret, in the writings of philosophers as in daily conversation. Political, economic, and social institutions are crumbling; the social structure, having become uninhabitable, is hindering, even preventing the development of the seeds which are being propagated within its damaged walls and being brought forth around them.

The need for a new life becomes apparent. The code of established morality, that which governs the greater number of people in their daily life, no longer seems sufficient. What formerly seemed just is now felt to be a crying injustice. The morality of yesterday is today recognized as revolting immorality. The conflict between new ideas and old traditions flames up in every class of society, in every possible environment, in the very bosom of the family. The son struggles against his father, he finds revolting what his father has all his life found natural; the daughter rebels against the principles which her mother has handed down to her as the result of long experience. Daily, the popular conscience rises up against the scandals which breed amidst the privileged and the leisured, against the crimes committed in the name of *the law of the stronger*, or in order to maintain these privileges. Those who long for the triumph of justice, those who would put new ideas into practice, are soon forced to recognize that the realization of their generous, humanitarian and regenerating ideas cannot take place in a society thus constituted; they perceive the necessity of a revolutionary whirlwind which will sweep away all this rottenness, revive sluggish hearts with its breath, and bring to mankind that spirit of devotion, self-denial, and heroism, without which society sinks through degradation and vileness into complete disintegration.

In periods of frenzied haste toward wealth, of feverish specula-

3

tion and of crisis, of the sudden downfall of great industries and the ephemeral expansion of other branches of production, of scandalous fortunes amassed in a few years and dissipated as quickly, it becomes evident that the economic institutions which control production and exchange are far from giving to society the prosperity which they are supposed to guarantee; they produce precisely the opposite result. Instead of order they bring forth chaos; instead of prosperity, poverty and insecurity; instead of reconciled interests, war; a perpetual war of the exploiter against the worker, of exploiters and of workers among themselves. Human society is seen to be splitting more and more into two hostile camps, and at the same time to be subdividing into thousands of small groups waging merciless war against each other. Weary of these wars, weary of the miseries which they cause, society rushes to seek a new organization; it clamors loudly for a complete remodelling of the system of property ownership, of production, of exchange and all economic relations which spring from it.

The machinery of government, entrusted with the maintenance of the existing order, continues to function, but at every turn of its deteriorated gears it slips and stops. Its working becomes more and more difficult, and the dissatisfaction caused by its defects grows continuously. Every day gives rise to a new demand. "Reform this," "reform that," is heard from all sides. "War, finance, taxes, courts, police, everything must be remodelled, reorganized, established on a new basis," say the reformers. And yet all know that it is impossible to make things over, to remodel anything at all because everything is interrelated; everything would have to be remade at once; and how can society be remodelled when it is divided into two openly hostile camps? To satisfy the discontented would be only to create new malcontents.

Incapable of undertaking reforms, since this would mean paving the way for revolution, and at the same time too impotent to be frankly reactionary, the governing bodies apply themselves to half-measures which can satisfy nobody, and only cause new dissatisfaction. The mediocrities who, in such transition periods, undertake to steer the ship of State, think of but one thing: to enrich themselves against the coming *débâcle*. Attacked from all sides they defend themselves awkwardly, they evade, they commit blunder upon blunder, and they soon succeed in cutting the last rope of salvation; they drown the prestige of the government in ridicule, caused by their own incapacity.

Such periods demand revolution. It becomes a social necessity; the situation itself is revolutionary.

When we study in the works of our greatest historians the genesis and development of vast revolutionary convulsions, we generally find under the heading, "The Cause of the Revolution," a gripping picture of the situation on the eve of events. The misery of the people, the general insecurity, the vexatious measures of the government, the odious scandals laying bare the immense vices of society, the new ideas struggling to come to the surface and repulsed by the incapacity of the supporters of the former régime,— nothing is omitted. Examining this picture, one arrives at the conviction that the revolution was indeed inevitable, and that there was no other way out than by the road of insurrection.

Take, for example, the situation before 1789 as the historians picture it. You can almost hear the peasant complaining of the salt tax, of the tithe, of the feudal payments, and vowing in his heart an implacable hatred towards the feudal baron, the monk, the monopolist, the bailiff. You can almost see the citizen bewailing the loss of his municipal liberties, and showering maledictions upon the king. The people censure the queen; they are revolted by the reports of ministerial action, and they cry out continually that the taxes are intolerable and revenue payments exorbitant, that crops are bad and winters hard, that provisions are too dear and the monopolists too grasping, that the village lawyer devours the peasant's crops and the village constable tries to play the role of a petty king, that even the mail service is badly organized and the employees too lazy. In short, nothing works well, everybody complains. "It can last no longer, it will come to a bad end," they cry everywhere.

But, between this pacific arguing and insurrection or revolt, there is a wide abyss,—that abyss which, for the greatest part of humanity, lies between reasoning and action, thought and will,—the urge to act. How has this abyss been bridged? How is it that men who only yesterday were complaining quietly of their lot as they smoked their pipes, and the next moment were humbly saluting the local guard and *gendarme* whom they had just been abusing,—how is it that these same men a few days later were capable of seizing their scythes and their iron-shod pikes and attacking in his castle the lord who only yesterday was so formidable? By what miracle were these men, whose wives justly called them cowards, transformed in a day into heroes, marching through bullets and cannon balls to the conquest of their rights? How was it that *words,* so often spoken and lost in the air like the empty chiming of bells, were changed into *actions?*

The answer is easy.

Action, the continuous action, ceaselessly renewed, of minorities brings about this transformation. Courage, devotion, the spirit of sacrifice, are as contagious as cowardice, submission, and panic.

What forms will this action take? All forms,—indeed, the most varied forms, dictated by circumstances, temperament, and the means at disposal. Sometimes tragic, sometimes humorous, but always daring; sometimes collective, sometimes purely individual, this policy of action will neglect none of the means at hand, no event of public life, in order to keep the spirit alive, to propagate and find expression for dissatisfaction, to excite hatred against exploiters, to ridicule the government and expose its weakness, and above all and always, by actual example, to awaken courage and fan the spirit of revolt.

When a revolutionary situation arises in a country, before the spirit of revolt is sufficiently awakened in the masses to express itself in violent demonstrations in the streets or by rebellions and uprisings, it is through *action* that minorities succeed in awakening that feeling of independence and that spirit of audacity without which no revolution can come to a head.

Men of courage, not satisfied with words, but ever searching for the means to transform them into action,—men of integrity for whom the act is one with the idea, for whom prison, exile, and death are preferable to a life contrary to their principles,—intrepid souls who know that it is necessary to *dare* in order to succeed,— these are the lonely sentinels who enter the battle long before the masses are sufficiently roused to raise openly the banner of insurrection and to march, arms in hand, to the conquest of their rights.

In the midst of discontent, talk, theoretical discussions, an individual or collective act of revolt supervenes, symbolizing the dominant aspirations. It is possible that at the beginning the masses will remain indifferent. It is possible that while admiring the courage of the individual or the group which takes the initiative, the masses will at first follow those who are prudent and cautious, who will immediately describe this act as "insanity" and say that "those madmen, those fanatics will endanger everything."

They have calculated so well, those prudent and cautious men, that their party, slowly pursuing its work would, in a hundred years, two hundred years, three hundred years perhaps, succeed in conquering the whole world,—and now the unexpected intrudes! The unexpected, of course, is whatever has not been expected by them,—those prudent and cautious ones! Whoever has a slight knowledge of history and a fairly clear head knows perfectly well from the beginning that theoretical propaganda for revolution will necessarily express itself in action long before the theoreticians have decided that the moment to act has come. Nevertheless, the cautious theoreticians are angry at these madmen, they excommunicate them, they anathematize them. But the madmen win sympathy, the mass of the people secretly applaud their courage, and they find imitators. In proportion as the pioneers go to fill the jails and the penal colonies, others continue their work; acts of illegal protest, of revolt, of vengeance, multiply.

Indifference from this point on is impossible. Those who at the beginning never so much as asked what the "madmen" wanted, are compelled to think about them, to discuss their ideas, to take sides for or against. By actions which compel general attention, the new idea seeps into people's minds and wins converts. One such act may, in a few days, make more propaganda than thousands of pamphlets.

Above all, it awakens the spirit of revolt: it breeds daring. The old order, supported by the police, the magistrates, the *gendarmes* and the soldiers, appeared unshakable, like the old fortress of the Bastille, which also appeared impregnable to the eyes of the unarmed people gathered beneath its high walls equipped with loaded cannon. But soon it became apparent that the established order has not the force one had supposed. One courageous act has sufficed to upset in a few days the entire governmental machinery, to make the colossus tremble; another revolt has stirred a whole province into turmoil, and the army, till now always so imposing, has retreated before a handful of peasants armed with sticks and stones. The people observe that the monster is not so terrible as they thought; they begin dimly to perceive that a few energetic efforts will be sufficient to throw it down. Hope is born in their hearts, and let us remember that if exasperation often drives men to revolt, it is always hope, the hope of victory, which makes revolutions.

The government resists; it is savage in its repressions. But, though formerly persecution killed the energy of the oppressed, now, in periods of excitement, it produces the opposite result. It provokes new acts of revolt, individual and collective; it drives the rebels to heroism; and in rapid succession these acts spread, become general, develop. The revolutionary party is strengthened by elements which up to this time were hostile or indifferent to it. The general disintegration penetrates into the government, the ruling classes, the privileged; some of them advocate resistance to the limit; others are in favor of concessions; others, again, go so far as to declare themselves ready to renounce their privileges for the moment, in order to appease the spirit of revolt, hoping to dominate again later on. The unity of the government and the privileged class is broken.

The ruling classes may also try to find safety in savage reaction. But it is now too late; the battle only becomes more bitter, more terrible, and the revolution which is looming will only be more bloody. On the other hand, the smallest concession of the governing classes, since it comes too late, since it has been snatched in struggle, only awakes the revolutionary spirit still more. The common people, who formerly would have been satisfied with the smallest concession, observe now that the enemy is wavering; they foresee victory, they feel their courage growing, and the same men who were formerly crushed by misery and were content to sigh in secret, now lift their heads and march proudly to the conquest of a better future.

Finally the revolution breaks out, the more terrible as the preceding struggles were bitter.

The direction which the revolution will take depends, no doubt, upon the sum total of the various circumstances that determine the coming of the cataclysm. But it can be predicted in advance, according to the vigor of revolutionary action displayed in the preparatory period by the different progressive parties.

One party may have developed more clearly the theories which it defines and the program which it desires to realize; it may have made propaganda actively, by speech and in print. But it may not have sufficiently expressed its aspirations in the open, on the street, by actions which *embody the thought it represents*; it has done little, or it has done nothing against those who are its principal enemies; it has not attacked the institutions which it wants to demolish; its strength has been in theory, not in action; it has contributed little to awaken the spirit of revolt, or it has neglected to direct that spirit against conditions which it particularly desires to attack at the time of the revolution. As a result, this party is less known; its aspirations have not been daily and continuously affirmed by actions, the glamor of which could reach even the remotest hut; they have not sufficiently penetrated into the consciousness of the people; they have not identified themselves with the crowd and the street; they have never found simple expression in a popular slogan.

The most active writers of such a party are known by their readers as thinkers of great merit, but they have neither the reputation nor the capacities of men of action; and on the day when the mobs pour through the streets they will prefer to follow the advice of those who have less precise theoretical ideas and not such great aspirations, but whom they know better because they have seen them act.

The party which has made most revolutionary propaganda and which has shown most spirit and daring will be listened to on the day when it is necessary to act, to march in front in order to realize the revolution. But that party which has not had the daring to affirm itself by revolutionary acts in the preparatory periods nor had a driving force strong enough to inspire men and groups to the sentiment of abnegation, to the irresistible desire to put their ideas into practice,—(if this desire had existed it would have expressed itself in action long before the mass of the people had joined the revolt)—and which did not know how to make its flag popular and its aspirations tangible and comprehensive,—that party will have only a small chance of realizing even the least part of its program. It will be pushed aside by the parties of action.

These things we learn from the history of the periods which precede great revolutions. The revolutionary *bourgeoisie* understood this perfectly,—it neglected no means of agitation to awaken the spirit of revolt when it tried to demolish the monarchical order. The French peasant of the eighteenth century understood it instinctively when it was a question of abolishing feudal rights; and the International acted in accordance with the same principles when it tried to awaken the spirit of revolt among the workers of the cities and to direct it against the natural enemy of the wage earner—the monopolizer of the means of production and of raw materials.

An Appeal to the Young

It is to the young that I wish to address myself. Let the old—I mean of course the old in heart and mind—lay this down without tiring their eyes in reading what will tell them nothing.

I assume that you are about eighteen or twenty years of age, that you have finished your apprenticeship or your studies, that you are just entering on life. I take it for granted that you have a mind free from the superstition which your teachers have sought to force upon you; that you do not fear the devil, and that you do not go to hear parsons and ministers rant. More, that you are not one of the fops, sad products of a society in decay, who display their well-cut trousers and their monkey faces in the park, and who even at their early age have only an insatiable longing for pleasure at any price . . . I assume on the contrary that you have a warm heart and for this reason I talk to you.

A first question, I know, occurs to you. You have often asked yourself—"What am I going to be?" In fact when a man is young he understands that after having studied a trade or a science for several years—at the cost of society, mark—he has not done this in order that he should make use of his acquirements as instruments of plunder for his own gain, and he must be depraved indeed and utterly cankered by vice, who has not dreamed that one day he would apply his intelligence, his abilities, his knowledge to help on the enfranchisement of those who today grovel in misery and in ignorance.

You are one of those who has had such a vision, are you not? Very well, let us see what you must do to make your dream a reality.

I do not know in what rank you were born. Perhaps, favored by fortune, you have turned your attention to the study of science; you are to be a doctor, a lawyer, a man of letters, or a scientific man. A wide field opens up before you. You enter upon life with extensive knowledge, with a trained intelligence. Or on the other hand, you are perhaps only an artisan whose knowledge of science is limited by the little you learned at school. But you have had the advantage of learning at first hand what a life of exhausting toil is the lot of the worker of our time.

To the "Intellectuals"

To Doctors

I stop at the first supposition, to return afterwards to the second; I assume then that you have received a scientific education. Let us suppose you intend to be a doctor.

Tomorrow a man attired in rough clothes will come to fetch you to see a sick woman. He will lead you into one of those alleys where the neighbors opposite can almost shake hands over the heads of the passers-by. You ascend into a foul atmosphere by the flickering light of a little ill-trimmed lamp. You climb two, three, four, five flights of filthy stairs, and in a dark, cold room you find the sick woman lying on a pallet covered with dirty rags. Pale, livid children, shivering under their scanty garments, gaze with their big eyes wide open. The husband has worked all his life twelve or thirteen hours a day at no matter what. Now he has been out of work for three months. To be out of employment is not rare in his trade; it happens every year, periodically. But formerly when he was out of work his wife went out as a charwoman—perhaps to wash your shirts; now she has been bedridden for two months, and misery glares upon the family in all its squalid hideousness.

What will you prescribe for the sick woman, doctor? You have seen at a glance that the cause of her illness is a general anaemia, want of good food, lack of fresh air. Say a good beefsteak every day? A little exercise in the country? A dry and well-ventilated bedroom? What irony! If she could have afforded it this would have been done long since without waiting for your advice.

If you have a good heart, a frank address, an honest face, the family will tell you many things. They will tell you that the woman on the other side of the partition, who coughs a cough which tears your heart, is a poor ironer; that a flight of stairs lower down all the children have the fever; that the washwoman who occupies the ground floor will not live to see the spring; and that in the house next door things are worse.

What will you say to all these sick people? Recommend them generous diet, change of air, less exhausting toil. . . . You only wish you could, but you daren't and you go out heartbroken with a curse on your lips.

The next day, as you still brood over the fate of the dwellers in this dog house, your partner tells you that yesterday a footman came to fetch him, this time in a carriage. It was for the owner of a fine house, for a lady worn out with sleepless nights, who devotes all her life to dressing, visits, balls, and squabbles with a stupid husband. Your friend has prescribed for her a less preposterous habit of life, a less heating diet, walks in the fresh air, an even temperament, and, in order to make up in some measure for the want of useful work, a little gymnastic exercise in her bedroom.

The one is dying because she has never had enough food nor enough rest in her whole life. The other pines because she has never known what work is since she was born.

If you are one of those characterless natures who adapt themselves to anything, who at the sight of the most revolting spectacles console themselves with a gentle sigh, then you will gradually become used to these contrasts, and the nature of the beast favoring your endeavors, your sole idea will be to maintain yourself in the ranks of pleasure-seekers, so that you may never find yourself among the wretched. But if you are a *Man*, if every sentiment is translated in your case into an action of the will, if in you the beast has not crushed the intelligent being, then you will return home one day saying to yourself: "No, it is unjust; this must not go on any longer. It is not enough to cure diseases; we must prevent them. A little good living and intellectual development would score off our lists half the patients and half the diseases. Throw physic to the dogs! Air, good diet, less crushing toil—that is how we must begin. Without this, the whole profession of a doctor is nothing but trickery and humbug."

That very day you will understand socialism. You will wish to know it thoroughly, and if altruism is not a word devoid of significance for you, if you apply to the study of the social question the rigid induction of the natural philosopher, you will end by finding yourself in our ranks, and you will work, as we work, to bring about the social revolution.

To Scientists

But perhaps you will say, "Mere practical business may go to the devil! As an astronomer, a physiologist, a chemist, I will devote myself to science. Such work as that always bears fruit, if only for future generations."

Let us first try to understand what you seek in devoting yourself to science. Is it only the pleasure—doubtless immense—which we derive from the study of nature and the exercise of our mental faculties? In that case I ask you in what respect does the philosopher, who pursues science in order that he may pass life pleasantly to himself, differ from that drunkard there, who only seeks the immediate gratification that gin affords him? The philosopher has, past all question, chosen his enjoyment more wisely, since it affords him a pleasure far deeper and more lasting than that of the toper. But that is all! Both one and the other have the same selfish end in view, personal gratification.

But no, you have no wish to lead this selfish life. By working at science you mean to work for humanity, and this is the idea which will guide you in your investigations. A charming illusion! Which of us has not hugged it for a moment when giving himself up for the first time to science?

But then, if you are really thinking about humanity, if it is the good of mankind at which you aim, a formidable question arises before you; for, however little you may have of critical spirit, you must at once note that in our society of today science is only an appendage to luxury, rendering life pleasanter for the few, but remaining absolutely inaccessible to the bulk of mankind.

More than a century has passed since science laid down sound propositions as to the origin of the universe, but how many have mastered them or possess the really scientific spirit of criticism? A few thousands at the outside, who are lost in the midst of hundreds of millions still steeped in prejudices and superstitions worthy of savages, who are consequently ever ready to serve as puppets for religious impostors.

Or, to go a step further, let us glance at what science has done to establish rational foundations for physical and moral health. Science tells us how we ought to live in order to preserve the health of our own bodies, how to maintain in good condition the crowded masses of our population. But does not all the vast amount of work done in these two directions remain a dead letter in our books? We know it does. And why? Because science today exists only for a handful of privileged persons, because social inequality, which divides society into two classes—the wage-slaves and the grabbers of capital—renders all its teachings as to the conditions of a rational existence only the bitterest irony to nine-tenths of mankind.

At the present moment we no longer need to accumulate scientific truths and discoveries. The most important thing is to spread the truths already acquired, to practice them in daily life, to make of them a common inheritance. We have to order things in such wise that all humanity may be capable of assimilating and applying them, so that science ceasing to be a luxury becomes the basis of everyday life. Justice requires this.

Furthermore, the very interests of science require it. Science only makes real progress when its truths find environments ready prepared for their reception. The theory of the mechanical origin of heat remained for eighty years buried in academic records until such knowledge of physics had spread widely enough to create a public capable of accepting it. Three generations had to go before the ideas of Erasmus Darwin on the variation of species could be favorably received from his grandson and admitted by academic philosophers, and even then not without pressure from public opinion. The philosopher like the poet or artist is always the product of the society in which he moves and teaches.

But if you are imbued with these ideas, you will understand that it is important above all to bring about a radical change in this state of affairs which today condemns the philosopher to be crammed with scientific truths, and almost the whole of the rest of human beings to remain what they were five or ten centuries ago,—that is to say, in the state of slaves and machines, incapable of mastering established truths. And the day when you are imbued with wide, deep, humane, and profoundly scientific truth, that day will you lose your taste for pure science. You will set to work to find out the means to effect this transformation, and if you bring to your investigations the impartiality which has guided you in your scientific researches, you will of necessity adopt the cause of socialism; you will make an end of sophisms and you will come among us. Weary of working to procure pleasures for this small group, which already has a large share of them, you will place your information and devotion at the service of the oppressed.

And be sure that the feeling of duty accomplished and of a real accord established between your sentiments and your actions, you will then find powers in yourself of whose existence you never even dreamed. When, too, one day—it is not far distant in any case, saving the presence of our professors—when one day, I say, the change for which you are working shall have been brought about, then, deriving new forces from collective scientific work, and from the powerful help of armies of laborers who will come to place their energies at its service, science will take a new bound forward, in comparison with which the slow progress of today will appear the simple exercise of tyros. Then you will enjoy science; that pleasure will be a pleasure for all.

To Lawyers

If you have finished reading law and are about to be called to the bar, perhaps you, too, have some illusions as to your future activity —I assume that you are one of the nobler spirits, that you know what altruism means. Perhaps you think, "To devote my life to an unceasing and vigorous struggle against all injustice; to apply my whole faculties to bringing about the triumph of law, the public expression of supreme justice—can any career be nobler!" You begin the real work of life confident in yourself and the profession you have chosen

Very well, let us turn to any page of the law reports and see what actual life will tell you.

Here we have a rich landowner. He demands the eviction of a farmer tenant who has not paid his rent. From a legal point of view the case is beyond dispute. Since the poor farmer can't pay, out he must go. But if we look into the facts we shall learn something like this. The landlord has squandered his rents persistently in rollicking pleasure; the tenant has worked hard all day and every day. The landlord has done nothing to improve his estate. Nevertheless, its value has trebled in fifty years owing to the rise in price of land due to the construction of a railway, to the making of new highroads, to the draining of a marsh, to the enclosure and cultivation of waste lands. But the tenant who has contributed largely towards this increase has ruined himself. He fell into the hands of usurers, and head over ears in debt, he can no longer pay the landlord. The law, always on the side of property, is quite clear; the landlord is in the right. But you, whose feeling of justice has not yet been stifled by legal fictions, what will you do? Will you contend that the farmer ought to be turned out upon the highroad—for that is what the law ordains—or will you urge that the landlord should pay back to the farmer the whole of the increase of value in his property which is due to the farmer's labor—this is what equity decrees? Which side will you take? For the law and against justice, or for justice and against the law?

Or when workmen have gone out on strike against a master, without notice, which side will you take then? The side of the law, that is to say the part of the master, who, taking advantage of a period of crisis, has made outrageous profits, or against the law but on the side of the workers who received during the whole time only miserable wages, and saw their wives and children fade away before their eyes? Will you stand up for that piece of chicanery which consists in affirming "freedom of contract"? Or will you uphold equity, according to which a contract entered into between a man who has dined well and a man who sells his labor for a bare subsistence, between the strong and the weak, is not a contract at all?

Take another case. Here in London a man was loitering near a butcher's shop. He stole a beefsteak and ran off with it. Arrested and questioned, it turns out that he is an artisan out of work, and that he and his family have had nothing to eat for four days. The butcher is asked to let the man off but he is all for the triumph of justice! He prosecutes and the man is sentenced to six months imprisonment. Does not your conscience revolt against society when you hear similar judgments pronounced every day?

Or again, will you call for the enforcement of the law against this man, who, badly brought up and ill-used from his childhood, has arrived at man's estate without having heard one sympathetic word, and completes his career by murdering his neighbor in order to rob him? Will you demand his execution, or, worse still, that he should be imprisoned for twenty years, when you know very well that he is rather a madman than a criminal, and, in any case, that his crime is the fault of our entire society?

Will you claim that these weavers should be thrown into prison who in a moment of desperation have set fire to a mill; that this man who shot at a crowned murderer should be imprisoned for life; that these insurgents should be shot down who plant the flag of the future on the barricades? No, a thousand times no!

If you *reason* instead of repeat what is taught you; if you analyze the law and strip off those cloudy fictions with which it has been draped in order to conceal its real origin, which is the right of the stronger, and its substance, which has ever been the consecration of all the tyrannies handed down to mankind through its long and bloody history; when you have comprehended this, your contempt for the law will be profound indeed. You will understand that to remain the servant of the written law is to place yourself every day in opposition to the law of conscience, and to make a bargain on the wrong side, and since this struggle cannot go on forever, you will either silence your conscience and become a scoundrel, or you will break with tradition, and you will work with us for the utter destruction of all this injustice, economic, social, and political. But then you will be a *socialist, you will be a revolutionist!*

To Engineers

And you, young engineer, who dream of bettering the lot of the workers by applying the inventions of science to industry, what a sad disenchantment, what deceptions await you. You devote the youthful energy of your intellect to working out the plan of some railway which, winding round by the edges of precipices, and piercing the heart of huge mountains, will unite two countries separated by nature. But when once the work is on foot you see whole regiments of workers decimated by privations and sickness in this gloomy tunnel, you see others returning home taking with them only a little money and the seeds of consumption, you will see each yard of the line marked off by human corpses, the result of grovelling greed, and finally, when the line is at last opened, you see it used as the highway for the artillery of an invading army.

You have devoted your youth to make a discovery destined to simplify production, and after many efforts, many sleepless nights, you have at last this valuable invention. You put it into practice and the result surpasses your expectations. Ten, twenty thousand beings are thrown out of work; those who remain, mostly children, are reduced to the condition of mere machines! Three, four, or maybe ten capitalists will make a fortune and drink champagne by the bottleful. Was that your dream?

Finally, you study recent industrial advances, and you see that the seamstress has gained nothing, absolutely nothing, by the invention of the sewing machine; that the laborer in the St. Gothard tunnel dies of ankylostomiasis, notwithstanding diamond drills; that the mason and the day laborer are out of work just as before. If you discuss social problems with the same independence of spirit which has guided you in your mechanical investigations, you necessarliy come to the conclusion that under the domination of private property and wage-slavery, every new invention, far from increasing the well-being of the worker, only makes his slavery heavier, his labor more degrading, the periods of slack work more frequent, the crisis sharper, and that the man who already has every conceivable pleasure for himself is the only one who profits by it.

What will you do when you have once come to this conclusion? Either you will begin by silencing your conscience by sophisms; then one fine day you will bid farewell to the honest dreams of your youth and you will try to obtain, for yourself, what commands pleasure and enjoyment—you will then go over to the camp of the exploiters. Or, if you have a tender heart, you will say to yourself: —"No, this is not the time for inventions. Let us work first to transform the domain of production. When private property is put to an end, then each new advance in industry will be made for the benefit of all mankind, and this mass of workers, mere machines as they are today, will then become thinking beings who apply to industry their intelligence, strengthened by study and skilled in manual labor, and thus mechanical progress will take a bound forward which will carry out in fifty years what now-a-days we cannot even dream of."

To Teachers

And what shall I say to the schoolmaster—not to the man who looks upon his profession as a wearisome business, but to him who, when surrounded by a joyous band of youngsters, feels exhilarated by their cheery looks and in the midst of their happy laughter; to him who tries to plant in their little heads those ideas of humanity which he cherished himself when he was young.

Often I see that you are sad, and I know what it is that makes you knit your brows. This very day, your favorite pupil, who is not very well up in Latin, it is true, but who has none the less an excellent heart, recited the story of William Tell with so much vigor! His eyes sparkled; he seemed to wish to stab all tyrants there and then; he gave with such fire the passionate lines of Schiller:—

> Before the slave when he breaks his chain,
> Before the free man tremble not.

But when he returned home, his mother, his father, his uncle, sharply rebuked him for want of respect to the minister or the rural policeman. They held forth to him by the hour on "prudence, respect for authority, submission to his betters," till he put Schiller aside in order to read *Self-Help*.

And then only yesterday you were told that your best pupils have all turned out badly. One does nothing but dream of becoming an officer; another in league with his master robs the workers of their slender wages; and you, who had such hopes of these young people, you now brood over the sad contrast between your ideal and life as it is.

You still brood over it. Then I foresee that in two years at the outside, after having suffered disappointment after disappointment, you will lay your favorite authors on the shelf, and you will end by saying that Tell was no doubt a very honest fellow, but after all a trifle cracked; that poetry is a first-rate thing for the fireside, especially when a man has been teaching the rule-of-three all day long, but still poets are always in the clouds and their views have nothing to do with the life of today, nor with the next visit of the inspector of schools. . . .

Or, on the other hand, the dreams of your youth will become the firm convictions of your mature age. You will wish to have wide, human education for all, in school and out of school. And seeing that this is impossible in existing conditions, you will attack the very foundations of *bourgeois* society. Then discharged as you will be by the board of education, you will leave your school and come among us and be of us. You will tell men of riper years but of smaller attainments than yourself how enticing knowledge is, what mankind ought to be, nay, what we could be. You will come and work with socialists for the complete transformation of the existing system, will strive side by side with us to attain true equality, true fraternity, never-ending liberty for the world.

To Artists

Lastly, you, young artist, sculptor, painter, poet, musician, do you not observe that the sacred fire which inspired your predecessors is wanting in the men of today; that art is commonplace and mediocrity reigns supreme?

Could it be otherwise? The delight at having rediscovered the ancient world, of having bathed afresh in the springs of nature which created the masterpieces of the Renaissance no longer exists for the art of our time. The revolutionary ideal has left it cold until now, and failing an ideal, our art fancies that it has found one in realism when it painfully photographs in colors the dewdrop on the leaf of a plant, imitates the muscles in the leg of a cow, or describes minutely in prose and in verse the suffocating filth of a sewer, the boudoir of a whore of high degree.

"But if this is so, what is to be done?" you say. If, I reply, the sacred fire that you say you possess is nothing better than a smouldering wick, then you will go on doing as you have done, and your art will speedily degenerate into the trade of decorator of tradesmen's shops, of a purveyor of libretti to third-rate operettas and tales for Christmas books—most of you are already running down that grade with a fine head of steam on. . . .

But, if your heart really beats in unison with that of humanity, if like a true poet you have an ear for Life, then, gazing out upon this sea of sorrow whose tide sweeps up around you, face to face with these people dying of hunger, in the presence of these corpses piled up in these mines, and these mutilated bodies lying in heaps on the barricades, in full view of this desperate battle which is being fought, amid the cries of pain from the conquered and the orgies of the victors, of heroism in conflict with cowardice, of noble determination face to face with contemptible cunning—you cannot remain neutral. You will come and take the side of the oppressed because you know that the beautiful, the sublime, the spirit of life itself are on the side of those who fight for light, for humanity, for justice!

What You Can Do

You stop me at last! "What the devil!" you say. "But if abstract science is a luxury and practice of medicine mere chicane; if law spells injustice, and mechanical invention is but a means of robbery; if the school, at variance with the wisdom of the 'practical man,' is sure to be overcome, and art without the revolutionary idea can only degenerate, what remains for me to do?"

A vast and most enthralling task, a work in which your actions will be in complete harmony with your conscience, an undertaking capable of rousing the noblest and most vigorous natures.

What work? I will now tell you.

Two courses are open to you. You can either tamper for ever with your conscience and finish one day by saying "Humanity can go to the devil as long as I am enjoying every pleasure to the full and so long as the people are foolish enough to let me do so." Or else you will join the ranks of the socialists and work with them for the complete transformation of society. Such is the necessary result of the analysis we have made. Such is the logical conclusion at which every intelligent being must arrive provided he judge impartially the things he sees around him, and disregard the sophisms suggested to him by his middle-class education and the interested views of his friends.

Having once reached this conclusion, the question which arises is "what is to be done?" The answer is easy. Quit the environment in which you are placed and in which it is customary to speak of the workers as a lot of brutes; go among the people, and the question will solve itself.

You will find that everywhere in England as in Germany, in Italy as in the United States, wherever there are privileged classes and oppressed, a tremendous movement is on foot among the working-classes, the aim of which is to destroy once and forever the slavery imposed by capitalists, and to lay the foundations of a new society based on the principles of justice and equality. It no longer suffices for the people to voice their misery in those songs whose melody breaks one's heart, and which the serfs of the eighteenth century sang. He works today fully conscious of what he has done, in spite of every obstacle to his enfranchisement. His thoughts are continually occupied in considering what to do so that life instead of being a mere curse to three-fourths of the human race may be a blessing to all. He attacks the most difficult problems of sociology, and strives to solve them with his sound common sense, his observation, and his sad experience. To come to a common understanding with his fellows in misfortune, he tries to form groups and to organize. He forms societies, sustained with difficulty by slender contributions. He tries to make terms with his fellows beyond the frontier. And he does more than all the loud-mouthed philanthropists to hasten the advent of the day when wars between nations will become impossible. To know what his brothers are doing, to improve his acquaintance with them, to elaborate and propagate his ideas, he sustains, at the cost of what efforts, his working-class press. What a ceaseless struggle! What labor, constantly requiring to be recommenced. Sometimes to fill the gaps made by desertion—the result of lassitude, of corruption, of persecutions; sometimes to reorganize the ranks decimated by fusillades and grape shot, sometimes to resume studies suddenly cut short by wholesale massacres.

The papers are conducted by men who have had to snatch from

society scraps of knowledge by depriving themselves of food and sleep. The agitation is supported with the pennies of the workers saved from the strict necessaries of life. And all this is done, shadowed by the continual apprehension of seeing their families plunged into destitution as soon as the master perceives that his worker, his slave, is a socialist.

These are the things you will see if you go among the people. And in this ceaseless struggle how often has the worker, sinking under the weight of difficulties, exclaimed in vain: "Where then are those young men who have been educated at our expense, whom we have clothed and fed while they studied? For whom, with backs bowed down under heavy loads, and with empty stomachs, we have built these houses, these academies, these museums? For whom we, with pallid faces, have printed those fine books we cannot so much as read? Where are they, those professors who claim to possess the science of humanity, and yet in whose eyes mankind is not worth a rare species of caterpillar? Where are those men who preach of liberty and who never rise to defend ours, daily trodden under foot? These writers, these poets, these painters, all this band of hypocrites, in short, who speak of the people with tears in their eyes, and who nevertheless never come among us to help us in our work?"

Some complacently enjoy their condition of cowardly indifference, others, the majority, despise the "rabble" and are ever ready to pounce down on it if it dare to attack their privileges.

From time to time, it is true, a young man appears on the scene who dreams of drums and barricades, and who is in search of sensational scenes and situations, but who deserts the cause of the people as soon as he perceives that the road to the barricades is long, that the laurels he counts on winning on the way are mixed with thorns. Generally these men are ambitious adventurers, who after failing in their first attempts, seek to obtain the votes of the people, but who later on will be the first to denounce it, if it dare to try and put into practice the principles they themselves advocated, and who perhaps will even point the cannon at the proletariat if it dare move before they, the leaders, have given the word of command.

Add to this stupid insults, haughty contempt, and cowardly calumny on the part of a great number, and you have all the help that the middle-class youth give the people in their powerful social evolution.

And then you ask, "what shall we do?" when there is everything to be done! When a whole army of young people would find plenty to employ the entire vigor of their youthful energy, the full force of their intelligence and their talents to help the people in the vast enterprise they have undertaken!

What shall we do? Listen.

You lovers of pure science, if you are imbued with the principles of socialism, if you have understood the real meaning of the revolution which is even now knocking at the door, do you not see that all science has to be recast in order to place it in harmony with the new principles? That it is your business to accomplish in this field a revolution far greater than that which was accomplished in every branch of science during the eighteenth century? Do you not understand that history—which today is an old woman's tale about great kings, great statesmen and great parliaments—that history itself has to be written from the point of view of the people in the long evolution of mankind? That social economy—which today is merely the sanctification of capitalist robbery—has to be worked out afresh in its fundamental principles as well as in its innumerable applications? That anthropology, sociology, ethics, must be completely recast, and that the natural sciences themselves, regarded from another point of view, must undergo a profound modification, alike in regard to the conception of natural phenomena and with respect to the method of exposition?

Very well, then, set to work! Place your abilities at the command of the good cause. Especially help us with your clear logic to combat prejudice and to lay by your synthesis the foundation of a better organization. Yet more, teach us to apply in our daily arguments the fearlessness of true scientific investigation, and show us as your predecessors did, how man dare sacrifice even life itself for the triumph of the truth.

You doctors who have learnt socialism by a bitter experience, never weary of telling us today, tomorrow, in and out of season, that humanity itself hurries onward to decay if man remain in the present conditions of existence and work; that all your medicaments must be powerless against disease while the majority of mankind vegetate in conditions absolutely contrary to those which science tells us are healthful. Convince the people that it is the causes of disease which must be uprooted, and show us all what is necessary to remove them.

Come with your scalpel and dissect for us with unerring hand this society of ours fast hastening to putrefaction. Tell us what a rational existence should and might be. Insist, as true surgeons, that a gangrenous limb must be amputated when it may poison the whole body.

You who have worked at the application of science to industry, come and tell us frankly what has been the outcome of your discoveries. Convince those who dare not march boldly towards the future what new inventions the knowledge we have already acquired carries in its womb, what industry could do under better conditions, what man might easily produce if he produced always with a view to enhance his own productions.

You poets, painters, sculptors, musicians, if you understand your true mission and the very interests of art itself, come with us. Place your pen, your pencil, your chisel, your ideas at the service of the revolution. Figure forth to us, in your eloquent style, or your impressive pictures, the heroic struggles of the people against their oppressors, fire the hearts of our youth with that glorious revolutionary enthusiasm which inflamed the souls of our ancestors. Tell women what a noble career is that of a husband who devotes his life to the great cause of social emancipation! Show the people how hideous is their actual life, and place your hands on the causes of its ugliness. Tell us what a rational life would be, if it did not encounter at every step the follies and the ignominies of our present social order.

Lastly, all of you who possess knowledge, talent, capacity, industry, if you have a spark of sympathy in your nature, come you, and your companions, come and place your services at the disposal of those who most need them. And remember, if you do come, that you come not as masters, but as comrades in the struggle; that you come not to govern but to gain strength for yourselves in a new life which sweeps upwards to the conquest of the future; that you come less to teach than to grasp the aspiration of the many; to divine them, to give them shape, and then to work, without rest and without haste, with all the fire of youth and all the judgment of age, to realize them in actual life. Then and then only, will you lead a complete, a noble, a rational existence. Then you will see that your every effort on this path bears with it fruit in abundance, and this sublime harmony once established between your actions and the dictates of your conscience will give you powers you never dreamt lay dormant in yourselves, the never-ceasing struggle for truth, justice, and equality among the people, whose gratitude you will earn—what nobler career can the youth of all nations desire than this?

It has taken me long to show you of the well-to-do classes that in view of the dilemma which life presents to you, you will be forced, if courageous and sincere, to come and work side by side with the socialists, and champion in their ranks, the cause of the social revolution.

And yet how simple this truth is after all! But when one is speaking to those who have suffered from the effects of *bourgeois* surroundings, how many sophisms must be combated, how many prejudices overcome, how many interested objections put aside!

To Working Class Youths

It is easy to be brief today in addressing you, the youth of the people. The very pressure of events impels you to become socialists, however little you may have the courage to reason and to act.

To rise from the ranks of the working people, and not devote oneself to bringing about the triumph of socialism, is to misconceive the real interests at stake, to give up the cause, and the true historic mission.

Do you remember the time, when still a mere lad, you went down one winter's day to play in your dark court? The cold nipped your shoulders through your thin clothes, and the mud worked into your worn-out shoes. Even then when you saw chubby children richly clad pass in the distance, looking at you with an air of contempt, you knew right well that these imps were not the equals of yourself and your comrades, either in intelligence, common sense, or energy. But later when you were forced to shut yourself up in a filthy factory from seven o'clock in the morning, to remain hours on end close to a whirling machine, and, a machine yourself, you were forced to follow day after day for whole years in succession its movements with relentless throbbing—during all this time they, the others, were going quietly to be taught at fine schools, at academies, at the universities. And now these same children, less intelligent, but better taught than you, have become your masters, are enjoying all the pleasures of life and all the advantages of civilization. And you? What sort of lot awaits you?

You return to little, dark, damp lodgings where five or six human beings pig together within a few square feet. Where your mother, sick of life, aged by care rather than years, offers you dry bread and potatoes as your only food, washed down by a blackish fluid called in irony "tea." And to distract your thoughts you have ever the same never-ending question, "How shall I be able to pay the baker tomorrow, and the landlord the day after?"

What! must you drag on the same weary existence as your father and mother for thirty and forty years? Must you toil your life long to procure for others all the pleasures of well-being, of knowledge, of art, and keep for yourself only the eternal anxiety as to whether you can get a bit of bread? Will you forever give up all that makes life so beautiful to devote yourself to providing every luxury for a handful of idlers? Will you wear yourself out with toil and have in return only trouble, if not misery, when hard times—the fearful hard times—come upon you? Is this what you long for in life?

Perhaps you will give up. Seeing no way whatever out of your condition, maybe you say to yourself, "Whole generations have undergone the same lot, and I, who can alter nothing in the matter, I must submit also. Let us work on then and endeavor to live as well as we can!"

Very well. In that case life itself will take pains to enlighten you. One day a crisis comes, one of those crises which are no longer mere passing phenomena, as they were formerly, but a crisis which destroys a whole industry, which plunges thousands of workers into misery, which crushes whole families. You struggle against the calamity like the rest. But you will soon see how your wife, your child, your friend, little by little succumb to privations, fade away under your very eyes. For sheer want of food, for lack of care and medical assistance, they end their days on the pauper's stretcher, whilst the life of the rich flows on joyously amidst the sunny streets of the great city, careless of those who starve and perish. You will then understand how utterly revolting is this society. You will then reflect upon the causes of this crisis, and your examinations will scrutinize to the depths that abomination which puts millions of human beings at the mercy of the brutal greed of a handful of useless triflers. Then you will understand that socialists are right when they say that our present society can be, that it must be, reorganized from top to bottom.

To pass from general crises to your particular case. One day when your master tries by a new reduction of wages to squeeze out of you a few more dollars in order to increase his fortune still further you will protest. But he will haughtily answer, "Go and eat grass, if you will not work at the price I offer." Then you will understand that your master not only tries to shear you like a sheep, but that he looks upon you as an inferior kind of animal altogether; that not content with holding you in his relentless grip by means of the wage system, he is further anxious to make you a slave in every respect. Then you will, perhaps, bow down before him, you will give up the feeling of human dignity, and you will end by suffering every possible humiliation. Or the blood will rush to your head, you shudder at the hideous slope on which you are slipping down, you will retort, and, turned out workless on the street, you will understand how right socialists are when they say, "Revolt! rise against this economic slavery!" Then you will come and take your place in the ranks of the socialists, and you will work with them for the complete destruction of all slavery—economic, social, and political.

Every one of you then, honest young people, men and women, peasants, laborers, artisans, and soldiers, you will understand what are your rights and you will come along with us. You will come in order to work with your brethren in the preparation of that revolution which is sweeping away every vestige of slavery, tearing the fetters asunder, breaking with the old worn-out traditions, and opening to all mankind a new and wider scope of joyous existence, and which shall at length establish true liberty, real equality, ungrudging fraternity throughout human society. Work with all, work for all—the full enjoyment of the fruits of their labor, the complete development of all their faculties, a rational, human, and happy life!

Don't let anyone tell us that we—but a small band—are too weak to attain unto the magnificent end at which we aim. Count and see how many there are who suffer this injustice. We peasants who work for others, and who mumble the straw while our master eats the wheat, we by ourselves are millions of men. We workers who weave silks and velvet in order that we may be clothed in rags, we, too, are a great multitude; and when the clang of the factories permits us a moment's repose, we overflow the streets and squares like the sea in a spring tide. We soldiers who are driven along to the word of command, or by blows, we who receive the bullets for which our officers get crosses and pensions, we, too, poor fools who have hitherto known no better than to shoot our brothers, why we have only to make a right about face towards these plumed and decorated personages who are so good as to command us, to see a ghastly pallor overspread their faces.

Ay, all of us together, we who suffer and are insulted daily, we are a multitude whom no man can number, we are the ocean that can embrace and swallow up all else. When we have but the will to do it, that very moment will justice be done; that very instant the tyrants of the earth shall bite the dust.

Law and Authority

I

"When ignorance reigns in society and disorder in the minds of men, laws are multiplied, legislation is expected to do everything, and each fresh law being a fresh miscalculation, men are continually led to demand from it what can proceed only from themselves, from their own education and their own morality." It is no revolutionist who says this, not even a reformer. It is the jurist, Dalloy, author of the collection of French law known as *Répertoire de la Législation*. And yet, though these lines were written by a man who was himself a maker and admirer of law, they perfectly represent the abnormal condition of our society.

In existing States a fresh law is looked upon as a remedy for evil. Instead of themselves altering what is bad, people begin by demanding a *law* to alter it. If the road between two villages is impassable, the peasant says, "There should be a law about parish roads." If a park-keeper takes advantage of the want of spirit in those who follow him with servile observance and insults one of them, the insulted man says, "There should be a law to enjoin more politeness upon park-keepers." If there is stagnation in agriculture or commerce, the husbandman, cattle-breeder, or corn speculator argues, "It is protective legislation that we require." Down to the old clothesman there is not one who does not demand a law to protect his own little trade. If the employer lowers wages or increases the hours of labor, the politician in embryo exclaims, "We must have a law to put all that to rights." In short, a law everywhere and for everything! A law about fashions, a law about mad dogs, a law about virtue, a law to put a stop to all the vices and all the evils which result from human indolence and cowardice.

We are so perverted by an education which from infancy seeks to kill in us the spirit of revolt, and to develop that of submission to authority; we are so perverted by this existence under the ferrule of a law, which regulates every event in life—our birth, our education, our development, our love, our friendship—that, if this state of things continues, we shall lose all initiative, all habit of thinking for ourselves. Our society seems no longer able to understand that it is possible to exist otherwise than under the reign of law, elaborated by a representative government and administered by a handful of rulers. And even when it has gone so far as to emancipate itself from the thralldom, its first care has been to reconstitute it immediately. "The Year I of Liberty" has never lasted more than a day, for after proclaiming it men put themselves the very next morning under the yoke of law and authority.

Indeed, for some thousands of years, those who govern us have done nothing but ring the changes upon "Respect for law, obedience to authority." This is the moral atmosphere in which parents bring up their children, and school only serves to confirm the impression. Cleverly assorted scraps of spurious science are inculcated upon the children to prove necessity of law; obedience to the law is made a religion; moral goodness and the law of the masters are fused into one and the same divinity. The historical hero of the schoolroom is the man who obeys the law, and defends it against rebels.

Later when we enter upon public life, society and literature, impressing us day by day and hour by hour as the water-drop hollows the stone, continue to inculcate the same prejudice. Books of history, of political science, of social economy, are stuffed with this respect for law. Even the physical sciences have been pressed into the service by introducing artificial modes of expression, borrowed from theology and arbitrary power, into knowledge which is purely the result of observation. Thus our intelligence is successfully befogged, and always to maintain our respect for law. The same work is done by newspapers. They have not an article which does not preach respect for law, even where the third page proves every day the imbecility of that law, and shows how it is dragged through every variety of mud and filth by those charged with its administration. Servility before the law has become a virtue, and I doubt if there was ever even a revolutionist who did not begin in his youth as the defender of law against what are generally called "abuses," although these last are inevitable consequences of the law itself.

Art pipes in unison with would-be science. The hero of the sculptor, the painter, the musician, shields Law beneath his buckler, and with flashing eyes and distended nostrils stands ever ready to strike down the man who would lay hands upon her. Temples are raised to her; revolutionists themselves hesitate to touch the high priests consecrated to her service, and when revolution is about to sweep away some ancient institution, it is still by law that it endeavors to sanctify the deed.

The confused mass of rules of conduct called law, which has been bequeathed to us by slavery, serfdom, feudalism, and royalty, has taken the place of those stone monsters, before whom human victims used to be immolated, and whom slavish savages dared not even touch lest they should be slain by the thunderbolts of heaven.

This new worship has been established with especial success since the rise to supreme power of the middle class—since the great French Revolution. Under the ancient *régime*, men spoke little of laws; unless, indeed, it were, with Montesquieu, Rousseau, and Voltaire, to oppose them to royal caprice. Obedience to the good pleasure of the king and his lackeys was compulsory on pain of hanging or imprisonment. But during and after the revolutions, when the lawyers rose to power, they did their best to strengthen the principle upon which their ascendancy depended. The middle class at once accepted it as a dyke to dam up the popular torrent. The priestly crew hastened to sanctify it, to save their bark from foundering amid the breakers. Finally the people received it as an improvement upon the arbitrary authority and violence of the past.

To understand this, we must transport ourselves in imagination into the eighteenth century. Our hearts must have ached at the story of the atrocities committed by the all-powerful nobles of that time upon the men and women of the people before we can understand what must have been the magic influence upon the peasant's mind of the words, "Equality before the law, obedience to the law without distinction of birth or fortune." He who until then had been treated more cruelly than a beast, he who had never had any rights, he who had never obtained justice against the most revolting actions on the part of a noble, unless in revenge he killed him and was hanged—he saw himself recognized by this maxim, at least in theory, at least with regard to his personal rights, as the equal of his lord. Whatever this law might be, it promised to affect lord and peasant alike; it proclaimed the equality of rich and poor before the judge. The promise was a lie, and today we know it; but at that period it was an advance, a homage to justice, as hypocrisy is a homage rendered to truth. This is the reason that when the saviors of the menaced middle class (the Robespierres and the Dantons) took their stand upon the writings of the Rousseaus and the Voltaires, and proclaimed "respect for law, the same for every man," the people accepted the compromise; for their revolutionary impetus had already spent its force in the contest with a foe whose ranks drew closer day by day; they bowed their neck beneath the yoke of law to save themselves from the arbitrary power of their lords.

The middle class has ever since continued to make the most of this maxim, which with another principle, that of representative government, sums up the whole philosophy of the *bourgeois* age, the nineteenth century. It has preached this doctrine in its schools, it has propagated it in its writings, it has moulded its art and science to the same purpose, it has thrust its beliefs into every hole and corner—like a pious Englishwoman, who slips tracts under the door—and it has done all this so successfully that today we behold the issue in the detestable fact that men who long for freedom begin the attempt to obtain it by entreating their masters to be kind enough to protect them by modifying the laws which these masters themselves have created!

But times and tempers are changed. Rebels are everywhere to be found who no longer wish to obey the law without knowing whence it comes, what are its uses, and whither arises the obligation to submit to it, and the reverence with which it is encompassed. The rebels of our day are criticizing the very foundations of society which have hitherto been held sacred, and first and foremost amongst them that fetish, law.

The critics analyze the sources of law, and find there either a god, product of the terrors of the savage, and stupid, paltry, and malicious as the priests who vouch for its supernatural origin, or else, bloodshed, conquest by fire and sword. They study the characteristics of law, and instead of perpetual growth corresponding to that of the human race, they find its distincitve trait to be immobility, a tendency to crystallize what should be modified and developed day by day. They ask how law has been maintained, and in its service they see the atrocities of Byzantinism, the cruelties of the Inquisition, the tortures of the middle ages, living flesh torn by the lash of the executioner, chains, clubs, axes, the gloomy dungeons of prisons, agony, curses, and tears. In our own days they see, as before, the axe, the cord, the rifle, the prison; on the one hand, the brutalized prisoner, reduced to the condition of a caged beast by the debasement of his whole moral being, and on the other, the judge, stripped of every feeling which does honor to human nature, living like a visionary in a world of legal fictions, reveling in the infliction of imprisonment and death, without even suspecting, in the cold malignity of his madness, the abyss of degradation into which he has himself fallen before the eyes of those whom he condemns.

They see a race of law-makers legislating without knowing what their laws are about; today voting a law on the sanitation of towns, without the faintest notion of hygiene, tomorrow making regulations for the armament of troops, without so much as understanding a gun; making laws about teaching and education without ever having given a lesson of any sort, or even an honest education to their own children; legislating at random in all directions, but never forgetting the penalties to be meted out to ragamuffins, the prison and the galleys, which are to be the portion of men a thousand times less immoral than these legislators themselves.

Finally, they see the jailer on the way to lose all human feeling, the detective trained as a blood-hound, the police spy despising himself; "informing," metamorphosed into a virtue; corruption, erected into a system; all the vices, all the evil qualities of mankind countenanced and cultivated to insure the triumph of law.

All this we see, and, therefore, instead of inanely repeating the old formula, "Respect the law," we say, "Despise law and all its attributes!" In place of the cowardly phrase, "Obey the law," our cry is "Revolt against all laws!"

Only compare the misdeeds accomplished in the name of each law with the good it has been able to effect, and weigh carefully both good and evil, and you will see if we are right.

II

Relatively speaking, law is a product of modern times. For ages and ages mankind lived without any written law, even that graved in symbols upon the entrance stones of a temple. During that period, human relations were simply regulated by customs, habits, and usages, made sacred by constant repetition, and acquired by each person in childhood, exactly as he learned how to obtain his food by hunting, cattle-rearing, or agriculture.

All human societies have passed through this primitive phase, and to this day a large proportion of mankind have no written law. Every tribe has its own manners and customs; customary law, as the jurists say. It has social habits, and that suffices to maintain cordial relations between the inhabitants of the village, the members of the tribe or community. Even amongst ourselves—the "civilized" nations—when we leave large towns, and go into the country, we see that there the mutual relations of the inhabitants are still regulated according to ancient and generally accepted customs, and not according to the written law of the legislators. The peasants of Russia, Italy, and Spain, and even of a large part of France and England, have no conception of written law. It only meddles with their lives to regulate their relations with the State. As to relations between themselves, though these are sometimes very complex, they are simply regulated according to ancient custom. Formerly, this was the case with mankind in general.

Two distinctly marked currents of custom are revealed by analysis of the usages of primitive people.

As man does not live in a solitary state, habits and feelings develop within him which are useful for the preservation of society and the propagation of the race. Without social feelings and usages, life in common would have been absolutely impossible. It is not law which has established them; they are anterior to all law. Neither is it religion which has ordained them; they are anterior to all religions. They are found amongst all animals living in society. They are spontaneously developed by the very nature of things, like those habits in animals which men call instinct. They spring from a process of evolution, which is useful, and, indeed, necessary to keep society together in the struggle it is forced to maintain for existence. Savages end by no longer eating one another because they find it in the long run more advantageous to devote themselves to some sort of cultivation than to enjoy the pleasure of feasting upon the flesh of an aged relative once a year. Many travelers have depicted the manners of absolutely independent tribes, where laws and chiefs are unknown, but where the members of the tribe have given up stabbing one another in every dispute, because the habit of living in society has ended by developing certain feelings of fraternity and oneness of interest, and they prefer appealing to a third person to settle their differences. The hospitality of primitive peoples, respect for human life, the sense of reciprocal obligation, compassion for the weak, courage, extending even to the sacrifice of self for others which is first learnt for the sake of children and friends, and later for that of members of the same community—all these qualities are developed in man anterior to all law, independently of all religion, as in the case of the social animals. Such feelings and practices are the inevitable results of social life. Without being, as say priests and metaphysicans, inherent in man, such qualities are the consequence of life in common.

But side by side with these customs, necessary to the life of societies and the preservation of the race, other desires, other passions, and therefore other habits and customs, are evolved in human association. The desire to dominate others and impose one's own will upon them; the desire to seize upon the products of the labor of a neighboring tribe; the desire to surround oneself with comforts without producing anything, while slaves provide their master with the means of procuring every sort of pleasure and luxury—these selfish, personal desires give rise to another current of habits and customs. The priest and the warrior, the charlatan who makes a profit out of superstition, and after freeing himself from the fear of the devil cultivates it in others; and the bully, who procures the invasion and pillage of his neighbors that he may return laden with booty and followed by slaves. These two, hand in hand, have succeeded in imposing upon primitive society customs advantageous to both of them, but tending to perpetuate their domination of the masses. Profiting by the indolence, the fears, the inertia of the crowd, and thanks to the continual repetition of the same acts, they have permanently established customs which have become a solid basis for their own domination.

For this purpose, they would have made use, in the first place, of that tendency to run in a groove, so highly developed in mankind. In children and all savages it attains striking proportions, and it may also be observed in animals. Man, when he is at all superstitious, is always afraid to introduce any sort of change into existing conditions; he generally venerates what is ancient. "Our fathers did so and so; they got on pretty well; they brought you up; they were not unhappy; do the same!" the old say to the young every time the latter wish to alter things. The unknown frightens them, they prefer to cling to the past even when that past represents poverty, oppression, and slavery.

It may even be said that the more miserable a man is, the more he dreads every sort of change, lest it may make him more wretched still. Some ray of hope, a few scraps of comfort, must penetrate his gloomy abode before he can begin to desire better things, to criticize the old ways of living, and prepare to imperil them for the sake of bringing about a change. So long as he is not imbued with hope, so long as he is not freed from the tutelage of those who utilize his superstition and his fears, he prefers remaining in his former position. If the young desire any change, the old raise a cry of alarm against the innovators. Some savages would rather die than transgress the customs of their country because they have been told from childhood that the least infraction of established routine would bring ill-luck and ruin the whole tribe. Even in the present day, what numbers of politicians, economists, and would-be revolutionists act under the same impression, and cling to a vanishing past. How many care only to seek for precedents. How many fiery innovators are mere copyists of bygone revolutions.

The spirit of routine, originating in superstition, indolence, and cowardice, has in all times been the mainstay of oppression. In primitive human societies it was cleverly turned to account by priests and military chiefs. They perpetuated customs useful only to themselves, and succeeded in imposing them on the whole tribe. So long as this conservative spirit could be exploited so as to assure the chief in his encroachments upon individual liberty, so long as the only inequalities between men were the work of nature, and these were not increased a hundred-fold by the concentration of power and wealth, there was no need for law and the formidable paraphernalia of tribunals and ever-augmenting penalties to enforce it.

But as society became more and more divided into two hostile classes, one seeking to establish its domination, the other struggling to escape, the strife began. Now the conqueror was in a hurry to secure the results of his actions in a permanent form, he tried to place them beyond question, to make them holy and venerable by every means in his power. Law made its appearance under the sanction of the priest, and the warrior's club was placed at its service. Its office was to render immutable such customs as were to the advantage of the dominant minority. Military authority undertook to ensure obedience. This new function was a fresh guarantee to the power of the warrior; now he had not only mere brute force at his service; he was the defender of law.

If law, however, presented nothing but a collection of prescriptions serviceable to rulers, it would find some difficulty in insuring acceptance and obedience. Well, the legislators confounded in one code the two currents of custom of which we have just been speaking, the maxims which represent principles of morality and social union wrought out as a result of life in common, and the mandates which are meant to ensure external existence to inequality. Customs, absolutely essential to the very being of society, are, in the code, cleverly intermingled with usages imposed by the ruling caste, and both claim equal respect from the crowd. "Do not kill," says the code, and hastens to add, "And pay tithes to the priest." "Do not steal," says the code, and immediately after, "He who refuses to pay taxes, shall have his hand struck off."

Such was law; and it has maintained its two-fold character to this day. Its origin is the desire of the ruling class to give permanence to customs imposed by themselves for their own advantage. Its character is the skillful commingling of customs useful to society, customs which have no need of law to insure respect, with other customs useful only to rulers, injurious to the mass of the people, and maintained only by the fear of punishment.

Like individual capital, which was born of fraud and violence, and developed under the auspices of authority, law has no title to the respect of men. Born of violence and superstition, and established in the interests of consumer, priest, and rich exploiter, it must be utterly destroyed on the day when the people desire to break their chains.

We shall be still better convinced of this when, later, we shall have analyzed the ulterior development of laws under the auspices of religion, authority, and the existing parliamentary system.

III

We have seen how law originated in established usage and custom, and how from the beginning it has represented a skillful mixture of social habits, necessary to the preservation of the human race, with other customs imposed by those who used popular superstition as well as the right of the strongest for their own advantage. This double character of law has determined its own later development during the growth of political organization. While in the course of ages the nucleus of social custom inscribed in law has been subjected to but slight and gradual modifications, the other portion has been largely developed in directions indicated by the interests of the dominant classes, and to the injury of the classes they oppress.

From time to time these dominant classes have allowed a law to be extorted from them which presented, or appeared to present, some guarantee for the disinherited. But then such laws have but repealed a previous law, made for the advantage of the ruling caste. "The best laws," says Buckle, "were those which repealed the preceding ones." But what terrible efforts have been needed, what rivers of blood have been spilt, every time there has been a question of the repeal of one of these fundamental enactments serving to hold the people in fetters. Before she could abolish the last vestiges of serfdom and feudal rights, and break up the power of the royal court, France was forced to pass through four years of revolution and twenty years of war. Decades of conflict are needful to repeal the least of the iniquitous laws, bequeathed us by the past, and even then they scarcely disappear except in periods of revolution.

The history of the genesis of capital has already been told by socialists many times. They have described how it was born of war and pillage, of slavery and serfdom, of modern fraud and exploitation. They have shown how it is nourished by the blood of the worker, and how little by little it has conquered the whole world. The same story, concerning the genesis and development of law has yet to be told. As usual, the popular intelligence has stolen a march upon men of books. It has already put together the philosophy of this history, and is busy laying down its essential landmarks.

Law, in its quality of guarantee of the results of pillage, slavery and exploitation, has followed the same phases of development as capital. Twin brother and sister, they have advanced hand in hand, sustaining one another with the suffering of mankind. In every country in Europe their history is approximately the same. It has differed only in detail; the main facts are alike; and to glance at the development of law in France or Germany is to know its essential traits and its phases of development in most of the European nations.

In the first instance, law was a national pact or contract. It is true that this contract was not always freely accepted. Even in the early days the rich and strong were imposing their will upon the rest. But at all events they encountered an obstacle to their encroachments in the mass of the people, who often made them feel their power in return.

But as the church on one side and the nobles on the other

succeeded in enthralling the people, the right of law-making escaped from the hands of the nation and passed into those of the privileged orders. Fortified by the wealth accumulating in her coffers, the church extended her authority. She tampered more and more with private life, and under pretext of saving souls, seized upon the labor of her serfs, she gathered taxes from every class, she increased her jurisdiction, she multiplied penalties, and enriched herself in proportion to the number of offenses committed, for the produce of every fine poured into her coffers. Laws had no longer any connection with the interest of the nation. "They might have been supposed to emanate rather from a council of religious fanatics than from legislators," observes an historian of French Law.

At the same time, as the baron likewise extended his authority over laborers in the fields and artisans in the towns, he, too, became legislator and judge. The few relics of national law dating from the tenth century are merely agreements regulating service, statute-labor, and tribute due from serfs and vassals to their lord. The legislators of that period were a handful of brigands organized for the plunder of a people daily becoming more peaceful as they applied themselves to agricultural pursuits. These robbers exploited the feelings for justice inherent in the people, they posed as the administrators of that justice, made a source of revenue for themselves out of its fundamental principles and concocted laws to maintain their own domination.

Later on, these laws collected and classified by jurists formed the foundation of our modern codes. And are we to talk about respecting these codes, the legacy of baron and priest?

The first revolution, the revolt of the townships, was successful in abolishing only a portion of these laws; the charters of enfranchised towns are, for the most part, a mere compromise between baronial and episcopal legislation, and the new relations created within the free borough itself. Yet what a difference between these laws and the laws we have now! The town did not take upon itself to imprison and execute citizens for reasons of State; it was content to expel anyone who plotted with the enemies of the city, and to raze his house to the ground. It confined itself to imposing fines for so-called "crimes and misdemeanors" and in the townships of the twelfth century may even be discerned the just principle today forgotten which holds the whole community responsible for the misdoing of each of its members. The societies of that time looked upon crime as an accident or misfortune; a conception common among the Russian peasantry at this moment. Therefore they did not admit of the principle of personal vengeance as preached by the Bible, but considered that the blame for each misdeed reverted to the whole society. It needed all the influence of the Byzantine church, which imported into the West the refined cruelties of Eastern despotism, to introduce into the manners of Gauls and Germans the penalty of death, and the horrible tortures afterwards inflicted on those regarded as criminals. Just in the same way, it needed all the influence of the Roman code, the product of the corruption of imperial Rome, to introduce the notions as to absolute property in land, which have overthrown the communistic customs of primitive people.

As we know, the free townships were not able to hold their own. Torn by internal dissensions between rich and poor, burgher and serf, they fell an easy prey to royalty. And as royalty acquired fresh strength, the right of legislation passed more and more into the hands of a clique of courtiers. Appeal to the nation was made only to sanction the taxes demanded by the king. Parliament summoned at intervals of two centuries, according to the good pleasure or caprice of the court, "Councils Extraordinary," assemblies of notables, ministers, scarce heeding the "grievances of the king's subjects"—these are the legislators of France. Later still, when all power is concentrated in a single man, who can say "I am the State," edicts are concocted in the "secret counsels of the prince," according to the whim of a minister, or of an imbecile king; and subjects must obey on pain of death. All judicial guarantees are abolished; the nation is the serf of royalty, and of a handful of courtiers. And at this period the most horrible penalties startle our gaze—the wheel, the stake, flaying alive, tortures of every description, invented by the sick fancy of monks and madmen, seeking delight in the sufferings of executed criminals.

The great Revolution began the demolition of this framework of law, bequeathed to us by feudalism and royalty. But after having demolished some portions of the ancient edifice, the Revolution delivered over the power of law-making to the *bourgeoisie*, who, in their turn, began to raise a fresh framework of laws intended to maintain and perpetuate middle-class domination among the masses. Their parliament makes laws right and left, and mountains of law accumulate with frightful rapidity. But what *are* all these laws at bottom?

The major portion have but one object—to protect private property, *i.e.*, wealth acquired by the exploitation of man by man. Their aim is to open out to capital fresh fields for exploitation, and to sanction the new forms which that exploitation continually assumes, as capital swallows up another branch of human activity, railways, telegraphs, electric light, chemical industries, the expression of man's thought in literature and science, etc. The object of the rest of these laws is fundamentally the same. They exist to keep up the machinery of government which serves to secure to capital the exploitation and monopoly of the wealth produced. Magistrature, police, army, public instruction, finance, all serve one God—capital; all have but one object—to facilitate the exploitation of the worker by the capitalist. Analyze all the laws passed and you will find nothing but this.

The protection of the person, which is put forward as the true mission of law, occupies an imperceptible space among them, for, in existing society, assaults upon the person directly dictated by hatred and brutality tend to disappear. Nowadays, if anyone is murdered, it is generally for the sake of robbing him; rarely because of personal vengeance. But if this class of crimes and misdemeanors is continually diminishing, we certainly do not owe the change to legislation. It is due to the growth of humanitarianism in our societies, to our increasingly social habits rather than to the prescriptions of our laws. Repeal tomorrow every law dealing with the protection of the person, and tomorrow stop all proceedings for assault, and the number of attempts dictated by personal vengeance and by brutality would not be augmented by one single instance.

It will perhaps be objected that during the last fifty years, a good many liberal laws have been enacted. But, if these laws are analyzed, it will be discovered that this liberal legislation consists in the repeal of the laws bequeathed to us by the barbarism of preceding centuries. Every liberal law, every radical program, may be summed up in these words,—abolition of laws grown irksome to the middle-class itself, and return and extension to all citizens of liberties enjoyed by the townships of the twelfth century. The abolition of capital punishment, trial by jury for all "crimes" (there was a more liberal jury in the twelfth century), the election of magistrates, the right of bringing public officials to trial, the abolition of standing armies, free instruction, etc., everything that is pointed out as an invention of modern liberalism, is but a return to the freedom which existed before church and king had laid hands upon every manifestation of human life.

Thus the protection of exploitation directly by laws on property, and indirectly by the maintenance of the State is both the spirit and the substance of our modern codes, and the one function of our costly legislative machinery. But it is time we gave up being satisfied with mere phrases, and learned to appreciate their real significance. The law, which on its first appearance presented itself as a compendium of customs useful for the preservation of society, is now perceived to be nothing but an instrument for the maintenance of exploitation and the domination of the toiling masses by rich idlers. At the present day its civilizing mission is *nil*; it has but one object,—to bolster up exploitation.

This is what is told us by history as to the development of law. Is it in virtue of this history that we are called upon to respect it? Certainly not. It has no more title to respect than capital, the fruit of pillage. And the first duty of the revolution will be to make a bonfire of all existing laws as it will of all titles to property.

IV

The millions of laws which exist for the regulation of humanity appear upon investigation to be divided into three principal categories: protection of property, protection of persons, protection of government. And by analyzing each of these three categories, we arrive at the same logical and necessary conclusion: *the uselessness and hurtfulness of law.*

Socialists know what is meant by protection of property. Laws on property are not made to guarantee either to the individual or to society the enjoyment of the produce of their own labor. On the contrary, they are made to rob the producer of a part of what he has created, and to secure to certain other people that portion of the produce which they have stolen either from the producer or from society as a whole. When, for example, the law establishes Mr. So-and-So's right to a house, it is not establishing his right to a cottage he has built for himself, or to a house he has erected with the help of some of his friends. In that case no one would have disputed his right. On the contrary, the law is establishing his right to a house which is *not* the product of his labor; first of all because he has had it built for him by others to whom he has not paid the full value of their work, and next because that house represents a social value which he could not have produced for himself. The law is establishing his right to what belongs to everybody in general and to nobody in particular. The same house built in the midst of Siberia would not have the value it possesses in a large town, and, as we know, that value arises from the labor of something like fifty generations of men who have built the town, beautified it, supplied it with water and gas, fine promenades, colleges, theatres, shops, railways, and roads leading in all directions. Thus, by recognizing the right of Mr. So-and-So to a particular house in Paris, London, or Rouen, the law is unjustly appropriating to him a certain portion of the produce of the labor of mankind in general. And it is precisely because this appropriation and all other forms of property bearing the same character are a crying injustice, that a whole arsenal of laws and a whole army of soldiers, policemen, and judges are needed to maintain it against the good sense and just feeling inherent in humanity.

Half our laws,—the civil code in each country,—serves no other purpose than to maintain this appropriation, this monopoly for the benefit of certain individuals against the whole of mankind. Three-fourths of the causes decided by the tribunals are nothing but quarrels between monopolists—two robbers disputing over their booty. And a great many of our criminal laws have the same object in view, their end being to keep the workman in a subordinate position towards his employer, and thus afford security for exploitation.

As for guaranteeing the product of his labor to the producer, there are no laws which even attempt such a thing. It is so simple and natural, so much a part of the manners and customs of mankind, that law has not given it so much as a thought. Open brigandage, sword in hand, is no feature of our age. Neither does one workman ever come and dispute the produce of his labor with another. If they have a misunderstanding they settle it by calling in a third person, without having recourse to law. The only person who exacts from another what that other has produced, is the proprietor, who comes in and deducts the lion's share. As for humanity in general, it everywhere respects the right of each to what he has created, without the interposition of any special laws.

As all the laws about property which make up thick volumes of codes and are the delight of our lawyers have no other object than to protect the unjust appropriation of human labor by certain monopolists, there is no reason for their existence, and, on the day of the revolution, social revolutionists are thoroughly determined to put an end to them. Indeed, a bonfire might be made with perfect justice of all laws bearing upon the so-called "rights of property." All title-deeds, all registers, in a word, of all that is in any way connected with an institution which will soon be looked upon as a blot in the history of humanity, as humiliating as the slavery and serfdom of past ages.

The remarks just made upon laws concerning property are quite as applicable to the second category of laws; those for the maintenance of government, *i.e.*, constitutional law.

It again is a complete arsenal of laws, decrees, ordinances, orders in council, and what not, all serving to protect the diverse forms of representative government, delegated or usurped, beneath which humanity is writhing. We know very well—anarchists have often enough pointed out in their perpetual criticism of the various forms of government—that the mission of all governments, monarchical, constitutional, or republican, is to protect and maintain by force the privileges of the classes in possession, the aristocracy, clergy, and traders. A good third of our laws—and each country possesses some tens of thousands of them—the fundamental laws on taxes, excise duties, the organization of ministerial departments and their offices, of the army, the police, the church, etc., have no other end than to maintain, patch up, and develop the administrative machine. And this machine in its turn serves almost entirely to protect the privileges of the possessing classes. Analyze all these laws, observe them in action day by day, and you will discover that not one is worth preserving.

About such laws there can be no two opinions. Not only anarchists, but more or less revolutionary radicals also, are agreed that the only use to be made of laws concerning the organization of government is to fling them into the fire.

The third category of law still remains to be considered; that relating to the protection of the person and the detection and prevention of "crime." This is the most important because most prejudices attach to it; because, if law enjoys a certain amount of consideration, it is in consequence of the belief that this species of law is absolutely indispensable to the maintenance of security in our societies. These are laws developed from the nucleus of customs useful to human communities, which have been turned to account by rulers to sanctify their own domination. The authority of the chiefs of tribes, of rich families in towns, and of the king, depended upon their judicial functions, and even down to the present day, whenever the necessity of government is spoken of, its function as supreme judge is the thing implied. "Without a government men would tear one another to pieces," argues the village orator. "The ultimate end of all government is to secure twelve honest jurymen to every accused person," said Burke.

Well, in spite of all the prejudices existing on this subject, it is quite time that anarchists should boldly declare this category of laws as useless and injurious as the preceding ones.

First of all, as to so-called "crimes"—assaults upon persons—it is well known that two-thirds, and often as many as three-fourths, of such "crimes" are instigated by the desire to obtain possession of someone's wealth. This immense class of so-called "crimes and misdemeanors" will disappear on the day on which private property ceases to exist. "But," it will be said, "there will always be brutes who will attempt the lives of their fellow citizens, who will lay their hands to a knife in every quarrel, and revenge the slightest offense by murder, if there are no laws to restrain and punishments to withhold them." This refrain is repeated every time the right of society *to punish* is called in question.

Yet there is one fact concerning this head which at the present time is thoroughly established; the severity of punishment does not diminish the amount of crime. Hang, and, if you like, quarter murderers, and the number of murders will not decrease by one. On the other hand, abolish the penalty of death, and there will not be one murder more; there will be fewer. Statistics prove it. But if the harvest is good, and bread cheap, and the weather fine, the number of murders immediately decreases. This again is proved by statistics. The amount of crime always augments and diminishes in proportion to the price of provisions and the state of the weather. Not that all murderers are actuated by hunger. That is not the case. But when the harvest is good, and provisions are at an obtainable price, and when the sun shines, men, lighter-hearted and less miserable than usual, do not give way to gloomy passions, do not from trivial motives plunge a knife into the bosom of a fellow creature.

Moreover, it is also a well known fact that the fear of punishment has never stopped a single murderer. He who kills his neighbor from revenge or misery does not reason much about consequences; and there have been few murderers who were not firmly convinced that they should escape prosecution.

Without speaking of a society in which a man will receive a better education, in which the development of all his faculties, and the possibility of exercising them, will procure him so many enjoyments that he will not seek to poison them by remorse—even in our society, even with those sad products of misery whom we see today in the public houses of great cities—on the day when no punishment is inflicted upon murderers, the number of murders will not be augmented by a single case. And it is extremely probable that it will be, on the contrary, diminished by all those cases which are due at present to habitual criminals, who have been brutalized in prisons.

We are continually being told of the benefits conferred by law, and the beneficial effect of penalties, but have the speakers ever attempted to strike a balance between the benefits attributed to laws and penalties, and the degrading effect of these penalties upon humanity? Only calculate all the evil passions awakened in mankind by the atrocious punishments formerly inflicted in our streets! Man is the cruelest animal upon earth. And who has pampered and developed the cruel instincts unknown, even among monkeys, if it is not the king, the judge, and the priests, armed with law, who caused flesh to be torn off in strips, boiling pitch to be poured into wounds, limbs to be dislocated, bones to be crushed, men to be sawn asunder to maintain their authority? Only estimate the torrent of depravity let loose in human society by the "informing" which is countenanced by judges, and paid in hard cash by governments, under pretext of assisting in the discovery of "crime." Only go into the jails and study what man becomes when he is deprived of freedom and shut up with other depraved beings, steeped in the vice and corruption which oozes from the very walls of our existing prisons. Only remember that the more these prisons are reformed, the more detestable they become. Our model modern penitentiaries are a hundred-fold more abominable than the dungeons of the middle ages. Finally, consider what corruption, what depravity of mind is kept up among men by the idea of obedience, the very essence of law; of chastisement; of authority having the right to punish, to judge irrespective of our conscience and the esteem of our friends; of the necessity for executioners, jailers, and informers —in a word, by all the attributes of law and authority. Consider all this, and you will assuredly agree with us in saying that a law inflicting penalties is an abomination which should cease to exist.

Peoples without political organization, and therefore less depraved than ourselves, have perfectly understood that the man who is called "criminal" is simply unfortunate; that the remedy is not to flog him, to chain him up, or to kill him on the scaffold or in prison, but to help him by the most brotherly care, by treatment based on equality, by the usages of life among honest men. In the next revolution we hope that this cry will go forth:

"Burn the guillotines; demolish the prisons; drive away the judges, policemen and informers—the impurest race upon the face of the earth; treat as a brother the man who has been led by passion to do ill to his fellow; above all, take from the ignoble products of middle-class idleness the possibility of displaying their vices in attractive colors; and be sure that but few crimes will mar our society."

The main supports of crime are idleness, law and authority; laws about property, laws about government, laws about penalties and misdemeanors; and authority, which takes upon itself to manufacture these laws and to apply them.

No more laws! No more judges! Liberty, equality, and practical human sympathy are the only effectual barriers we can oppose to the anti-social instincts of certain among us.

Prisons and Their
Moral Influence on Prisoners

After the economic problem and after the problem of the State, perhaps the most important of all is that concerning the control of anti-social acts. The meting out of justice was always the principal instrument for creating rights and privilege, since it was based on solid foundations of constituted rights; the problem of what is to be done with those who commit anti-social acts therefore contains within itself the great problem of government and the State.

It is time to ask if condemnation to death or to prison is just. Does it attain the dual end it has as its goal—that of preventing the repetition of the anti-social deed, and (as regards prisons) that of reforming the offender?

They are grave questions. On their answers depend not only the happiness of thousands of prisoners, not only the fate of miserable women and children, whose husbands and fathers are helpless to aid them from behind their bars, but also the happiness of humanity. Every injustice committed against one individual is, in the end, experienced by humanity as a whole.

Having had occasion to become acquainted with two prisons in France and several in Russia, having been led by various circumstances in my life to return to the study of penal questions, I think it is my duty to state openly what prisons are,—to relate my observations and my beliefs as a result of these observations.

The Prison as a School of Crime

Once a man has been in prison, he will return. It is inevitable, and statistics prove it. The annual reports of the administration of criminal justice in France show that one-half of all those tried by juries and two-fifths of all those who yearly get into the police courts for minor offenses received their education in prisons. Nearly half of all those tried for murder and three-fourths of those tried for burglary are repeaters. As for the central prisons, more than one-third of the prisoners released from these supposedly cor-

44

rectional institutions are reimprisoned in the course of twelve months after their liberation.

Another significant angle is that the offense for which a man returns to prison is always more serious than his first. If, before, it was petty thieving, he returns now for some daring burglary, if he was imprisoned for the first time for some act of violence, often he will return as a murderer. All writers on criminology are in accord with this observation. Former offenders have become a great problem in Europe. And you know how France has solved it; she ordains their wholesale destruction by the fevers of Cayenne, an extermination which begins on the voyage.

The Futility of Prisons

In spite of all the reforms made up to the present,—in spite of all the experiments of different prison systems, the results are always the same. On the one hand, the number of offenses against existing laws neither increases nor diminishes, *no matter what the system of punishments is*—the knout has been abolished in Russia and the death penalty in Italy, and the number of murders there has remained the same. The cruelty of the judges grows or lessens, the cruelty of the Jesuitical penal system changes, but the number of acts designated as crimes remains constant. It is affected only by other causes which I shall shortly mention. On the other hand, no matter what changes are introduced in the prison *régime*, the problem of second offenders does not decrease. That is inevitable;—*it must be so;*—the prison kills all the qualities in a man which make him best adapted to community life. It makes him the kind of a person who will inevitably return to prison to end his days in one of those stone tombs over which is engraved—"House of Detention and Correction." There is only one answer to the question, "What can be done to better this penal system?" Nothing. A prison cannot be improved. With the exception of a few unimportant little improvements, there is absolutely nothing to do but demolish it.

I might propose that a Pestalozzi be placed at the head of each prison. I refer to the great Swiss pedagogue who used to take in abandoned children and make good citizens of them. I might also propose that in the place of the present guards, ex-soldiers and ex-policemen, sixty Pestalozzis be substituted. But, you will ask, "Where are we to find them?"—a pertinent question. The great Swiss teacher would certainly refuse to be a prison guard, for, basically, the principle of all prisons is wrong because it deprives man of liberty. So long as you deprive a man of his liberty, you will not make him better. You will cultivate habitual criminals: that is what I shall now prove.

The Criminals in Prison and Outside

To begin with, there is the fact that none of the prisoners recognize the justice of the punishment inflicted on them. This is in itself a condemnation of our whole judicial system. Speak to an imprisoned man or to some great swindler. He will say. "The little swindlers are here but the big ones are free and enjoy public respect." What can you answer, knowing the existence of great financial companies expressly designed to take the last pennies of the savings of the poor, with the founders retiring in time to make good legal hauls out of these small fortunes? We all know these great stock-issuing companies with their lying circulars and their huge swindles. What can we answer the prisoner except that he is right?

Or this man, imprisoned for robbing a till, will tell you, "I simply wasn't clever enough; that's all." And what can you answer, knowing what goes on in important places, and how, following terrible scandals, the verdict "not guilty" is handed out to these great robbers? How many times have you heard prisoners say, "It's the big thieves who are holding us here; we are the little ones." Who can dispute this when he knows the incredible swindles perpetrated in the realm of high finance and commerce; when he knows that the thirst for riches, acquired by every possible means, is the very essence of *bourgeois* society. When he has examined this immense quantity of suspicious transactions divided between the honest man (according to *bourgeois* standards) and the criminal, when he has seen all this, he must be convinced that jails are made for the unskillful, not for criminals. This is the standard on the outside. As for the standard in the prison itself, it is needless to dwell on it long. We know well enough what it is. Whether in regard to food or the distribution of favors, in the words of the prisoners, from San Francisco to Kamchatka, "The biggest thieves are those who hold us here, not ourselves."

Prison Labor

Everyone knows the evil influence of laziness. Work relieves a man. But there is work and work. There is the work of the free individual which makes him feel a part of the immense whole. And there is that of the slave which degrades. Convict labor is unwillingly done, done only through fear of worse punishment. The work, which has no attraction in itself because it does not exercise any of the mental faculties of the worker, is so badly paid that it is looked upon as a punishment.

When my anarchist friends at Clairvaux made corsets or mother of pearl buttons and received twelve cents for ten hours labor, of which four cents were retained by the State, we can understand very well the disgust which this work aroused in a man condemned to it. When he receives thirty-six cents at the end of a week, he is right to say, "Those who keep us here are thieves, not we."

The Effect of Cutting Off Social Contacts

And what inspiration can a prisoner get to work for the common good, deprived as he is of all connections with life outside? By a refinement of cruelty, those who planned our prisons did everything they could to break all relationships of the prisoner with society. In England the prisoner's wife and children can see him only once every three months, and the letters he is allowed to write are really preposterous. The philanthropists have even at times carried defiance of human nature so far as to restrict a prisoner from writing anything but his signature on a printed circular. The best influence to which a prisoner could be subjected, the only one which could bring him a ray of light, a softer element in his life,—the relationship with his kin,—is systematically prevented.

In the sombre life of the prisoner which flows by without passion or emotion, all the finer sentiments rapidly become atrophied. The skilled workers who loved their trade lose their taste for work. Bodily energy slowly disappears. The mind no longer has the energy for sustained attention; thought is less rapid, and in any case less persistent. It loses depth. It seems to me that the lowering of nervous energy in prisons is due, above all, to the lack of varied impressions. In ordinary life a thousand sounds and colors strike our senses daily, a thousand little facts come to our consciousness and stimulate the activity of our brains. No such things strike the prisoners' senses. Their impressions are few and always the same.

The Theory of Will Power

There is another important cause of demoralization in prisons. All transgressions of accepted moral standards may be ascribed to lack of a strong will. The majority of the inmates of prisons are people who did not have sufficient strength to resist the temptations surrounding them or to control a passion which momentarily carried them away. In prisons as in monasteries, everything is done to kill a man's will. He generally has no choice between one of two acts. The rare occasions on which he can exercise his will are very brief. His whole life is regulated and ordered in advance. He has only to swim with the current, to obey under pain of severe punishment.

Under these conditions all the will power that he may have had on entering disappears. And where will he find the strength with which to resist the temptations which will arise before him, as if by magic, when he is free of the prison walls? Where will he find the strength to resist the first impulse to a passionate outbreak, if during several years everything was done to kill this inner strength, to make him a docile tool in the hands of those who control him? This fact is, according to my mind, *the most terrible condemnation of the whole penal system based on the deprivation of individual liberty.*

The origin of this suppression of individual will, which is the essence of all prisons, is easy to see. It springs from the desire of guarding the greatest number of prisoners with the fewest possible guards. The ideal of prison officials would be thousands of automatons, arising, working, eating and going to sleep by means of electric currents switched on by one of the guards. Economies might then be made in the budget, but no astonishment should be expressed that men, reduced to machines, are not, on their release, the type which society wants. As soon as a prisoner is released, his old companions await him. He is fraternally received and once again engulfed by the current which once swept him to prison. Protective organizations can do nothing. All that they can do to combat the evil influence of the prison is to counterbalance some of those results in the liberated men.

And what a contrast between the reception by his old companions and that of the people in philanthropic work for released prisoners! Who of them will invite him to his home and say to him simply, "Here is a room, here is work, sit down at this table, and become part of the family"? The released man is only looking for the outstretched hand of warm friendship. But society, after having done everything it could to make an enemy of him, having inoculated him with the vices of the prison, rejects him. He is condemned to become a "repeater."

The Effect of Prison Clothes and Discipline

Everyone knows the influence of decent clothing. Even an animal is ashamed to appear before his fellow creatures if something makes him look ridiculous. A cat whom somebody has painted black and yellow will not dare mingle with other cats. But men begin by giving the clothes of a lunatic to those whom they profess to want to reform.

During all his prison life the prisoner is subjected to treatment which shows the greatest contempt of his feelings. A prisoner is not accorded the single respect due a human being. He is a thing, a number, and he is treated like a numbered thing. If he yields to the most human of all desires, that of communicating with a comrade, he is guilty of a breach of discipline. Before entering prison he may not have lied or deceived, but in prison he will learn to lie and deceive so that it will become second nature to him.

And it goes hard with those who do not submit. If being searched is humiliating, if a man finds the food distasteful, if he shows disgust in the keeper's trafficking in tobacco, if he divides his bread with his neighbor, if he still has enough dignity to be irritated by an insult, if he is honest enough to be revolted by the petty intrigues, prison will be a hell for him. He will be overburdened with work unless he is sent to rot in solitary confinement. The slightest infraction of discipline will bring down the severest punishment. And each punishment will lead to another. He will be driven to madness through persecution. He can consider himself lucky to leave prison otherwise than in a coffin.

Prison Guards

It is easy to write in the newspapers that the guards must be carefully watched, that the wardens must be chosen from good men. Nothing is easier than to build administrative utopias. But man will remain man—guard as well as prisoner. And when these guards are condemned to spend the rest of their lives in these false positions, they suffer the consequences. They become fussy. Nowhere, save in monasteries or convents, does such a spirit of petty intrigue reign. Nowhere are scandal and tale-bearing so well developed as among prison guards.

You cannot give an individual any authority without corrupting him. He will abuse it. He will be less scrupulous and feel his authority even more when his sphere of action is limited. Forced to live in any enemy's camp, the guards cannot become models of kindness. To the league of prisoners there is opposed the league of jailers. It is the institution which makes them what they are—petty, mean persecutors. Put a Pestalozzi in their place and he will soon become a prison guard.

Quickly rancor against society gets into the prisoner's heart. He becomes accustomed to detesting those who oppress him. He divides the world into two parts,—one in which he and his comrades belong, the other, the external world, represented by the guards and their superiors. A league is formed by the prisoners against all those who do not wear prison garb. These are their enemies and everything that can be done to deceive them is right.

As soon as he is freed, the prisoner puts this code into practice. Before going to prison he could commit his offenses unthinkingly. Now he has a philosophy, which can be summed up in the words of Zola, "What rascals these honest men are."

If we take into consideration all the different influences of the prison on the prisoner, we will be convinced that they make a man less and less fitted for life in society. On the other hand, none of these influences raises the intellectual and moral faculties of the prisoner, or leads him to a higher conception of life. Prison does not improve the prisoner. And furthermore, we have seen that it does not prevent him from committing other crimes. It does not then achieve any of the ends which it has set itself.

How Shall We Deal with Offenders?

That is why the question must be asked, "What should be done with those who break the laws?" I do not mean the written laws— they are a sad heritage of a sad past—but the principles of morality which are engraved on the hearts of each one of us.

There was a time when medicine was the art of administering some drugs, gropingly discovered through experiment. But our times have attacked the medical problem from a new angle. Instead of curing diseases medicine now seeks primarily to prevent them. Hygiene is the best of all medicines.

We have yet to do the same thing for this great social phenomenon which we still call "crime" but which our children will call a "social disease." To prevent this illness will be the best of cures. And this conclusion has already become the watchword of a whole school of modern thinkers concerned with "crime." In the works published by these innovators we have all the elements necessary for taking a new stand towards those whom society, until now, has in cowardly fashion decapitated, hanged, or imprisoned.

Causes of Crime

Three great categories of causes produce these anti-social acts called crimes. They are social, physiological, and physical. I shall begin with the last-named causes. They are less well known, but their influence is indisputable.

Physical Causes

When one sees a friend mail a letter which he has forgotten to address, one says this is an accident—it is unforeseen. These accidents, these unexpected events, occur in human societies with the same regularity as those which can be foreseen. The number of unaddressed letters which will be mailed continues from year to year with astounding regularity. Their number may vary slightly each year, but only slightly. Here we have so capricious a factor as absentmindedness. However, this factor is subject to laws that are just as rigorous as those governing the movements of the planets.

The same is true for the number of murders committed from year to year. With the statistics for previous years in hand, anyone can predict in advance, with striking exactitude, the approximate number of murders that will be committed in the course of the year in every country of Europe.

The influence of physical causes on our actions is still far from being completely analyzed. It is, however, known that acts of violence predominate in summer whereas in winter acts against property take the lead. When one examines the curves traced by Prof. Enrico Ferri and when one observes the curve for acts of violence rise and fall with the curve for temperature, one is vividly impressed by the similarity of the two curves and one understands how much of a machine man is. Man who boasts of his free will is as dependent on the temperature, the winds, and the rain as any other organism. Who will doubt these influences? When the weather is fine and the harvest good, and when the villagers feel at their ease, certainly they will be less likely to end their petty squabbles with knife thrusts. When the weather is bad and the harvest poor, the villagers become morose and their quarrels will take on a more violent character.

Physiological Causes

The physiological causes, those which depend on the brain structure, the digestive organs, and the nervous system, are certainly more important than the physical causes. The influence of inherited capacities as well as of physical organization on our acts has been the object of such searching investigation that we can form a fairly correct idea of its importance.

When Cesare Lombroso maintains that the majority of our prison inmates have some defect of their brain structure, we can accept this declaration on condition that we compare the brains of those who died in prison with those who died outside under generally bad living conditions. When he demonstrates that the most brutal murders are perpetrated by individuals who have some serious mental defect, we agree because this statement has been confirmed by observation. But when Lombroso declares that society has the right to take measures against the defectives, we refuse to follow him. Society has no right to exterminate those who have diseased brains. We admit that many of those who commit these atrocious acts are almost idiots. But not all idiots become murderers.

In many families, in palaces as well as insane asylums, idiots were found with the same traits which Lombroso considers characteristic of "criminal insanity." The only difference between them and those sent to the gallows is the environment in which they lived. Cerebral diseases can certainly stimulate the development of an inclination to murder, but it is not inevitable. Everything depends on the circumstances in which the individual suffering from a mental disease is placed.

Every intelligent person can see from the accumulated facts that the majority of those now treated as criminals are people suffering from some malady, and that, consequently, it is necessary to cure them by the best of care instead of sending them to prison where the disease will only be aggravated.

If each one of us subjects himself to a severe analysis, he will see that at times there pass through his mind the germs of ideas, quick as a flash, which constitute the foundations for evil deeds. We repudiated these ideas, but if they had found a favorable response in our circumstances, or, if other sentiments, such as love, pity and the sense of brotherhood had not counteracted these flashes of egoistic and brutal thoughts, they would have ended by leading to an evil act. In brief, the physiological causes play an important part in leading men to prison, but they are not the causes of "criminality" properly speaking. These affections of the mind, the cerebrospinal system, etc., might be found in their incipience among us all. The great majority of us have some one of these maladies. But they do not lead a person to commit an anti-social act unless external circumstances give them a morbid turn.

The Social Causes

But if physical causes have so strong an influence on our actions, if our physiology so often becomes the cause of the anti-social deeds we commit, how much more potent are the social causes. The most forward-looking and intelligent minds of our time proclaim that society as a whole is responsible for every anti-social act committed. We have our part in the glory of our heroes and geniuses; we also share in the acts of our assassins. It is we who have made them what they are,—the one as well as the other.

Year in and year out thousands of children grow up in the midst of the moral and material filth of our great cities, in the midst of a population demoralized by hand to mouth living. These children do not know a real home. Their home is a wretched lodging today, the streets tomorrow. They grow up without any decent outlets for their young energies. When we see the child population of large cities grow up in this fashion, we can only be astonished that so few of them become highwaymen and murderers. What surprises me is the depth of the social sentiments among humanity, the warm friendliness of even the worst neighborhoods. Without it, the number of these that would declare open warfare on society would be even greater. Without this friendliness, this aversion to violence, not a stone would be left of our sumptuous city palaces.

And at the other end of the ladder, what does the child growing up on the streets see? Luxury, stupid and insensate, smart shops, reading matter devoted to exhibiting wealth, a money-worshipping cult developing a thirst for riches, a passion for living at the expense of others. The watchword is: "Get rich. Destroy everything that stands in your way, and do it by any means save those that will land you in jail." Manual labor is despised to a point where our ruling classes prefer to indulge in gymnastics than handle a spade or a saw. A calloused hand is considered a sign of inferiority and a silk dress of superiority.

Society itself daily creates these people incapable of leading a life of honest labor, and filled with anti-social desires. She glorifies them when their crimes are crowned with financial success. She sends them to prison when they have not "succeeded." We will no longer have any use for prisons, executioners, or judges when the social revolution will have wholly changed the relations between capital and labor, when there are no more idlers, when each can work according to his inclination for the common good, when every child will be taught to work with his hands at the same time that his mind and soul get normal development.

Man is the result of the environment in which he grows up and spends his life. If he is accustomed to work from childhood, to being considered as a part of society as a whole, to understanding that he cannot injure anyone without finally feeling the effects himself, then there will be found few cases of violation of moral laws.

Two-thirds of the acts condemned as crimes today are acts

against property. They will disappear along with private property. As for acts of violence against people, they already decrease in proportion to the growth of the social sense and they will disappear when we attack the causes instead of the effects.

How Shall Offenders Be Cured?

Until now, penal institutions, so dear to the lawyers, were a compromise between the Biblical idea of vengeance, the belief of the middle ages in the devil, the modern lawyers' idea of terrorization, and the idea of the prevention of crime by punishment.

It is not insane asylums that must be built instead of prisons. Such an execrable idea is far from my mind. The insane asylum is always a prison. Far from my mind also is the idea, launched from time to time by the philanthropists, that the prison be kept but entrusted to physicians and teachers. What prisoners have not found today in society is a helping hand, simple and friendly, which would aid them from childhood to develop the higher faculties of their minds and souls;—faculties whose natural development has been impeded either by an organic defect or by the evil social conditions which society itself creates for millions of people. But these superior faculties of the mind and heart cannot be exercised by a person deprived of his liberty, if he never has choice of action. The physicians' prison, the insane asylum, would be much worse than our present jails. Human fraternity and liberty are the only correctives to apply to those diseases of the human organism which lead to so-called crime.

Of course in every society, no matter how well organized, people will be found with easily aroused passions, who may, from time to time, commit anti-social deeds. But what is necessary to prevent this is to give their passions a healthy direction, another outlet.

Today we live too isolated. Private property has led us to an egoistic individualism in all our mutual relations. We know one another only slightly; our points of contact are too rare. But we have seen in history examples of a communal life which is more intimately bound together,—the "composite family" in China, the agrarian communes, for example. These people really know one another. By force of circumstances they must aid one another materially and morally.

Family life, based on the original community, has disappeared. A new family, based on community of aspirations, will take its place. In this family people will be obliged to know one another, to aid one another and to lean on one another for moral support on every occasion. And this mutual prop will prevent the great number of anti-social acts which we see today.

It will be said, however, there will always remain some people, the sick, if you wish to call them that, who constitute a danger to society. Will it not be necessary somehow to rid ourselves of them, or at least prevent their harming others?

No society, no matter how little intelligent, will need such an absurd solution, and this is why. Formerly the insane were looked upon as possessed by demons and were treated accordingly. They were kept in chains in places like stables, riveted to the walls like wild beasts. But along came Pinel, a man of the Great Revolution, who dared to remove their chains and tried treating them as brothers. "You will be devoured by them," cried the keepers. But Pinel dared. Those who were believed to be wild beasts gathered around Pinel and proved by their attitude that he was right in believing in the better side of human nature even when the intelligence is clouded by disease. Then the cause was won. They stopped chaining the insane.

Then the peasants of the little Belgian village, Gheel, found something better. They said: "Send us your insane. We will give them absolute freedom." They adopted them into their families, they gave them places at their tables, chance alongside them to cultivate their fields and a place among their young people at their country balls. "Eat, drink, and dance with us. Work, run about the fields, and be free." That was the system, that was all the science the Belgian peasant had. (I am speaking of the early days. Today the treatment of the insane at Gheel has become a profession and where it is a profession for profit, what significance can there be in it?) And liberty worked a miracle. The insane became cured. Even those who had incurable, organic lesions became sweet, tractable members of the family like the rest. The diseased mind would always work in an abnormal fashion but the heart was in the right place. They cried that it was a miracle. The cures were attributed to a saint and a virgin. But this virgin was liberty and the saint was work in the fields and fraternal treatment.

At one of the extremes of the immense "space between mental disease and crime" of which Maudsley speaks, liberty and fraternal treatment have worked their miracle. They will do the same at the other extreme.

To Sum Up

The prison does not prevent anti-social acts from taking place. It increases their numbers. It does not improve those who enter its walls. However it is reformed it will always remain a place of restraint, an artificial environment, like a monastery, which will make the prisoner less and less fit for life in the community. It does not achieve its end. It degrades society. It must disappear. It is a survival of barbarism mixed with Jesuitical philanthropy.

The first duty of the revolution will be to abolish prisons,—those monuments of human hyprocrisy and cowardice. Anti-social acts need not be feared in a society of equals, in the midst of a free people, all of whom have acquired a healthy education and the habit of mutually aiding one another. The greater number of these acts will no longer have any *raison d'être*. The others will be nipped in the bud.

As for those individuals with evil tendencies whom existing society will pass on to us after the revolution, it will be our task to prevent their exercising these tendencies. This is already accomplished quite efficiently by the solidarity of all the members of the community against such aggressors. If we do not succeed in all cases, the only practical corrective still will be fraternal treatment and moral support.

This is not Utopia. It is already done by isolated individuals and it will become the general practice. And such means will be far more powerful to protect society from anti-social acts than the existing system of punishment which is an ever-fertile source of new crimes.

Modern Science and Anarchism

Anarchism like socialism is general, and like every other social movement, has not of course developed out of science or out of some philosophical school. The social sciences are still very far removed from the time when they shall be as exact as are physics and chemistry. Even in meteorology we cannot yet predict the weather a month or even one week in advance. It would be unreasonable, therefore, to expect of the young social sciences, which are concerned with phenomena much more complex than winds and rain, that they should foretell social events with any approach to certainty. Besides, it must not be forgotten that men of science, too, are but human, and that most of them either belong by descent to the possessing classes and are steeped in the prejudices of their class, or else are in the actual service of the government. Not out of the universities therefore does anarchism come.

Like socialism in general, and like all other social movements, anarchism was born *among the people*; and it will continue to be full of life and creative power only as long as it remains a thing of the people.

At all times two tendencies were continually at war in human society. On the one hand, the masses were developing in the form of customs a number of institutions which were necessary to make social life at all possible—to insure peace amongst men, to settle any disputes that might arise, and to help one another in everything requiring cooperative effort. The savage clan at its earliest stage, the village community, the hunters', and later on, the industrial guilds of the free town-republics of the middle ages, the beginnings of international law that these cities worked out with their mutual relations in those early periods, and many other institutions,—were elaborated, not by legislators, but by the creative power of the people.

And at all times, too, there appeared sorcerers, prophets, priests, and heads of military organizations, who endeavored to establish and to strengthen their authority over the people. They supported one another, concluded alliances in order that they might reign over the people, hold them in subjection and compel them to work for the masters.

Anarchism is obviously the representative of the first tendency—that is, of the creative, constructive power of the people themselves who aimed at developing institutions of common law in order to protect them from the power-seeking minority. By means of the same popular creative power and constructive activity, based upon modern science and technique, anarchism tries now as well to develop institutions which would insure a free evolution of society. In this sense, therefore, anarchists and governmentalists have existed through all historic times.

Then again it always happened that institutions—even those established originally with the object of securing equality, peace, and mutual aid—in the course of time became petrified, lost their original meaning, came under the control of the ruling minority, and became in the end a constraint upon the individual in his endeavors for further development. Then men would rise against these institutions. But while some of these discontented endeavored to throw off the yoke of the old institutions—of caste, commune, or guild—only in order that they themselves might rise over the rest and enrich themselves at their expense, others aimed at a modification of the institutions in the interest of all, especially in order to shake off the authority which had fixed its hold upon society. All really serious reformers—political, religious, and economic—have belonged to this class. And among them there always appeared persons who, without waiting for the time when all their fellow-countrymen, or even a majority of them, shall have become imbued with the same views, moved onward in the struggle against oppression, in mass where it was possible, and single-handed where it could not be done otherwise. These were the revolutionists, and them too we meet at all times.

But the revolutionists themselves generally appeared under two different aspects. Some of them in rising against the established authority endeavored not to abolish it but to take it in their own hands. In place of the authority which had become oppressive, these reformers sought to create a new one, promising that if they exercised it they would have the interests of the people dearly at heart, and would ever represent the people themselves. In this way, however, the authority of the Caesars was established in Imperial Rome, the power of the church rose in the first centuries after the fall of the Roman Empire, and the tyranny of dictators grew up in the medieval communes at the time of their decay. Of the same tendency, too, the kings and the czars availed themselves to constitute their power at the end of the feudal period. The belief in an emperor "for the people," that is, Caesarism, has not died out even yet.

But all the while another tendency was ever manifest. At all times, beginning with ancient Greece, there were persons and popular movements that aimed not at the substitution of one government for another, but at the abolition of authority altogether. They proclaimed the supreme rights of the individual and the people, and endeavored to free popular institutions from forces which were foreign and harmful to them, in order that the unhampered creative genius of the people might remould these institutions in accordance with the new requirements. In the history of the ancient Greek republics, and especially in that of the medieval commonwealths, we find numerous examples of this struggle. In this sense, therefore, Jacobinists and anarchists have existed at all times among reformers and revolutionists.

In past ages there were even great popular movements of this latter (anarchist) character. Many thousands of people then rose against authority—its tools, its courts, and its laws—and proclaimed the supreme rights of man. Discarding all written laws, the promoters of these movements endeavored to establish a new society based on equality and labor and on the government of each by his own conscience. In the Christian movement against Roman law, Roman government, Roman morality (or, rather, Roman immorality), which began in Judea in the reign of Augustus, there undoubtedly existed much that was essentially anarchistic. Only by degrees it degenerated into an ecclesiastical movement, modeled upon the ancient Hebrew church and upon Imperial Rome itself, which killed the anarchistic germ, assumed Roman governmental forms, and became in time the chief bulwark of government authority, slavery, and oppression.

Likewise, in the Anabaptist movement (which really laid the foundation for the Reformation) there was a considerable element of anarchism. But, stifled as it was by those of the reformers who, under Luther's leadership, joined the princes against the revolting peasants, it died out after wholesale massacres of the peasants had been carried out in Holland and Germany. Thereupon, the moderate reformers degenerated by degrees into those compromisers between conscience and government who exist today under the name of Protestants.

Anarchism consequently, to summarize, owes its origin to the constructive, creative activity of the people, by which all institutions of communal life were developed in the past, and to a protest —a revolt against the external force which had thrust itself upon these institutions; the aim of this protest being to give new scope to the creative activity of the people in order that it might work out the necessary institutions with fresh vigor.

In our own time anarchism arose from the same critical and revolutionary protest that called forth socialism in general. Only that some of the socialists, having reached the negation of capital and of our social organization based upon the exploitation of labor, went no further. They did not denounce what in our opinion constitutes the chief bulwark of capital; namely, government and its chief supports: centralization, law (always written by a minority in the interest of that minority), and courts of justice (established mainly for the defense of authority and capital).

Anarchism does not exclude these institutions from its criticism. It attacks not only capital, but also the main sources of the power of capitalism: law, authority, and the State.

But, though anarchism, like all other revolutionary movements, was born among the people—in the struggles of real life, and not in the philosopher's studio,—it is none the less important to know what place it occupies among the various scientific and philosophic streams of thought now prevalent: what is its relation to them; upon which of them principally does it rest; what method it employs in its researches—in other words, to which school of philosophy of law it belongs, and to which of the now existing tendencies in science it has the greatest affinity.

The Place of Anarchism in Modern Science

Anarchism is a world-concept based upon a mechanical explanation of all phenomena, embracing the whole of nature—that is, including in it the life of human societies and their economic, political, and moral problems. Its method of investigation is that of the exact natural sciences, and, if it pretends to be scientific, every conclusion it comes to must be verified by the method by which every scientific conclusion must be verified. Its aim is to construct a synthetic philosophy comprehending in one generalization all the phenomena of nature—and therefore also the life of societies.

It is therefore natural that to most of the questions of modern life anarchism should give new answers, and hold with regard to them a position differing from those of all political and to a certain extent of all socialistic parties which have not yet freed themselves from the metaphysical fictions of old.

Of course the elaboration of a complete mechanical world-conception has hardly been begun in its sociological part—in that part, that is, which deals with the life and the evolution of societies. But the little that has been done undoubtedly bears a marked though often not fully conscious character. In the domain of philosophy of law, in the theory of morality, in political economy, in history, both of nations and institutions, anarchism has already shown that it will not content itself with metaphysical conclusions, but will seek in every case a basis in the realm of natural science.

In the same way as the metaphysical conceptions of a Universal

Spirit, or of a Creative Force in Nature, the Incarnation of the Idea, Nature's Goal, the Aim of Existence, the Unknowable, Mankind (conceived as having a separate spiritualized existence), and so on—in the same way as all these have been brushed aside by the materialist philosophy of today, while the embryos of generalizations concealed beneath these misty terms are being translated into the concrete language of natural sciences,—so we proceed in dealing with the facts of social life. Here also we try to sweep away the metaphysical cobwebs, and to see what embryos of generalizations —if any—may have been concealed beneath all sorts of misty words.

When the metaphysicians try to convince the naturalist that the mental and moral life of man develops in accordance with certain "In-dwelling Laws of the Spirit," the latter shrugs his shoulders and continues his physiological study of the phenomena of life, of intelligence, and of emotions and passions, with a view to showing that they can all be resolved into chemical and physical phenomena. He endeavors to discover the natural laws on which they are based. Similarly, when the anarchists are told, for instance, that every development consists of a thesis, an antithesis, and a synthesis; or that "the object of law is the establishment of justice, which represents the realization of the highest idea;" or, again, when they are asked what, in their opinion, is "the object of life?", they, too, simply shrug their shoulders and wonder how, at the present state of development of natural science, old-fashioned people can still be found who continue to believe in "words" like these and still express themselves in the language of primitive anthropomorphism (the conception of nature as a thing governed by a being endowed with human attributes). Anarchists are not to be deceived by sonorous phrases, because they know that these words simply conceal either ignorance—that is, uncompleted investigation—or, what is much worse, mere superstition. They therefore pass on and continue their study of past and present social ideas and institutions according to the scientific method of induction. And in doing so they find of course that the development of social life is incomparably more complicated, and incomparably more interesting for practical purposes, than we should be led to believe if we judged by metaphysical formulae.

We have heard much of late about "the dialectic method," which was recommended for formulating the socialist ideal. Such a method we do not recognize, neither would the modern natural sciences have anything to do with it. "The dialectic method" reminds the modern naturalist of something long since passed—of something outlived and now happily forgotten by science. The discoveries of the nineteenth century in mechanics, physics, chemistry, biology, physical psychology, anthropology, psychology of nations, etc., were made—not by the dialectic method, but by the natural-scientific method, the method of induction and deduction. And since man is part of nature, and since the life of his "spirit," personal as well as social, is just as much a phenomenon of nature as is the growth of a flower or the evolution of social life amongst the ants and the bees, there is no cause for suddenly changing our method of investigation when we pass from the flower to man, or from a settlement of beavers to a human town.

The inductive method has proved its merits so well, that the nineteenth century, which has applied it, has caused science to advance more in a hundred years than it had advanced during the two thousand years that went before. And when in the second half of the century this method began to be applied to the investigation of human society, no point was ever reached where it was found necessary to abandon it and again adopt medieval scholasticism. Besides, when philistine naturalists, seemingly basing their arguments on "Darwinism," began to teach, "Crush whoever is weaker than yourself, such is the law of nature," it was easy for us to prove first, that this was *not* Darwin's conclusion, and by the same scientific method to show that these scientists were on the wrong path; that no such law exists; that the life of animals teaches us something entirely different; and that their conclusions were absolutely unscientific. They were just as unscientific as for instance the assertion that the inequality of wealth is a law of nature, or that capitalism is the most advantageous form of social life calculated to promote progress. Precisely this natural-scientific method applied to economic facts, enables us to prove that the so-called "laws" of middle-class sociology, including also their political economy, are not laws at all, but simply guesses, or mere assertions which have never been verified at all.

Moreover every investigation bears fruit only when it has a definite aim—when it is undertaken for the purpose of obtaining an answer to a definite and clearly-worded question. And it is the more fruitful the more clearly the explorer sees the connection that exists between his problem and his general concept of the universe. The better he understands the importance of the problem in the general concept, the easier will the answer be. The questions then which anarchism puts to itself may be stated thus: "What forms of social life assure to a given society, and then to mankind generally, the greatest amount of happiness, and hence also the greatest amount of vitality?" "What forms of social life are most likely to allow this amount of happiness to grow and to develop, quantitatively as well as qualitatively,—that is, to become more complete and more varied?" (from which, let us note in passing, a definition of *progress* is derived). The desire to promote evolution in this direction determines the scientific as well as the social and artistic activity of the anarchist. And this activity, in its turn, precisely on account of its falling in with the development of society in this direction, becomes a source of increased vitality, vigor, sense of oneness with mankind and its best vital forces.

It therefore becomes a source of increased vitality and happiness for the individual.

The Anarchist Ideal and the Preceding Revolutions

Anarchism originated, as has already been said, from the demands of practical life.

At the time of the great French Revolution of 1789–1793, Godwin had the opportunity of himself seeing how the governmental authority created during the revolution and by the revolution itself acted as a retarding force upon the revolutionary movement. And he knew too what was then taking place in England, under cover of Parliament,—the confiscation of public lands, the kidnapping of poor workhouse children by factory agents and their deportation to weavers' mills, where they perished wholesale. He understood that a government, even the government of the "One and Undivided" Jacobinist Republic would not bring about the necessary revolution; that the revolutionary government itself, from the very fact of its being a guardian of the State, and of the privileges every State has to defend, was an obstacle to emancipation; that to insure the success of the revolution, people ought to part, first of all, with their belief in law, authority, uniformity, order, property, and other superstitions inherited by us from our servile past. And with this purpose in view he wrote *Political Justice.*

The theorist of anarchism who followed Godwin—Proudhon— had himself lived through the Revolution of 1848 and had seen with his own eyes the crimes perpetrated by the revolutionary republican government, and the impotence of state socialism. Fresh from the impressions of what he had witnessed, Proudhon penned his admirable works, *A General Idea of the Social Revolution* and *Confessions of a Revolutionist,* in which he boldly advocated the abolition of the State and proclaimed anarchism.

And finally the idea of anarchism reappeared again in the International Working Men's Association, after the revolution that was attempted in the Paris Commune of 1871. The eyes of many were opened by the complete failure of the Council of the Commune and its incapacity to act as a revolutionary body—although it consisted, in due proportion, of representatives of every revolutionary faction of the time—and, on the other hand, by the incapacity of the London General Council of the International and its ludicrous and even harmful pretension to direct the Paris insurrection by orders sent from England. They led many members of the International, including Bakunin, to reflect upon the harmfulness of every kind of authority, of government—even when it had been as freely elected as that of the Commune and the International Working Men's Association. A few months later the resolution, passed by the same General Council of the Association at a secret conference held in London in 1871 instead of at an annual congress, made the dangers of having a government in the International still more evident. By this dire resolution they decided to turn the entire labor movement into another channel and to convert it from an economic revolutionary movement—from a direct struggle of the workingmen's organizations against capitalism—into an elective parliamentary and political movement. This decision led to open revolt on the part of the Italian, Spanish, Swiss, and partly also of the Belgian Federations against the London General Council, and out of this rebellion modern anarchism subsequently developed.

Every time, then, the anarchist movement sprang up in response to the lessons of actual life and originated from the practical tendencies of events. And, under the impulse thus given it, anarchism set to work out its theoretic, scientific basis. Scientific—not in the sense of adopting an incomprehensible terminology, or by clinging to ancient metaphysics, but in the sense of finding a basis for its principles in the natural sciences of the time, and of becoming one of their departments.

At the same time it worked out its ideal. No struggle can be successful if it does not render itself a clear and concise account of its aim. No destruction of the existing order is possible, if at the time of the overthrow, or of the struggle leading to the overthrow, the idea of what is to take the place of what is to be destroyed is not always present in the mind. Even the theoretical criticism of the existing conditions is impossible, unless the critic has in his mind a more or less distinct picture of what he would have in place of the existing state. Consciously or unconsciously, the *ideal*, the conception of something better is forming in the mind of everyone who criticizes social institutions.

This is even more the case with a man of action. To tell people, "First let us abolish autocracy or capitalism, and then we will discuss what to put in its place," means simply to deceive oneself and others. And *power* is never created by deception. The very man who deprecates ideals and sneers at them always has, nevertheless, some ideal of what he would like to take the place of what he is attacking. Among those who work for the abolition—let us say, of autocracy—some inevitably think of a constitution like that of England or Germany, while others think of a republic, either placed under the powerful dictatorship of their own party or modeled after the French empire-republic, or, again, of a federal republic as in the United States.

And when people attack capitalism, they always have a certain conception, a vague or definite idea, of what they hope to see in the place of capitalism: state capitalism, or some sort of state communism, or a federation of free communist association for the production, the exchange, and the consumption of commodities.

Every party thus has its ideal of the future, which serves it as a criterion in all events of political and economic life, as well as a basis for determining its proper modes of action. Anarchism, too, has conceived its own ideal; and this very ideal has led it to find its own immediate aims and its own methods of action different from those of all other political parties and also to some extent from those of the socialist parties which have retained the old Roman and ecclesiastic ideals of governmental organization.

It is seen from the foregoing that a variety of considerations, historical, ethnological, and economic, have brought the anarchists to conceive a society very different from what is considered as an ideal by the authoritarian political parties. The anarchists conceive a society in which all the mutual relations of its members are regulated, not by laws, not by authorities, whether self-imposed or elected, but by mutual agreements between the members of that society and by a sum of social customs and habits—not petrified by law, routine, or superstition, but continually developing and continually readjusted in accordance with the ever-growing requirements of a free life stimulated by the progress of science, invention, and the steady growth of higher ideals.

No ruling authorities, then. No government of man by man; no crystallization and immobility, but a continual evolution—such as we see in nature. Free play for the individual, for the full development of his individual gifts—*for his individualization*. In other words, no actions are *imposed* upon the individual by a fear of punishment; none is required from him by society, but those which receive his free acceptance. *In a society of equals* this would be quite sufficient for preventing those unsociable actions that might be harmful to other individuals and to society itself, and for favoring the steady moral growth of that society.

This is the conception developed and advocated by the anarchists.

Of course, up till now no society has existed which would have realized these principles in full, although the striving towards a partial realization of such principles has always been at work in mankind. We may say, therefore, that anarchism is a certain *ideal* of society and that this ideal is different from the ideal of society which has hitherto been advocated by most philosophers, scientists, and leaders of political parties, who pretended to rule mankind and to govern men.

But it would not be fair to describe such a conception as a Utopia, because the word "Utopia" in our current language conveys the idea of something that *cannot* be realized.

Taken in its usual current sense, therefore, the word "Utopia" ought to be limited to those conceptions only which are based on merely theoretical reasonings as to what is *desirable* from the writers' points of view, but not on what *is already developing* in human agglomerations. Such were, for instance, the Utopias of the Catholic Empire of the Popes, the Napoleonic Empire, the Messianism of Mickiewicz, and so on. But it cannot be applied to a conception of society which is based, as anarchism is, on an analysis of *tendencies of an evolution that is already going on in society,* and on *inductions* therefrom as to the future—those tendencies which have been, as we saw, for thousands of years the mainspring for the growth of sociable habits and customs, known in science under the name of customary law, and which affirm themselves more and more definitely in modern society.

When we look into the origin of the anarchist conception of society, we see that it has had a double origin: the criticism, on the one side, of the hierarchical organizations and the authoritarian conceptions of society; and on the other side, the analysis of the tendencies that are seen in the progressive movements of mankind, both in the past, and still more so at the present time.

Growth of Anarchist Ideas

From the remotest, stone-age antiquity, men must have realized the evils that resulted from letting some of them acquire personal authority—even if they were the most intelligent, the bravest, or the wisest. Consequently they developed in the primitive clan, the village community, the medieval guild (neighbors' guilds, arts and crafts' guilds, traders', hunters', and so on), and finally in the free medieval city, such institutions as enabled them to resist the encroachments upon their life and fortunes both of those strangers who conquered them, and of those clansmen of their own who endeavored to establish their personal authority. The same popular tendency was self evident in the religious movements of the masses in Europe during the earlier portions of the Reform movement and its Hussite and Anabaptist forerunners. At a much later period, namely in 1793, the same current of thought and of action found its expression in the strikingly independent, freely federated activity of the "Sections" of Paris and all great cities and many small "Communes" during the French Revolution. And later still, the labor combinations which developed in England and France, notwithstanding Draconic laws, as soon as the factory system began to grow up, were an outcome of the same popular resistance to the growing power of the few—the capitalists in this case.

These were the main popular anarchist currents which we know of in history, and it is self-evident that these movements could not but find their expression in literature. So they did, beginning with Lao-tse in China, and some of the earliest Greek philosophers (Aristippus and the Cynics, Zeno and some of the Stoics). However, being born in the masses, and not in any centers of learning, these popular movements, both when they were revolutionary and when they were deeply constructive, found little sympathy among the learned men—far less than the authoritarian hierarchical tendencies.

It was Godwin, in his *Enquiry Concerning Political Justice*, who stated in 1793 in a quite definite form the political and economic principles of anarchism. He did not use the word "anarchism" itself, but he very forcibly laid down its principles, boldly attacking the laws, proving the uselessness of the State, and maintaining that only with the abolition of courts would true *justice*—the only real foundation of all society—become possible. As regards property, he openly advocated communism.

Proudhon was the first to use the word "an-archy" (no-government) and to submit to a powerful criticism the fruitless efforts of men to give themselves such a government as would prevent the rich ones from dominating the poor, and at the same time always remain under the control of the governed ones. The repeated attempts of France, since 1793, at giving herself such a constitution, and the failure of the Revolution of 1848, gave him rich material for his criticism.

Being an enemy of all forms of state socialism, of which the communists of those years (the forties and fifties of the nineteenth century) represented a mere subdivision, Proudhon fiercely attacked all such attempts; and taking Robert Owen's system of labor checks representing hours of labor, he developed a conception of *mutualism*, in which any sort of political government would be useless.

The values of all the commodities being measured by the amount of labor necessary to produce them, all the exchanges between the producers could be carried on by means of a national bank, which would accept payment in labor checks—a clearing house establishing the daily balance of exchanges between the thousands of branches of this bank.

The services exchanged by different men would thus be *equivalent*; and as the bank would be able to lend the labor checks' money without interest, and every association would be able to borrow it on payment of only one per cent or less to cover the administration costs, capital would lose its pernicious power; it could be used no more as an instrument of exploitation.

Proudhon gave to the system of mutualism a very full development in connection with his anti-government and anti-state ideas; but it must be said that the mutualist portion of his program had already been developed in England by William Thompson (he was a mutualist prior to his becoming a communist) and the English followers of Thompson—John Gray (1825, 1831) and J. F. Bray (1839).

In the United States, the same direction was represented by Josiah Warren, who, after having taken part in Robert Owen's colony, "New Harmony," turned against communism, and in 1827 founded, in Cincinnati, a "store" in which goods were exchanged on the principle of time-value and labor checks. Such institutions remained in existence up till 1865 under the names of "equity stores," "equity village," and "house of equity."

The same ideas of labor-value and exchange at labor-cost were advocated in Germany, in 1843 and 1845, by Moses Hess and Karl Grün; and in Switzerland by Wilhelm Marr, who opposed the authoritarian communist teachings of Weitling.

On the other side, in opposition to the strongly authoritarian communism of Weitling, which had found a great number of adherents among workingmen in Germany, there appeared in 1845 the work of a German Hegelian, Max Stirner (Johann Kaspar Schmidt was his real name), *The Ego and His Own*, which was lately rediscovered, so to say, by J. H. Mackay, and very much spoken of in anarchist circles as a sort of manifesto of the individualist anarchists.

Stirner's work is a revolt against both the State and the new tyranny which would have been imposed upon man if authoritarian communism were introduced. Reasoning on Hegelian metaphysical lines, Stirner preaches, therefore, the rehabilitation of the "I" and the supremacy of the individual; and he comes in this way to advocate complete "a-moralism" (no-morality) and an "association of egoists."

It is easy to see, however,—as has been indicated more than once by anarchist writers, and lately by the French professor, V. Basch, in an interesting work, *Anarchist Individualism: Max Stirner* (1904, in French)—that this sort of individualism, aiming as it does at the "full development," not of all members of society, but of those only who would be considered as the most gifted ones, without caring for the right of full development for *all*—is merely a disguised return towards the now-existing education-monopoly of the few. It simply means a "right to their full development" for the privileged minorities. But, as such monopolies cannot be maintained otherwise than under the protection of a monopolist legislation and an organized coercion by the State, the claims of these individualists necessarily end in a return to the state idea and to that same coercion which they so fiercely attack themselves. Their position is thus the same as that of Spencer, and of all the so-called "Manchester school" of economists, who also begin by a severe criticism of the State and end in its full recognition in order to maintain the property monopolies, of which the State is the necessary stronghold.

Such was the growth of anarchist ideas, from the French Revolution and Godwin to Proudhon. The next step was made within the great "International Working Men's Association," which so much inspired the working-classes with hope, and the middle classes with terror, in the years 1868–1870—just before the Franco-German War.

That this association was not founded by Marx, or any other personality, as the hero-worshippers would like us to believe, is self-evident. It was the outcome of the meeting, at London, in 1862, of a delegation of French workingmen who had come to visit the Second International Exhibition, with representatives of British Trade Unions and Radicals who received that delegation.

Anarchism and the Free Commune

With the Franco-German War came the crushing defeat of France, the provisory government of Gambetta and Thiers, and the Commune of Paris, followed by similar attempts at Saint Etienne in France, and at Barcelona and Cartagena in Spain. And these popular insurrections brought into evidence what the *political* aspect of a social revolution ought to be.

Not a democratic republic, as was said in 1848, but *the free, independent Communist Commune.*

The Paris Commune itself suffered from the confusion of ideas as to the economic and political steps to be taken by the revolution, which prevailed, as we saw, in the International. Both the Jacobinists and the communalists—*i.e.*, the centralists and the federalists—

were represented in the uprising, and necessarily they came into conflict with each other. The most warlike elements were the Jacobinists and the Blanquists, but the economic, communist ideals of Babeuf had already faded among their middle-class leaders. They treated the economic question as a secondary one, which would be attended to later on, *after* the triumph of the Commune, and this idea prevailed. But the crushing defeat which soon followed, and the bloodthirsty revenge taken by the middle class, proved once more that the triumph of a popular commune was materially impossible without a parallel triumph of the people in the economic field.

For the Latin nations, the Commune of Paris, followed by similar attempts at Cartagena and Barcelona, settled the ideas of the revolutionary protetariat.

This was the form that the social revolution must take—the independent commune. Let all the country and all the world be against it; but once its inhibitants have decided that they *will* communalize the consumption of commodities, their exchange, and their production, *they must realize it among themselves*. And in so doing, they will find such forces as never could be called into life and to the service of a great cause, if they attempted to take in the sway of the revolution the whole country including its most backward or indifferent regions. Better to fight such strongholds of reaction openly than to drag them as so many chains rivetted to the feet of the fighter.

More than that. We made one step more. We understood that if no central government was needed to rule the independent communes, if the national government is thrown overboard and national unity is obtained by free federation, then a central *municipal* government becomes equally useless and noxious. The same federative principle would do within the commune.

The uprising of the Paris Commune thus brought with it the solution of a question which tormented every true revolutionist. Twice had France tried to bring about some sort of socialist revolution by imposing it through a central government more or less disposed to accept it: in 1793–94, when she tried to introduce *l'égalité de fait*—real, economic equality—by means of strong Jacobinist measures; and in 1848, when she tried to impose a "Democratic Socialist Republic." And each time she failed. But now a new solution was indicated. The free commune must do it on its own territory, and with this grew up a new ideal—anarchism.

We understood then that at the bottom of Proudhon's *Idée Générale sur la Revolution au Dix-neuvième Siècle* (unfortunately not yet translated into English) lay a deeply *practical* idea—that of anarchism. And in the Latin countries the thought of the more advanced men began to work in this direction.

Alas! in Latin countries only: in France, in Spain, in Italy, in the French-speaking part of Switzerland, and the Wallonic part of Belgium. The Germans, on the contrary, drew from their victory over France quite another lesson and quite different ideals—the worship of the centralized State.

The centralized State, hostile even to national tendencies of independence; the power of centralization and a strong central authority—these were the lessons they drew from the victories of the German Empire, and to these lessons they cling even now, without understanding that this was only a victory of a military mass, of the universal obligatory military service of the Germans over the recruiting system of the French and over the rottenness of the second Napoleonic Empire approaching a revolution which would have benefitted mankind, if it had not been hindered by the German invasion.

In the Latin countries, then, the lesson of the Paris and the Cartagena communes laid the foundations for the development of anarchism. And the authoritarian tendencies of the General council of the International Working Men's Association, which soon became evident and worked fatally against the unity of action of the great association, still more reinforced the anarchist current of thought. The more so as that council, led by Marx, Engels, and some French Blanquist refugees—all pure Jacobinists—used its powers to make a *coup d'état* in the International. It substituted in the program of the association parliamentary political action *in lieu* of the economic struggle of labor against capital, which hitherto had been the essence of the International. And in this way it provoked an open revolt against its authority in the Spanish, Italian, Jurassic, and East Belgian Federations, and among a certain section of the English Internationalists.

Bakunin and the State

In Mikhail Bakunin, the anarchist tendency, now growing within the International, found a powerful, gifted, and inspired exponent; while round Bakunin and his Jura friends gathered a small circle of talented young Italians and Spaniards, who further developed his ideas. Largely drawing upon his wide knowledge of history and philosophy, Bakunin established in a series of powerful pamphlets and letters the leading principles of modern anarchism.

The complete abolition of the State, with all its organization and ideals, was the watchword he boldly proclaimed. The State has been in the past a historical necessity which grew out of the authority won by the religious castes. But its complete extinction is now, in its turn, a historical necessity because the State represents the negation of liberty and spoils even what it undertakes to do for the sake of general well-being. All legislation made within the State, even when it issues from the so-called universal suffrage, has to be repudiated because it always has been made with regard to the interests of the privileged classes. Every nation, every region, every commune must be absolutely free to organize itself, politically and economically, as it likes, so long as it is not a menace to its neighbors. "Federalism" and "autonomy" are not enough. These are only words, used to mask the State authority. Full independence of the communes, their free federation, and the social revolution within the communes—this was, he proved, the ideal now rising before our civilization from the mists of the past. The individual understands that he will be really free in proportion only as all the others round him become free.

As to his economic conceptions, Bakunin was at heart a communist; but, in common with his federalist comrades of the International, and as a concession to the antagonism to communism that the authoritarian communists had inspired in France, he described himself as a "collectivist anarchist." But, of course, he was not a "collectivist" in the sense of Vidal or Pecqueur, or of their modern followers, who simply aim at "state capitalism;" he understood it in the above-mentioned sense of *not* determining in advance what form of distribution the producers should adopt in their different groups—whether the communist solution, or the labor checks, or equal salaries, or any other method. And with these views, he was an ardent preacher of the social revolution, the near approach of which was foreseen then by all socialists, and which he foretold in fiery words.

The State is an institution which was developed for the very purpose of establishing monopolies in favor of the slave and serf owners, the landed proprietors, canonic and laic, the merchant guilds and the money-lenders, the kings, the military commanders, the noblemen, and finally, in the nineteenth century, the industrial capitalist, whom the State supplied with "hands" driven away from the land. Consequently the State would be, to say the least, a useless institution, once these monopolies ceased to exist. *Life would be simplified*, once the mechanism created for the exploitation of the poor by the rich would have been done away with.

The idea of independent communes for the territorial organization, and of federations of trade unions for the organization of men in accordance with their different functions, gave a *concrete* conception of society regenerated by a social revolution. There remained only to add to these two modes of organization a third, which we saw rapidly developing during the last fifty years, since a little liberty was conquered in this direction: the thousands upon thousands of free combines and societies growing up everywhere for the satisfaction of all possible and imaginable needs, economic, sanitary, and educational; from mutual protection, for the propaganda of ideas, for art, for amusement, and so on. All of them covering each other, and all of them always ready to meet the new needs by new organizations and adjustments.

More than that. It begins to be understood now that if human societies go on developing on these lines, coercion and punishment must necessarily fall into decay. The greatest obstacle to the maintenance of a certain moral level in our present societies lies in the absence of social equality. Without *real* equality, the sense of justice can never be universally developed, because *justice implies the recognition of equality*; while in a society in which the principles of justice would not be contradicted at every step by the existing inequalities of rights and possibilities of development, they would be bound to spread and to enter into the habits of the people.

In such a case the individual would be *free*, in the sense that his freedom would not be limited any more by *fear:* by the fear of a social or a mystical punishment, or by obedience, either to other men reputed to be his superiors, or to mystical and metaphysical entities—which leads in both cases to intellectual servility (one of the greatest curses of mankind) and to the lowering of the moral level of men.

In free surroundings based upon equality, man might with full confidence let himself be guided by his own reason (which, of course, by necessity, would bear the stamp of his social surroundings). And he might also attain the full development of his individuality; while the "individualism" considered now by middle-class intellectuals as the *means* for the development of the better-gifted individuals, is, as every one may himself see, the chief *obstacle* to this development. Not only because, with a low productivity, which is kept at a low level by capitalism and the State, the immense majority of gifted men have neither the leisure nor the chance to develop their higher gifts; but also because those who have that leisure are recognized and rewarded by the present society on the condition of never going "too far" in their criticisms of that society, and especially never going over to acts that may lead to its destruction, or even to a serious reform. Those only are allowed to attain a certain "development of their individualities" who are not dangerous in this respect—those who are merely "interesting," but not dangerous to the Philistine.

The anarchists, we have said, build their previsions of the future upon those data which are supplied by the observation of life at the present time.

Thus, when we examine the tendencies that have prevailed in the life of civilized countries since the end of the eighteenth century, we certainly do not fail to see how strong the centralizing and authoritarian tendency was during that time, both among the middle classes and those workingmen who have been educated in the ideas of the middle classes and now strive to enter the ranks of their present rulers and exploiters.

But at the same time it is a fact that the anti-centralist and anti-militarist ideas, as well as the ideas of a free understanding, grow stronger and stronger nowadays both among the workingmen and the better educated and more or less intellectually free portions of the middle classes—especially in Western Europe.

I have shown, indeed, elsewhere (in *The Conquest of Bread* and in *Mutual Aid*) how strong at the present time is the tendency to constitute freely, *outside the State and the churches,* thousands upon thousands of free organizations for all sorts of needs: economic (agreements between the railway companies, the labor syndicates, trusts of employers, agricultural cooperation, cooperation for export, etc.), political, intellectual, artistic, educational, and so on. What formerly belonged without a shadow of doubt to the functions of the State, or the church, enters now into the domain of free organization.

This tendency develops with a striking rapidity under our very eyes. It was sufficient that a breath of emancipation should have slightly limited the powers of church and State in their never-satisfied tendency towards further extension—and voluntary organizations have already germinated by the thousand. And we may be sure that every new limitation that may be imposed upon State and church—the two inveterate enemies of freedom—will still further widen the sphere of action of the free organizations.

Future progress lies in this direction, and anarchism works precisely that way.

Economic Views of Anarchism

Passing now to the economic views of anarchists, three different conceptions must be distinguished.

So long as socialism was understood in its wide, generic, and true sense—as an effort to *abolish* the exploitation of labor by capital —the anarchists were marching hand-in-hand with the socialists of that time. But they were compelled to separate from them when the socialists began to say that there is no possibility of *abolishing* capitalist exploitation within the lifetime of our generation: that *during that phase of economic evolution which we are now living through* we have only to *mitigate* the exploitation, and to impose upon the capitalists certain legal limitations.

Contrarily to this tendency of the present-day socialists, we maintain that already now, without waiting for the coming of new phases and forms of the capitalist exploitation of labor, we must work for its *abolition*. We must, already now, tend to transfer all that is needed for production—the soil, the mines, the factories, the means of communication, and the means of existence, too—from the hands of the individual capitalist into those of the communities of producers and consumers.

As for the *political* organization—*i.e.*, the forms of the commonwealth in the midst of which an economic revolution could be accomplished—we entirely differ from all the sections of state socialists in that we do not see in the system of *state capitalism,* which is now preached under the name of collectivism, a solution of the social question. We see in the organization of the posts and telegraphs, in the State railways, and the like—which are represented as illustrations of a society without capitalists—nothing but a new, perhaps improved, but still undesirable form of the wage system. We even think that such a solution of the social problem would so much run against the present libertarian tendencies of civilized mankind, that it simply would be unrealizable.

We maintain that the State organization, having been the force to which the minorities resorted for establishing and organizing their power over the masses, cannot be the force which will serve to destroy these privileges. The lessons of history tell us that a new form of economic life always calls forth a new form of political organization; and a socialist society (whether communist or collectivist) cannot be an exception to this rule. Just as the churches cannot be utilized for freeing man from his old superstitions, and just as the feeling of human solidarity will have to find other channels for its expression besides the churches, so also the economic and political liberation of man will have to create new forms for its expression in life, instead of those established by the State.

Consequently, the chief aim of anarchism is to awaken those constructive powers of the laboring masses of the people which at all great moments of history came forward to accomplish the necessary changes, and which, aided by the now accumulated knowledge, will accomplish the change that is called forth by all the best men of our own time.

This is also why the anarchists refuse to accept the functions of legislators or servants of the State. We know that the social revolution will not be accomplished by means of *laws*. Laws can only *follow* the accomplished facts; and even if they honestly do follow them—which usually is *not* the case—a law remains a dead letter so long as there are not on the spot the living forces required for making of the *tendencies* expressed in the law an accomplished *fact*.

On the other hand, since the times of the International Working Men's Association, the anarchists have always advised taking an active part in those workers' organizations which carry on the *direct* struggle of labor against capital and its protector,—the State.

Such a struggle, they say, better than any other indirect means, permits the worker to obtain some temporary improvements in the present conditions of work, while it opens his eyes to the evil that is done by capitalism and the State that supports it, and wakes up his thoughts concerning the possibility of organizing consumption, production, and exchange without the intervention of the capitalist and the State.

Remuneration of Labor

The opinions of the anarchists concerning the form which *the remuneration of labor* may take in a society freed from the yoke of capital and State still remain divided.

To begin with, all are agreed in repudiating the new form of the wage system which would be established if the State became the owner of all the land, the mines, the factories, the railways, and so on, and the great organizer and manager of agriculture and all the industries. If these powers were added to those which the State already possesses (taxes, defence of the territory, subsidized religions, etc.), we should create a new tyranny even more terrible than the old one.

The greater number of anarchists accept the communist solution. They see that the only form of communism that would be acceptable in a civilized society is one which would exist without the continual interference of government, *i.e.*, the anarchist form. And they realize also that an anarchist society of a large size would be impossible, unless it would begin by guaranteeing to all its members a certain minimum of well-being produced in common. Communism and anarchism thus complete each other.

However, by the side of this main current there are those who see in anarchism a rehabilitation of individualism.

This last current is, in our opinion, a survival from those times when the power of production of food-stuffs and of all industrial commodities had not yet reached the perfection they have attained now. In those times communism was truly considered as equivalent to general poverty and misery, and well-being was looked at as something which is accessible to a very small number only. But this quite real and extremely important obstacle to communism exists no more. Owing to the immense productivity of human labor which has been reached nowadays in all directions—agricultural and industrial—it is quite certain, on the contrary, that a very high degree of well-being can easily be obtained in a few years by communist work.

Be this as it may, the individualist anarchists subdivide into two branches. There are, first, the pure individualists, in the sense of Max Stirner, who have lately gained some support in the beautiful poetical form of the writings of Nietzsche. But we have already said once how metaphysical and remote from real life is this "self-assertion of the individual;" how it runs against the feelings of equality of most of us; and how it brings the would-be "individualists" dangerously near to those who imagine themselves to represent a "superior breed"—those to whom we owe the State, the church, modern legislation, the police, militarism, imperialism, and all other forms of oppression.

The other branch of individualist anarchists comprises the *mutualists*, in the sense of Proudhon. However, there will always be against this system the objection that it could hardly be compatible with a system of common ownership of land and the necessaries for production. Communism in the possession of land, factories, etc. and individualism in production are too contradictory to coexist in the same society—to say nothing of the difficulty of estimating the *market* value or the *selling* value of a product by the average time that is necessary, or the time that was actually used, in producing it. To bring men to agree upon such an estimation of their work would already require a deep penetration of the communist principle into their ideas—at least, for all produce of first necessity. And if a community introduced, as a further concession to individualism, a higher payment for skilled work, or chances of promotion in a hierarchy of functionaries, this would reintroduce all those inconveniences of the present wage system which are combatted now by the workers.

To some extent the same remark applies to the American anarchist individualists who were represented in the fifties by S. P. Andrews and W. Greene, later on by Lysander Spooner, and now are represented by Benjamin Tucker, the well-known editor of the New York *Liberty*. Their ideas are partly those of Proudhon, but partly also those of Herbert Spencer. They start from the principle that the only law which is obligatory for the anarchist is to mind his own business, and not to meddle with that of others; that each individual and each group has the *right* to oppress all mankind—if they have the *force* to do so; and that if this only law, of minding one's own business, had received a *general* and *complete* application, it would offer no danger, because the rights of each individual would have been limited by the equal rights of all others.

But to reason in this way is to pay, in our opinion, too large a tribute to metaphysical dialectics, and to ignore the facts of real life. It is impossible to conceive a society in which the affairs of any one of its members would not concern many other members, if not all; still less a society in which a continual contact between its members would not have established an interest of every one towards all others, which would render it *impossible* to act without thinking of the effects which our actions may have on others.

This is why Tucker, like Spencer, after his admirable criticism of the State and a vigorous defense of the rights of the individual, comes to recognize the right of *defense* of its members by the State. But it was precisely by assuming the function of "defense" of its weaker members that the State in its historical evolution developed all its *aggressive* functions, which Spencer and Tucker have so brilliantly criticized.

This contradiction is probably the reason why anarchist individualism, while it finds followers amongst the middle-class intellectuals, does not spread amongst the workers. It must be said, however, that it renders a real service in preventing the anarchist communists from making too many concessions to the old idea of State officialism. Old ideas are so difficult to get rid of.

As to anarchist communism, it is certain that this solution wins more and more ground nowadays among those workingmen who try to get a clear conception as to the forthcoming revolutionary action. The syndicalist and trade union movements, which permit the workingmen to realize their solidarity and to feel the community of their interests much better than any elections, prepare the way for these conceptions. And it is hardly too much to hope that when some serious movement for the emancipation of labor begins in Europe and America, attempts will be made, at least in the Latin countries, in the anarchist-communist direction—much deeper than anything that was done by the French nation in 1793–94.

Anarchism and the Law

When we are told that Law (written with a capital letter) "is the objectification of Truth;" or that "the principles underlying the development of Law are the same as those underlying the development of the human spirit;" or that "Law and Morality are identical and differ only formally;" we feel as little respect for these assertions as does Mephistopheles in Goethe's *Faust*. We are aware that those who make such seemingly profound statements as these have expended much thought upon these questions. But they have taken a wrong path; and hence we see in these high-flown sentences mere attempts at unconscious generalization based upon inadequate foundations and confused moreover by words chosen to hypnotize men by their obscurity. In olden times they tried to give "Law" a divine origin; later they began to seek a metaphysical basis for it; now, however, we are able to study its anthropological origin. And, availing ourselves of the results obtained by the anthropological school, we take up the study of social customs, beginning with those of the primitive savages, and trace the origin and the development of the laws at different epochs.

In this way we come to the conclusion already expressed, namely, that all laws have a twofold origin, and in this very respect differ from those institutions established by custom which are generally recognized as the moral code of a given society at a given time. Law confirms and crystallizes these customs, but while doing so it takes advantage of this fact to establish (for the most part in a disguised form) the germs of slavery and class distinction, the authority of priest and warrior, serfdom and various other institutions, in the interests of the armed and would-be ruling minority. In this way a yoke has imperceptibly been placed upon man, of which he could only rid himself by means of subsequent bloody revolutions. And this is the course of events down to the present moment —even in contemporary "labor legislation" which, along with "protection of labor," covertly introduces the idea of *compulsory* State arbitration in case of strikes, a *compulsory* working day of so many hours, military exploitation of the railroads during strikes, legal sanction for the dispossession of the peasants in Ireland, and so on. And this will continue to be so as long as *one* portion of society goes on framing laws for *all* society, and thereby strengthens the power of the State, which forms the chief support of capitalism.

It is plain, therefore, why anarchism,—although the anarchists, more than any legislators, aspire to *Justice*, which is equivalent to *Equality*, and impossible without it,—has from the time of Godwin rejected all written *laws*.

When, however, we are told that by rejecting law we reject all morality, we answer that the very wording of this objection is to us strange and incomprehensible. It is as strange and incomprehensible to us as it would be to every naturalist engaged in the study of the phenomena of morality. In answer to this argument, we ask: "What do you really mean? Can you not translate your statements into comprehensible language?"

Now, what does a man who takes his stand on "universal law" really mean? Does he mean that *there is* in all men the conception that one ought not to do to another what he would not have done to himself—that it would be better even to return good for evil? If so, well and good. Let us, then, study the origin of these moral ideas in man, and their course of development. Let us extend our studies also to prehuman times. Then, we may analyze to what extent the idea of *Justice* implies that of *Equality*. The question is an important one, because only those who regard *others* as their equals can accept the rule, "Do not to others what you would not have done to yourself." The landlord and the slave-owner, who did not look upon "the serf" and the negro as their equals, did not recognize "the universal law" as applicable to these unhappy members of the human family. And then, if this observation of ours be correct, we shall see whether it is at all possible to inculcate morality while teaching the doctrine of inequality.

We shall finally analyze, as Mark Guyau did, the facts of self-sacrifice. And then we shall consider what has most promoted the development in man of moral feelings—first, of those which are expressed in the commandment concerning our neighbor, and then of the other feelings which lead to self-sacrifice; and after this consideration we shall be able to deduce from our study exactly what social conditions and what institutions promise the best results for the future. Is this development promoted by religion, and to what extent? Is it promoted by inequality—economic and political —and by a division into classes? Is it promoted by law? By punishment? By prisons? By the judge? The jailer? The hangman?

Let us study all this in detail, and then only may we speak again of morality and moralization by means of laws, law courts, jailers, spies, and police. But we had better give up using the sonorous words which only conceal the superficiality of our semi-learning. In their time the use of these words was, perhaps, unavoidable—their application could never have been useful. But now that we are able to approach the study of burning social questions in exactly the same manner as the gardener and the physiologist take up the study of the conditions most favorable for the growth of a plant—let us do so!

Economic Laws

Likewise, when certain economists tell us that "in a perfectly free market the price of commodities is measured by the amount of labor socially necessary for their production," we do not take this assertion on faith because it is made by certain authorities or because it may seem to us "tremendously socialistic." It may be so, we say. But do you not notice that by this very statement you maintain that value and the necessary labor *are proportional to each other*—just as the speed of a falling body is proportional to the number of seconds it has been falling? Thus you maintain a *quantitative relation* between these two magnitudes; whereas a quantitative relation can be proved *only* by quantitative measurements. To confine yourself to the remark that the exchange-value of commodities "generally" increases when a greater expenditure of labor is required, and then to assert that *therefore* the two quantities are proportional to each other, is to make as great a mistake as the man who would assert that the quantity of rainfall is measured by the fall of the barometer below its average height. He who first observed that, generally speaking, when the barometer is falling a greater amount of rain falls than when it is rising; or, that there is a certain relation between the speed of a falling stone and the height from which it fell—that man surely made a scientific discovery. But the person who would come after him and assert that the amount of rainfall is *measured* by the fall of the barometer below its average height, or that the space through which a falling body has passed is *proportional* to the time of fall and is measured by it,— that person would not only talk nonsense, but would prove by his very words that the method of scientific research is absolutely strange to him; that his work is unscientific, full as it may be of scientific expressions. The absence of data is clearly no excuse. Hundreds if not thousands of similar relationships are known to science in which we see the dependence of one magnitude upon another—for example, the recoil of a cannon depending upon the quantity of powder in the charge, or the growth of a plant depending upon the amount of heat or light received by it. But no scientific man will presume to affirm the proportion of these magnitudes without having investigated their relations quantitatively, and still less would he represent this proportion as a scientific *law*. In most instances the dependence is very complex—as it is, indeed, in the theory of value. The necessary amount of labor and value are by no means proportional.

The same remark refers to almost every economic doctrine that is current today in certain circles and is being presented with wonderful naiveté as an invariable law. We not only find most of these so-called laws grossly erroneous, but maintain also that those who believe in them will themselves become convinced of their error as soon as they come to see the necessity of verifying their quantitative deductions by quantitative investigation.

Moreover, the whole of political economy appears to us in a different light from that in which it is seen by modern economists of both the middle-class and the social-democratic camps. The scientific method (the inductive method of natural sciences) being utterly unknown to them, they fail to give themselves any definite account of what constitutes "a law of nature," although they delight in using the term. They do not know—or if they know they continually forget—that every law of nature has a *conditional* character. In fact every natural law always means this: "If certain conditions in nature are at work, certain things will happen." "If one line intersects another, forming right angles on both its sides at the crossing point, the consequences will be such and such." "If two bodies are acted upon by such movements only as exist in interstellar space, and there is not, within measurable distance of them, a third body or a fourth body acting upon the two, then their centers of gravity will approach each other at a certain speed (the law of gravitation)." And so on. In every case there is an *"if"*—a condition.

In consequence of this, all the so-called laws and theories of political economy are in reality no more than statements of the following nature: "Granting that there are always in a country a considerable number of people who cannot subsist a month, or even a fortnight, without earning a salary and accepting for that purpose the conditions of work imposed upon them by the State, or offered to them by those whom the State recognizes as owners of land, factories, railways, etc., then the results will be so and so."

So far academic political economy has been only an enumeration of what happens under the just-mentioned conditions—without distinctly stating the conditions themselves. And then, having described *the facts* which arise in our society under these conditions, they represent to us these *facts* as rigid, *inevitable economic laws.* As to socialist political economy, although it criticizes some of these deductions, or explains others somewhat differently,—it has not yet been original enough to find a path of its own. It still follows in the old grooves, and in most cases repeats the very same mistakes.

And yet, in our opinion, political economy must have an entirely different problem in view. It ought to occupy with respect to human societies a place in science similar to that held by physiology in relation to plants and animals. It must become *the physiology of society.* It should aim at *studying the needs of society and the various means, both hitherto used and available under the present state of scientific knowledge, for their satisfaction.* It should try to analyze how far the present means are expedient and satisfactory, economic or wasteful; and then, since the ultimate end of every science (as Bacon had already stated) is obviously prediction and practical application to the demands of life, it should concern itself with the discovery of means *for the satisfaction of these needs with the smallest possible waste of labor and with the greatest benefit to mankind in general.* Such means would be, in fact, mere corollaries from the relative investigation mentioned above, provided this last had been made on scientific lines.

Pursuing the same method, anarchism arrives at its own conclusions concerning the different forms of society, especially the State. It could not rest content with current metaphysical assertions like the following: "The State is the affirmation of the idea of the highest justice in society;" or "The State is the instigation and the instrument of progress;" or, "Without the State, society is impossible."

Anarchism has approached the study of the State exactly in the manner the naturalist approaches the study of social life among bees and ants, or among the migratory birds which hatch their young on the shores of subarctic lakes. It would be useless to repeat here the conclusions to which this study has brought us with reference to the history of the different political forms (and to their desirable or probable evolution in the future). If I were to do so, I should have to repeat what has been written by anarchists from the time of Godwin, and what may be found with all necessary explanations, in a whole series of books and pamphlets.

I will say only that the State is a form of social life which has developed in our European civilization, under the influence of a series of causes, only since the end of the sixteenth century. Before the sixteenth century the State, in its Roman form, did not exist—or, more exactly, it existed only in the minds of the historians who trace the genealogy of Russian autocracy to Rurik and that of France to the Merovingian kings.

Furthermore, the State (state-justice, state-church, state-army) and capitalism are, in our opinion, inseparable concepts. In history these institutions developed side by side, mutually supporting and re-enforcing each other. They are bound together, not by a mere coincidence of contemporaneous development, but by the bond of cause and effect, effect and cause. Thus the State appears to us as a society for the mutual insurance of the landlord, the warrior, the judge, and the priest, constituted in order to enable every one of them to assert his respective authority over the people and to exploit the poor.

Such was the origin of the State; such was its history; and such is its present essence.

Consequently, to imagine that capitalism may be abolished while the State is maintained, and with the aid of the State—while the latter was founded for forwarding the development of capitalism and was always growing in power and solidity, in proportion as the power of capitalism grew up—to cherish such an illusion is as unreasonable, in our opinion, as it was to expect the emancipation of labor from the church, or from Caesarism or imperialism. Certainly, in the first half of the nineteenth century, there have been many socialists who had such dreams; but to live in the same dreamland now that we enter in the twentieth century, is really too childish.

A new form of economic organization will necessarily require a new form of political structure. And, whether the change be accomplished suddenly, by a revolution, or slowly, by the way of a gradual evolution, the two changes, political and economic, must go on abreast, hand in hand.

Each step towards economic freedom, each victory won over capitalism will be at the same time a step towards political liberty—towards liberation from the yoke of the State by means of free agreement, territorial, professional, and functional. And each step made towards taking from the State any one of its powers and attributes will be helping the masses to win a victory over capitalism.

The Means of Action

It is obvious that, since anarchism differs so widely in its method of investigation and in its fundamental principles, both from the academic sociologists and from its social-democratic fraternity, it must of necessity equally differ from them all in its means of action.

Understanding law, right, and the State as we do, we cannot see any guarantee of progress, still less an approach to the required social changes, in the submission of the individual to the State. We are therefore no longer able to say, as do the superficial interpreters of social phenomena when they require the State management of industries, that modern capitalism has come into being through "the anarchy of exploitation," through "the theory of non-interference," which—we are told—the States have carried out by practicing the formula of "let them do as they like" (*laissez faire, laissez passer*). We know that this is not true. While giving the capitalist any degree of free scope to amass his wealth at the expense of the helpless laborers, the government has *nowhere* and *never* during the whole nineteenth century afforded the laborers the opportunity "to do as they pleased." The terrible revolutionary, that is, Jacobinist, convention treated strikes as a coalition and legislated, "For strikes, for forming a State within the State—death!" In 1813 people were hanged in England for going out on strike, and in 1831 they were deported to Australia for forming the Great Trades' Union (Union of all Trades) of Robert Owen. In the sixties people were still condemned to hard labor for participating in strikes, and even now trade unions are prosecuted for damages for picketing—for having dissuaded laborers from working in times of strike. What is one to say, then, of France, Belgium, Switzerland, and especially of Germany and Russia? It is needless also to tell how by means of taxes the State brings laborers to the verge of poverty which puts them body and soul in the power of the factory boss; how the communal lands have been robbed from the people. Or must we remind the reader how even at the present moment, all the States without exception are creating directly all kinds of monopolies—in railroads, tramways, telephones, gasworks, waterworks, electric works, schools, etc. In short, the system of non-interference—*laissez faire* —has never been applied for one single hour by any government.

And therefore if it is permissible for middle-class economists to affirm that the system of "non-interference" is practiced (since they endeavor to prove that poverty is a law of nature), it is simply shameful that socialists should speak thus to the workers. *Freedom to oppose exploitation has so far never and nowhere existed.* Everywhere it had to be taken by force, step by step, at the cost of countless sacrifices. "Non-interference," and more than non-interference,—direct support, help and protection,—existed *only* in the interests of the exploiters. *Nor could it be otherwise.* The mission of the church has been to hold the people in intellectual slavery. The mission of the State was to hold them, half starved, in economic slavery.

The State was established for the precise purpose of imposing the rule of the landowners, the employers of industry, the warrior class, and the clergy upon the peasants on the land and the artisans in the city. And the rich perfectly well know that if the machinery of the State ceased to protect them, their power over the laboring classes would be gone immediately.

Socialism, we have said—whatever form it may take in its evolution towards communism—must find *its own form* of political organization. Serfdom and absolute monarchy have always marched hand-in-hand. The one rendered the other a necessity. The same is true of capitalist rule, whose political form is representative government, either in a republic or in a monarchy. This is why socialism *cannot* utilize representative government as a weapon for liberating labor, just as it cannot utilize the church and its theory of divine right, or imperialism and Caesarism, with its theory of hierarchy of functionaries, for the same purpose.

A new form of political organization has to be worked out the moment that socialist principles shall enter into our life. And it is self–evident that this new form will have to be *more popular, more decentralized, and nearer to the folkmote self–government* than representative government can ever be.

Knowing this, we cannot see a guarantee of progress in a still greater submission of all to the State. We seek progress in the fullest emancipation of the individual from the authority of the State; in the greatest development of individual initiative and in the limitation of all the governmental functions, but surely not in their extension. The march forward in political institutions appears to us to consist in abolishing in the first place the State authority which has fixed itself upon society and which now tries to extend its functions more and more; and in the second place, in allowing the broadest possible development for the principle of free agreement, and in acknowledging the independence of all possible associations formed for definite ends, embracing in their federations the whole of society. The life of society itself we understand, not as something complete and rigid, but as something never perfect—something ever striving for new forms, and ever changing these forms in accordance with the needs of the time. This is what *life* is in nature.

Such a conception of human progress and of what we think desirable in the future (what, in our opinion, can increase the sum of happiness) leads us inevitably to our own special tactics in the struggle. It induces us to strive for the greatest possible development of personal initiative in every individual and group, and to secure unity of action, not through discipline, but through the unity of aims and the mutual confidence which never fail to develop when a great number of persons have consciously embraced some common idea.

Then we assert and endeavor to prove that it devolves upon every new economic form of social life to develop *its own* new form of political relations. It has been so in the past, and so it undoubtedly will be in the future. New forms are already germinating all round.

Feudal right and autocracy, or at least the almost unlimited power of a czar or a king, have moved hand in hand in history. They depended on each other in this development. Exactly in the same way the rule of the capitalists has evolved its own characteristic political order—representative government—both in strictly centralized monarchies and in republics.

Socialism, whatever may be the form in which it will appear, and in whatever degree it may approach to its unavoidable goal,—communism,—will also have to choose *its own* form of political structure. Of the old form *it cannot make use*, no more than it could avail itself of the hierarchy of the church or of autocracy. The State bureaucracy and centralization are as irreconcilable with socialism as was autocracy with capitalist rule. One way or another, socialism must become *more popular*, more communalistic, and less dependent upon indirect government through elected representatives. It must become more *self-governing*.

Besides, when we closely observe the modern life of France, Spain, England, and the United States, we notice in these countries the evident tendency to form into groups of entirely independent communes, towns, and villages, which would combine by means of free federation, in order to satisfy innumerable needs and attain certain immediate ends. In actual life this tendency manifests itself in thousands of attempts at organization outside the State, fully independent of it; as well as in attempts to take hold of various functions which had been previously usurped by the State and which, of course, it has never properly performed. And then as a great social phenomenon of universal import, this tendency found expression in the Paris Commune of 1871 and in a whole series of similar uprisings in France and Spain; while in the domain of thought—of ideas spreading through society—this view has already acquired the force of an extremely important factor of future history. The future revolutions in France and Spain will be *communalist*—not centralist.

On the strength of all this, we are convinced that to work in favor of a centralized state-capitalism and to see in it a *desideratum*, means to work *against* the tendency of progress already manifest. We see in such work as this a gross misunderstanding of the historic mission of socialism itself—a great historical mistake, and we make war upon it. To assure the laborers that they will be able to establish socialism, or even to take the first steps on the road to socialism, by retaining the entire government machinery, and changing only the persons who manage it; not to promote but even to retard the day on which the working people's minds shall be bent upon discovering their own new forms of political life,—this is in our eyes a colossal historical blunder which borders upon crime.

Finally, since we represent a revolutionary party, we try to study the history of the origin and development of past revolutions. We endeavor, first of all, to free the histories of revolutions written up till now from the partisan, and for the most part false, governmental coloring that has been given them. In the histories hitherto written we do not yet see *the people*, nor do we see how revolutions began. The stereotyped phrases about the desperate condition of people previous to revolutions fail to explain whence amid this desperation came the hope of something better—whence came the revolutionary spirit. And therefore after reading these histories, we put them aside, and going back to first sources, try to learn from them what caused the people to rise and what was its true part in revolutions, what advantages it obtained from a revolution, what ideas it launched into circulation, what faults of tactics it committed.

Thus, we understand the Great French Revolution not at all as it is pictured by Louis Blanc, who presents it chiefly as a great political movement directed by the Jacobin Club. We see in it first of all a chaotic *popular* movement, chiefly of the peasant folk ("Every village had its Robespierre," as the Abbé Grégoire, who *knew* the people's revolt, remarked to the historian Schlosser). This movement aimed chiefly at the destruction of every vestige of *feudal rights* and of redemptions that had been imposed for the abolition of some of them, as well as at the recovery of the *lands* which had been seized from the village communes by vultures of various kinds. And in so far the peasant movement was successful.

Then, upon this foundation of revolutionary tumult, of increased pulsation of life and of disorganization of all the powers of the State, we find on the one hand developing among the town laborers a tendency towards a vaguely understood socialist equality and the admirable forms of voluntary popular organization for a variety of functions, economic and political, that they worked out in the "sections" of the great cities and small municipalities; and on the other hand the middle classes working hard and successfully in order to establish their own authority upon the ruins of that of royalty and nobility. To this end the middle classes fought stubbornly and desperately that they might create a powerful, all-inclusive, centralized government, which would preserve and assure to them their right of property (gained partly by plunder before and during the Revolution) and afford them the full opportunity of exploiting the poor without any legal restrictions. We study the development and the struggle of these two powers and try to find out why the latter gained the upper hand over the former. And we see how in the State centralization which was created by the revolutionary Jacobinists, Napoleon found an excellent soil for establishing his empire. From this centralized authority which kills all local life, France is suffering even to this very day, and the first attempt to throw off its yoke—an attempt which opened a new era in history—was made by the proletariat of Paris only in 1871.

Without entering here upon an analysis of other revolutionary movements, it is sufficient to say that we understand the social revolution, not at all as a Jacobinist dictatorship—not at all as a reform of the social institutions by means of laws issued by a convention or a senate or a dictator. Such revolutions have never occurred, and a movement which should take this form would be doomed to inevitable death. We understand the revolution as a widespread popular movement, during which in every town and village within the region of the revolt, the masses will have to take upon themselves the task of rebuilding society—will have to take up themselves *the work of construction upon communistic bases,* without awaiting any orders and directions from above. That is, first of all they will have to organize, one way or another, the means of supplying food to everyone and of providing dwellings for all, and then produce whatever will be found necessary for feeding, clothing, and sheltering everybody.

They may not be—they are sure not to be the *majority* of the nation. But if they are a respectably numerous minority of cities and villages scattered over the country, starting life on their own new socialist lines, they will be able to win the right to pursue their own course. In all probability they will draw towards them a notable portion of the land, as was the case in France in 1793–94.

As to representative government, whether self-appointed or elected—be it "the dictatorship of the proletariat," or an elected "temporary government," or again a Jacobinist "convention,"—we place in it no hopes whatever. We know beforehand that it will be able to do nothing to accomplish the revolution so long as the people themselves do not accomplish the change by working out on the spot the necessary new institutions. We say so, not because we have a personal dislike of governments, but because nowhere and never in history do we find that people carried into government by a revolutionary wave, have proved equal to the occasion.

In the task of reconstructing society on new principles, separate men, however intelligent and devoted they may be, are sure to fail. The collective spirit of the masses is necessary for this purpose. Isolated men can sometimes find the legal expression to sum up the destruction of old social forms—when the destruction is already proceeding. At the utmost, they may widen, perhaps, the sphere of the reconstructive work, extending what is being done in a part of the country, over a larger part of the territory. But to impose the reconstruction by law is absolutely impossible, as was proved, among other examples, by the whole history of the French Revolution. Many thousands of the *laws* passed by the revolutionary convention had not even been put into force when reaction came and flung those laws into the waste-paper basket.

During a revolution new forms of life will always germinate on the ruins of the old forms, but no government will ever be able to find their expression *so long as these forms will not have taken a definite shape during the work itself of reconstruction* which must be going on in thousands of spots at the same time. It is impossible to legislate for *the future.* All we can do is to guess vaguely its essential tendencies and clear the road for it.

Looking upon the problems of the revolution in this light, anarchism obviously cannot take a sympathetic attitude toward the program which aims at "the conquest of power in present society." We know that by peaceful, parliamentary means in the present State such a conquest as this is impossible. The middle class will not give up its power without a struggle. It will resist. And in proportion as the socialists become a power in the present *bourgeois* society and State, their socialism must die out. Otherwise the middle classes, which are much more powerful both intellectually and numerically than is admitted in the socialist press, will not recognize them as their rulers. And we know also that were a revolution to give France or England or Germany a socialist government, the respective governments would be absolutely powerless without the activity of the people themselves, and that, necessarily, they would soon begin to act fatally as a bridle upon the revolution.

Finally our studies of the preparatory stages of all revolutions bring us to the conclusion that not a single revolution has originated in parliaments or in any other representative assembly. *All began with the people.* And no revolution has appeared in full armor—born, like Minerva out of the head of Jupiter, in a day. They all had their periods of incubation during which the masses were very slowly becoming imbued with the revolutionary spirit, grew bolder, commenced *to hope*, and step by step emerged from their former indifference and resignation. And the awakening of the revolutionary spirit always took place in such a manner that at first single individuals, deeply moved by the existing state of things, protested against it, one by one. Many perished, "uselessly" the armchair critic would say. But the indifference of society was shaken by these progenitors. The dullest and most narrow-minded people were compelled to reflect, "Why should men, young, sincere, and full of strength, sacrifice their lives in this way?" It was impossible to remain indifferent; it was necessary to take a stand, for or against: thought was awakening. Then little by little small groups came to be imbued with the same spirit of revolt. They also rebelled —sometimes in the hope of local success—in strikes or in small revolts against some official whom they disliked, or in order to get food for their hungry children, but frequently also without any hope of success, simply because the conditions grew unbearable. Not one, or two, or tens, but *hundreds* of similar revolts have preceded *and must precede* every revolution. Without these no revolution was ever wrought.

Without the menace contained in such revolts not a single concession was ever made by the ruling classes. Even the famous "peaceful" abolition of serfdom in Russia, of which Tolstoy often speaks as of a peaceful conquest, was forced upon the government by a series of peasant uprisings, beginning with the early fifties, spreading from year to year, and gaining in importance so as to attain proportions hitherto unknown, until 1857. Alexander Herzen's words, "Better to abolish serfdom from above than to wait until the abolition comes from below,"—repeated by Alexander II before the serf-owners of Moscow—were not mere phrases but expressed the real state of affairs. This was all the more true as to the eve of every revolution. Hundreds of partial revolts preceded every one of them. And it may be stated as a general rule that the character of every revolution is determined by the character and the aim of the uprisings by which it is preceded.

To wait therefore for a *social* revolution to come as a birthday present, without a whole series of protests on the part of the individual conscience, and without hundreds of preliminary revolts by which the very nature of the revolution is determined, is to say the least, absurd. But to assure the working people that they will gain all the benefits of a socialist revolution by confining themselves to electoral agitation, and to attack vehemently every act of individual revolt and all minor preliminary mass-revolts—means to become as great an obstacle to the development of the revolutionary spirit and to all progress as was and is the Christian Church.

Conclusion

Without entering into further discussion of the principles of anarchism and the anarchist program of action, enough has been said, I think, to show the place of anarchism among the modern sociological sciences.

Anarchism is an attempt to apply to the study of human institutions the generalizations gained by means of the natural-scientific inductive method; and an attempt to foresee the future steps of mankind on the road to liberty, equality, and fraternity, with a view to realizing the greatest sum of happiness for every unit of human society.

It is the inevitable result of that natural-scientific, intellectual movement which began at the close of the eighteenth century, was hampered for half a century by the reaction that set in throughout Europe after the French Revolution, and has been appearing again in full vigor ever since the end of the fifties. Its roots lie in the natural-scientific philosophy of the century mentioned. Its complete scientific basis, however, it could receive only after that awakening of naturalism which brought into being the natural-scientific study of human social institutions.

In anarchism there is no room for those pseudo-scientific laws with which the German metaphysicians of the first thirty years of the nineteenth century had to content themselves. Anarchism does not recognize any method other than the natural-scientific, and it applies this method to all the so-called humanitarian sciences. Availing itself of this method as well as of all researches which have recently been called forth by it, anarchism endeavors to reconstruct all the sciences dealing with man and to revise every current idea of right and justice on the bases which have served for the revision of all natural sciences. Its object is to form a scientific concept of the universe embracing the whole of nature and including man.

This world-concept determines the position anarchism has taken in practical life. In the struggle between the individual and the State, anarchism, like its predecessors of the eighteenth century, takes the side of the individual as against the State, of society as against the authority which oppresses it. And availing itself of the historical data collected by modern science, it has shown that the State—whose sphere of authority there is now a tendency among its admirers to increase, and a tendency to limit in actual life—is in reality a superstructure—as harmful as it is unnecessary, and for us Europeans of a comparatively recent origin. A superstructure in the interests of capitalism—agrarian, industrial, and financial—which in ancient history caused the decay of politically free Rome and Greece, and which caused the death of all other despotic centers of civilization of the east and of Egypt.

The power which was created for the purpose of welding together the interests of the landlord, the judge, the warrior, and the priest, and has been opposed throughout history to every attempt of mankind to create for themselves a more assured and freer mode of life,—this power cannot become an instrument for emancipation, any more than imperialism or the church can become the instrument for a social revolution.

In the economic field anarchism has come to the conclusion that the root of modern evil lies not in the fact that the capitalist appropriates the profits or the surplus-value, but in the very possibility of these profits, which accrue only because millions of people have literally nothing to subsist upon without selling their labor-power at a price which makes profits and the creation of "surplus values" possible.

Anarchism understands therefore that in political economy attention must be directed first of all to so-called "consumption," and that the first concern of the revolution must be to reorganize that so as to provide food, clothing, and shelter for all. "Production," on the other hand, must be so adapted as to satisfy this primary, fundamental need of society. Therefore anarchism cannot see in the next coming revolution a mere exchange of monetary symbols for labor-checks, or an exchange of present capitalism for state-capitalism. It sees in it the first step on the road to no-government communism.

Whether or not anarchism is right in its conclusions will be shown by a scientific criticism of its bases and by the practical life of the future. But in one thing it is absolutely right: in that it has included the study of social institutions in the sphere of natural-scientific investigations; has forever parted company with metaphysics; and makes use of the method by which modern natural science and modern materialist philosophy were developed. Owing to this, the very mistakes which anarchism may have made in its researches can be detected the more readily. But its conclusions can be verified only by the same natural-scientific, inductive method by which every science and every scientific concept of the universe is created.

The Wage System

Representative Government and Wages

In their plans for the reconstruction of society, the Collectivists commit, in our opinion, a double error. Whilst speaking of the abolition of the rule of capital, they wish, nevertheless, to maintain two institutions which form the very basis of that rule, namely, representative government and the wage system.

As for representative government, it remains absolutely incomprehensible to us how intelligent men (and they are not wanting amongst the Collectivists) can continue to be the partisans of national and municipal parliaments, after all the lessons on this subject bestowed on us by history, whether in England or in France, in Germany, Switzerland, or the United States. Whilst parliamentary rule is seen to be everywhere falling to pieces; whilst its principles in themselves—and no longer merely their applications—are being criticised in every direction, how can intelligent men, calling themselves Revolutionary Socialists, seek to maintain a system already condemned to death?

Representative government is a system which was elaborated by the middle class to make headway against royalty and, at the same time, to maintain and augment their domination of the workers. It is the characteristic form of middle-class rule. But even its most ardent admirers have never seriously contended that a parliament or municipal body does actually represent a nation or a city; the more intelligent are aware that this is impossible. By upholding parliamentary rule the middle class have been simply seeking to oppose a dam betwixt themselves and royalty, or betwixt themselves and the territorial aristocracy, without giving liberty to the people. It is moreover plain that, as the people become conscious of their interests, and as the variety of those interests increases, the system becomes unworkable. And this is why the democrats of all countries are seeking for different palliatives or correctives and cannot find them. They are trying the *Referendum*, and discovering that it is worthless; they prate of proportional representation, of the representation of minorities, and other parliamentary utopias. In a word, they are striving to discover the undiscoverable; that is to say, a method of delegation which shall represent the myriad varied

94

interests of the nation; but they are being forced to recognise that they are upon a false track, and confidence in government by delegation is passing away.

It is only the Social Democrats and Collectivists who are not losing this confidence, who are attempting to maintain so-called national representation; and this is what we cannot understand.

If our Anarchist principles do not suit them, if they think them inapplicable, they ought, at least, as it seems to us, to try to discover what other system of organisation could well correspond to a society without capitalists or landlords. But to take the middle-class system—a system already in its decadence, a vicious system if ever there was one—and to proclaim this system (with a few innocent corrections, such as the imperative mandate, or the *Referendum*, the uselessness of which has been demonstrated already) good for a society that has passed through the Social Revolution, is what seems to us absolutely incomprehensible, unless under the name of Social Revolution they understand something very different from Revolution, some petty botching of existing middle-class rule.

The same with regard to the wage system. After having proclaimed the abolition of private property and the possession in common of the instruments of production, how can they sanction the maintenance of the wage system under any form? And yet this is what the Collectivists are doing when they praise the efficiency of labor notes.

That the English Socialists of the early part of this century should invent labor notes is comprehensible. They were simply trying to reconcile Capital and Labor. They repudiated all idea of laying violent hands upon the property of the capitalists. They were so little of revolutionaries that they declared themselves ready to submit even to imperial rule, if that rule would favour their co-operative societies. They remained middle class men at bottom, if charitable ones; and this is why (Engels has said so in his preface to the Communist Manifesto of 1848) the Socialists of that period were to be found amongst the middle class, whilst the advanced workmen were Communists.

If later Proudhon took up this same idea, that again is easy to understand. What was he seeking in his Mutualist system, if not to render capital less offensive, despite the maintenance of private property, which he detested to the bottom of his heart, but which he believed necessary to guarantee the individual against the state? Further, if economists, belonging more or less to the middle class, also admit labor notes, it is not surprising. It matters little to them whether the worker be paid in labor notes or in coin stamped with the effigy of king or republic. They want to save, in the coming overthrow, private property in inhabited houses, the soil, the mills;

or, at least, in inhabited houses and the capital necessary for the production of manufactures. And to maintain this property, labor notes will answer very well.

If the labor note can be exchanged for jewels and carriages, the owner of house property will willingly accept it as rent. And as long as the inhabited house, the field and the mill belong to individual owners, so long will it be requisite to pay them in some way before they will allow you to work in their fields or their mills, or to lodge in their houses. And it will also be requisite to pay wages to the worker, either in gold or in paper money or in labor notes exchangeable for all sorts of commodities.

But how can this new form of wages, the labor note, be sanctioned by those who admit that houses, fields, mills are no longer private property, that they belong to the commune or the nation?

The Collectivist Wage System

Let us examine more closely this system for the remuneration of labor, as set forth by the English, French, German, and Italian Collectivists.[1]

It comes very much to this: Every one works, be it in fields, in factories, in schools, in hospitals, or what not. The working day is regulated by the state, to which belong the soil, factories, means of communication, and all the rest. Each worker, having done a day's work, receives a labor note, stamped, let us say, with these words: *eight hours of labor*. With this note he can procure any sort of goods in the shops of the state or the various corporations. The note is divisible in such a way that one hour's worth of meat, ten minutes' worth of matches, or half-an-hour's worth of tobacco can be purchased. Instead of saying, "two pennyworth of soap," after the Collectivist Revolution they will say, "five minutes' worth of soap."

Most Collectivists, faithful to the distinction established by the middle-class economists (and Marx also) between *qualified* (skilled) and *simple* (unskilled) labor, tell us that qualified or professional toil should be paid a certain number of times more than simple toil. Thus, one hour of the doctor's work should be considered as equivalent to two or three hours of the work of the nurse, or three hours of that of the navvy. "Professional or qualified labor will be a multiple of simple labor," says the Collectivist

---

1. The Spanish Anarchists, who continue to call themselves Collectivists, understand by this term common possession of the instruments of labor and "liberty for each group to share the produce of labor as they think fit," on Communist principles or in any other way.

Grönlund, because this sort of labor demands a longer or shorter apprenticeship.

Other Collectivists, the French Marxists for example, do not make this distinction. They proclaim "equality of wages." The doctor, the schoolmaster, and the professor will be paid (in labor notes) at the same rate as the navvy. Eight hours spent in walking the hospitals will be worth the same as eight hours spent in navvies' work or in the mine or the factory.

Some make a further concession; they admit that disagreeable or unhealthy labor, such as that in the sewers, should be paid at a higher rate than work which is agreeable. One hour of service in the sewers may count, they say, for two hours of the labor of the professor.

Let us add that certain Collectivists advocate the wholesale remuneration of trade societies. Thus, one society may say: "Here are a hundred tons of steel. To produce them one hundred workers of our society have taken ten days; as our day consisted of eight hours, that makes eight thousand hours of labor for one hundred tons of steel; eighty hours a ton." Upon which the State will pay them eight thousand labor notes of one hour each, and these eight thousand notes will be distributed amongst the fellow-workers in the foundry as seems best to themselves.

Or again, if one hundred miners have spent twenty days in hewing eight thousand tons of coal, the coal will be worth two hours a ton, and the sixteen thousand labor notes for one hour each received by the miners' union will be divided amongst them as they think fair.

If there be disputes, if the miners protest and say that a ton of steel ought to cost six hours of labor instead of eight, or if the professor rate his day twice as high as the nurse, then the State must step in and regulate their differences.

Such, in a few words, is the organisation which the Collectivists desire to see arising from the Social Revolution. As we have seen, their principles are: collective property in the instruments of labor, and remuneration of each worker according to the time spent in productive toil, taking into account the productiveness of his work. As for their political system, it would be parliamentary rule, ameliorated by the change of men in power, the imperative mandate, and the *referendum*—i.e., the general vote of Yes or No upon questions submitted to the popular decision.

Now, we must at once say that this system seems to us absolutely incapable of realisation.

The Collectivists begin by proclaiming a revolutionary principle —the abolition of private property—and, as soon as proclaimed, they deny it, by maintaining an organisation of production and consumption springing from private property.

They proclaim a revolutionary principle and ignore the consequences it must necessarily bring about. They forget that the very fact of abolishing individual property in the instruments of production (land, factories, means of communication, capital) must cause society to set out in a new direction; that it must change production from top to bottom, change not only its method but its ends; that all the everyday relations between individuals must be modified as soon as land, machinery, and the rest are considered as common possessions.

They say, "No private property," and immediately they hasten to maintain private property in its everyday forms. "For productive purposes you are a commune," they say; "the fields, the tools, the machinery, all that has been made up to this day—manufactures, railways, wharves, mines—belong to all of you in common. Not the slightest distinction will be made concerning the share of each one in this collective property.

"But from tomorrow you are minutely to discuss the part that each one of you is to take in making the new machines, digging the new mines. From tomorrow you are to endeavour to weigh exactly the portion which will accrue to each one from the new produce. You are to count your minutes of work, you are to be on the watch lest one moment of your neighbour's toil may purchase more than yours.

"You are to calculate your hours and your minutes of labor, and since the hour measures nothing,—since in one factory a workman can watch four looms at once, whilst in another he only watches two, you are to weigh the muscular force, the energy of brain, the energy of nerve expended. You are scrupulously to count up the years of apprenticeship, that you may value precisely the share of each one amongst you in the production of the future. And all this, after you have declared that you leave entirely out of your reckoning the share he has taken in the past."

Well, it is evident to us that a society cannot organise itself upon two absolutely opposing principles, two principles which contradict one another at every step. And the nation or the commune which should give to itself such an organisation would be forced either to return to private property or else to transform itself immediately into a communist society.

Unequal Remuneration

We have said that most Collectivist writers demand that in a Socialist society remuneration should be based upon a distinction between qualified or professional labor and simple labor. They assert that an hour of the engineer's, the architect's, or the doctor's work should be counted as two or three hours' work from the blacksmith, the mason, or the nurse. And the same distinction, say they, ought to be established between workers whose trades require a longer or shorter apprenticeship and those who are mere day laborers.

This is the case in the present middle-class society; it must be the case in the future society of Collectivism.

Yes, but to establish this distinction is to maintain all the inequalities of our existing society. It is to trace out beforehand a demarcation between the worker and those who claim to rule him. It is still to divide society into two clearly defined classes; an aristocracy of knowledge above, a horny-handed democracy below; one class devoted to the service of the other; one class toiling with its hands to nourish and clothe the other, whilst that other profits by its leisure to learn how to dominate those who toil for it.

This is to take the distinctive features of middle-class society and sanction them by a social revolution. It is to erect into a principle an abuse which today is condemned in the society that is breaking up.

We know very well what will be said in answer. We shall be told about "Scientific Socialism." The middle-class economists, and Marx too, will be cited to prove that there is a good reason for a scale of wages, for the "labor force" of the engineer costs society more than the "labor force" of the navvy. And, indeed, have not the economists striven to prove that, if the engineer is paid twenty times more than the navvy, it is because the cost necessary to produce an engineer is more considerable than that necessary to produce a navvy? And has not Marx maintained that the like distinction bteween various sorts of manual labor is of equal logical necessity? He could come to no other conclusion, since he took up Ricardo's theory of value and insisted that products exchange in proportion to the quantity of the work socially necessary to produce them.

But we know also how much of all this to believe. We know that if the engineer, the scientist, and the doctor are paid today ten or a hundred times more than the laborer, and the weaver earns three times as much as the toiler in the fields and ten times as much as a match girl, it is not because what they receive is in proportion to their various costs of production. Rather it is in proportion to the extent of monopoly in education and in industry. The engineer, the scientist, and the doctor simply draw their profits from their own sort of capital—their degree, their certificates—just as the manufacturer draws a profit from a mill, or as a nobleman used to do from his birth and title.

When the employer pays the engineer twenty times more than the workman, he makes this very simple calculation: if an engineer can save him £ 4,000 a year in cost of production, he will pay him £ 800 a year to do it. And if he sees a foreman is a clever sweater and can save him £ 400 in handicraft, he at once offers him £ 80 or £ 90 a year. He expends £ 100 where he counts upon gaining £ 1,000; that is the essence of the capitalist system. And the like holds good of the differences in various trades.

Where then is the sense of talking of the cost of production of labor force, and saying that a student who passes a merry youth at the University, has a *right* to ten times higher wages than the son of a miner who has pined in a pit since he was eleven? Or that a weaver has a *right* to wages three or four times higher than those of an agricultural laborer? The expenditure needed to produce a weaver is not four times as great as the necessary cost of producing a field worker. The weaver simply benefits by the advantageous position which industry enjoys in Europe as compared with parts of the world where at present there is no industrial development.

No one has ever estimated the real cost of production of labor force. And if an idler costs society much more than an honest workman, it still remains to be known if, when all is told (infant mortality amongst the workers, the ravages of anemia, the premature deaths) a sturdy day laborer does not cost society more than an artisan.

Are we to be told that, for example, the 1s. a day of a London workwoman and the 3d. a day of the Auvergne peasant who blinds herself over lace-making, represent the cost of production of these women? We are perfectly aware that they often work for even less, but we know also that they do it entirely because, thanks to our splendid social organisation, they would die of hunger without these ridiculous wages.

The existing scale of wages seems to us a highly complex product of taxation, government interference, monopoly and capitalistic greed–in a word, of the State and the capitalist system. In our opinion all the theories made by economists about the scale of wages have been invented after the event to justify existing injustices. It is needless to regard them.

We are, however, certain to be informed that the Collectivist wage scale will, at all events, be an improvement. "You must admit," we shall be told, "that it will, at least, be better to have a class of workers paid at twice or three times the ordinary rate than to have Rothschilds, who put into their pockets in one day more than a workman can in a year. It will be a step towards equality."

To us it seems a step away from it. To introduce into a Socialist society the distinction between ordinary and professional labor would be to sanction by the Revolution and erect into a principle a brutal fact, to which we merely submit today, considering it all the while as unjust. It would be acting after the manner of those gentlemen of the Fourth of August, 1789, who proclaimed, in high sounding phraseology, the abolition of feudal rights, and on the Eighth of August sanctioned those very rights by imposing upon the peasants the dues by which they were to be redeemed from the nobles. Or again, like the Russian government at the time of the emancipation of the serfs, when it proclaimed that the land henceforth belonged to the nobility, whereas previously it was considered an abuse that the land which belonged to the peasants should be bought and sold by private persons.

Or, to take a better known example, when the Commune of 1871 decided to pay the members of the Communal Council 12s. 6d. a day, whilst the National Guards on the ramparts had only 1s. 3d., certain persons applauded this decision as an act of grand democratic equality. But, in reality, the Commune did nothing thereby but sanction the ancient inequality between officials and soldiers, governors and governed. For an Opportunist parliament such a decision might have seemed splendid, but for the Commune it was a negation of its own principles. The Commune was false to its own revolutionary principle, and by that very fact condemned it.

In the present state of society, when we see Cabinet Ministers paying themselves thousands a year, whilst the workman has to content himself with less than a hundred; when we see the foreman paid twice or three times as much as the ordinary hand, and when amongst workers themselves there are all sorts of gradations, from 7s. or 8s. a day down to the 3d. of the sempstress, we disapprove the large salary of the minister, and also the difference between the artisan's eight-shillings and the sempstress' three-pence. And we say, "Let us have done with privileges of education as well as of birth." We are Anarchists just because such privileges disgust us.

How can we then raise these privileges into a principle? How can we proclaim that privileges of education are to be the basis of an equal Society, without striking a blow at that very Society? What is submitted to today, will be submitted to no longer in a society based on equality. The general above the soldier, the rich engineer above the workman, the doctor above the nurse, already disgust us. Can we suffer them in a society which starts by proclaiming equality?

Evidently not. The popular conscience, inspired by the idea of equality, will revolt against such an injustice, it will not tolerate it. It is not worth while to make the attempt.

That is why certain Collectivists, understanding the impossibility of maintaining a scale of wages in a society inspired by the influence of the Revolution, zealously advocate equality in wages. But they only stumble against fresh difficulties, and their equality of wages becomes a Utopia, as incapable of realisation as the wage scale of the others.

A society that has seized upon all social wealth, and has plainly announced that all have a right to this wealth, whatever may be the part they have taken in creating it in the past, will be obliged to give up all idea of wages, either in money or in labor notes.

Equal Wages versus Free Communism

"To each according to his deeds," say the Collectivists, or rather according to his share of service rendered to society. And this is the principle they recommend as the basis of economic organisation, after the Revolution shall have made all the instruments of labor and all that is necessary for production common property!

Well, if the Social Revolution should be so unfortunate as to proclaim this principle, it would be stemming the tide of human progress; it would be leaving unsolved the huge social problem cast by past centuries upon our shoulders.

It is true that in such a society as ours, where the more a man works the less he is paid, this principle may seem, at first sight, an aspiration towards justice. But at bottom it is but the consecration of past injustice. It is with this principle that the wage-system started, to end where it is today, in crying inequalities and all the abominations of the present state of things. And it has ended thus because, from the day on which society began to value services in the money or any other sort of wages, from the day on which it was said that each should have only what he could succeed in getting paid for his work, the whole history of Capitalism (the State aiding therein) was written beforehand; its germ was enclosed in this principle.

Must we then return to our point of departure and pass once more through the same process of capitalist evolution? These theorists seem to desire it; but happily it is impossible; the Revolution will be Communistic; or it will be drowned in blood, and must be begun all over again.

Service rendered to society, be it labor in factory or field, or moral service cannot be valued in monetary units. There cannot be an exact measure of its value, either of what has been improperly called its "value in exchange" or of its value in use. If we see two individuals, both working for years, for five hours daily, for the community, at two different occupations equally pleasing to them, we can say that, taken all in all, their labors are roughly equivalent. But their work could not be broken up into fractions, so that the product of each day, each hour or each minute of the labor of one should be worth the produce of each minute and each hour of that of the other.

Broadly speaking, we can say that a man who during his whole life deprives himself of leisure for ten hours daily has given much more to society than he who has deprived himself of but five hours a day, or has not deprived himself of any leisure at all. But we cannot take what one man has done during any two hours and say that this produce is worth exactly twice as much as the produce of one hour's work from another individual and reward each proportionately. To do this would be to ignore all that is complex in the industry, the agriculture, the entire life of society as it is; it would be to ignore the extent to which all individual work is the outcome of the former and present labors of society as a whole. It would be to fancy oneself in the Stone Age, when we are living in the Age of Steel.

Go into a coal mine and see that man stationed at the huge machine that hoists and lowers the cage. In his hand he holds a lever whereby to check or reverse the action of the machinery. He lowers the handle, and in a second the cage changes the direction of its giddy rush up or down the shaft. His eyes are attentively fixed upon an indicator in front of him which shows exactly the point the cage has reached; no sooner does it touch the given level than at his gentlest pressure it stops dead short, not a foot above or below the required place. And scarcely are the full trucks discharged or the empties loaded before, at a touch to the handle, the cage is again swinging up or down the shaft.

For eight or ten hours at a time he thus concentrates his attention. Let his brain relax but for an instant, and the cage would fly up and shatter the wheels, break the rope, crush the men, bring all the work of the mine to a stand-still. Let him lose three seconds upon each reverse of the lever and, in a mine with all the modern improvements, the output will be reduced by from twenty to fifty tons a day.

Well, is it he who renders the greatest service in the mine? Or is it, perhaps, that boy who rings from below the signal for the mounting of the cage? Or is it the miner who risks his life every moment in the depths of the mine and will end one day by being killed by fire-damp? Or, again, the engineer who would lose the coal seam and set men hewing bare rock, if he merely made a mistake in the addition of his calculations? Or, finally is it the owner, who has put all his patrimony into the concern, and who perhaps has said, in opposition to all previous anticipations, "Dig there, you will find excellent coal"?

All the workers engaged in the mine contribute to the raising of coal in proportion to their strength, their energy, their knowledge, their intelligence, and their skill. And we can say that all have the right to *live*, to satisfy their needs, and even gratify their whims, after the more imperious needs of every one are satisfied. But how can we exactly value what they have each done?

Further, is the coal that they have extracted entirely the result of *their* work? Is it not also the outcome of the work of the men who constructed the railway leading to the mine, and the roads branching off on all sides from the stations? And what of the work of those who have tilled and sown the fields which supply the miners with food, smelted the iron, cut the wood in the forest, made the machines which will consume the coal, and so on?

No hard and fast line can be drawn between the work of one and the work of another. To measure them by results leads to absurdity. To divide them into fractions and measure them by hours of labor leads to absurdity also. (One course remains: not to measure them at all, but to recognise the right of all who take part in productive labor first of all to live, and then to enjoy the comforts of life.)

Take any other branch of human activity, take our existence as a whole, and say which of us can claim the highest reward for his deeds?

The doctor who has divined the disease or the nurse who has assured its cure by her sanitary cares? The inventor of the first steam engine or the boy who one day, tired of pulling the cord which formerly served to open the valve admitting the steam beneath the piston, tied his cord to the lever of the machine, and went to play with his companions, without imagining that he had invented the mechanism essential to all modern machinery—the automatic valve? The inventor of the locomotive or that Newcastle workman who suggested that wooden sleepers should take the place of the stones which were formerly put under the rails and threw trains off the line by their want of elasticity? The driver of the locomotive or the signalman who stops the train or opens the way for it?

To whom do we owe the trans-Atlantic cable? To the engineer who persisted in declaring that the cable would transmit telegrams, whilst the learned electricians declared that it was impossible? To Maury, the scientist, who advised the disuse of thick cables and the substitution of one no bigger than a walking stick? Or, after all, is it to those volunteers, from no one knows where, who spent day and night on the deck of the *Great Eastern*, minutely examining every yard of cable and taking out the nails that the shareholders of the maritime companies had stupidly caused to be driven through the isolating coat of the cable to render it useless?

And, in a still wider field, the vast tract of human life, with its joys, its sorrows, and its varied incidents, cannot each of us mention some one who during his life has rendered him some service so great, so important, that if it were proposed to value it in money he would be filled with indignation? This service may have been a word, nothing but a word in season, or it may have been months or years of devotion. Are you going to estimate these, the most important of all services, in labor notes?

"The deeds of each"! But human societies could not live for two successive generations, they would disappear in fifty years, if each one did not give infinitely more than will be returned to him in money, in "notes" or in civic rewards. It would be the extinction of the race if the mother did not expend her life to preserve her children, if every man did not give some things without counting the cost, if human beings did not give most where they look for no reward.

If middle-class society is going to ruin; if we are today in a blind alley from which there is no escape without applying axe and torch to the institutions of the past, that is just because we have calculated too much. It is just because we have allowed ourselves to be drawn into giving that we may receive; because we have desired to make society into a commercial company based upon debit and credit.

Moreover, the Collectivists know it. They vaguely comprehend that a society cannot exist if it logically carries out the principle, "To each according to his deeds." They suspect that the *needs* (we are not speaking of the whims) of the individual do not always correspond to his deeds. Accordingly, De Paepe tells us:—

> This eminently individualistic principle will be *tempered* by social intervention for the purpose of the education of children and young people (including their maintenance and nurture) and by social organisations for the assistance of the sick and infirm, asylums for aged workers, etc.

Even Collectivists suspect that a man of forty, the father of three children, has greater needs than a youth of twenty. They suspect that a woman who is suckling her child and spends sleepless nights by its cot, cannot get through so much work as a man who has enjoyed tranquil slumber.

They seem to understand that a man or woman worn out by

having perhaps, worked over hard for society in general may find themselves incapable of performing so many "deeds" as those who take their hours of labor quietly and pocket their "notes" in the privileged offices of State statisticians.

And they hasten to *temper* their principle. Oh, certainly, they say, society will feed and bring up its children. Oh, certainly it will assist the old and infirm. Oh, certainly *needs* not *deeds* will be the measure of the cost which society will impose on itself to temper the principle of deeds.

What, Charity? Yes, our old friend, "Christian Charity," organised by the State.

Improve the foundling hospital, organise insurance against age and sickness, and the principle of deeds will be "tempered." "Wound that they may heal," they can get no further.

Thus, then, after having forsworn Communism, after having sneered at their ease at the formula, "To each according to his needs," is it not obvious that they, the great economists, also perceive that they have forgotten something, *i.e.*, the needs of the producers? And thereupon they hasten to recognise these needs. Only it is to be the State by which they are to be estimated; it is to be the State which will undertake to find out if needs are disproportionate to deeds.

It is to be the State that will give alms to him who is willing to recognise his inferiority. From thence to the Poor Law and the Workhouse is but a stone's throw.

There is but a stone's throw, for even this step-mother of a society, against which we are in revolt, has found it necessary to temper its individualistic principle. It too has had to make concessons in a Communistic sense, and in this same form of charity.

It also distributes halfpenny dinners to prevent the pillage of its shops. It also builds hospitals, often bad enough, but sometimes splendid, to prevent the ravages of contagious disease. It also, after having paid for nothing but the hours of labor, receives the children of those whom it has itself reduced to the extremity of distress. It also takes account of needs—as a charity.

Poverty, the existence of the poor, was the first cause of riches. This it was which created the earliest capitalist. For, before the surplus value, about which people are so fond of talking, could begin to be accumulated it was necessary that there should be poverty-stricken wretches who would consent to sell their labor force rather than die of hunger. It is poverty that has made the rich. And if poverty had advanced by such rapid strides by the end of the Middle Ages, it was chiefly because the invasions and wars, the creation of States and the development of their authority, the wealth gained by exploitation in the East, and many other causes of a like nature, broke the bonds which once united agrarian and urban communities, and led them, in place of the solidarity which they once practised, to adopt the principle of the wage-system.

Is this principle to be the outcome of the Revolution? Dare we dignify by the name of a Social Revolution—that name so dear to the hungry, the suffering and the oppressed—the triumph of such a principle as this?

It cannot be so. For, on the day when ancient institutions splinter into fragments before the axe of the proletariat, voices will be heard shouting: Bread for all! Lodging for all! Right for all to the comforts of life!

And these voices will be heeded. The people will say to themselves: "Let us begin by satisfying our thirst for the life, the joy, the liberty we have never known. And when all have tasted happiness, we will set to work; the work of demolishing the last vestiges of middle-class rule, with its account-book morality, its philosophy of debit and credit, its institutions of mine and thine." "While we throw down we shall be building," as Proudhon said; we shall build in the name of Communism and of Anarchy.

Anarchism

Anarchism (from the Gr. ἀν-, and ἀρχή, contrary to authority), is the name given to a principle or theory of life and conduct under which society is conceived without government—harmony in such a society being obtained, not by submission to law, or by obedience to any authority, but by free agreements concluded between the various groups, territorial and professional, freely constituted for the sake of production and consumption, as also for the satisfaction of the infinite variety of needs and aspirations of a civilized being.

In a society developed on these lines, the voluntary associations which already now begin to cover all the fields of human activity would take a still greater extension so as to substitute themselves for the State in all its functions. They would represent an interwoven network, composed of an infinite variety of groups and federations of all sizes and degrees, local, regional, national, and international—temporary or more or less permanent—for all possible purposes: production, consumption and exchange, communications, sanitary arrangements, education, mutual protection, defense of the territory, and so on; and, on the other side, for the satisfaction of an ever-increasing number of scientific, artistic, literary, and sociable needs.

Moreover, such a society would represent nothing immutable. On the contrary—as is seen in organic life at large—harmony would (it is contended) result from an ever-changing adjustment and readjustment of equilibrium between the multitudes of forces and influences, and this adjustment would be the easier to obtain as none of the forces would enjoy a special protection from the State.

If, it is contended, society were organized on these principles, man would not be limited in the free exercise of his powers in productive work by a capitalist monopoly, maintained by the State; nor would he be limited in the exercise of his will by a fear of punishment, or by obedience towards individuals or metaphysical entities, which both lead to depression of initiative and servility of mind. He would be guided in his actions by his own understanding, which necessarily would bear the impression of a free action and reaction between his own self and the ethical conceptions of his surroundings. Man would thus be enabled to obtain the full devel-

* From the eleventh edition of the *Encyclopædia Britannica*.

opment of all his faculties, intellectual, artistic, and moral, without being hampered by overwork for the monopolists, or by the servility and inertia of mind of the great number. He would thus be able to reach full *individualization*, which is not possible either under the present system of *individualism*, or under any system of State socialism in the so-called Volksstaat (popular State).

The anarchist writers consider, moreover, that their conception is not a Utopia, constructed on the *a priori* method, after a few desiderata have been taken as postulates. It is derived, they maintain, from an *analysis of tendencies* that are at work already, even though state socialism may find a temporary favor with the reformers. The progress of modern technics, which wonderfully simplifies the production of all the necessaries of life; the growing spirit of independence, and the rapid spread of free initiative and free understanding in all branches of activity—including those which formerly were considered as the proper attribution of church and State—are steadily reinforcing the no-government tendency.

As to their economical conceptions, the anarchists, in common with all socialists, of whom they constitute the left wing, maintain that the now prevailing system of private ownership in land, and our capitalist production for the sake of profits, represent a monopoly which runs against both the principles of justice and the dictates of utility. They are the main obstacle which prevents the successes of modern technics from being brought into the service of all, so as to produce general well-being. The anarchists consider the wage-system and capitalist production altogether as an obstacle to progress. But they point out also that the State was, and continues to be, the chief instrument for permitting the few to monopolize the land, and the capitalists to appropriate for themselves a quite disproportionate share of the yearly accumulated surplus of production. Consequently, while combating the present monopolization of land, and capitalism altogether, the anarchists combat with the same energy the State as the main support of that system. Not this or that special form, but the State altogether, whether it be a monarchy or even a republic governed by means of the *referendum*.

The State organization, having always been, both in ancient and modern history (Macedonian empire, Roman empire, modern European states grown up on the ruins of the autonomous cities), the instrument for establishing monopolies in favor of the ruling minorities, cannot be made to work for the destruction of these monopolies. The anarchists consider, therefore, that to hand over to the State all the main sources of economic life—the land, the mines, the railways, banking, insurance, and so on—as also the management of all the main branches of industry, in addition to all the functions already accumulated in its hands (education, State-supported religions, defense of the territory, etc.), would mean to create a new instrument of tyranny. State capitalism would only increase the powers of bureaucracy and capitalism. True progress lies in the direction of decentralization, both *territorial* and *functional*, in the development of the spirit of local and personal initiative, and of free federation from the simple to the compound, *in lieu* of the present hierarchy from the center to the periphery.

In common with most socialists, the anarchists recognize that, like all evolution in nature, the slow evolution of society is followed from time to time by periods of accelerated evolution which are called revolutions; and they think that the era of revolutions is not yet closed. Periods of rapid changes will follow the periods of slow evolution, and these periods must be taken advantage of—not for increasing and widening the powers of the State, but for reducing them, through the organization in every township or commune of the local groups of producers and consumers, as also the regional, and eventually the international, federations of these groups.

In virtue of the above principles the anarchists refuse to be party to the present-State organization and to support it by infusing fresh blood into it. They do not seek to constitute, and invite the workingmen not to constitute, political parties in the parliaments. Accordingly, since the foundation of the International Working Men's Association in 1864–1866, they have endeavored to promote their ideas directly amongst the labor organizations and to induce those unions to a direct struggle against capital, without placing their faith in parliamentary legislation.

The Historical Development of Anarchism

The conception of society just sketched, and the tendency which is its dynamic expression, have always existed in mankind, in opposition to the governing hierarchic conception and tendency—now the one and now the other taking the upper hand at different periods of history. To the former tendency we owe the evolution, by the masses themselves, of those institutions—the clan, the village community, the guild, the free medieval city—by means of which the masses resisted the encroachments of the conquerors and the power-seeking minorities. The same tendency asserted itself with great energy in the great religious movements of medieval times, especially in the early movements of the reform and its forerunners. At the same time it evidently found its expression in the writings of some thinkers, since the times of Lao-tze, although, owing to its non-scholastic and popular origin, it obviously found less sympathy among the scholars than the opposed tendency.

As has been pointed out by Prof. Adler in his *Geschichte des Sozialismus und Kommunismus,* Aristippus (430 B.C.), one of the founders of the Cyrenaic school, already taught that the wise must not give up their liberty to the State, and in reply to a question by Socrates he said that he did not desire to belong either to the governing or the governed class. Such an attitude, however, seems to have been dictated merely by an Epicurean attitude towards the life of the masses.

The best exponent of anarchist philosophy in ancient Greece was Zeno (342–267 or 270 B.C.), from Crete, the founder of the Stoic philosophy, who distinctly opposed his conception of a free community without government to the state-Utopia of Plato. He repudiated the omnipotence of the State, its intervention and regimentation, and proclaimed the sovereignty of the moral law of the individual—remarking already that, while the necessary instinct of self-preservation leads man to egoism, nature has supplied a corrective to it by providing man with another instinct—that of sociability. When men are reasonable enough to follow their natural instincts, they will unite across the frontiers and constitute the Cosmos. They will have no need of law-courts or police, will have no temples and no public worship, and use no money—free gifts taking the place of the exchanges. Unfortunately, the writings of Zeno have not reached us and are only known through fragmentary quotations. However, the fact that his very wording is similar to the wording now in use, shows how deeply is laid the tendency of human nature of which he was the mouth-piece.

In medieval times we find the same views on the State expressed by the illustrious bishop of Alba, Marco Girolamo Vida, in his first dialogue *De dignitate reipublicae* (Ferd. Cavalli, in *Men. dell' Istituto Vaento,* xiii.; Dr. E. Nys, *Researches in the History of Economics*). But it is especially in several early Christian movements, beginning with the ninth century in Armenia, and in the preachings of the early Hussites, particularly Chojecki, and the early Anabaptists, especially Hans Denk (cf. Keller, *Ein Apostel der Wiedertäufer*), that one finds the same ideas forcibly expressed—special stress being laid of course on their moral aspects.

Rabelais and Fénelon, in their Utopias, have also expressed similar ideas, and they were also current in the eighteenth century amongst the French Encyclopaedists, as may be concluded from separate expressions occasionally met with in the writings of Rousseau, from Diderot's Preface to the *Voyage* of Bougainville, and so on. However, in all probability such ideas could not be developed then, owing to the rigorous censorship of the Roman Catholic Church.

These ideas found their expression later during the great French

Revolution. While the Jacobins did all in their power to centralize everything in the hands of the government, it appears now, from recently published documents, that the masses of the people, in their municipalities and "sections," accomplished a considerable constructive work. They appropriated for themselves the election of the judges, the organization of supplies and equipment for the army, as also for the large cities, work for the unemployed, the management of charities, and so on. They even tried to establish a direct correspondence between the 36,000 communes of France through the intermediary of a special board, outside the National Assembly (cf. Sigismund Lacroix, *Actes de la commune de Paris*).

It was Godwin, in his *Enquiry concerning Political Justice* (2 vols., 1973), who was the first to formulate the political and economical conceptions of anarchism, even though he did not give that name to the ideas developed in his remarkable work. Laws, he wrote, are not a product of the wisdom of our ancestors; they are the product of their passions, their timidity, their jealousies and their ambition. The remedy they offer is worse than the evils they pretend to cure. If and only if all laws and courts were abolished, and the decisions in the arising contests were left to reasonable men chosen for that purpose, real justice would gradually be evolved. As to the State, Godwin frankly claimed its abolition. A society, he wrote, can perfectly well exist without any government, only the communities should be small and perfectly autonomous. Speaking of property, he stated that the rights of every one "to every substance capable of contributing to the benefit of a human being" must be regulated by justice alone, the substance must go "to him who most wants it." His conclusion was communism. Godwin, however, had not the courage to maintain his opinions. He entirely rewrote later on his chapter on property and mitigated his communist views in the second edition of *Political Justice* (8 vols., 1796).

Proudhon was the first to use, in 1840 (*Qu'est-ce que la propriété?* first memoir), the name of anarchy with application to the no-government state of society. The name of "anarchists" had been freely applied during the French Revolution by the Girondists to those revolutionaries who did not consider that the task of the Revolution was accomplished with the overthrow of Louis XVI, and insisted upon a series of economical measures being taken (the abolition of feudal rights without redemption, the return to the village communities of the communal lands enclosed since 1669, the limitation of landed property to 120 acres, progressive income-tax, the national organization of exchanges on a just value basis, which already received a beginning of practical realization, and so on).

Now Proudhon advocated a society without government, and used the word anarchy to describe it. Proudhon repudiated, as is known, all schemes of communism, according to which mankind would be driven into communistic monasteries or barracks, as also all the schemes of state or state-aided socialism which were advocated by Louis Blanc and the collectivists. When he proclaimed in his first memoir on property that "Property is theft," he meant only property in its present, Roman-law, sense of "right of use and abuse;" in property-rights, on the other hand, understood in the limited sense of *possession*, he saw the best protection against the encroachments of the State. At the same time he did not want violently to dispossess the present owners of land, dwelling-houses, mines, factories, and so on. He preferred to attain the same end by rendering capital incapable of earning interest; and this he proposed to obtain by means of a national bank, based on the mutual confidence of all those who are engaged in production, who would agree to exchange among themselves their produces at cost-value, by means of labor checks representing the hours of labor required to produce every given commodity. Under such a system, which Proudhon described as "Mutuellisme," all the exchanges of services would be strictly equivalent. Besides, such a bank would be enabled to lend money without interest, levying only something like 1 per cent, or even less, for covering the cost of administration. Every one being thus enabled to borrow the money that would be required to buy a house, nobody would agree to pay any more a yearly rent for the use of it. A general "social liquidation" would thus be rendered easy, without expropriation. The same applied to mines, railways, factories, and so on.

In a society of this type the State would be useless. The chief relations between citizens would be based on free agreement and regulated by mere account keeping. The contests might be settled by arbitration. A penetrating criticism of the State and all possible forms of government and a deep insight into all economic problems, were well-known characteristics of Proudhon's work.

It is worth noticing that French mutualism had its precursor in England, in William Thompson, who began by mutualism before he become a communist, and in his followers John Gray (A *Lecture on Human Happiness*, 1825; *The Social System*, 1831) and J. F. Bray (*Labour's Wrongs and Labour's Remedy*, 1839). It had also its precursor in America. Josiah Warren, who was born in 1798 (cf. W. Bailie, *Josiah Warren, the First American Anarchist*, Boston, 1900), and belonged to Owen's "New Harmony," considered that the failure of this enterprise was chiefly due to the suppression of individuality and the lack of initiative and responsiblity. These defects, he taught, were inherent to every scheme based

upon authority and the community of goods. He advocated, therefore, complete individual liberty. In 1827 he opened in Cincinnati a
little country store which was the first "Equity Store," and which
the people called "Time Store," because it was based on labor being
exchanged hour for hour in all sorts of produce. "Cost—the limit
of price," and consequently "no interest," was the motto of his
store, and later on of his "Equity Village," near New York, which
was still in existence in 1865. Mr. Keith's "House of Equity" at
Boston, founded in 1855, is also worthy of notice.

While the economic, and especially the mutual-banking, ideas of
Proudhon found supporters and even a practical application in the
United States, his political conception of anarchy found but little
echo in France, where the christian socialism of Lamennais and the
Fourierists, and the state socialism of Louis Blanc and the followers of Saint-Simon, were dominating. These ideas found, however,
some temporary support among the left-wing Hegelians in Germany, Moses Hess in 1843, and Karl Grün in 1845, who advocated
anarchism. Besides, the authoritarian communism of Wilhelm
Weitling having given origin to opposition amongst the Swiss workingmen, Wilhelm Marr gave expression to it in the forties.

On the other side, individualist anarchism found, also in Germany, its fullest expression in Max Stirner (Kaspar Schmidt),
whose remarkable works (*Der Einzige und sein Eigenthum* and
articles contributed to the *Rheinische Zeitung*) remained quite
overlooked until they were brought into prominence by John Henry
Mackay.

Prof. V. Basch, in a very able introduction to his interesting
book, *L'Individualisme anarchiste: Max Stirner* (1904), has shown
how the development of the German philosophy from Kant to
Hegel, and "the absolute" of Schelling and the *Geist* of Hegel,
necessarily provoked, when the anti-Hegelian revolt began, the
preaching of the same "absolute" in the camp of the rebels. This
was done by Stirner, who advocated, not only a complete revolt
against the State and against the servitude which authoritarian
communism would impose upon men, but also the full liberation of
the individual from all social and moral bonds—the rehabilitation
of the "I," the supremacy of the individual, complete "a-moralism,"
and the "association of the egoists." The final conclusion of that
sort of individual anarchism has been indicated by Prof. Basch. It
maintains that the aim of all superior civilization is, not to permit
all members of the community to develop in a normal way, but to
permit certain better endowed individuals "fully to develop," even
at the cost of the happiness and the very existence of the mass of
mankind. It is thus a return towards the most common individualism, advocated by all the would-be superior minorities, to which

indeed man owes in his history precisely the State and the rest, which these individualists combat. Their individualism goes so far as to end in a negation of their own starting-point,—to say nothing of the impossibility for the individual to attain a really full development in the conditions of oppression of the masses by the "beautiful aristocracies." His development would remain uni-lateral. This is why this direction of thought, notwithstanding its undoubtedly correct and useful advocacy of the full development of each individuality, finds a hearing only in limited artistic and literary circles.

Anarchism in the International Working Men's Association

A general depression in the propaganda of all fractions of socialism followed, as is known, after the defeat of the uprising of the Paris workingmen in June 1848 and the fall of the Republic. All the socialist press was gagged during the reaction period, which lasted fully twenty years. Nevertheless, even anarchist thought began to make some progress, namely in the writings of Bellegarrique (*Coeurderoy*), and especially Joseph Déjacque (*Les Lazaréennes, L'Humanisphère*, an anarchist-communist Utopia, lately discovered and reprinted). The socialist movement revived only after 1864, when some French workingmen, all "mutualists," meeting in London during the Universal Exhibition with English followers of Robert Owen, founded the International Working Men's Association. This association developed very rapidly and adopted a policy of direct economic struggle against capitalism, without interfering in the political parliamentary agitation, and this policy was followed until 1871. However, after the Franco-German War, when the International Association was prohibited in France after the uprising of the Commune, the German workingmen, who had received manhood suffrage for elections to the newly constituted imperial parliament, insisted upon modifying the tactics of the International, and began to build up a social-democratic political party. This soon led to a division in the Working Men's Association, and the Latin federations, Spanish, Italian, Belgian, and Jurassic (France could not be represented), constituted among themselves a federal union which broke entirely with the Marxist general council of the International. Within these federations developed now what may be described as *modern anarchism*. After the names of "federalists" and "anti-authoritarians" had been used for some time by these federations the name of "anarchists," which their adversaries insisted upon applying to them, prevailed, and finally it was revindicated.

Bakunin soon became the leading spirit among these Latin federations for the development of the principles of anarchism, which he **did** in a number of writings, pamphlets, and letters. He demanded the complete abolition of the State, which—he wrote—is a product of religion, belongs to a lower state of civilization, represents the negation of liberty, and spoils even that which it undertakes to do for the sake of general well-being. The State was an historically necessary evil, but its complete extinction will be, sooner or later, equally necessary. Repudiating all legislation, even when issuing from universal suffrage, Bakunin claimed for each nation, each region and each commune, full autonomy, so long as it is not a menace to its neighbors, and full independence for the individual, adding that one becomes really free only when, and in proportion as, all others are free. Free federations of the communes would constitute free nations.

As to his economic conceptions, Bakunin described himself, in common with his federalist comrades of the International, a "collectivist anarchist"—not in the sense of Vidal and Pecqueur in the forties, or of their modern social-democratic followers, but to express a state of things in which all necessaries for production are owned in common by the labor groups and the free communes, while the ways of retribution of labor, communist or otherwise, would be settled by each group for itself. Social revolution, the near approach of which was foretold at that time by all socialists, would be the means of bringing into life the new conditions.

The Jurassic, the Spanish, and the Italian federations and sections of the International Working Men's Association, as also the French, the German, and the American anarchist groups, were for the next years the chief centers of anarchist thought and propaganda. They refrained from any participation in parliamentary politics, and always kept in close contact with the labor organizations. However, in the second half of the eighties and the early nineties of the nineteenth century, when the influence of the anarchists began to be felt in strikes, in the first of May demonstrations, where they promoted the idea of a general strike for an eight hours' day, and in the anti-militarist propaganda in the army, violent prosecutions were directed against them, especially in the Latin countries (including physical torture in the Barcelona Castle) and the United States (the execution of five Chicago anarchists in 1887). Against these prosecutions the anarchists retaliated by acts of violence which in their turn were followed by more executions from above, and new acts of revenge from below. This created in the general public the impression that violence is the substance of anarchism, a view repudiated by its supporters, who hold that in reality violence is resorted to by all parties in proportion as their open action is obstructed by repression, and exceptional laws render them outlaws.

Anarchism continued to develop, partly in the direction of Proudhonian "Mutuellisme," but chiefly as communist-anarchism, to which a third direction, christian-anarchism, was added by Leo Tolstoy, and a fourth, which might be described as literary-anarchism, began amongst some prominent modern writers.

The ideas of Proudhon, especially as regards mutual banking, corresponding with those of Josiah Warren, found a considerable following in the United States, creating quite a school, of which the main writers are Stephen Pearl Andrews, William Greene, Lysander Spooner (who began to write in 1850, and whose unfinished work, *Natural Law*, was full of promise), and several others, whose names will be found in Dr. Nettlau's *Bibliographie de l'anarchie*.

A prominent position among the individualist anarchists in America has been occupied by Benjamin R. Tucker, whose journal *Liberty* was started in 1881 and whose conceptions are a combination of those of Proudhon with those of Herbert Spencer. Starting from the statement that anarchists are egoists, strictly speaking, and that every group of individuals, be it a secret league of a few persons, or the Congress of the United States, has the right to oppress all mankind, provided it has the power to do so, that equal liberty for all and absolute equality ought to be the law, and "mind every one your own business" is the unique moral law of anarchism, Tucker goes on to prove that a general and thorough application of these principles would be beneficial and would offer no danger, because the powers of every individual would be limited by the exercise of the equal rights of all others. He further indicated (following H. Spencer) the difference which exists between the encroachment on somebody's rights and resistance to such an encroachment; between domination and defense: the former being equally condemnable, whether it be encroachment of a criminal upon an individual, or the encroachment of one upon all others, or of all others upon one; while resistance to encroachment is defensible and necessary. For their self-defense, both the citizen and the group have the right to any violence, including capital punishment. Violence is also justified for enforcing the duty of keeping an agreement. Tucker thus follows Spencer, and, like him, opens (in the present writer's opinion) the way for reconstituting under the heading of "defense" all the functions of the State. His criticism of the present State is very searching, and his defense of the rights of the individual very powerful. As regards his economic views B. R. Tucker follows Proudhon.

The individualist anarchism of the American Proudhonians finds, however, but little sympathy amongst the working masses. Those who profess it—they are chiefly "intellectuals"—soon realize that the *individualization* they so highly praise is not attainable by individual efforts, and either abandon the ranks of the anarchists, and are driven into the liberal individualism of the classical economists, or they retire into a sort of Epicurean a-moralism, or super-man-theory, similar to that of Stirner and Nietzsche. The great bulk of the anarchist workingmen prefer the anarchist-communist ideas which have gradually evolved out of the anarchist collectivism of the International Working Men's Association. To this direction belong—to name only the better known exponents of anarchism—Élisée Reclus, Jean Grave, Sebastien Fauré, Emile Pouget in France; Enrico Malatesta and Covelli in Italy; R. Mella, A. Lorenzo, and the mostly unknown authors of many excellent manifestos in Spain; John Most amongst the Germans; Spies, Parsons, and their followers in the United States, and so on; while Domela Nieuwenhuis occupies an intermediate position in Holland. The chief anarchist papers which have been published since 1880 also belong to that direction; while a number of anarchists of this direction have joined the so-called syndicalist movement—the French name for the non-political labor movement, devoted to direct struggle with capitalism, which has lately become so prominent in Europe.

As one of the anarchist-communist direction, the present writer for many years endeavored to develop the following ideas: to show the intimate, logical connection which exists between the modern philosophy of natural sciences and anarchism; to put anarchism on a scientific basis by the study of the tendencies that are apparent now in society and may indicate its further evolution; and to work out the basis of anarchist ethics. As regards the substance of anarchism itself, it was Kropotkin's aim to prove that communism—at least partial—has more chances of being established than collectivism, especially in communes taking the lead, and that free, or anarchist-communism is the only form of communism that has any chance of being accepted in civilized societies; communism and anarchy are therefore two terms of evolution which complete each other, the one rendering the other possible and acceptable. He has tried, moreover, to indicate how, during a revolutionary period, a large city—if its inhabitants have accepted the idea—could organize itself on the lines of free communism; the city guaranteeing to every inhabitant dwelling, food, and clothing to an extent corresponding to the comfort now available to the middle classes only, in exchange for a half-day's, or a five-hours' work; and how all those things which would be considered as luxuries might be obtained by every one if he joins for the other half of the day all sorts of free associations pursuing all possible aims—educational, literary, scientific, artistic, sports, and so on. In order to prove the first of these assertions he has analyzed the possibilities of agriculture and industrial work, both being combined with brain work. And in order to elucidate the main factors of human evolution, he has analyzed the part played in history by the popular constructive agencies of mutual aid and the historical role of the State.

Without naming himself an anarchist, Leo Tolstoy, like his predecessors in the popular religious movements of the fifteenth and sixteenth centuries, Chojecki, Denk, and many others, took the anarchist position as regards the State and property rights, deducing his conclusions from the general spirit of the teachings of the Christ and from the necessary dictates of reason. With all the might of his talent he made (especially in *The Kingdom of God in Yourselves*) a powerful criticism of the church, the State, and law altogether, and especially of the present property laws. He describes the State as the domination of the wicked ones, supported by brutal force. Robbers, he says, are far less dangerous than a well-organized government. He makes a searching criticism of the prejudices which are current now concerning the benefits conferred upon men by the church, the State, and the existing distribution of property, and from the teachings of the Christ he deduces the rule of nonresistance and the absolute condemnation of all wars. His religious arguments are, however, so well combined with arguments borrowed from a dispassionate observation of the present evils, that the anarchist portions of his works appeal to the religious and the nonreligious reader alike.

It would be impossible to represent here, in a short sketch, the penetration, on the one hand, of anarchist ideas into modern literature, and the influence, on the other hand, which the libertarian ideas of the best comtemporary writers have exercised upon the development of anarchism. One ought to consult the ten big volumes of the *Supplément littéraire* to the paper *La Révolte* and later the *Temps Nouveaux*, which contain reproductions from the works of hundreds of modern authors expressing anarchist ideas, in order to realize how closely anarchism is connected with all the intellectual movement of our own times. J. S. Mill's *Liberty*, Spencer's *Individual versus The State*, Marc Guyau's *Morality without Obligation or Sanction*, and Fouillée's *La morale, l'art et la religion*, the works of Multatuli (E. Douwes Dekker), Richard Wagner's *Art and Revolution*, the works of Nietzsche, Emerson, W. Lloyd Garrison, Thoreau, Alexander Herzen, Edward Carpenter, and so on; and in the domain of fiction, the dramas of Ibsen, the poetry of Walt Whitman, Tolstoy's *War and Peace*, Zola's *Paris* and *Le*

Travail, the latest works of Merezhkovsky, and an infinity of works of less known authors,—are full of ideas which show how closely anarchism is interwoven with the work that is going on in modern thought in the same direction of enfranchisement of man from the bonds of the State as well as from those of capitalism.

Part II

Selections from
Memoirs of a Revolutionist

* * *

The five years that I spent in Siberia were for me a genuine education in life and human character. I was brought into contact with men of all descriptions: the best and the worst; those who stood at the top of society and those who vegetated at the very bottom,—the tramps and the so-called incorrigible criminals. I had ample opportunities to watch the ways and habits of the peasants in their daily life, and still more opportunities to appreciate how little the state administration could give to them, even if it was animated by the very best intentions. Finally, my extensive journeys, during which I traveled over fifty thousand miles in carts, on board steamers, in boats, but chiefly on horseback, had a wonderful effect in strengthening my health. They also taught me how little man really needs as soon as he comes out of the enchanted circle of conventional civilization. With a few pounds of bread and a few ounces of tea in a leather bag, a kettle and a hatchet hanging at the side of the saddle, and under the saddle a blanket, to be spread at the camp-fire upon a bed of freshly cut spruce twigs, a man feels wonderfully independent, even amidst unknown mountains thickly clothed with woods, or capped with snow. A book might be written about this part of my life, but I must rapidly glide over it here, there being so much more to say about the later periods.

Siberia is not the frozen land buried in snow and peopled with exiles only, that it is imagined to be, even by many Russians. In its southern parts it is as rich in natural productions as are the southern parts of Canada, which it resembles so much in its physical aspects; and beside half a million of natives, it has a population of more than four millions of Russians. The southern parts of West Siberia are as thoroughly Russian as the provinces to the north of Moscow. In 1862 the upper administration of Siberia was far more enlightened and far better all round than that of any province of Russia proper. For several years the post of governor-general of East Siberia had been occupied by a remarkable personage, Count N. N. Muravioff, who annexed the Amur region to Russia. He was

123

very intelligent, very active, extremely amiable, and desirous to work for the good of the country. Like all men of action of the governmental school, he was a despot at the bottom of his heart; but he held advanced opinions, and a democratic republic would not have quite satisfied him. He had succeeded to a great extent in getting rid of the old staff of civil service officials, who considered Siberia a camp to be plundered, and he had gathered around him a number of young officials, quite honest, and many of them animated by the same excellent intentions as himself. In his own study, the young officers, with the exile Bakunin among them (he escaped from Siberia in the autumn of 1861), discussed the chances of creating the United States of Siberia, federated across the Pacific Ocean with the United States of America.

When I came to Irkutsk, the capital of East Siberia, the wave of reaction which I saw rising at St. Petersburg had not yet reached these distant dominions. I was very well received by the young governor-general, Korsakoff, who had just succeeded Muravioff, and he told me that he was delighted to have about him men of liberal opinions. As to the commander of the general staff, Kukel, —a young general not yet thirty-five years old, whose personal aide-de-camp I became,—he at once took me to a room in his house, where I found, together with the best Russian reviews, complete collections of the London revolutionary editions of Herzen. We were soon warm friends.

General Kukel temporarily occupied at that time the post of governor of Transbaikalia, and a few weeks later we crossed the beautiful Lake Baikal and went further east, to the little town of Chita, the capital of the province. There I had to give myself, heart and soul, without loss of time, to the great reforms which were then under discussion. The St. Petersburg ministries had applied to the local authorities, asking them to work out schemes of complete reform in the administration of the provinces, the organization of the police, the tribunals, the prisons, the system of exile, the self-government of the townships,—all on broadly liberal bases laid down by the Emperor in his manifestoes.

Kukel, supported by an intelligent and practical man, Colonel Pedashenko, and a couple of well-meaning civil service officials, worked all day long, and often a good deal of the night. I became the secretary of two committees,—for the reform of the prisons and the whole system of exile, and for preparing a scheme of municipal self-government,—and I set to work with all the enthusiasm of a youth of nineteen years. I read much about the historical development of these institutions in Russia and their present condition abroad, excellent works and papers dealing with these subjects hav-

.ing been published by the ministries of the interior and of justice; but what we did in Transbaikalia was by no means merely theoretical. I discussed first the general outlines, and subsequently every point of detail, with practical men, well acquainted with the real needs and the local possibilities; and for that purpose I met a considerable number of men both in town and in the province. Then the conclusions we arrived at were re-discussed with Kukel and Pedashenko; and when I had put the results into a preliminary shape, every point was again very thoroughly thrashed out in the committees. One of these committees, for preparing the municipal government scheme, was composed of citizens of Chita, elected by all the population, as freely as they might have been elected in the United States. In short, our work was very serious; and even now, looking back at it through the perspective of so many years, I can say in full confidence that if municipal self-government had been granted then, in the modest shape which we gave to it, the towns of Siberia would be very different from what they are. But nothing came of it all, as will presently be seen.

There was no lack of other incidental occupations. Money had to be found for the support of charitable institutions; an economic description of the province had to be written in connection with a local agricultural exhibition; or some serious inquiry had to be made. "It is a good epoch we live in; work, my dear friend; remember that you are the secretary of all existing and future committees," Kukel would sometimes say to me,—and I worked with doubled energy.

An example or two will show with what results. There was in our province a "district chief"—that is, a police officer invested with very wide and indeterminate rights—who was simply a disgrace. He robbed the peasants and flogged them right and left,—even women, which was against the law; and when a criminal affair fell into his hands, it might lie there for months, men being kept in the meantime in prison till they gave him a bribe. Kukel would have dismissed this man long before, but the governor-general did not like the idea of it, because he had strong protectors at St. Petersburg. After much hesitation, it was decided at last that I should go to make an investigation on the spot, and collect evidence against the man. This was not by any means easy, because the peasants, terrorized by him, and well knowing an old Russian saying, "God is far away, while your chief is your next-door neighbor," did not dare to testify. Even the woman he had flogged was afraid at first to make a written statement. It was only after I had stayed a fortnight with the peasants, and had won their confidence, that the misdeeds of their chief could be brought to light. I collected crushing evidence, and the district chief was dismissed. We congratulated ourselves on having got rid of such a pest. What was, however, our astonishment when, a few months later, we learned that this same man had been nominated to a higher post in Kamchatka! There he could plunder the natives free of any control, and so he did. A few years later he returned to St. Petersburg a rich man. The articles he occasionally contributes now to the reactionary press are, as one might expect, full of high "patriotic" spirit.

The wave of reaction, as I have already said, had not then reached Siberia, and the political exiles continued to be treated with all possible leniency, as in Muravioff's time. When, in 1861, the poet Mikhailoff was condemned to hard labor for a revolutionary proclamation which he had issued, and was sent to Siberia, the governor of the first Siberian town on his way, Tobolsk, gave a dinner in his honor, in which all the officials took part. In Transbaikalia he was not kept at hard labor, but was allowed officially to stay in the hospital prison of a small mining village. His health being very poor,—he was dying from consumption, and did actually die a few months later,—General Kukel gave him permission to stay in the house of his brother, a mining engineer, who had rented a gold mine from the Crown on his own account. Unofficially that was well known all over Siberia. But one day we learned from Irkutsk that, in consequence of a secret denunciation, the general of the gendarmes (state police) was on his way to Chita, to make a strict inquiry into the affair. An aide-de-camp of the governor-general brought us the news. I was dispatched in great haste to warn Mikhailoff, and to tell him that he must return at once to the hospital prison, while the general of the gendarmes was kept at Chita. As that gentleman found himself every night the winner of considerable sums of money at the green table in Kukel's house, he soon decided not to exchange this pleasant pastime for a long journey to the mines in a temperature which was then a dozen degrees below the freezing-point of mercury, and eventually went back to Irkutsk, quite satisfied with his lucrative mission.

The storm, however, was coming nearer and nearer, and it swept everything before it soon after the insurrection broke out in Poland.

In January, 1863, Poland rose against Russian rule. Insurrectionary bands were formed, and a war began which lasted for full eighteen months. The London refugees had implored the Polish revolutionary committees to postpone the movement. They foresaw that it would be crushed, and would put an end to the reform period in Russia. But it could not be helped. The repression of the nationalist manifestations which took place at Warsaw in 1861, and the cruel, quite unprovoked executions which followed, exasperated the Poles. The die was cast.

Never before had the Polish cause so many sympathizers in Russia as at that time. I do not speak of the revolutionists; but even among the more moderate elements of Russian society it was thought, and was openly said, that it would be a benefit for Russia to have in Poland a friendly neighbor instead of a hostile subject. Poland will never lose her national character, it is too strongly developed; she has, and will have, her own literature, her own art and industry. Russia can keep her in servitude only by means of sheer force and oppression,—a condition of things which has hitherto favored, and necessarily will favor, oppression in Russia herself. Even the peaceful Slavophiles were of that opinion; and while I was at school, St. Petersburg society greeted with full approval the "dream" which the Slavophile Ivan Aksakoff had the courage to print in his paper, "The Day." His dream was that the Russian troops had evacuated Poland, and he discussed the excellent results which would follow.

When the revolution of 1863 broke out, several Russian officers refused to march against the Poles, while others openly took their part, and died either on the scaffold or on the battlefield. Funds for the insurrection were collected all over Russia,—quite openly in Siberia,—and in the Russian universities the students equipped those of their comrades who were going to join the revolutionists.

Then, amidst this effervescence, the news spread over Russia that, during the night of January 10, bands of insurgents had fallen upon the soldiers who were cantoned in the villages, and had murdered them in their beds, although on the very eve of that day the relations of the troops with the Poles seemed to be quite friendly. There was some exaggeration in the report, but unfortunately there was also truth in it, and the impression it produced in Russia was most disastrous. The old antipathies between the two nations, so akin in their origins, but so different in their national characters, woke once more.

Gradually the bad feeling faded away to some extent. The gallant fight of the always brave sons of Poland, and the indomitable energy with which they resisted a formidable army, won sympathy for that heroic nation. But it became known that the Polish revolutionary committee, in its demand for the re-establishment of Poland with its old frontiers, included the Little Russian or Ukrainian provinces, the Greek Orthodox population of which hated its Polish rulers, and more than once in the course of the last three centuries had slaughtered them wholesale. Moreover, Napoleon III began to menace Russia with a new war,—a vain menace, which did more harm to the Poles than all other things put together. And finally, the radical elements of Russia saw with regret that now the purely nationalist elements of Poland had got the upper hand, the revolutionary government did not care in the least to grant the land to the serfs,—a blunder of which the Russian government did not fail to take advantage, in order to appear in the position of protector of the peasants against their Polish landlords.

When the revolution broke out in Poland, it was generally believed in Russia that it would take a democratic, republican turn; and that the liberation of the serfs on a broad democratic basis would be the first thing which a revolutionary government, fighting for the independence of the country, would accomplish.

The emancipation law, as it had been enacted at St. Petersburg in 1861, provided ample opportunity for such a course of action. The personal obligations of the serfs to their owners came to an end only on the 19th of February, 1863. Then, a very slow process had to be gone through in order to obtain a sort of agreement between the landlords and the serfs as to the size and the location of the land allotments which were to be given to the liberated serfs. The yearly payments for these allotments (disproportionally high) were fixed by law at so much per acre; but the peasants had also to pay an additional sum for their homesteads, and of this sum the maximum only had been fixed by the statute,—it having been thought that the landlords might be induced to forego that additional payment, or to be satisfied with only a part of it. As to the so-called "redemption" of the land,—in which case the government undertook to pay the landlord its full value in state bonds, and the peasants, receiving the land, had to pay in return, for forty-nine years, six per cent. on that sum as interest and annuities,—not only were these payments extravagant and ruinous for the peasants, but no time was fixed for the redemption. It was left to the will of the landlord, and in an immense number of cases the redemption arrangements had not even been entered upon, twenty years after the emancipation.

Under such conditions a revolutionary government had ample opportunity for immensely improving upon the Russian law. It was bound to accomplish an act of justice towards the serfs—whose condition in Poland was as bad as, and often worse than in Russia itself—by granting them better and more definite terms of emancipation. But nothing of the sort was done. The purely nationalist party and the aristocratic party having obtained the upper hand in the movement, this fundamentally important matter was left out of sight. This made it easy for the Russian government to win the peasants to its side.

Full advantage was taken of this mistake when Nicholas Milutin was sent to Poland by Alexander II with the mission of liberating the peasants in the way he intended doing it in Russia,—whether the landlords were ruined in consequence or not. "Go to Poland; apply there your Red programme against the Polish landlords," said Alexander II to him; and Milutin, together with Prince Cherkassky and many others, really did their best to take the land from the landlords and give good-sized allotments to the peasants.

I once met one of the Russian functionaries who went to Poland under Milutin and Prince Cherkassky. "We had full liberty," he said to me, "to turn over the land to the peasants. My usual plan was to go and to convoke the peasants' assembly. 'Tell me first,' I would say, 'what land do you hold at this moment?' They would point it out to me. 'Is this all the land you ever held?' I would then ask. 'Surely not,' they would reply with one voice. 'Years ago these meadows were ours; this wood was once in our possession; these fields, too,' they would say. I would let them go on talking all over and then would ask, 'Now, which of you can certify under oath that this land or that land has ever been held by you?' Of course there would be nobody forthcoming,—it was all too long ago. At last, some old man would be thrust out from the crowd, the rest saying, 'He knows all about it; he can swear to it.' The old man would begin a long story about what he knew in his youth, or had heard from his father, but I would cut the story short. . . . 'State on oath what you know to have been held by the *gmina* (the village community), and the land is yours.' And as soon as he took the oath—one could trust that oath implicitly—I wrote out the papers and declared to the assembly, 'Now, this land is yours. You stand no longer under any obligations whatever to your late masters: you are simply their neighbors; all you will have to do is to pay the redemption tax, so much every year, to the government. Your homesteads go with the land: you get them free.' "

One can imagine the effect which such a policy had upon the peasants. A cousin of mine, Petr Nikolaevich Kropotkin, a brother of the aide-de-camp whom I have mentioned, was in Poland or in Lithuania with his regiment of *uhlans* of the guard. The revolution was so serious that even the regiments of the guard had been sent from St. Petersburg against it, and it is now known that when Mikhael Muravioff was sent to Lithuania and came to take leave of the Empress Marie, she said to him, "Save at least Lithuania for Russia!" Poland was regarded as lost.

"The armed bands of the revolutionists held the country," my cousin said to me, "and we were powerless to defeat them, or even to find them. Small bands over and over again attacked our small detachments, and as they fought admirably, and knew the country, and found support in the population, they often had the best of the skirmishes. We were thus compelled to march in large columns only. We would cross a region, marching through the woods, without finding any trace of the bands; but when we marched back again, we learned that bands had reappeared in our rear; that they had levied the patriotic tax in the country; and if some peasant had rendered himself useful in any way to our troops, we found him hanged on a tree by the revolutionary bands. So it went on for months, with no chance of improvement, until Milutin and Cherkassky came and freed the peasants, giving them the land. Then— all was over. The peasants sided with us; they helped us to capture the bands, and the insurrection came to an end."

I often spoke with the Polish exiles in Siberia upon this subject, and some of them understood the mistake that had been made. A revolution, from its very outset, must be an act of justice towards "the downtrodden and the oppressed," not a promise of such reparation later on; otherwise it is sure to fail. Unfortunately, it often happens that the leaders are so much absorbed with mere questions of military tactics that they forget the main thing. For revolutionists not to succeed in proving to the masses that a new era has really begun for them is to insure the certain failure of their cause.

The disastrous consequences for Poland of this revolution are known; they belong to the domain of history. How many thousand men perished in battle, how many hundreds were hanged, and how many scores of thousands were transported to various provinces of Russia and Siberia is not yet fully known. But even the official figures which were printed in Russia a few years ago show that in the Lithuanian provinces alone—not to speak of Poland proper— that terrible man, Mikhael Muravioff, to whom the Russian government has just erected a monument at Wilno, hanged by his own authority 128 Poles, and transported to Russia and Siberia 9423 men and women. Official lists, also published in Russia, give 18,672 men and women exiled to Siberia from Poland, of whom 10,407 were sent to East Siberia. I remember that the governor-general of East Siberia mentioned to me the same number, about 11,000 persons, sent to hard labor or exile in his domains. I saw them there, and witnessed their sufferings. Altogether, something like 60,000 or 70,000 persons, if not more, were torn out of Poland and transported to different provinces of Russia, to the Urals, to Caucasus, and to Siberia.

For Russia the consequences were equally disastrous. The Polish insurrection was the definitive close of the reform period. True, the law of provincial self-government (*Zemstvos*) and the reform of the law courts were promulgated in 1864 and 1866; but both were ready in 1862, and, moreover, at the last moment Alexander II gave preference to the scheme of self-government which had been prepared by the reactionary party of Valueff, as against the scheme that had been prepared by Nicholas Milutin; and immediately after the promulgation of both reforms, their importance was reduced, and in some cases destroyed, by the enactment of a number of by-laws.

Worst of all, public opinion itself took a further step backward. The hero of the hour was Katkoff, the leader of the serfdom party, who appeared now as a Russian "patriot," and carried with him most of the St. Petersburg and Moscow society. After that time, those who dared to speak of reforms were at once classed by Katkoff as "traitors to Russia."

The wave of reaction soon reached our remote province. One day in March a paper was brought by a special messenger from Irkutsk. It intimated to General Kukel that he was at once to leave the post of governor of Transbaikalia and go to Irkutsk, waiting there for further orders, and that he was not to reassume the post of commander of the general staff.

Why? What did that mean? There was not a word of explanation. Even the governor-general, a personal friend of Kukel, had not run the risk of adding a single word to the mysterious order. Did it mean that Kukel was going to be taken between two gendarmes to St. Petersburg, and immured in that huge stone coffin, the fortress of St. Peter and St. Paul? All was possible. Later on we learned that such was indeed the intention; and so it would have been done but for the energetic intervention of Count Nicholas Muravioff, "the conqueror of the Amur," who personally implored the Tsar that Kukel should be spared that fate.

Our parting with Kukel and his charming family was like a funeral. My heart was very heavy. I not only lost in him a dear personal friend, but I felt also that this parting was the burial of a whole epoch, full of long-cherished hopes,—"full of illusions," as it became the fashion to say.

So it was. A new governor came,—a good-natured, "leave-me-in-peace" man. With renewed energy, seeing that there was no time to lose, I completed our plans for the reform of the system of exile and municipal self-government. The governor made a few objections here and there for formality's sake, but finally signed the schemes, and they were sent to headquarters. But at St. Petersburg reforms were no longer wanted. There our projects lie buried still, with hundreds of similar ones from all parts of Russia. A few "improved" prisons, even more terrible than the old unimproved ones, have been built in the capitals, to be shown during prison congresses to distinguished foreigners; but the remainder, and the whole system of exile, were found by George Kennan in 1886 in exactly the same state in which I left them in 1862. Only now, after thirty-five years have passed away, the authorities are introducing the reformed tribunals and a parody of self-government in Siberia, and committees have been nominated again to inquire into the system of exile.

When Kennan came back to London from his journey to Siberia, he managed, on the very next day after his arrival in London, to hunt up Stepniak, Tchaykovsky, myself, and another Russian refugee. In the evening we all met at Kennan's room in a small hotel near Charing Cross. We saw him for the first time, and having no excess of confidence in enterprising Englishmen who had previously undertaken to learn all about the Siberian prisons without even learning a word of Russian, we began to cross-examine Kennan. To our astonishment, he not only spoke excellent Russian, but he knew everything worth knowing about Siberia. One or another of us had been acquainted with the greater proportion of all political exiles in Siberia, and we besieged Kennan with questions: "Where is So and So? Is he married? Is he happy in his marriage? Does he still keep fresh in spirit?" We were soon satisfied that Kennan knew all about every one of them.

When this questioning was over, and we were preparing to leave, I asked, "Do you know, Mr. Kennan, if they have built a watch-tower for the fire brigade at Chita?" Stepniak looked at me, as if to reproach me for abusing Kennan's goodwill. Kennan, however, began to laugh, and I soon joined him. And with much laughter we tossed each other questions and answers: "Why, do you know about that?" "And you too?" "Built?" "Yes, double estimates!" and so on, till at last Stepniak interfered, and in his most severely good-natured way objected: "Tell us at least what you were laughing about." Whereupon Kennan told the story of that watchtower which his readers must remember. In 1859 the Chita people wanted to build a watchtower, and collected the money for it; but their estimates had to be sent to St. Petersburg. So they went to the ministry of the interior; but when they came back, two years later, duly approved, all the prices for timber and work had gone up in that rising young town. This was in 1862, while I was at Chita. New estimates were made and sent to St. Petersburg, and the story was repeated for full twenty-five years, till at last the Chita people, losing patience, put in their estimates prices nearly double the real ones. These fantastic estimates were solemnly considered at St. Petersburg, and approved. This is how Chita got its watchtower.

It has often been said that Alexander II committed a great fault, and brought about his own ruin, by raising so many hopes which later on he did not satisfy. It is seen from what I have just said— and the story of little Chita was the story of all Russia—that he did worse than that. It was not merely that he raised hopes. Yielding for a moment to the current of public opinion around him, he induced men all over Russia to set to work, to issue from the domain of mere hopes and dreams, and to touch with the finger the reforms that were required. He made them realize what could be done immediately, and how easy it was to do it; he induced them to sacrifice whatever of their ideals could not be immediately realized, and to demand only what was practically possible at the time. And when they had framed their ideas, and had shaped them into laws which merely required his signature to become realities, then he refused that signature. No reactionist could raise, or ever has raised, his voice to assert that what was left—the unreformed tribunals, the absence of municipal self-government, or the system of exile— was good and was worth maintaining: no one has dared to say that. And yet, owing to the fear of doing anything, all was left as it was; for thirty-five years those who ventured to mention the necessity of a change were treated as "suspects;" and institutions unanimously recognized as bad were permitted to continue in existence only that nothing more might be heard of that abhorred word "reform."

Seeing that there was nothing more to be done at Chita in the way of reforms, I gladly accepted the offer to visit the Amur that same summer of 1863.

The immense domain on the left (northern) bank of the Amur, and along the Pacific coast as far south as the bay of Peter the Great (Vladivostok), had been annexed to Russia by Count Muravioff, almost against the will of the St. Petersbug authorities and certainly without much help from them. When he conceived the bold plan of taking possession of the great river whose southern position and fertile lands had for the last two hundred years always attracted the Siberians; and when, on the eve of the opening of Japan to Europe, he decided to take for Russia a strong position on the Pacific coast, and to join hands with the United States, he had almost everybody against him at St. Petersburg: the ministry of war, which had no men to dispose of; the ministry of finance, which had no money for annexations; and especially the ministry of foreign affairs, always guided by its preoccupation of avoiding "diplomatic complications." Muravioff had thus to act on his own responsibility, and to rely upon the scanty means which thinly populated Eastern Siberia could afford for this grand enterprise. Moreover, everything had to be done in a hurry, in order to oppose the "accomplished fact" to the protests of the West European diplomatists, which would certainly be raised.

A nominal occupation would have been of no avail, and the idea was to have on the whole length of the great river and of its southern tributary, the Usuri,—full 2500 miles,—a chain of self-supporting settlements, and thus to establish a regular communication between Siberia and the Pacific coast. Men were wanted for these settlements, and as the scanty population of East Siberia could not supply them, Muravioff was forced to unusual measures. Released convicts who, after having served their time, had become serfs to the imperial mines, were freed and organized as Transbaikalian Cossacks, part of whom were settled along the Amur and the Usuri, forming two new Cossack communities. Then Muravioff obtained the release of a thousand hard-labor convicts (mostly robbers and murderers), who were to be settled as free men on the lower Amur. He came himself to see them off, and as they were going to leave, addressed them on the beach: "Go, my children, be free there, cultivate the land, make it Russian soil, start a new life," and so on. The Russian peasant women nearly always, of their own free will, follow their husbands, if the latter happen to be sent to hard labor in Siberia, and many of the would-be colonists had thus their families with them. But those who had none ventured to remark to Muravioff: "What is agriculture without a wife! We ought to be married." Whereupon Muravioff ordered the release of all the hard-labor convict women of the place—about a hundred—and offered them their choice of the men. But there was little time to lose; the high water in the river was rapidly going down, the rafts had to start, and Muravioff, asking the people to stand in pairs on the beach, blessed them, saying: "I marry you, children. Be kind to each other; you men, don't ill-treat your wives,—and be happy."

I saw these settlers some six years after that scene. Their villages were poor, the land they had been settled on having had to be cleared from under virgin forests; but, all things considered, their settlements were not a failure; and the Muravioff marriages were not less happy than marriages are on the average. That excellent, intelligent man, Innocentus, bishop of the Amur, afterward recognized these marriages, as well as the children that were born, as quite legal, and had them inscribed on the church registers.

Muravioff was less successful, however, with another batch of men that he added to the population of East Siberia. In his penury of men, he had accepted a couple of thousand soldiers from the punishment battalions. They were incorporated as "adopted sons" in the families of the Cossacks, or were settled in joint households in the villages of the Siberians. But ten or twenty years of barrack life under the horrid discipline of Nicholas I's time surely were not a preparation for an agricultural life. The "sons" deserted their adopted fathers, and constituted the floating population of the towns, living from hand to mouth on occasional jobs, spending chiefly in drink what they earned, and then waiting as care-free as birds for new jobs to turn up.

The motley crowd of Transbaikalian Cossacks, of ex-convicts, and "sons"—all settled in a hurry, and often in a haphazard way, along the banks of the Amur—certainly did not attain prosperity, especially in the lower parts of the river and on the Usuri, where almost every square yard of land had to be won from a virgin subtropical forest, and where deluges of rain brought by the monsoons in July, inundations on a gigantic scale, millions of migrating birds, and the like, continually destroyed the crops, finally reducing whole populations to sheer despair and apathy.

Considerable supplies of salt, flour, cured meat, and so on had therefore to be shipped every year, to support both the regular troops and the settlements on the lower Amur, and for that purpose some hundred and fifty barges were yearly built at Chita and floated with the early spring high water down the Ingoda, the Shilka, and the Amur. The whole flotilla was divided into detachments of from twenty to thirty barges, which were placed under the orders of a number of Cossack and civil-service officers. Most of these did not know much about navigation, but they could be trusted, at least, not to steal the provisions and then report them as lost. I was nominated assistant to the chief of all that flotilla,—let me name him,—Major Marovsky.

My first experiences in my new capacity of navigator were not entirely successful. It so happened that I had to proceed with a few barges as rapidly as possible to a certain point on the Amur, and there to hand over my vessels. For that purpose I had to hire men from among those very "sons" whom I have already mentioned. None of them had ever had any experience in river navigation; nor had I. On the morning of our start my crew had to be collected from the public houses of the place, most of them being so drunk at that early hour that they had to be bathed in the river to bring them back to their senses. When we were afloat, I had to teach them everything that was to be done. Still, things went pretty well during the day; the barges, carried along by a swift current, floated down the river, and my crew, inexperienced though they were, had no interest in throwing their vessels upon the shore: that would have required special exertion. But when dusk came, and it was time to bring our huge, heavily laden barges to the shore and fasten them for the night, one of them, which was far ahead of the one that carried me, was stopped only when it was fast upon a rock, at the foot of a tremendously high, insurmountable cliff. There it stood immovable, while the level of the river, temporarily swollen by rains, was rapidly going down. My ten men evidently could not move it. I rowed down to the next village to ask assistance from the Cossacks, and at the same time dispatched a messenger to a friend, a Cossack officer who was staying some twenty miles away, and who had had experience in such things.

The morning came; a hundred Cossacks—men and women—had

come to my aid, but there was no means whatever of connecting the barge with the shore, in order to unload it, so deep was the water under the cliff. And, as soon as we attempted to push it off the rock, its bottom was broken in, and the water freely entered, sweeping away the flour and salt which formed the cargo. To my great horror I perceived numbers of small fish entering through the hole and swimming about in the barge, and I stood there helpless, without knowing what to do next. There is a very simple and effective remedy for such emergencies. A sack of flour is forced into the hole, to the shape of which it soon adapts itself, while the outer crust of paste which is formed in the sack prevents water from penetrating through the flour; but none of us knew this at the time.

Happily for me, a few minutes later a barge was sighted coming down the river towards us. The appearance of the swan which carried Lohengrin was not greeted with more enthusiasm by the despairing Elsa than that clumsy vessel was greeted by me. The haze which covered the beautiful Shilka at that early hour in the morning added even more to the poetry of the vision. It was my friend, the Cossack officer, who had realized by my description that no human force could drag my barge off the rock,—that it was lost,—and was bringing an empty barge which by chance was at hand, to take away the cargo of my doomed craft.

Now the hole was stopped, the water was pumped out, the cargo was transferred to the new barge, and next morning I could continue my journey. This little experience was of great profit to me, and I soon reached my destination on the Amur without further adventures worth mentioning. Every night we found some stretch of steep but relatively low shore where to stop with the barges, and our fires were soon lighted on the bank of the swift and clear river, amidst the most beautiful mountain scenery. In daytime, one could hardly imagine a more pleasant journey than on board a barge, which floats leisurely down, without any of the noise of the steamer; one or two strokes being occasionally given with its immense stern sweep to keep it in the main current. For the lover of nature, the lower part of the Shilka and the upper part of the Amur, where one sees a most beautiful, wide, and swift river flowing amidst mountains rising in steep, wooded cliffs a couple of thousand feet above the water, offer some of the most delightful scenes in the world. But these same cliffs make communication along the shore on horseback, by way of a narrow trail, extremely difficult. I learned this that very autumn at my own expense. In East Siberia the seven last stations along the Shilka (about 120 miles) were known as the Seven Mortal Sins. This stretch of the Trans-Siberian railway—if it is ever built—will cost unimaginable sums of money; much more than the stretch of the Canadian Pacific line in the Rocky Mountains, in the canyon of the Fraser River, has cost.

After I had delivered my barges, I made about a thousand miles down the Amur in one of the post boats which are used on the river. The stern of the boat was covered in, and in the bow was a box filled with earth upon which a fire was kept to cook the food. My crew consisted of three men. We had to make haste, and therefore used to row in turns all day long, while at night the boat was left to float with the current, and I kept the watch for three or four hours to maintain the boat in the middle of the river, and to prevent it from being drawn into some side channel. These watches —the full moon shining above and the dark hills reflected in the river—were beautiful beyond description. My rowers were taken from the aforementioned "sons;" they were three tramps, who had the reputation of being incorrigible thieves and robbers,—and I carried with me a heavy sack full of banknotes, silver, and copper. In Western Europe such a journey, on a lonely river, would have been considered risky; not so in East Siberia. I made it without even having so much as an old pistol, and I found my three tramps excellent company. Only, as we approached Blagoveschensk, they became restless. "Khanshina" (the Chinese brandy) "is cheap there," they reasoned, with deep sighs. "We are sure to get into trouble! It's cheap, and it knocks you over in no time, from want of being used to it!" I offered to leave the money which was due to them with a friend who would see them off with the first steamer. "That would not help us," they replied mournfully. "Somebody will offer a glass,—it's cheap,—and a glass knocks you over!" they persisted in saying. They were really perplexed, and when, a few months later, I returned through the town, I learned that one of "my sons," as people called them in town, had really got into trouble. When he had sold the last pair of boots to get the poisonous drink, he had committed some theft and had been locked up. My friend finally obtained his release and shipped him back.

Only those who have seen the Amur, or know the Mississippi or the Yang-tse-kiang, can imagine what an immense river the Amur becomes after it has joined the Sungari, and can realize what tremendous waves roll over its bed if the weather is stormy. When the rainy season, due to the monsoons, comes in July, the Sungari, the Usuri, and the Amur are swollen by unimaginable quantities of water; thousands of low islands usually covered with willow thickets are inundated or washed away, and the width of the river attains in places two, three, and even five miles; water rushes into the side channels and the lakes which spread in the low lands along the main channel; and when a fresh wind blows from an easterly quarter, against the current, tremendous waves, even higher than those which one sees in the estuary of the St. Lawrence, roll up both the main river and the side channels. Still worse is it when a typhoon blows from the Chinese Sea and spreads over the Amur region.

We experienced such a typhoon. I was then on board a large decked boat, with Major Marovsky, whom I joined at Blagoveschensk. He had rigged his boat so that she would sail close to the wind, and when the storm began we managed to bring our boat to the sheltered side of the river, and to find refuge in a small tributary. There we stayed for two days, while the storm raged with such fury that, when I ventured for a few hundred yards into the surrounding forest, I had to retreat on account of the number of immense trees which the wind was blowing down around me. We began to feel very uneasy for our barges. It was evident that if they had been afloat that morning, they never would have been able to reach the sheltered side of the river, but must have been driven by the storm to the bank exposed to the full rage of the wind, and there destroyed. A disaster was almost certain.

We sailed out as soon as the fury of the storm had abated. We knew that we ought soon to overtake two detachments of barges; but we sailed one day, two days, and found no trace of them. My friend Marovsky lost both sleep and appetite, and looked as if he had just had a serious illness. He sat whole days on the deck, motionless, murmuring, "All is lost, all is lost." The villages are few and far between on this part of the Amur, and nobody could give us any information. A new storm came on, and finally, reaching a village at daybreak, we learned that no barges had passed, but that quantities of wreckage had been seen floating down the river during the previous day. It was evident that at least forty barges, which carried a cargo of about two thousand tons, must have been lost. It meant a certain famine next spring on the lower Amur if no supplies were brought in time, for it was late in the season, navigation would soon come to a close, and there was then no telegraph along the river.

We held a council, and decided that Marovsky should sail as quickly as possible to the mouth of the Amur. Some purchases of grain might perhaps be made in Japan before the close of navigation. Meanwhile I was to go with all possible speed up the river, to determine the losses, and do my best to cover the two thousand miles up the Amur and the Shilka,—in boats, on horseback, or on board steamer if I met one. The sooner I could warn the Chita authorities, and dispatch any amount of provisions available, the better it would be. Perhaps part of them would this same autumn reach the upper Amur, whence it would be easier to ship them in the early spring to the low lands. If only a few weeks or even days could be saved, it might make an immense difference in case of a famine.

I began my two thousand miles' journey in a row-boat, changing rowers at each village, every twenty miles or so. It was very slow progress, but there might be no steamer coming up the river for a fortnight, and in the meantime I could reach the places where the barges were wrecked, and see if any of the provisions had been saved. Then, at the mouth of the Usuri (Khabarovsk) I might secure a steamer. The boats which I found at the villages were miserable, and the weather was very stormy. We kept along the shore, of course, but we had to cross some branches of the Amur, of considerable width, and the waves driven by the high wind continually threatened to swamp our little craft. One day we had to cross a branch of the river nearly half a mile wide. Choppy waves rose like mountains as they rolled up that branch. My rowers, two peasants, were seized with terror; their faces were white as paper; their blue lips trembled; they murmured prayers. But a boy of fifteen, who held the rudder, calmly kept a watchful eye upon the waves. He glided between them as they seemed to sink around us for a moment, but when he saw them rising to a menacing height in front of us, he gave a slight turn to the boat and steadied it across the waves. The boat shipped water from each wave, and I bailed it out with an old ladle, noting at times that it accumulated more rapidly than I could throw it out. There was a moment, when the boat shipped two such big waves, that at a sign from one of the trembling rowers I unfastened the heavy sack, full of copper and silver, that I carried across my shoulder. . . . For several days in succession we had such crossings. I never forced the men to cross, but they themselves, knowing why I had to hurry, would decide at a given moment that an attempt must be made. "There are not seven deaths in one's life, and one cannot be avoided," they would say, and, signing themselves with the cross, they would seize the oars and pull over.

I soon reached the place where the main destruction of our barges had taken place. Forty-four of them had been wrecked by the storm. Unloading had been impossible, and very little of the cargo had been saved. Two thousand tons of flour had been destroyed. With this news I continued my journey.

A few days later, a steamer slowly creeping up the river overtook me, and when I boarded her, the passengers told me that the captain had drunk himself into a delirium and jumped overboard. He was saved, however, and was now lying ill in his cabin. They asked me to take command of the steamer, and I had to consent; but soon I found to my great astonishment that everything went on by itself in such an excellent routine way that, though I paraded all day on the bridge, I had almost nothing to do. Apart from a few minutes of real responsibility, when the steamer had to be brought to the landing-places, where we took wood for fuel, and saying a word or two now and then to encourage the stokers to start as soon as the dawn permitted us faintly to distinguish the outlines of the shores, matters took care of themselves. A pilot who would have been able to interpret the map would have managed as well.

Traveling by steamer and a great deal on horseback, I reached at last Transbaikalia. The idea of a famine that might break out next spring on the lower Amur oppressed me all the time. I found that on the Shilka the small steamer did not progress up the swift river rapidly enough; so I abandoned it and rode with a Cossack a couple of hundred miles up the Argun, along one of the wildest mountain tracks in Siberia, never stopping to light our camp-fire until midnight had overtaken us in the woods. Even the ten or twenty hours that I might gain by this exertion were not to be despised, for every day brought nearer the close of navigation; ice was already forming on the river at night. At last I met the Governor of Transbaikalia and my friend Colonel Pedashenko on the Shilka, at the convict settlement of Kara, and the latter took in hand the care of shipping immediately all available provisions. As for me, I left immediately to report all about the matter at Irkutsk.

People at Irkutsk wondered that I had managed to make this long journey so rapidly; but I was quite worn out. However, I recuperated by sleeping, for a week's time, such a number of hours every day that I should be ashamed to mention it now.

"Have you taken enough rest?" the governor-general asked me, a week or so after my arrival. "Could you start tomorrow for St. Petersburg, as a courier, to report there yourself upon the loss of the barges?"

It meant to cover in twenty days—not one day more—another distance of 3200 miles between Irkutsk and Nijni Novgorod, where I could take the railway to St. Petersburg; to gallop day and night in post carts, which had to be changed at every station, because no carriage would stand such a journey full speed over the frozen roads. But to see my brother Alexander was too great an attraction for me not to accept the offer, and I started the next night. When I reached the low lands of West Siberia and the Urals, the journey really became a torture. There were days when the wheels of the carts would be broken in the frozen ruts at every successive station. The rivers were freezing, and I had to cross the Ob in a boat amidst floating ice, which threatened at every moment to crush our small craft. When I reached the Tom River, on which the floating ice had just frozen together during the preceding night, the peasants refused for some time to take me over, asking me to give them "a receipt."

"What sort of receipt do you want?"

"Well, you write on a paper: 'I, the undersigned, hereby testify that I was drowned by the will of God, and through no fault of the peasants,' and you give us that paper."

"With pleasure—on the other shore."

At last they took me over. A boy—a brave, bright boy whom I had selected in the crowd—headed the procession, testing the strength of the ice with a pole; I followed him, carrying my dispatch box on my shoulders, and we two were attached to long lines, which five peasants held, following us at a distance,—one of them carrying a bundle of straw, to be thrown on the ice where it did not seem strong enough.

Finally I reached Moscow, where my brother met me at the station, and thence we proceeded at once to St. Petersburg.

Youth is a grand thing. After such a journey, which lasted twenty-four days and nights, arriving early in the morning at St. Petersburg, I went the same day to deliver my dispatches, and did not fail also to call upon an aunt, or rather upon a cousin of mine. She was radiant. "We have a dancing party tonight. Will you come?" she said. Of course I would! And not only come, but dance until an early hour in the morning.

When I reached St. Petersburg and saw the authorities, I understood why I had been sent to make the report. Nobody would believe the possibility of such a destruction of the barges. "Have you been on the spot?" "Did you see the destruction with your own eyes?" "Are you perfectly sure that 'they' have not simply stolen the provisions, and shown you the wreck of some barges?" Such were the questions I had to answer.

The high functionaries who stood at the head of Siberian affairs at St. Petersburg were simply charming in their innocent ignorance of Siberia. "*Mais, mon cher,*" one of them said to me,—he always spoke French,—"how *is* it possible that forty barges should be destroyed on the Neva without any one rushing to save them?" "The Neva!" I exclaimed, "put three—four Nevas side by side and you will have the lower Amur!"

"Is it really as big as that?" And two minutes later he was chatting, in excellent French, about all sorts of things. "When did you last see Schwartz, the painter? Is not his 'Ivan the Terrible' a wonderful picture? Do you know why they were going to arrest Kukel?" and he told me all about a letter that had been addressed to him, asking his support for the Polish insurrection. "Do you know that Chernyshevsky has been arrested? He is now in the fortress."

"What for? What has he done?" I asked.

"Nothing in particular, nothing! But, *mon cher*, you know,— State considerations! . . . Such a clever man, awfully clever! And such an influence he has upon the youth. You understand that a government cannot tolerate that: that's impossible! *intolérable, mon cher, dans un Etat bien ordonné!*"

Count Ignatieff asked no such questions; he knew the Amur very well,—and he knew St. Petersburg, too. Amidst all sorts of jokes and witty remarks about Siberia, which he made with an astounding vivacity, he said to me, "It is a very lucky thing that you were there on the spot and saw the wrecks. And 'they' were clever to send you with the report. Well done! At first nobody wanted to believe about the barges. 'Some new swindling,' it was thought. But now people say that you were well known as a page, and you have only been a few months in Siberia; so you would not shelter the people there, if it were swindling; they trust in you."

The Minister of War, Dmitri Milutin, was the only man high in the administration at St. Petersburg who took the matter seriously. He asked me many questions, all to the point. He mastered the subject at once, and all our conversation went on in short sentences, without hurry, but without any waste of words. "The coast settlements to be supplied from the sea, you mean? The remainder only from Chita? Quite right. But if a storm happens next year,— will there be the same destruction once more?" "No, if there are two small tugs to convoy the barges." "Will it do?" "Yes; with one tug the loss would not have been half so heavy." "Very probably. Write to me, please; state all you have said; quite plainly—no formalities."

I did not stay long at St. Petersburg, but returned to Irkutsk the same winter. My brother was going to join me there in a few months: he was accepted as an officer of the Irkutsk Cossacks.

Traveling across Siberia in the winter is supposed to be a terrible experience; but, all things considered, it is on the whole more comfortable than at any other season of the year. The snow-covered roads are excellent, and although the cold is intense, one can stand it well enough. Lying full length in the sledge, as every one does in Siberia, wrapped in fur blankets, fur inside and fur outside, one does not suffer much from the cold, even when the temperature is forty or sixty degrees below zero, Fahrenheit. Traveling in courier fashion,—that is, rapidly changing horses at each station and stopping only once a day for one hour to take a meal, —I reached Irkutsk nineteen days after leaving St. Petersburg. Two hundred miles a day is the normal speed in such cases, and I remember having covered the last 660 miles of my journey in seventy hours. The frost was not severe then, the roads were in an excellent condition, the drivers were kept in good spirits by a free allowance of silver coins, and the team of three small and light horses seemed to enjoy running swiftly over hill and vale, across rivers frozen as hard as steel, and through forests glistening in their silver attire under the rays of the sun.

I was now appointed *attaché* to the Governor-General of East Siberia for Cossack affairs, and had to reside at Irkutsk; but there was nothing in particular to do. To let everything go on according to the established routine, with no more reference to changes,—such was the watchword that came now from St. Petersburg. I therefore gladly accepted the proposal to undertake geographical exploration in Manchuria.

If one casts a glance on a map of Asia, one sees that the Russian frontier which runs in Siberia, broadly speaking, along the fiftieth degree of latitude, suddenly bends in Transbaikalia to the north. It follows for three hundred miles the Argun River; then, on reaching the Amur, it turns southeastward, the town of Blagoveschensk, which was the capital of the Amur land, being situated again in about the same latitude of fifty degrees. Between the southeastern corner of Transbaikalia (New Tsurukhaitu) and Blagoveschensk on the Amur, the distance west to east is only five hundred miles; but along the Argun and the Amur it is over a thousand miles, and moreover communication along the Argun, which is not navigable, is extremely difficult. In its lower parts there is nothing but a mountain track of the wildest description.

Transbaikalia is very rich in cattle, and the Cossacks who occupy its southeastern corner and are wealthy cattlebreeders wanted to establish a direct communication with the middle Amur, which would be a good market for their cattle. They used to trade with the Mongols, and they had heard from them that it would not be difficult to reach the Amur, traveling eastward across the Great Khingan. Going straight towards the east, they were told, one would fall in with an old Chinese route which crosses the Khingan and leads to the Manchurian town of Merghen (on the Nonni River, a tributary to the Sungari), whence there is an excellent road to the middle Amur.

I was offered the leadership of a trading caravan which the Cossacks intended to organize in order to find that route, and I accepted it with enthusiasm. No European had ever visited that region; and a Russian topographer who went that way a few years before was killed. Only two Jesuits, in the times of the Emperor Kan-si, had penetrated from the south as far as Merghen, and had determined its latitude. All the immense region to the north of it, five hundred miles wide, and seven hundred miles deep, was totally, absolutely unknown. I consulted all the available sources about this region. Nobody, not even the Chinese geographers, knew anything about it. Besides, the very fact of connecting the middle Amur with Transbaikalia had its importance, and Tsurukhaitu is now going to be the head of the Trans-Manchuria Railway. We were thus the pioneers of that great enterprise.

There was, however, one difficulty. The treaty with China granted to the Russians free trade with the "Empire of China, and Mongolia." Manchuria was not mentioned in it, and could as well be excluded as included in the treaty. The Chinese frontier authorities interpreted it one way, and the Russians the other way. Moreover, only trade being mentioned, an officer would not be allowed to enter Manchuria. I had thus to go as a trader; so I bought at Irkutsk various goods and went disguised as a merchant. The governor-general delivered me a passport 'To the Irkutsk second guild merchant, Petr Alexeiev, and his companions;' and he warned me that if the Chinese authorities arrested me and took me to Pekin, and thence across the Gobi to the Russian frontier,—in a cage, on a camel's back, was their way of conveying prisoners across Mongolia,—I must not betray him by naming myself. I accepted, of course, all the conditions, the temptation to visit a country which no European had ever seen being too great for an explorer to resist.

It would not have been easy to conceal my identity while I was in Transbaikalia. The Cossacks are an extremely inquisitive people, —real Mongols,—and as soon as a stranger comes to their villages, while treating him with the greatest hospitality, the master of the house where he stays subjects him to a formal interrogatory.

"A tedious journey, I suppose," he begins; "a long way from Chita, is it not? And then, perhaps, longer still for one who comes from some place beyond Chita. Maybe from Irkutsk? Trading there, I believe. Many tradesmen come this way. You are going also to Nerchinsk, are you not? Yes, people are often married at your age: and you, too, must have left a family, I suppose. Many children? Not all boys, I should say?" And so on for quite half an hour.

The local commander of the Cossacks, Captain Buxhovden, knew his people, and consequently we had taken our precautions. At Chita and at Irkutsk we often had had amateur theatricals, playing by preference dramas of Ostrovsky, in which the scene of action is nearly always amongst the merchant classes. I played several times in such dramas, and found so great pleasure in acting that I even wrote on one occasion to my brother an enthusiastic letter confessing to him my passionate desire to abandon my military career and to go on the stage. I played mostly young merchants, and had acquired sufficiently well their ways of talking and gesticulating and tea-drinking from the saucer,—I learned those ways in my Nikolskoye experiences,—and now I had a good opportunity to act it all out in reality for useful purposes.

"Take your seat, Petr Alexeievich," Captain Buxhovden would say to me when the boiling tea urn, throwing out clouds of steam, was placed on the table.

"Thank you; we will stay here," I would reply, sitting on the edge of a chair at a distance, and beginning to drink my tea in true Moscow merchant fashion, Buxhovden meanwhile nearly exploding with laughter, as I blew upon my saucer with "staring eyes" and bit off in a special way microscopic particles from a small lump of sugar which was to serve for half a dozen cups.

We knew that the Cossacks would soon make out the truth about me, but the important thing was to win a few days, and to cross the frontier while my identity was still undiscovered. I must have played my part pretty well, for the Cossacks treated me like a petty merchant. In one village an old woman beckoned to me as I passed, and asked, "Are there more people coming behind you on the road, my dear?"

"None, grandmother, that we heard of."

"They said a prince, Rapotsky, was going to come. Is he coming?"

"Oh, I see. You are right, grandmother. His highness intended to go, too, from Irkutsk. But how can 'they'? Such a journey! Not suitable for them. So they remained where they were."

"Of course, how can he!"

To be brief, we crossed the frontier unmolested. We were eleven Cossacks, one Tungus, and myself, all on horseback. We had with us about forty horses for sale and two carts,—one of which, two-wheeled, belonged to me, and contained the cloth, the velveteen, the gold braid, and so on, which I had taken in my capacity of merchant. I attended to my cart and my horses entirely myself, while we chose one of the Cossacks to be the "elder" of our caravan. He had to manage all the diplomatic talk with the Chinese authorities. All the Cossacks spoke Mongolian, and the Tungus understood Manchurian. The Cossacks of the caravan knew of course who I was,—one of them knew me at Irkutsk,—but they never betrayed that knowledge, understanding that the success of the expedition depended upon it. I wore a long blue cotton dress, like all the others, and the Chinese paid no attention to me, so that, unnoticed by them, I could make the compass survey of the route. On the first day, when all sorts of Chinese soldiers hung about us, in the hope of getting a glass of whiskey, I had often to cast only a furtive glance at my compass, and to jot down the bearings and the distances inside of my pocket, without taking my paper out. We had with us no arms whatever. Only our Tungus, who was going to be married, had taken his matchlock gun and used it to hunt fallow deer, bringing us meat for supper, and securing furs with which to pay for his future wife.

When there was no more whiskey to be obtained from us, the Chinese soldiers left us alone. So we went straight eastward, finding our way as best we could across hill and dale, and after a four or five days march we actually fell in with the Chinese track which would take us across the Khingan to Merghen.

To our astonishment, we found that the crossing of the great ridge, which looked so black and terrible on the maps, was very easy. We overtook on the road an old Chinese functionary, miserably wretched, traveling in a two-wheeled cart. For the last two days the road was up-hill, and the country bore testimony to its high altitude. The ground became marshy, and the road muddy; the grass was very poor, and the trees grew thin, undeveloped, often crippled, and covered with lichens. Mountains bare of forests rose to right and left, and we were thinking already of the difficulties we should experience in crossing the ridge, when we saw the old Chinese functionary alighting from his cart before an *obo*,—that is, a heap of stones and branches of trees to which bundles of horsehair and small rags had been attached. He drew several hairs out of the mane of his horse, and attached them to the branches. "What is that?" we asked. "The *obo*; the waters before us flow now to the Amur." "Is that all of the Khingan?" "It's all! No more mountains to cross until we reach the Amur, only hills!"

Quite a commotion spread in our caravan. "The rivers flow to the Amur, the Amur!" shouted the Cossacks to one another. All their lives they had heard the old Cossacks talking about the great river where the vine grows wild, where the prairies extend for hundreds of miles and could give wealth to millions of men; then, after the Amur had been annexed to Russia, they heard of the long journey to it, the difficulties of the first settlers, and the prosperity of their relatives settled in the upper Amur; and now we had found the short way to them! We had before us a steep slope, the road leading downwards in zigzags to a small river which pierced its way through a choppy sea of mountains, and led to the Amur. No more obstacles lay between us and the great river. A traveler will imagine my delight at this unexpected geographical discovery. As to the Cossacks, they hastened to dismount and to attach in their turn bundles of hair taken from their horses to the branches thrown on the *obo*. The Siberians in general have a sort of awe of the gods of the heathens. They do not think much of them, but these gods, they say, are wicked creatures, bent on mischief, and it is never good to be on bad terms with them. It is far better to bribe them with small tokens of respect.

"Look, here is a strange tree; it must be an oak," they exclaimed, as we descended the steep slope. The oak does not grow in Siberia at all, and is not found until the eastern slope of the high plateau has been reached. "Look, nut trees!" they exclaimed next. "And what tree is that?" they said, seeing a lime-tree, or some other trees which do not grow in Russia, and which I knew as part of the Manchurian flora. The northerners, who for many years had dreamed of warmer lands, and now saw them, were delighted. Lying upon the ground covered with rich grass, they caressed it with their eyes,—they would have kissed it. Now they burned with the desire to reach the Amur as soon as possible. And when a fortnight later, we stopped at our last camp-fire within twenty miles of the river, they grew impatient like children. They began to saddle their horses shortly after midnight, and made me start long before daybreak; and when at last from an eminence we caught a sight of the mighty stream, the eyes of these unimpressionable Siberians, generally devoid of poetical feeling, gleamed with a poet's ardor as they looked upon the blue waters of the majestic Amur. It was evident that, sooner or later, with or without the support, or even against the wish, of the Russian government, both banks of this river, a desert now but rich with possibilities, as well as the immense unpopulated stretches of North Manchuria, would be invaded by Russian settlers, just as the shores of the Mississippi were colonized by the Canadian *voyageurs*.

In the meantime, the old half-blind Chinese functionary with whom we had cross the Khingan, having donned his blue coat and official hat with a glass button on its top, declared to us next morning that he would not let us go further. Our "elder" had received him and his clerk in our tent, and the old man, repeating what the clerk whispered to him, raised all sorts of objections to our further progress. He wanted us to camp on the spot while he should send our pass to Pekin to get orders,—which we absolutely refused to do. Then he sought to quarrel with our passport.

"What sort of a passport is that?" he said, looking with disdain at our pass, which was written in a few lines on a plain sheet of foolscap paper, in Russian and Mongolian, and had a simple sealing-wax seal. "You may have written it yourselves and sealed it with a copper," he remarked. "Look at my pass; this is worth something," and he unrolled before us a sheet of paper, two feet long, covered with Chinese characters.

I sat quietly aside during this conference, packing something in my box, when a sheet of the "Moscow Gazette" fell under my hand. The "Gazette," being the property of the Moscow University, had an eagle printed on its title-heading. "Show him this," I said to our elder. He unfolded the immense sheet and pointed out the eagle. "That pass was to show to you," our elder said, "but this is what we have for ourselves." "Why, is it all written about you?" the old man asked, with terror. "All about us," our elder replied, without even a twinkle in his eyes.

The old man—a true functionary—looked quite dumfounded at seeing such a proficiency of writing. He examined every one of us, nodding with his head. But the clerk was still whispering something to his chief, who finally declared that he would not let us continue the journey.

"Enough of talking," I said to the elder; "give the order to saddle the horses." The Cossacks were of the same opinion, and in no time our caravan started, bidding good-by to the old functionary, and promising him to report that short of resorting to violence —which he was not able to do—he had done all in his power to prevent us from entering Manchuria, and that it was our fault if we went nevertheless.

A few days later we were at Merghen, where we traded a little, and soon reached the Chinese town Aigun on the right bank of the Amur, and the Russian town of Blagoveschensk on the left bank. We had discovered the direct route and many interesting things besides: the border-ridge character of the Great Khingan, the ease with which it can be crossed, the tertiary volcanoes of the Uyun Kholdontsi region which had so long been a puzzle in geographical literature, and so on. I cannot say that I was a sharp tradesman, for at Merghen I persisted (in broken Chinese) in asking thirty-five rubles for a watch, when the Chinese buyer had already offered me forty-five; but the Cossacks traded all right. They sold all their horses very well, and when my horses, my goods, and the like were sold by the Cossacks, it appeared that the expedition had cost the government the modest sum of twenty-two rubles,—eleven dollars.

All this summer I traveled on the Amur. I went as far as its mouth, or rather its estuary,—Nikolaevsk,—to join the governor-general, whom I accompanied in a steamer up the Usuri; and after that, in the autumn, I made a still more interesting journey up the Sungari, to the very heart of Manchuria, as far as Ghirin (or Kirin, according to the southern pronunciation).

Many rivers in Asia are made by the junction of two equally important streams, so that it is difficult for the geographer to say which of the two is the main one, and which is a tributary. The Ingoda and the Onon join to make the Shilka; the Shilka and the

Argun join to make the Amur; and the Amur joins the Sungari to form that mighty stream which flows northeastward and enters the Pacific in the inhospitable latitudes of the Tartar strait.

Up to the year 1864, the great river of Manchuria remained very little known. All information about it dated from the times of the Jesuits, and that was scanty. Now that a revival in the exploration of Mongolia and Manchuria was going to take place, and the fear of China which had hitherto been entertained in Russia appeared to be exaggerated, all of us younger people pressed upon the governor-general the necessity of exploring the Sungari. To have next door to the Amur an immense region, almost as little known as an African desert, seemed to us provoking. Suddenly General Korsakoff decided to send a steamer up the Sungari, under the pretext of carrying some message of friendship to the governor-general of the Ghirin province. A Russian consul from Urga had to carry the message. A doctor, an astronomer, and myself, all under the command of a Colonel Chernyaeff, were sent upon the expedition in a tiny steamer, Usuri, which took in tow a barge with coal. Twenty-five soldiers, whose rifles were carefully concealed in the coal, went with us, on the barge.

All was organized very hurriedly, and there was no accommodation on the small steamer to receive such a numerous company; but we were all full of enthusiasm, and huddled as best we could in the tiny cabins. One of us had to sleep on a table, and when we started we found that there were not even knives and forks for all of us,—not to speak of other necessaries. One of us resorted to his penknife at dinner time, and my Chinese knife with two sticks, serving as a fork, was a welcome addition to our equipment.

It was not an easy task to go up the Sungari. The great river in its lower parts, where it flows through the same low lands as the Amur, is very shallow, and although our steamer drew only three feet, we often could not find a channel deep enough for us. There were days when we advanced but some forty miles, and scraped as many times the sandy bottom of the river with our keel; over and over again a rowboat was sent out to find the necessary depth. But our young captain had made up his mind that he would reach Ghirin that autumn, and we progressed every day. As we ascended higher and higher, we found the river more and more beautiful, and more and more easy of navigation; and when we had passed the sandy deserts at its junction with its sister river, the Nonni, progress became easy and pleasant. In a few weeks we thus reached the capital of that province of Manchuria. An excellent map of the river was made by the topographers. There was no time to spare, unfortunately, and so we very seldom landed in any village or town. The villages along the banks of the river are few and far between, and on its lower parts we found only low lands, which are inundated every year; higher up we sailed for a hundred miles amidst sand dunes; and it was only when we reached the upper Sungari and began to approach Ghirin, that we found a dense population.

If our aim had been to establish friendly relations with Manchuria, and not simply to learn what the Sungari is, our expedition might well have been considered a dead failure. The Manchurian authorities had it fresh in their memories how, eight years before, the "visit" of Muravioff ended in the annexation of the Amur and the Usuri, and they could not but look with suspicion on this new and uncalled-for visitation. The twenty-five rifles concealed in the coal, which had been duly reported to the Chinese authorities before we left, still more provoked their suspicions; and when our steamer cast her anchor in front of the populous city of Ghirin, we found all its merchants armed with rusty swords from some old arsenal. We were not prevented, however, from walking in the streets, but all shops were closed as soon as we landed, and the merchants were not allowed to sell anything. Some provisions were sent to us on board the steamer as a gift, but no money was taken in return.

The autumn was rapidly coming to its end, the frosts had begun already, and we had to hurry back, as we could not winter on the Sungari. In short, we saw Ghirin, but spoke to no one but the two interpreters who came every morning on board our steamer. Our aim, however, was fulfilled: we had ascertained that the river is navigable, and an excellent map of it was made, from its mouth to Ghirin, with the aid of which we were able to steam on our return journey at full speed without any accident. At one time our steamer ran upon a sandbank. But the Ghirin officials, desirous above all things that we should not be compelled to winter on the river, sent two hundred Chinese, who aided us in getting off. When I jumped into the water, and, taking a stick, began to sing our river-song, "Dubinushka," which helps all present to give a sudden push at the same moment, the Chinese enjoyed immensely the fun of it, and after several such pushes the steamer was soon afloat. The most cordial relations were established between ourselves and the Chinese by this little adventure. I mean, of course, the people, who seemed to dislike very much their arrogant Manchurian officials.

We called at several Chinese villages, peopled with exiles from the Celestial Empire, and were received in the most cordial way. One evening especially impressed itself on my memory. We came to a picturesque little village as night was already falling. Some of us landed, and I went alone through the village. A thick crowd of about a hundred Chinese soon surrounded me, and although I knew not a word of their tongue, and they knew as little of mine, we chatted in the most amicable way by mimicry, and we understood one another. To pat one on the shoulders in sign of friendship is decidedly international language. To offer one another tobacco and to be offered a light is again an international expression of friendship. One thing interested them,—why had I, though young, a beard? They wear none before they are sixty. And when I told them by signs that in case I should have nothing to eat I might eat it, the joke was transmitted from one to the other through the whole crowd. They roared with laughter, and began to pat me even more caressingly on the shoulders; they took me about, showing me their houses; every one offered me his pipe, and the whole crowd accompanied me as a friend to the steamer. I must say that there was not one single *boshko* (policeman) in that village. In other villages our soldiers and myself always made friends with the Chinese, but as soon as a *boshko* appeared, all was spoiled. In return, one should have seen what "faces" they used to make at the *boshko* behind his back! They evidently hated this representative of authority.

This expedition has since been forgotten. The astronomer Th. Usoltzeff and I published reports about it in the Memoirs of the Siberian Geographical Society; but a few years later a terrible conflagration at Irkutsk destroyed all the copies left of the Memoirs, as well as the original map of the Sungari; and it was only last year, when work upon the Trans-Manchurian Railway was beginning, that Russian geographers unearthed our reports, and found that the great river had been explored five-and-thirty years ago by our expedition.

As there was nothing more to be done in the direction of reform, I tried to do what seemed to be possible under the existing circumstances,—only to become convinced of the absolute uselessness of such efforts. In my new capacity of *attaché* to the governor-general for Cossack affairs, I made, for instance, a most thorough investigation of the economical conditions of the Usuri Cossacks, whose crops used to be lost every year, so that the government had every winter to feed them in order to save them from famine. When I returned from the Usuri with my report, I received congratulations on all sides, I was promoted, I got special rewards. All the measures I recommended were accepted, and special grants of money were given for aiding the emigration of some and for supplying cattle to others, as I had suggested. But the practical realization of the measures went into the hands of some old drunkard, who would squander the money and pitilessly flog the unfortunate Cossacks for the purpose of converting them into good agriculturalists. And thus it went on in all directions, beginning with the Winter Palace at St. Petersburg, and ending with the Usuri and Kamchatka.

The higher administration of Siberia was influenced by excellent intentions, and I can only repeat that, everything considered, it was far better, far more enlightened, and far more interested in the welfare of the country than the administration of any other province of Russia. But it was an administration,—a branch of the tree which had its root at St. Petersburg, and that was quite sufficient to paralyze all its excellent intentions, and to make it interfere with all beginnings of local spontaneous life and progress. Whatever was started for the good of the country by local men was looked at with distrust, and was immediately paralyzed by hosts of difficulties which came, not so much from the bad intentions of men,—men, as a rule, are better than institutions,—but simply because they belonged to a pyramidal, centralized administration. The very fact of its being a government which had its source in a distant capital caused it to look upon everything from the point of view of a functionary of the government who thinks, first of all, about what his superiors will say, and how this or that will appear in the administrative machinery, and not of the interests of the country.

Gradually I turned my energy more and more toward scientific exploration. In 1865 I explored the western Sayans, where I got a new glimpse into the structure of the Siberian highlands, and came upon another important volcanic region on the Chinese frontier; and finally, next year, I undertook a long journey to discover a direct communication between the gold mines of the Yakutsk province (on the Vitim and the Olokma) and Transbaikalia. For several years (1860–64) the members of the Siberian expedition had tried to find such a passage, and had endeavored to cross the series of very wild stony parallel ridges which separate these mines from Transbaikalia; but when they reached that region, coming from the south, and saw before them these dreary mountains spreading for hundreds of miles northward, all of them, save one who was killed by natives, returned southward. It was evident that, in order to be successful, the expedition must move from the north to the south, —from the dreary and unknown wilderness to the warmer and populated regions. It also happened that while I was preparing for the expedition, I was shown a map which a native had traced with his knife on a piece of bark. This little map—a splendid example, by the way, of the usefulness of the geometrical sense in the lowest stages of civilization, and one which would consequently interest A. R. Wallace—so struck me by its seeming truth to nature that I fully trusted to it, and began my journey, following the indications of the map. In company with a young and promising naturalist, Polakoff, and a topographer, I went first down the Lena to the northern gold mines. There we equipped our expedition, taking provisions for three months, and started southward. An old Yakut hunter, who twenty years before had once followed the passage indicated on the Tungus map, undertook to act for us as guide, and to cross the mountain region,—full 250 miles wide,—following the river valleys and gorges indicated by the knife of the Tungus on the birch-bark map. He really accomplished this wonderful feat, although there was no track of any sort to follow, and all the valleys that one sees from the top of a mountain pass, all equally filled with woods, seem, to the unpracticed eye, to be absolutely alike.

This time the passage was found. For three months we wandered in the almost totally uninhabited mountain deserts and over the marshy plateau, till at last we reached our destination, Chita. I am told that this passage is now of value for bringing cattle from the south to the gold mines; as for me, the journey helped me immensely afterward in finding the key to the structure of the mountains and plateaus of Siberia,—but I am not writing a book of travel, and must stop.

The years that I spent in Siberia taught me many lessons which I could hardly have learned elsewhere. I soon realized the absolute impossibility of doing anything really useful for the mass of the people by means of the administrative machinery. With this illusion I parted forever. Then I began to understand not only men and human character, but also the inner springs of the life of human society. The constructive work of the unknown masses, which so seldom finds any mention in books, and the importance of that constructive work in the growth of forms of society, fully appeared before my eyes. To witness, for instance, the ways in which the communities of Dukhobortsy (brothers of those who are now going to settle in Canada, and who find such a hearty support in the United States) migrated to the Amur region, to see the immense advantages which they got from their semi-communistic brotherly organization, and to realize what a wonderful success their colonization was, amidst all the failures of state colonization, was learning something which cannot be learned from books. Again, to live with natives, to see at work all the complex forms of social organization which they have elaborated far away from the influence of any civilization, was, as it were, to store up floods of light which illuminated my subsequent reading. The part which the unknown masses play in the accomplishment of all important historical events, and even in war, became evident to me from direct observation, and I came to hold ideas similar to those which Tolstoy expresses concerning the leaders and the masses in his monumental work, *War and Peace.*

Having been brought up in a serf-owner's family, I entered active life, like all young men of my time, with a great deal of confidence in the necessity of commanding, ordering, scolding, punishing, and the like. But when, at an early stage, I had to manage serious enterprises and to deal with men, and when each mistake would lead at once to heavy consequences, I began to appreciate the difference between acting on the principle of command and discipline and acting on the principle of common understanding. The former works admirably in a military parade, but it is worth nothing where real life is concerned, and the aim can be achieved only through the severe effort of many converging wills. Although I did not then formulate my observations in terms borrowed from party struggles, I may say now that I lost in Siberia whatever faith in state discipline I had cherished before. I was prepared to become an anarchist.

From the age of nineteen to twenty-five I had to work out important schemes of reform, to deal with hundreds of men on the Amur, to prepare and to make risky expeditions with ridiculously small means, and so on; and if all these things ended more or less successfully, I account for it only by the fact that I soon understood that in serious work commanding and discipline are of little avail. Men of initiative are required everywhere; but once the impulse has been given, the enterprise must be conducted, especially in Russia, not in military fashion, but in a sort of communal way, by means of common understanding. I wish that all framers of plans of state discipline could pass through the school of real life before they begin to frame their state Utopias. We should then hear far less than at present of schemes of military and pyramidal organization of society.

With all that, life in Siberia became less and less attractive to me, although my brother Alexander had joined me in 1864 at Irkutsk, where he commanded a squadron of Cossacks. We were happy to be together; we read a great deal, and discussed all the philosophical, scientific, and sociological questions of the day; but we both longed after intellectual life, and there was none in Siberia. The occasional passage through Irkutsk of Raphael Pumpelly or of Adolph Bastian —the only two men of science who visited our capital during my stay there—was quite an event for both of us. The scientific and especially the political life of Western Europe, of which we heard through the papers, attracted us, and the return to Russia was the subject to which we continually came back in our conversations. Finally, the insurrection of the Polish exiles in 1866 opened our eyes to the false position we both occupied as officers of the Russian army.

I was far away, in the Vitim mountains, when the Polish exiles, who were employed in excavating a new road in the cliffs round Lake Baikal, made a desperate attempt to break their chains, and to force their way to China across Mongolia. Troops were sent out against them, and a Russian officer—whom I will call Potaloff— was killed by the insurgents. I heard of it on my return to Irkutsk, where some fifty Poles were to be tried by court-martial. The sittings of courts-martial being open in Russia, I followed this, taking detailed notes of the proceedings, which I sent to a St. Petersburg paper, and which were published in full, to the great dissatisfaction of the governor-general.

Eleven thousand Poles, men and women, had been transported to East Siberia alone, in consequence of the insurrection of 1863. They were chiefly students, artists, ex-officers, nobles, and especially skilled artisans from the intelligent and highly developed workers' population of Warsaw and other towns. A great number of them were kept at hard labor, while the remainder were settled all over the country, in villages where they could find no work whatever, and lived in a state of semi-starvation. Those who were at hard labor worked either at Chita, building the barges for the Amur,—these were the happiest,—or in iron works of the Crown, or in salt works. I saw some of the latter, on the Lena, standing half-naked in a shanty, around an immense cauldron filled with salt-brine, and mixing the thick, boiling brine with long shovels, in an infernal temperature, while the gates of the shanty were wide open, to make a strong current of glacial air. After two years of such work these martyrs were sure to die from consumption.

Afterward, a considerable number of Polish exiles were employed as navvies building a road along the southern coast of Lake Baikal. This narrow Alpine lake, four hundred miles long, surrounded by beautiful mountains rising three to five thousand feet above its level, cuts off Transbaikalia and the Amur from Irkutsk. In winter it may be crossed upon the ice, and in summer there are steamers; but for six weeks in the spring and another six weeks in the autumn the only way to reach Chita and Kyakhta (for Pekin) from Irkutsk is to travel on horseback a long, circuitous route, across mountains 7000 to 8000 feet in altitude. I once traveled along this track, greatly enjoying the scenery of the mountains, which were snow-clad in May, but otherwise the journey was really awful. To climb eight miles only, to the top of the main pass, Khamar-daban, it took me the whole day from three in the morning till eight at night. Our horses continually fell through the thawing snow, plunging with their riders many times a day into the icy water which flowed underneath the snow crust. It was decided accordingly to build a permanent road along the southern coast of the lake, blasting out a passage in the steep, almost vertical cliffs which rise along the shore, and spanning with bridges a hundred wild torrents that furiously rush from the mountains into the lake. Polish exiles were employed at this hard work.

Several batches of Russian political exiles had been sent during the last century to Siberia, but with the submissiveness to fate which is characteristic of the Russians, they never revolted; they allowed themselves to be killed inch by inch without ever attempting to free themselves. The Poles, on the contrary,—to their honor be it said,—were never so submissive as that, and this time they broke into open revolt. It was evident that they had no chance of success, but they revolted nevertheless. They had before them the great lake, and behind them a girdle of absolutely impracticable mountains, beyond which spread the wildernesses of North Mongolia; but they conceived the idea of disarming the soldiers who guarded them, forging those terrible weapons of the Polish insurrections,—scythes fastened as pikes on long poles,—and making their way across the mountains and across Mongolia, towards China, where they would find English ships to take them. One day the news came to Irkutsk that part of those Poles who were at work on the Baikal road had disarmed a dozen soldiers and broken out into revolt. Eighty soldiers were all that could be dispatched against them from Irkutsk; crossing the Baikal, in a steamer, they went to meet the insurgents on the other side of the lake.

The winter of 1866 had been unusually dull at Irkutsk. In the Siberian capital there is no such distinction between the different classes as one sees in Russian provincial towns, and Irkutsk "society," composed of numerous officers and officials, together with the wives and daughters of local traders and even clergymen, met during the winter, every Thursday, at the Assembly rooms. This winter, however, there was no "go" in the evening parties. Amateur theatricals, too, were not successful; and gambling, which usually flourished on a grand scale at Irkutsk, only dragged along; a serious want of money was felt among the officials, and even the arrival of several mining officers was not signalized by the heaps of banknotes with which these privileged gentlemen commonly enlivened the knights of the green tables. The season was decidedly dull,—just the season for starting spiritualistic experiences with talking tables and talkative spirits. A gentleman who had been the pet of Irkutsk society the previous winter for the tales from popular life which he recited with great talent, seeing that interest in himself and his tales was failing, took now to spiritualism as a new amusement. He was clever, and in a week's time all Irkutsk society was mad over talking spirits. A new life was infused into those who did not know how to kill time. Talking tables appeared in every drawing-room, and love-making went hand in hand with spirit rapping. Lieutenant Potaloff took it all in deadly earnest,—talking tables and love. Perhaps he was less fortunate with the latter than with the tables; at any rate, when the news of the Polish insurrection came, he asked to be sent to the spot with the eighty soldiers. He hoped to return with a halo of military glory.

"I go against the Poles," he wrote in his diary; "it would be so interesting to be slightly wounded!"

He was killed. He rode on horseback by the side of the colonel who commanded the soldiers, when "the battle with the insurgents" —the glowing description of which may be found in the annals of the general staff—began. The soldiers were slowly advancing along the road when they met some fifty Poles, five or six of whom were armed with rifles and the remainder with sticks and scythes. The Poles occupied the forest and from time to time fired their guns. The file of soldiers returned the fire. Potaloff twice asked the permission of the colonel to dismount and dash into the forest. The colonel very angrily ordered him to stay where he was. Notwithstanding this, the next moment the lieutenant had disappeared. Several shots resounded in the wood in succession, followed by wild cries; the soldiers rushed that way, and found the lieutenant bleeding on the grass. The Poles fired their last shots and surrendered; the battle was over, and Potaloff was dead. He had rushed, revolver in hand, into the thicket, where he found several Poles armed with scythes. He fired upon them all his shots, in a haphazard way, wounding one of them, whereupon the others rushed upon him with their scythes.

At the other end of the road, on this side of the lake, two Russian officers behaved in the most abominable way towards the Poles who were building the same road, but took no part in the insurrection. One of the two officers rushed into their tent, swearing and firing his revolver at the peaceful exiles, two of whom he badly wounded.

Now, the logic of the Siberian military authorities was that as a Russian officer had been killed, several Poles must be executed. The court-martial condemned five of them to death: Szaramowicz, a pianist, a fine looking man of thirty, who was the leader of the insurrection; Celinski, a man of sixty, who had once been an officer in the Russian army; and three others whose names I do not remember.

The governor-general telegraphed to St. Petersburg asking permission to reprieve the condemned insurgents; but no answer came. He had promised us not to execute them, but after having waited several days for the reply, he ordered the sentence to be carried out in secrecy, early in the morning. The reply from St. Petersburg came four weeks later, by post: the governor was left to act "according to the best of his understanding." In the mean time five brave men had been shot.

The insurrection, people said, was foolish. And yet this brave handful of insurgents had obtained something. The news of it reached Europe. The executions, the brutalities of the two officers, which became known through the proceedings of the court, produced a commotion in Austria, and Austria interfered in favor of the Galicians who had taken part in the revolution of 1863 and had been sent to Siberia. Soon after the insurrection, the fate of the Polish exiles in Siberia was substantially bettered, and they owed it to the insurgents,—to those five brave men who were shot at Irkutsk, and those who had taken arms by their side.

For my brother and myself this insurrection was a great lesson. We realized what it meant to belong in any way to the army. I was far away, but my brother was at Irkutsk, and his squadron was dispatched against the insurgents. Happily, the commander of the regiment to which my brother belonged knew him well, and, under some pretext, he ordered another officer to take command of the mobilized part of the squadron. Otherwise, Alexander, of course, would have refused to march. If I had been at Irkutsk, I should have done the same.

We decided then to leave the military service and to return to Russia. This was not an easy matter, especially as Alexander had married in Siberia; but at last all was arranged, and early in 1867 we were on our way to St. Petersburg.

Early in the autumn of 1867 my brother and I, with his family, were settled at St. Petersburg. I entered the university, and sat on the benches among young men, almost boys, much younger than myself. What I so longed for five years before was accomplished,— I could study; and, acting upon the idea that a thorough training in mathematics is the only solid basis for all subsequent work and thought, I joined the physico-mathematical faculty in its mathematical section. My brother entered the military academy for jurisprudence, whilst I entirely gave up military service, to the great dissatisfaction of my father, who hated the very sight of a civilian dress. We both had now to rely entirely upon ourselves.

Study at the university and scientific work absorbed all my time for the next five years. A student of the mathematical faculty has, of course, very much to do, but my previous studies in higher mathematics permitted me to devote part of my time to geography; and, moreover, I had not lost in Siberia the habit of hard work.

The report of my last expedition was in print; but in the meantime a vast problem rose before me. The journeys that I had made in Siberia had convinced me that the mountains which at that time were drawn on the maps of Northern Asia were mostly fantastic, and gave no idea whatever of the structure of the country. The great plateaus which are so prominent a feature of Asia were not even suspected by those who drew the maps. Instead of them, several great ridges, such as, for instance, the eastern portion of the Stanovoi, which used to be drawn on the maps as a black worm creeping eastward, had grown up in the topographic bureaus, contrary to the indications and even to the sketches of such explorers as L. Schwartz. These ridges have no existence in nature. The heads of the rivers which flow toward the Arctic Ocean on the one side, and toward the Pacific on the other, lie intermingled on the surface of a vast plateau; they rise in the same marshes. But, in the European topographer's imagination, the highest mountain ridges must run along the chief water-partings, and the topographers had drawn there the highest Alps, of which there is no trace in reality. Many such imaginary mountains were made to intersect the maps of Northern Asia in all directions.

To discover the true leading principles in the disposition of the mountains of Asia—the harmony of mountain formation—now became a question which for years absorbed my attention. For a considerable time the old maps, and still more the generalizations of Alexander von Humboldt, who, after a long study of Chinese sources, had covered Asia with a network of mountains running along the meridians and parallels, hampered me in my researches, until at last I saw that even Humboldt's generalizations, stimulating though they had been, did not agree with the facts.

Beginning, then, with the beginning, in a purely inductive way, I collected all the barometrical observations of previous travelers, and from them calculated hundreds of altitudes; I marked on a large scale map all geological and physical observations that had been made by different travelers,—the facts, not the hypotheses; and I tried to find out what structural lines would answer best to the observed realities. This preparatory work took me more than two years; and then followed months of intense thought, in order to find out what all the bewildering chaos of scattered observations meant, until one day, all of a sudden, the whole became clear and comprehensible, as if it were illuminated with a flash of light. The main structural lines of Asia are *not* north and south, or west and east; they are from the southwest to the northeast,—just as, in the Rocky Mountains and the plateaus of America, the lines are northwest to southeast; only secondary ridges shoot out northwest. Moreover, the mountains of Asia are not bundles of independent ridges, like the Alps, but are subordinated to an immense plateau, an old continent which once pointed toward Bering Strait. High border ridges have towered up along its fringes, and in the course of ages terraces, formed by later sediments, have emerged from the sea, thus adding on both sides to the width of that primitive backbone of Asia.

There are not many joys in human life equal to the joy of the sudden birth of a generalization, illuminating the mind after a long period of patient research. What has seemed for years so chaotic, so contradictory, and so problematic takes at once its proper position within an harmonious whole. Out of a wild confusion of facts and from behind the fog of guesses,—contradicted almost as soon as they are born,—a stately picture makes its appearance, like an Alpine chain suddenly emerging in all its grandeur from the mists which concealed it the moment before, glittering under the rays of the sun in all its simplicity and variety, in all its mightiness and beauty. And when the generalization is put to a test, by applying it to hundreds of separate facts which had seemed to be hopelessly contradictory the moment before, each of them assumes its due position, increasing the impressiveness of the picture, accentuating some characteristic outline, or adding an unsuspected detail full of meaning. The generalization gains in strength and extent; its foundations grow in width and solidity; while in the distance, through the far-off mist on the horizon, the eye detects the outlines of new and still wider generalizations.

He who has once in his life experienced this joy of scientific creation will never forget it; he will be longing to renew it; and he cannot but feel with pain that this sort of happiness is the lot of so few of us, while so many could also live through it,—on a small or on a grand scale,—if scientific methods and leisure were not limited to a handful of men.

This work I consider my chief contribution to science. My first intention was to produce a bulky volume, in which the new ideas about the mountains and plateaus of Northern Asia should be supported by a detailed examination of each separate region; but in 1873, when I saw that I should soon be arrested, I only prepared a map which embodied my views and wrote an explanatory paper. Both were published by the Geographical Society, under the supervision of my brother, while I was already in the fortress of St. Peter and St. Paul. Petermann, who was then preparing a map of Asia, and knew my preliminary work, adopted my scheme for his map, and it has been accepted since by most cartographers. The map of Asia, as it is now understood, explains, I believe, the main physical features of the great continent, as well as the distribution of its climates, faunas, and floras, and even its history. It reveals, also, as I was able to see during my last journey to America, striking analogies between the structure and the geological growth of the two continents of the northern hemisphere. Very few cartographers could say now whence all these changes in the map of Asia have come; but in science it is better that new ideas should make their way independently of any name attached to them. The errors, which are unavoidable in a first generalization, are easier to rectify.

At the same time I worked a great deal for the Russian Geographical Society in my capacity of secretary to its section of physical geography.

Great interest was taken then in the exploration of Turkestan and the Pamirs. Syevertsoff had just returned after several years of travel. A great zoologist, a gifted geographer, and one of the most intelligent men I ever came across, he, like so many Russians, disliked writing. When he had made an oral communication at a meeting of the society, he could not be induced to write anything beyond revising the reports of his communication, so that all that has been published over his signature is very far from doing full justice to the real value of the observations and the generalizations he had made. This reluctance to put down in writing the results of thought and observation is unfortunately not uncommon in Russia. The remarks on the orography of Turkestan, on the geographical distribution of plants and animals, on the part played by hybrids in the production of new species of birds, and so on, which I have heard Syevertsoff make, and the observations on the importance of mutual support in the progressive development of species which I have found just mentioned in a couple of lines in some report of a meeting,—these bore the stamp of more than ordinary talent and originality; but he did not possess the exuberant force of exposition in an appropriately beautiful form which might have made of him one of the most prominent men of science of our time.

Miklukho-Maklay, well known in Australia, which towards the end of his life became the country of his adoption, belonged to the same order of men: the men who have had so much more to say than they have said in print. He was a tiny, nervous man, always suffering from malaria, who had just returned from the coasts of the Red Sea when I made his acquaintance. A follower of Haeckel, he had worked a great deal upon the marine invertebrates in their natural surroundings. The Geographical Society managed next to get him taken on board a Russian man-of-war to some unknown part of the coast of New Guinea, where he wanted to study the most primitive savages. Accompanied by one sailor only, he was left on this inhospitable shore, the inhabitants of which had the reputation of terrible cannibals. A hut was built for the two Crusoes, and they lived eighteen months or more near a native village on excellent terms with the natives. Always to be straightforward towards them, and never to deceive them,—not even in the most trifling matters, not even for scientific purposes,—was the point on which he was most scrupulous. When he was traveling some time later in the Malayan archipelago, he had with him a native who had entered into his service on the express condition of never being photographed. The natives, as every one knows, consider that something is taken out of them when their likeness is taken by photography. One day when the native was fast asleep, Maklay, who was collecting anthropological materials, confessed that he was awfully tempted to photograph his native, the more so as he was a typical representative of his tribe and would never have known that he had been photographed. But he remembered his agreement and refrained. When he left New Guinea, the natives made him promise to return; and a few years later, although he was severely ill, he kept his word and did return. This remarkable man has, however, published only an infinitesimal part of the truly invaluable observations he made.

Fedchenko, who had made extensive zoological observations in Turkestan,—in company with his wife, Olga Fedchenko, also a naturalist,—was, as we used to say, a "West European." He worked hard to bring out in an elaborated form the results of his observations; but he was, unfortunately, killed in climbing a mountain in Switzerland. Glowing with youthful ardor after his journeys in the Turkestan highlands, and full of confidence in his own powers, he undertook an ascent without proper guides, and perished in a snowstorm. His wife, happily, completed the publication of his *Travels* after his death, and I believe she has now a son who continues the work of his father and mother.

I also saw a great deal of Prjevalsky, or rather Przewalski, as his Polish name ought to be spelled, although he himself preferred to appear as a "Russian patriot." He was a passionate hunter, and the enthusiasm with which he made his explorations of Central Asia was almost as much the result of his desire to hunt all sorts of difficult game,—bucks, wild camels, wild horses, and so on,—as of his desire to discover lands, new and difficult to approach. When he was induced to speak of his discoveries, he would soon interrupt his modest descriptions with an enthusiastic exclamation: "But what game there! What hunting!" And he would describe enthusiastically how he crept such and such a distance to approach a wild horse within shooting range. No sooner was he back at St. Petersburg than he planned a new expedition, and parsimoniously laying aside all his money, tried to increase it by stock exchange operations for that purpose. He was the type of a traveler in his strong physique, and in his capacity for living for years the rough life of a mountain hunter. He delighted in leading such a life. He made his first journey with only three comrades, and always kept on excellent terms with the natives. However, as his subsequent expeditions took on more of a military character, he began unfortunately to rely more upon the force of his armed escort than upon peaceful intercourse with the natives, and I heard it said in well-informed quarters that even if he had not died at the very start of his Tibet expedition,—so admirably and peacefully conducted after his death by his companions, Pyevtsoff, Roborovsky, and Kozloff,—he very probably would not have returned alive.

There was considerable activity at that time in the Geographical Society, and many were the geographical questions in which our section, and consequently its secretary, took a lively interest. Most of them were too technical to be mentioned in this place, but I must allude to the awakening of interest in the Russian settlements, the fisheries, and the trade in the Russian portion of the Arctic Ocean, which took place in these years. A Siberian merchant and gold miner, Sidoroff, made the most persevering efforts to awaken that interest. He foresaw that with a little aid in the shape of naval schools, the exploration of the White Sea, and so on, the Russian fisheries and Russian navigation could be largely developed. But that little, unfortunately, had to be done entirely through St. Petersburg; and the ruling powers of that courtly, bureaucratic, literary, artistic, and cosmopolitan city could not be moved to take an interest in anything provincial. Poor Sidoroff was simply ridiculed for his efforts. Interest in our far north had to be enforced upon the Russian Geographical Society from abroad.

In the years 1869–71 the bold Norwegian seal-hunters had quite unexpectedly opened the Kara Sea to navigation. To our extreme astonishment, we learned one day at the society that that sea, which lies between the island of Novaya Zemlya and the Siberian coast, and which we used confidently to describe in our writings as "an ice cellar permanently stocked with ice," had been entered by a number of small Norwegian schooners and crossed by them in all directions. Even the wintering place of the famous Dutchman Barentz, which we believed to be concealed forever from the eyes of man by ice fields hundreds of years old, had been visited by these adventurous Norsemen.

"Exceptional seasons and an exceptional state of the ice," was what our old navigators said. But to a few of us it was quite evident that, with their small schooners and their small crews, the bold Norwegian hunters, who feel at home amidst the ice, had ventured to pierce the floating ice which usually bars the way to the Kara Sea, while the commanders of government ships, hampered by the responsibilities of the naval service, had never risked doing so.

A general interest in arctic exploration was awakened by these discoveries. In fact, it was the seal-hunters who opened the new era of arctic enthusiasm which culminated in Nordenskjold's circumnavigation of Asia, in the permanent establishment of the north-eastern passage to Siberia, in Peary's discovery of North Greenland, and in Nansen's Fram expedition. Our Russian Geographical Society also began to move, and a committee was appointed to prepare the scheme of a Russian arctic expedition, and to indicate the scientific work that could be done by it. Specialists undertook to write each of the special scientific chapters of this report; but, as often happens, a few chapters only, on botany, geology, and meterorology, were ready in time, and the secretary of the committee —that is, myself—had to write the remainder. Several subjects, such as marine zoology, the tides, pendulum observations, and terrestrial magnetism, were quite new to me; but the amount of work which a healthy man can accomplish in a short time, if he strains all his forces and goes straight to the root of the subject, no one would suppose beforehand,—and so my report was ready.

It concluded by advocating a great scientific expedition, which would awaken in Russia a permanent interest in arctic questions and arctic navigation, and in the meantime a reconnoitering expedition on board a schooner chartered in Norway with its captain, pushing north or northeast of Novaya Zemlya. This expedition, we suggested, might also try to reach, or at least to sight, an unknown land which must be situated at no great distance from Novaya Zemlya. The probable existence of such a land had been indicated by an officer of the Russian navy, Baron Schilling, in an excellent but little known paper on the currents in the Arctic Ocean. When I read this paper, as also Lutke's journey to Novaya Zemlya, and made myself acquainted with the general conditions of this part of the Arctic Ocean, I saw at once that the supposition must be correct. There must be a land to the northwest of Novaya Zemlya, and it must reach a higher latitude than Spitzbergen. The steady position of the ice at the west of Novaya Zemlya, the mud and stones on it, and various other smaller indications confirmed the hypothesis. Besides, if such a land were not located there, the ice current which flows westward from the meridian of Bering Strait to Greenland (the current of the Fram's drift) would, as Baron Schilling had truly remarked, reach the North Cape and cover the coasts of Laponia with masses of ice, just as it covers the northern extremity of Greenland. The warm current alone—a feeble continuation of the Gulf Stream—could not have prevented the accumulation of ice on the coasts of Northern Europe. This land, as is known, was discovered a couple of years later by the Austrian expedition, and named Franz Josef Land.

The arctic report had a quite unexpected result for me. I was offered the leadership of the reconnoitering expedition, on board a Norwegian schooner chartered for the purpose. I replied, of course, that I had never been to sea; but I was told that by combining the experience of a Carlsen or a Johansen with the initiative of a man of science, something valuable could be done; and I would have accepted, had not the ministry of finance at this juncture interposed with its veto. It replied that the exchequer could not grant the three or four thousand pounds which would be required for the expedition. Since that time Russia has taken no part in the exploration of the arctic seas. The land which we distinguished through the subpolar mists was discovered by Payer and Weyprecht, and the archipelagoes which must exist to the northeast of Novaya Zemlya—I am even more firmly persuaded of it now than I was then—remain undiscovered.

Instead of joining an arctic expedition, I was sent out by the Geographical Society for a modest tour in Finland and Sweden, to explore the glacial deposits; and that journey drifted me in a quite different direction.

The Russian Academy of Sciences sent out that summer two of its members—the old geologist General Helmersen and Frederick Schmidt, the indefatigable explorer of Siberia—to study the structure of those long ridges of drift which are known as *asar* in Sweden and Finland, and as *eskers, kames,* and so on, in the British Isles. The Geographical Society sent me to Finland for the same purpose. We visited, all three, the beautiful ridge of Pungaharju and then separated. I worked hard during the summer. I traveled a great deal in Finland, and crossed over to Sweden, where I spent many happy hours in the company of A. Nordenskjold. As early as then—1871—he mentioned to me his schemes for reaching the mouths of the Siberian rivers, and even the Bering Strait, by the northern route. Returning to Finland I continued my researches till late in the autumn, and collected a mass of most interesting observations relative to the glaciation of the country. But I also thought a great deal during this journey about social matters, and these thoughts had a decisive influence upon my subsequent development.

All sorts of valuable materials relative to the geography of Russia passed through my hands in the Geographical Society, and the idea gradually came to me of writing an exhaustive physical geography of that immense part of the world. My intention was to give a thorough geographical description of the country, basing it upon the main lines of the surface structure, which I began to disentangle for European Russia; and to sketch, in that description, the different forms of economic life which ought to prevail in different physical regions. Take, for instance, the wide prairies of Southern Russia, so often visited by droughts and failure of crops. These droughts and failures must not be treated as accidental calamities:

they are as much a natural feature of that region as its position on a southern slope, its fertility, and the rest; and the whole of the economic life of the southern prairies ought to be organized in prevision of the unavoidable recurrence of periodical droughts. Each region of the Russian Empire ought to be treated in the same scientific way, just as Karl Ritter has treated parts of Asia in his beautiful monographs.

But such a work would have required plenty of time and full freedom for the writer, and I often thought how helpful to this end it would be were I to occupy some day the position of secretary to the Geographical Society. Now, in the autumn of 1871, as I was working in Finland, slowly moving on foot toward the seacoast along the newly built railway, and closely watching the spot where the first unmistakable traces of the former extension of the post-glacial sea would appear, I received a telegram from the Geographical Society: "The council begs you to accept the position of secretary to the Society." At the same time the outgoing secretary strongly urged me to accept the proposal.

My hopes were realized. But in the meantime other thoughts and other longings had pervaded my mind. I seriously thought over the reply, and wired, "Most cordial thanks, but cannot accept."

It often happens that men pull in a certain political, social, or familiar harness simply because they never have time to ask themselves whether the position they stand in and the work they accomplish are right; whether their occupations really suit their inner desires and capacities, and give them the satisfaction which every one has the right to expect from his work. Active men are especially liable to find themselves in such a position. Every day brings with it a fresh batch of work, and a man throws himself into his bed late at night without having completed what he had expected to do; then in the morning he hurries to the unfinished task of the previous day. Life goes, and there is no time left to think, no time to consider the direction that one's life is taking. So it was with me.

But now, during my journey in Finland, I had leisure. When I was crossing in a Finnish two-wheeled *karria* some plain which offered no interest to the geologist, or when I was walking, hammer on shoulder, from one gravel-pit to another, I could think; and amidst the undoubtedly interesting geological work I was carrying on, one idea, which appealed far more strongly to my inner self than geology, persistently worked in my mind.

I saw what an immense amount of labor the Finnish peasant spends in clearing the land and in breaking up the hard boulder-clay, and I said to myself: "I will write the physical geography of this part of Russia, and tell the peasant the best means of cultivating this soil. Here an American stump-extractor would be invaluable; there certain methods of manuring would be indicated by science. . . . But what is the use of talking to this peasant about American machines, when he has barely enough bread to live upon from one crop to the next; when the rent which he has to pay for that boulder-clay grows heavier and heavier in proportion to his success in improving the soil? He gnaws at his hard-as-a-stone rye-flour cake which he bakes twice a year; he has with it a morsel of fearfully salted cod and a drink of skimmed milk. How dare I talk to him of American machines, when all that he can raise must be sold to pay rent and taxes? He needs me to live with him, to help him to become the owner or the free occupier of that land. Then he will read books with profit, but not now."

And my thoughts wandered from Finland to our Nikolskoye peasants, whom I had lately seen. Now they are free, and they value freedom very much. But they have no meadows. In one way or another, the landlords have got all the meadows for themselves. When I was a child, the Savokhins used to send out six horses for night pasture, the Tolkachoffs had seven. Now, these families have only three horses each; other families, which formerly had three horses, have only one, or none. What can be done with one miserable horse? No meadows, no horses, no manure! How can I talk to them of grass-sowing? They are already ruined,—poor as Lazarus, —and in a few years they will be made still poorer by a foolish taxation. How happy they were when I told them that my father gave them permission to mow the grass in the small open spaces in his Kostino forest! "Your Nikolskoye peasants are *ferocious* for work,"—that is the common saying about them in our neighborhood; but the arable land, which our stepmother has taken out of their allotments in virtue of the "law of minimum,"—that diabolic clause introduced by the serf-owners when they were allowed to revise the emancipation law,—is now a forest of thistles, and the "ferocious" workers are not allowed to till it. And the same sort of thing goes on throughout all Russia. Even at that time it was evident, and official commissioners gave warning of it, that the first serious failure of crops in Middle Russia would result in a terrible famine,—and famine came, in 1876, in 1884, in 1891, in 1895, and again in 1898.

Science is an excellent thing. I knew its joys and valued them,— perhaps more than many of my colleagues did. Even now, as I was looking on the lakes and the hillocks of Finland, new and beautiful generalizations arose before my eyes. I saw in a remote past, at the very dawn of mankind, the ice accumulating from year to year in the northern archipelagoes, over Scandinavia and Finland. An im-

mense growth of ice invaded the north of Europe and slowly spread
as far as its middle portions. Life dwindled in that part of the
northern hemisphere, and, wretchedly poor, uncertain, it fled further and further south before the icy breath which came from that
immense frozen mass. Man—miserable, weak, ignorant—had every
difficulty in maintaining a precarious existence. Ages passed away,
till the melting of the ice began, and with it came the lake period,
when countless lakes were formed in the cavities, and a wretched
subpolar vegetation began timidly to invade the unfathomable
marshes with which every lake was surrounded. Another series of
ages passed before an extremely slow process of drying up set in,
and vegetation began its slow invasion from the south. And now we
are fully in the period of a rapid desiccation, accompanied by the
formation of dry prairies and steppes, and man has to find out the
means to put a check to that desiccation to which Central Asia
already has fallen a victim, and which menaces Southeastern
Europe.

Belief in an ice-cap reaching Middle Europe was at that time
rank heresy; but before my eyes a grand picture was rising, and I
wanted to draw it, with the thousands of details I saw in it; to use it
as a key to the present distribution of floras and faunas; to open
new horizons for geology and physical geography.

But what right had I to these highest joys, when all around me
was nothing but misery and struggle for a mouldy bit of bread;
when whatsoever I should spend to enable me to live in that world
of higher emotions must needs be taken from the very mouths of
those who grew the wheat and had not bread enough for their
children? From somebody's mouth it must be taken, because the
aggregate production of mankind remains still so low.

Knowledge is an immense power. Man must know. But we already know much! What if that knowledge—and only that—should
become the possession of all? Would not science itself progress in
leaps, and cause mankind to make strides in production, invention,
and social creation, of which we are hardly in a condition now to
measure the speed?

The masses want to know: they are willing to learn; they *can*
learn. There, on the crest of that immense moraine which runs
between the lakes, as if giants had heaped it up in a hurry to
connect the two shores, there stands a Finnish peasant plunged in
contemplation of the beautiful lakes, studded with islands, which lie
before him. Not one of these peasants, poor and downtrodden
though they may be, will pass this spot without stopping to admire
the scene. Or there, on the shore of a lake, stands another peasant,
and sings something so beautiful that the best musician would envy
him his melody, for its feeling and its meditative power. Both

deeply feel, both meditate, both think; they are ready to widen their knowledge,—only give it to them, only give them the means of getting leisure.

This is the direction in which, and these are the kind of people for whom, I must work. All those sonorous phrases about making mankind progress, while at the same time the progress-makers stand aloof from those whom they pretend to push onwards, are mere sophisms made up by minds anxious to shake off a fretting contradiction.

So I sent my negative reply to the Geographical Society.

Selections from
Mutual Aid

Mutual Aid in the Mediaeval City

I

Sociability and need of mutual aid and support are such inherent parts of human nature that at no time of history can we discover men living in small isolated families, fighting each other for the means of subsistence. On the contrary, modern research . . . proves that since the very beginning of their prehistoric life men used to agglomerate into *gentes*, clans, or tribes, maintained by an idea of common descent and by worship of common ancestors. For thousands and thousands of years this organization has kept men together, even though there was no authority whatever to impose it. It has deeply impressed all subsequent development of mankind; and when the bonds of common descent had been loosened by migrations on a grand scale, while the development of the separated family within the clan itself had destroyed the old unity of the clan, a new form of union, territorial in its principle—the village community—was called into existence by the social genius of man. This institution, again, kept men together for a number of centuries, permitting them to further develop their social institutions and to pass through some of the darkest periods of history, without being dissolved into loose aggregations of families and individuals, to make a further step in their evolution, and to work out a number of secondary social institutions, several of which have survived down to the present time. We have now to follow the further developments of the same ever-living tendency for mutual aid. Taking the village communities of the so-called barbarians at a time when they were making a new start of civilization after the fall of the Roman Empire, we have to study the new aspects taken by the sociable wants of the masses in the middle ages, and especially in the mediaeval guilds and the mediaeval city.

Far from being the fighting animals they have often been compared to, the barbarians of the first centuries of our era (like so many Mongolians, Africans, Arabs, and so on, who still continue in the same barbarian stage) invariably preferred peace to war. With the exception of a few tribes which had been driven during the great migrations into unproductive deserts or highlands, and were thus compelled periodically to prey upon their better-favoured neighbours—apart from these, the great bulk of the Teutons, the Saxons, the Celts, the Slavonians, and so on, very soon after they had settled in their newly-conquered abodes, reverted to the spade or to their herds. The earliest barbarian codes already represent to us societies composed of peaceful agricultural communities, not hordes of men at war with each other. These barbarians covered the country with villages and farmhouses; they cleared the forests, bridged the torrents, and colonized the formerly quite uninhabited wilderness; and they left the uncertain warlike pursuits to brother-hoods, *scholae*, or "trusts" of unruly men, gathered round temporary chieftains, who wandered about, offering their adventurous spirit, their arms, and their knowledge of warfare for the protection of populations, only too anxious to be left in peace. The warrior bands came and went, prosecuting their family feuds; but the great mass continued to till the soil, taking but little notice of their would-be rulers, so long as they did not interfere with the independence of their village communities. The new occupiers of Europe evolved the systems of land tenure and soil culture which are still in force with hundreds of millions of men; they worked out their systems of compensation for wrongs, instead of the old tribal blood-revenge; they learned the first rudiments of industry; and while they fortified their villages with palisaded walls, or erected towers and earthen forts whereto to repair in case of a new invasion, they soon abandoned the task of defending these towers and forts to those who made of war a speciality.

The very peacefulness of the barbarians, certainly not their supposed warlike instincts, thus became the source of their subsequent subjection to the military chieftains. It is evident that the very mode of life of the armed brotherhoods offered them more facilities for enrichment than the tillers of the soil could find in their agricultural communities. Even now we see that armed men occasionally came together to shoot down Matabeles and to rob them of their droves of cattle, though the Matabeles only want peace and are ready to buy it at a high price. The *scholae* of old certainly were not more scrupulous than the *scholae* of our own time. Droves of cattle, iron (which was extremely costly at that time[1]), and slaves were appro-

---

1. According to the Riparian law, the sword, the spear, and the iron armour of a warrior attained the value of at least twenty-five cows, or two years of a free-man's labour. A cuirass alone was valued in the Salic law at as much as thirty-six bushels of wheat.

priated in this way; and although most acquisitions were wasted on the spot in those glorious feasts of which epic poetry has so much to say—still some part of the robbed riches was used for further enrichment. There was plenty of waste land, and no lack of men ready to till it, if only they could obtain the necessary cattle and implements. Whole villages, ruined by murrains, pests, fires, or raids of new immigrants, were often abandoned by their inhabitants, who went anywhere in search of new abodes. They still do so in Russia in similar circumstances. And if one of the *hirdmen* of the armed brotherhoods offered the peasants some cattle for a fresh start, some iron to make a plough, if not the plough itself, his protection from further raids, and a number of years free from all obligations, before they should begin to repay the contracted debt, they settled upon the land. And when, after a hard fight with bad crops, inundations and pestilences, those pioneers began to repay their debts, they fell into servile obligations towards the protector of the territory. Wealth undoubtedly did accumulate in this way, and power always follows wealth. And yet, the more we penetrate into the life of those times, the sixth and seventh centuries of our era, the more we see that another element, besides wealth and military force, was required to constitute the authority of the few. It was an element of law and right, a desire of the masses to maintain peace, and to establish what they considered to be justice, which gave to the chieftains of the *scholae*—kings, dukes, *knyazes*, and the like—the force they acquired two or three hundred years later. That same idea of justice, conceived as an adequate revenge for the wrong done, which had grown in the tribal stage, now passed as a red thread through the history of subsequent institutions, and, much more even than military or economic causes, it became the basis upon which the authority of the kings and the feudal lords was founded.

In fact, one of the chief preoccupations of the barbarian village community always was, as it still is with our barbarian contemporaries, to put a speedy end to the feuds which arose from the then current conception of justice. When a quarrel took place, the community at once interfered, and after the folkmote had heard the case, it settled the amount of composition (*wergeld*) to be paid to the wronged person, or to his family, as well as the *fred*, or fine for breach of peace, which had to be paid to the community. Interior quarrels were easily appeased in this way. But when feuds broke out between two different tribes, or two confederations of tribes, notwithstanding all measures taken to prevent them, the difficulty was to find an arbiter or sentence-finder whose decision should be accepted by both parties alike, both for his impartiality and for his knowledge of the oldest law. The difficulty was the greater as the customary laws of different tribes and confederations were at variance as to the compensation due in different cases. It therefore became habitual to take the sentence-finder from among such families, or such tribes, as were reputed for keeping the law of old in its purity; of being versed in the songs, triads, sagas, etc., by means of which law was perpetuated in memory; and to retain law in this way became a sort of art, a "mystery," carefully transmitted in certain families from generation to generation. Thus in Iceland, and in other Scandinavian lands, at every *Allthing*, or national folkmote, a *lövsögmathr* used to recite the whole law from memory for the enlightening of the assembly; and in Ireland there was, as is known, a special class of men reputed for the knowledge of the old traditions, and therefore enjoying a great authority as judges. Again, when we are told by the Russian annals that some stems of North-West Russia, moved by the growing disorder which resulted from "clans rising against clans," appealed to Norman *varingiar* to be their judges and commanders of warrior *scholae;* and when we see the *knyazes*, or dukes, elected for the next two hundred years always from the same Norman family, we cannot but recognize that the Slavonians trusted to the Normans for a better knowledge of the law which would be equally recognized as good by different Slavonian kins. In this case the possession of runes, used for the transmission of old customs, was a decided advantage in favour of the Normans; but in other cases there are faint indications that the "eldest" branch of the stem, the supposed mother-branch, was appealed to to supply the judges, and its decisions were relied upon as just; while at a later epoch we see a distinct tendency towards taking the sentence-finders from the Christian clergy, which, at that time, kept still to the fundamental, now forgotten, principle of Christianity, that retaliation is no act of justice. At that time the Christian clergy opened the churches as places of asylum for those who fled from blood revenge, and they willingly acted as arbiters in criminal cases, always opposing the old tribal principle of life for life and wound for wound. In short, the deeper we penetrate into the history of early institutions, the less we find grounds for the military theory of origin of authority. Even that power which later on became such a source of oppression seems, on the contrary, to have found its origin in the peaceful inclinations of the masses.

In all these cases the *fred*, which often amounted to half the compensation, went to the folkmote, and from times immemorial it used to be applied to works of common utility and defence. It has still the same destination (the erection of towers) among the Kabyles and certain Mongolian stems; and we have direct evidence that even several centuries later the judicial fines, in Pskov and several French and German cities, continued to be used for the repair of the city walls.[2] It was thus quite natural that the fines should be handed over to the sentence-finder, who was bound, in return, both to maintain the *schola* of armed men to whom the defence of the territory was trusted, and to execute the sentences. This became a universal custom in the eighth and ninth centuries, even when the sentence-finder was an elected bishop. The germ of a combination of what we should now call the judicial power and the executive thus made its appearance. But to these two functions the attributions of the duke or king were strictly limited. He was no ruler of the people—the supreme power still belonging to the folkmote—not even a commander of the popular militia; when the folk took to arms, it marched under a separate, also elected, commander, who was not a subordinate, but an equal to the king. The king was a lord on his personal domain only. In fact, in barbarian language, the word *konung, koning,* or *cyning,* synonymous with the Latin *rex,* had no other meaning than that of a temporary leader or chieftain of a band of men. The commander of a flotilla of boats, or even of a single pirate boat, was also a *konung,* and till the present day the commander of fishing in Norway is named *Not-kong*—"the king of the nets." The veneration attached later on to the personality of a king did not yet exist, and while treason to the kin was punished by death, the slaying of a king could be recouped by the payment of compensation: a king simply was valued so much more than a freeman.[3] And when King Knu (or Canute) had killed one man of his own *schola,* the saga represents him convoking his comrades to a *thing* where he stood on his knees imploring pardon. He was pardoned, but not till he had agreed to pay nine times the regular composition, of which one-third went to himself for the loss of one of his men, one-third to the relatives of the slain man, and one-third (the *fred*) to the *schola.* In reality, a complete change had to be accomplished in the current conceptions, under the double influence of the Church and the students of Roman law, before an idea of sanctity began to be attached to the personality of the king.

However, it lies beyond the scope of these essays to follow the gradual development of authority out of the elements just indicated. Historians, such as Mr. and Mrs. Green for this country, Augustin

2. It was distinctly stated in the charter of St. Quentin of the year 1002 that the ransom for houses which had to be demolished for crimes went for the city walls. The same destination was given to the *Ungeld* in German cities. At Pskov the cathedral was the bank for the fines, and from this fund money was taken for the walls.

3. Thirty-six times more than a noble, according to the Anglo-Saxon law. In the Code of Rothari the slaying of a king is, however, punished by death; but (apart from Roman influence) this new disposition was introduced (in 646) in the Lombardian law—as remarked by Leo and Botta—to cover the king from blood revenge. The king being at that time the executioner of his own sentences (as the tribe formerly was of its own sentences), he had to be protected by a special disposition, the more so as several Lombardian kings before Rothari had been slain in succession.

Thierry, Michelet, and Luchaire for France, Kaufmann, Janssen, W. Arnold, and even Nietzsche, for Germany, Leo and Botta for Italy, Byelaeff, Kostomaroff, and their followers for Russia, and many others, have fully told that tale. They have shown how populations, once free, and simply agreeing "to feed" a certain portion of their military defenders, gradually became the serfs of these protectors; how "commendation" to the Church, or to a lord, became a hard necessity for the freeman; how each lord's and bishop's castle became a robber's nest—how feudalism was imposed, in a word—and how the crusades, by freeing the serfs who wore the cross, gave the first impulse to popular emancipation. All this need not be retold in this place, our chief aim being to follow the *constructive* genius of the masses in their mutual-aid institutions.

At a time when the last vestiges of barbarian freedom seemed to disappear, and Europe, fallen under the dominion of thousands of petty rulers, was marching towards the constitution of such theocracies and despotic States as had followed the barbarian stage during the previous starts of civilization, or of barbarian monarchies, such as we see now in Africa, life in Europe took another direction. It went on on lines similar to those it had once taken in the cities of antique Greece. With a unanimity which seems almost incomprehensible, and for a long time was not understood by historians, the urban agglomerations, down to the smallest burgs, began to shake off the yoke of their worldly and clerical lords. The fortified village rose against the lord's castle, defied it first, attacked it next, and finally destroyed it. The movement spread from spot to spot, involving every town on the surface of Europe, and in less than a hundred years free cities had been called into existence on the coasts of the Mediterranean, the North Sea, the Baltic, the Atlantic Ocean, down to the fjords of Scandinavia; at the feet of the Apennines, the Alps, the Black Forest, the Grampians, and the Carpathians; in the plains of Russia, Hungary, France, and Spain. Everywhere the same revolt took place, with the same features, passing through the same phases, leading to the same results. Wherever men had found, or expected to find, some protection behind their town walls, they instituted their "co-jurations," their "fraternities," their "friendships," united in one common idea, and boldly marching towards a new life of mutual support and liberty. And they succeeded so well that in three or four hundred years they had changed the very face of Europe. They had covered the country with beautiful sumptuous buildings, expressing the genius of free unions of free men, unrivalled since for their beauty and expressiveness; and they bequeathed to the following generations all the arts, all the industries, of which our present civilization, with all its achievements and promises for the future, is only a further development. And when we now look to the forces which have produced these grand results, we find them—not in the genius of individual heroes, not in the mighty organization of huge States or the political capacities of their rulers, but in the very same current of mutual aid and support which we saw at work in the village community, and which was vivified and reinforced in the Middle Ages by a new form of unions, inspired by the very same spirit but shaped on a new model—the guilds.

It is well known by this time that feudalism did not imply a dissolution of the village community. Although the lord had succeeded in imposing servile labour upon the peasants, and had appropriated for himself such rights as were formerly vested in the village community alone (taxes, mortmain, duties on inheritances and marriages), the peasants had, nevertheless, maintained the two fundamental rights of their communities: the common possession of the land, and self-jurisdiction. In olden times, when a king sent his *vogt* to a village, the peasants received him with flowers in one hand and arms in the other, and asked him—which law he intended to apply: the one he found in the village, or the one he brought with him? And, in the first case, they handed him the flowers and accepted him; while in the second case they fought him. Now, they accepted the king's or the lord's official whom they could not refuse; but they maintained the folkmote's jurisdiction, and themselves nominated six, seven, or twelve judges, who acted with the lord's judge, in the presence of the folkmote, as arbiters and sentence-finders. In most cases the official had nothing left to him but to confirm the sentence and to levy the customary *fred*. This precious right of self-jurisdiction, which, at that time, meant self-administration and self-legislation, had been maintained through all the struggles; and even the lawyers by whom Karl the Great was surrounded could not abolish it; they were bound to confirm it. At the same time, in all matters concerning the community's domain, the folkmote retained its supremacy and (as shown by Maurer) often claimed submission from the lord himself in land tenure matters. No growth of feudalism could break this resistance; the village community kept its ground; and when, in the ninth and tenth centuries, the invasions of the Normans, the Arabs, and the Ugrians had demonstrated that military *scholae* were of little value for protecting the land, a general movement began all over Europe for fortifying the villages with stone walls and citadels. Thousands of fortified centres were then built by the energies of the village communities; and, once they had built their walls, once a common interest had been created in this new sanctuary—the town walls—

they soon understood that they could henceforward resist the encroachments of the inner enemies, the lords, as well as the invasions of foreigners. A new life of freedom began to develop within the fortified enclosures. The mediaeval city was born.[4]

No period of history could better illustrate the constructive powers of the popular masses than the tenth and eleventh centuries, when the fortified villages and market-places, representing so many "oases amidst the feudal forest," began to free themselves from their lord's yoke, and slowly elaborated the future city organization; but, unhappily, this is a period about which historical information is especially scarce: we know the results, but little has reached us about the means by which they were achieved. Under the protection of their walls the cities' folkmotes—either quite independent, or led by the chief noble or merchant families—conquered and maintained the right of electing the military *defensor* and supreme judge of the town, or at least of choosing between those who pretended to occupy this position. In Italy the young communes were continually sending away their *defensors* or *domini*, fighting those who refused to go. The same went on in the East. In Bohemia, rich and poor alike (*Bohemicae gentis magni et parvi, nobiles et ignobiles*) took part in the election; while the *vyeches* (folkmotes) of the Russian cities regularly elected their dukes—always from the same Rurik family—covenanted with them, and sent the *knyaz* away if he had provoked discontent. At the same time in most cities of Western and Southern Europe, the tendency was to take for *defensor* a bishop whom the city had elected itself; and so many bishops took the lead in protecting the "immunities" of the towns and in defending their liberties, that numbers of them were considered, after their death, as saints and special patrons of different cities. St. Uthelred of Winchester, St. Ulrik of Augsburg, St. Wolfgang of Ratisbon, St. Heribert of Cologne, St. Adalbert of Prague, and so on, as well as many abbots and monks, became so many cities' saints for having acted in defence of popular rights. And under the new *defensors*, whether laic or clerical, the citizens conquered full self-jurisdiction and self-administration for their folkmotes.[5]

4. The fact is, that whenever mankind made a new start in civilization, in Greece, Rome, or middle Europe, it passed through the same stages—the tribe, the village community, the free city, the state—each one naturally evolving out of the preceding stage. Of course, the experience of each preceding civilization was never lost. Greece (itself influenced by Eastern civilizations) influenced Rome, and Rome influenced our civilization; but each of them began from the same beginning—the tribe. And just as we cannot say that our states are *continuations* of the Roman state, so also can we not say that the mediaeval cities of Europe (including Scandinavia and Russia) were a continuation of the Roman cities. They were a continuation of the barbarian village community, influenced to a certain extent by the traditions of the Roman towns.

5. It must, however, be remarked that in royal cities the folkmote never attained the independence which is assumed elsewhere. It is even certain that Moscow

The whole process of liberation progressed by a series of imperceptible acts of devotion to the common cause, accomplished by men who came out of the masses—by unknown heroes whose very names have not been preserved by history. The wonderful movement of the God's peace (*tregua Dei*) by which the popular masses endeavoured to put a limit to the endless family feuds of the noble families, was born in the young towns, the bishops and the citizens trying to extend to the nobles the peace they had established within their town walls. Already at that period, the commercial cities of Italy, and especially Amalfi (which had its elected consuls since 844, and frequently changed its doges in the tenth century) worked out the customary maritime and commercial law which later on became a model for all Europe; Ravenna elaborated its craft organization, and Milan, which had made its first revolution in 980, became a great centre of commerce, its trades enjoying a full independence since the eleventh century. So also Brügge and Ghent; so also several cities of France in which the *Mahl* or *forum* had become a quite independent institution. And already during that period began the work of artistic decoration of the towns by works of architecture, which we still admire and which loudly testify of the intellectual movement of the times. "The basilicae were then renewed in almost all the universe," Raoul Glaber wrote in his chronicle, and some of the finest monuments of mediaeval architecture date from that period: the wonderful old church of Bremen was built in the ninth century, Saint Marc of Venice was finished in 1071, and the beautiful dome of Pisa in 1063. In fact, the intellectual movement which has been described as the Twelfth Century Renaissance and the Twelfth Century Rationalism—the precursor of the Reform—date from that period, when most cities were still simple agglomerations of small village communities enclosed by walls.

However, another element, besides the village-community principle, was required to give to these growing centres of liberty and enlightenment the unity of thought and action, and the powers of initiative, which made their force in the twelfth and thirteenth centuries. With the growing diversity of occupations, crafts and arts, and with the growing commerce in distant lands, some new form of union was required, and this necessary new element was supplied by the *guilds*. Volumes and volumes have been written about these unions which, under the name of guilds, brotherhoods, friendships and *druzhestva, minne, artels* in Russia, *esnaifs* in

---

and Paris were chosen by the kings and the Church as the cradles of the future royal authority in the State, because they did not possess the tradition of folkmotes accustomed to act as sovereign in all matters.

Servia and Turkey, *amkari* in Georgia, and so on, took such a formidable development in mediaeval times and played such an important part in the emancipation of the cities. But it took historians more than sixty years before the universality of this institution and its true characters were understood. Only now, when hundreds of guild statutes have been published and studied, and their relationship to the Roman *collegiae*, and the earlier unions in Greece and in India, is known, can we maintain with full confidence that these brotherhoods were but a further development of the same principles which we saw at work in the *gens* and the village community.

Nothing illustrates better these mediaeval brotherhoods than those temporary guilds which were formed on board ships. When a ship of the Hansa had accomplished her first half-day passage after having left the port, the captain (*Schiffer*) gathered all crew and passengers on the deck, and held the following language, as reported by a contemporary:—

'As we are now at the mercy of God and waves,' he said, 'each one must be equal to each other. And as we are surrounded by storms, high waves, pirates and other dangers, we must keep a strict order that we may bring our voyage to a good end. That is why we shall pronounce the prayer for a good wind and good success, and, according to marine law, we shall name the occupiers of the judges' seats (*Schöffenstellen*).' Thereupon the crew elected a *Vogt* and four *scabini*, to act as their judges. At the end of the voyage the *Vogt* and the *scabini* abdicated their functions and addressed the crew as follows:—'What has happened on board ship, we must pardon to each other and consider as dead (*todt und ab sein lassen*). What we have judged right, was for the sake of justice. This is why we beg you all, in the name of honest justice, to forget all the animosity one may nourish against another, and to swear on bread and salt that he will not think of it in a bad spirit. If any one, however, considers himself wronged, he must appeal to the land *Vogt* and ask justice from him before sunset.' On landing, the Stock with the *fred*-fines was handed over to the *Vogt* of the sea-port for distribution among the poor.

This simple narrative, perhaps better than anything else, depicts the spirit of the mediaeval guilds. Like organizations came into existence wherever a group of men—fishermen, hunters, travelling merchants, builders, or settled craftsmen—came together for a common pursuit. Thus, there was on board ship the naval authority of the captain; but, for the very success of the common enterprise, all men on board, rich and poor, masters and crew, captain and sailors, agreed to be equals in their mutual relations, to be simply men, bound to aid each other and to settle their possible disputes before judges elected by all of them. So also when a number of

craftsmen—masons, carpenters, stone-cutters, etc.—came together
for building, say, a cathedral, they all belonged to a city which had
its political organization, and each of them belonged moreover to
his own craft; but they were united besides by their common enterprise, which they knew better than any one else, and they joined
into a body united by closer, although temporary, bonds; they
founded the guild for the building of the cathedral. We may see the
same till now in the Kabylian *çof:* the Kabyles have their village
community; but this union is not sufficient for all political, commercial, and personal needs of union, and [so] the closer brotherhood of the *çof* is constituted.

As to the social characters of the mediaeval guild, any guild-
statute may illustrate them. Taking, for instance, the *skraa* of some
early Danish guild, we read in it, first, a statement of the general
brotherly feelings which must reign in the guild; next come the
regulations relative to self-jurisdiction in cases of quarrels arising
between two brothers, or a brother and a stranger; and then, the
social duties of the brethren are enumerated. If a brother's house is
burned, or he has lost his ship, or has suffered on a pilgrim's
voyage, all the brethren must come to his aid. If a brother falls
dangerously ill, two brethren must keep watch by his bed till he is
out of danger, and if he dies, the brethren must bury him—a great
affair in those times of pestilences—and follow him to the church
and the grave. After his death they must provide for his children, if
necessary; very often the widow becomes a sister to the guild.

These two leading features appeared in every brotherhood
formed for any possible purpose. In each case the members treated
each other as, and named each other, brother and sister;[6] all were
equals before the guild. They owned some "chattel" (cattle, land,
buildings, places of worship, or "stock") in common. All brothers
took the oath of abandoning all feuds of old; and, without imposing
upon each other the obligation of never quarrelling again, they
agreed that no quarrel should degenerate into a feud, or into a law-
suit before another court than the tribunal of the brothers themselves. And if a brother was involved in a quarrel with a stranger to
the guild, they agreed to support him for bad and for good; that is,
whether he was unjustly accused of aggression, or really was the
aggressor, they had to support him, and to bring things to a peaceful end. So long as his was not a secret aggression—in which case
he would have been treated as an outlaw—the brotherhood stood
by him.[7] If the relatives of the wronged man wanted to revenge the

6. Upon the position of women in guilds,
see Miss Toulmin Smith's introductory
remarks to the *English Guilds* of her
father. One of the Cambridge statutes of
the year 1503 is quite positive in the following sentence: "The statute is made by
the comyne assent of all the bretherne
and sisterne of alhallowe yelde."
7. In mediaeval times, only secret aggression was treated as a murder. Blood-

offence at once by a new aggression, the brotherhood supplied him with a horse to run away, or with a boat, a pair of oars, a knife, and a steel for striking light; if he remained in town, twelve brothers accompanied him to protect him; and in the meantime they arranged the composition. They went to court to support by oath the truthfulness of his statements, and if he was found guilty they did not let him go to full ruin and become a slave through not paying the due compensation: they all paid it, just as the *gens* did in olden times. Only when a brother had broken the faith towards his guild-brethren, or other people, he was excluded from the brotherhood "with a Nothing's name" (*tha scal han maeles af brödrescap met nidings nafn*).

Such were the leading ideas of those brotherhoods which gradually covered the whole of mediaeval life. In fact, we know of guilds among all possible professions: guilds of serfs,[8] guilds of freemen, and guilds of both serfs and freemen; guilds called into life for the special purpose of hunting, fishing, or a trading expedition, and dissolved when the special purpose had been achieved; and guilds lasting for centuries in a given craft or trade. And, in proportion as life took an always greater variety of pursuits, the variety in the guilds grew in proportion. So we see not only merchants, draftsmen, hunters, and peasants united in guilds; we also see guilds of priests, painters, teachers of primary schools and universities, guilds for performing the passion play, for building a church, for developing the "mystery" of a given school of art or craft, or for a special recreation—even guilds among beggars, executioners, and lost women, all organized on the same double principle of self-jurisdiction and mutual support.[9] For Russia we have positive evidence showing that the very "making of Russia" was as much the work of its hunters', fishermen's, and traders' *artels* as of the budding village communities, and up to the present day the country is covered with *artels*.

revenge in broad daylight was justice; and slaying in a quarrel was not murder, once the aggressor showed his willingness to repent and to repair the wrong he had done. Deep traces of this distinction still exist in modern criminal law, especially in Russia.

8. They played an important part in the revolts of the serfs, and were therefore prohibited several times in succession in the second half of the ninth century. Of course, the king's prohibitions remained a dead letter.

9. The mediaeval Italian painters were also organized in guilds, which became at a later epoch Academies of art. If the Italian art of those times is impressed with so much individuality that we distinguish, even now, between the different schools of Padua, Bassano, Treviso, Verona, and so on, although all these cities were under the sway of Venice, this was due—J. Paul Richter remarks—to the fact that the painters of each city belonged to a separate guild, friendly with the guilds of other towns, but leading a separate existence. The oldest guild-statute known is that of Verona, dating from 1303, but evidently copied from some much older statute. "Fraternal assistance in necessity of whatever kind," "hospitality towards strangers, when passing through the town, as thus information may be obtained about matters which one may like to learn," and "obligation of offering comfort in case of debility" are among the obligations of the members (*Nineteenth Century*, Nov. 1890, and Aug. 1892).

These few remarks show how incorrect was the view taken by some early explorers of the guilds when they wanted to see the essence of the institution in its yearly festival. In reality, the day of the common meal was always the day, or the morrow of the day, of election of aldermen, of discussion of alterations in the statutes, and very often the day of judgment of quarrels that had risen among the brethren,[1] or of renewed allegiance to the guild. The common meal, like the festival at the old tribal folkmote—the *mahl* or *malum*—or the Buryate *aba*, or the parish feast and the harvest supper, was simply an affirmation of brotherhood. It symbolized the times when everything was kept in common by the clan. This day, at least, all belonged to all; all sat at the same table and partook of the same meal. Even at a much later time the inmate of the almshouse of a London guild sat this day by the side of the rich alderman. As to the distinction which several explorers have tried to establish between the old Saxon "frith guild" and the so-called "social" or "religious" guilds—all were frith guilds in the sense above mentioned, and all were religious in the sense in which a village community or a city placed under the protection of a special saint is social and religious. If the institution of the guild has taken such an immense extension in Asia, Africa, and Europe, if it has lived thousands of years, reappearing again and again when similar conditions called it into existence, it is because it was much more than an eating association, or an association for going to church on a certain day, or a burial club. It answered to a deeply inrooted want of human nature; and it embodied all the attributes which the State appropriated later on for its bureaucracy and police, and much more than that. It was an association for mutual support in all circumstances and in all accidents of life, "by deed and advice," and it was an organization for maintaining justice—with this difference from the State, that on all these occasions a humane, a brotherly element was introduced instead of the formal element which is the essential characteristic of State interference. Even when appearing before the guild tribunal, the guild-brother answered before men who knew him well and had stood by him before in their daily work, at the common meal, in the performance of their brotherly duties: men who were his equals and brethren

1. See, for instance, the texts of the Cambridge guilds given by Toulmin Smith (*English Guilds*, London, 1870), from which it appears that the "generall and principall day" was the "eleccioun day." It appears very probable that when the guilds began to be prosecuted, many of them inscribed in their statues the meal day only, or their pious duties, and only alluded to the judicial function of the guild in vague words; but this function did not disappear till a very much later time. The question, "Who will be my judge?" has no meaning now, since the State has appropriated for its bureaucracy the organization of justice; but it was of primordial importance in mediaeval times, the more so as self-jurisdiction meant self-administration. It must also be remarked that the translation of the Saxon and Danish "guild-brethren," or "brodrae," by the Latin *convivii* must also have contributed to the above confusion.

indeed, not theorists of law nor defenders of some one else's interests.

It is evident that an institution so well suited to serve the need of union, without depriving the individual of his initiative, could but spread, grow, and fortify. The difficulty was only to find such form as would permit to federate the unions of the guilds without interfering with the unions of the village communities, and to federate all these into one harmonious whole. And when this form of combination had been found, and a series of favourable circumstances permitted the cities to affirm their independence, they did so with a unity of thought which can but excite our admiration, even in our century of railways, telegraphs, and printing. Hundreds of charters in which the cities inscribed their liberation have reached us, and through all of them—notwithstanding the infinite variety of details, which depended upon the more or less greater fulness of emancipation—the same leading ideas run. The city organized itself as a federation of both small village communities and guilds.

"All those who belong to the friendship of the town"—so runs a charter given in 1188 to the burghesses of Aire by Philip, Count of Flanders—"have promised and confirmed by faith and oath that they will aid each other as brethren, in whatever is useful and honest. That if one commits against another an offence in words or in deeds, the one who has suffered therefrom will not take revenge, either himself or his people . . . he will lodge a complaint and the offender will make good for his offence, according to what will be pronounced by twelve elected judges acting as arbiters. And if the offender or the offended, after having been warned thrice, does not submit to the decision of the arbiters, he will be excluded from the friendship as a wicked man and a perjuror."

"Each one of the men of the commune will be faithful to his con-juror, and will give him aid and advice, according to what justice will dictate him"—the Amiens and Abbeville charters say. "All will aid each other, according to their powers, within the boundaries of the Commune, and will not suffer that any one takes anything from any one of them, or makes one pay contributions"—do we read in the charters of Soissons, Compiègne, Senlis, and many others of the same type. And so on with countless variations on the same theme.

"The Commune," Guilbert de Nogent wrote, "is an oath of mutual aid (*mutui adjutorii conjuratio*) . . . A new and detestable word. Through it the serfs (*capite sensi*) are freed from all serfdom; through it, they can only be condemned to a legally determined fine for breaches of the law; through it, they cease to be liable to payments which the serfs always used to pay."

The same wave of emancipation ran, in the twelfth century, through all parts of the continent, involving both rich cities and the poorest towns. And if we may say that, as a rule, the Italian cities were the first to free themselves, we can assign no centre from which the movement would have spread. Very often a small burg in central Europe took the lead for its region, and big agglomerations accepted the little town's charter as a model for their own. Thus, the charter of a small town, Lorris, was adopted by eighty-three towns in south-west France, and that of Beaumont became the model for over five hundred towns and cities in Belgium and France. Special deputies were dispatched by the cities to their neighbours to obtain a copy from their charter, and the constitution was framed upon that model. However, they did not simply copy each other: they framed their own charters in accordance with the concessions they had obtained from their lords; and the result was that, as remarked by an historian, the charters of the mediaeval communes offer the same variety as the Gothic architecture of their churches and cathedrals. The same leading ideas in all of them— the cathedral symbolizing the union of parish and guild in the city,—and the same infinitely rich variety of detail.

Self-jurisdiction was the essential point, and self-jurisdiction meant self-administration. But the commune was not simply an "autonomous" part of the State—such ambiguous words had not yet been invented by that time—it was a State in itself. It had the right of war and peace, of federation and alliance with its neighbours. It was sovereign in its own affairs, and mixed with no others. The supreme political power could be vested entirely in a democratic forum, as was the case in Pskov, whose *vyeche* sent and received ambassadors, concluded treaties, accepted and sent away princes, or went on without them for dozens of years; or it was vested in, or usurped by, an aristocracy of merchants or even nobles, as was the case of hundreds of Italian and middle European cities. The principle, nevertheless, remained the same: the city was a State and—what was perhaps still more remarkable—when the power in the city was usurped by an aristocracy of merchants or even nobles, the inner life of the city and the democratism of its daily life did not disappear: they depended but little upon what may be called the political form of the State.

The secret of this seeming anomaly lies in the fact that a mediaeval city was not a centralized State. During the first centuries of its existence, the city hardly could be named a State as regards its interior organization, because the middle ages knew no more of the present centralization of functions than of the present territorial centralization. Each group had its share of sovereignty. The city was usually divided into four quarters, or into five to seven sections radiating from a centre, each quarter or section roughly corresponding to a certain trade or profession which prevailed in it, but nevertheless containing inhabitants of different social positions and occupations—nobles, merchants, artisans, or even half-serfs; and each section or quarter constituted a quite independent agglomeration. In Venice, each island was an independent political community. It had its own organized trades, its own commerce in salt, its own jurisdiction and administration, its own forum; and the nomination of a doge by the city changed nothing in the inner independence of the units. In Cologne, we see the inhabitants divided into *Geburschaften* and *Heimschaften* (*viciniae*), *i.e.* neighbour guilds, which dated from the Franconian period. Each of them had its judge (*Burrichter*) and the usual twelve elected sentence-finders (*Schöffen*), its *Vogt*, and its *greve* or commander of the local militia. The story of early London before the Conquest—Mr. Green says—is that "of a number of little groups scattered here and there over the area within the walls, each growing up with its own life and institutions, guilds, sokes, religious houses, and the like, and only slowly drawing together into a municipal union." And if we refer to the annals of the Russian cities, Novgorod and Pskov, both of which are relatively rich in local details, we find the section (*konets*) consisting of independent streets (*ulitsa*), each of which, though chiefly peopled with artisans of a certain craft, had also merchants and landowners among its inhabitants, and was a separate community. It had the communal responsibility of all members in case of crime, its own jurisdiction and administration by street aldermen (*ulichanskiye starosty*), its own seal and, in case of need, its own forum; its own militia, as also its self-elected priests and its own collective life and collective enterprise.

The mediaeval city thus appears as a double federation: of all householders united into small territorial unions—the street, the parish, the section—and of individuals united by oath into guilds according to their professions; the former being a produce of the village-community origin of the city, while the second is a subsequent growth called to life by new conditions.

To guarantee liberty, self-administration, and peace was the chief aim of the mediaeval city; and labour, as we shall presently see when speaking of the craft guilds, was its chief foundation. But "production" did not absorb the whole attention of the mediaeval economist. With his practical mind, he understood that "consumption" must be guaranteed in order to obtain production; and therefore, to provide for "the common first food and lodging of poor and rich alike" (*Gemeine notdurft vnd gemach armer vnd richer*) was the fundamental principle in each city. The purchase of food supplies and other first necessaries (coal, wood, etc.) before they had reached the market, or altogether in especially favourable conditions from which others would be excluded—the *preempcio*, in a word—was entirely prohibited. Everything had to go to the market and be offered there for every one's purchase, till the ringing of the bell had closed the market. Then only could the retailer buy the remainder, and even then his profit should be an "honest profit" only.[2] Moreover, when corn was bought by a baker wholesale after the close of the market, every citizen had the right to claim part of the corn (about half-a-quarter) for his own use, at wholesale price, if he did so before the final conclusion of the bargain; and reciprocally, every baker could claim the same if the citizen purchased corn for re-selling it. In the first case, the corn had only to be brought to the town mill to be ground in its proper turn for a settled price, and the bread could be baked in the *four banal*, or communal oven.[3] In short, if a scarcity visited the city, all had to suffer from it more or less; but apart from the calamities, so long as the free cities existed no one could die in their midst from starvation, as is unhappily too often the case in our own times.

However, all such regulations belong to later periods of the cities' life, while at an earlier period it was the city itself which used to buy all food supplies for the use of the citizens. The documents recently published by Mr. Gross are quite positive on this point and fully support his conclusion to the effect that the cargoes of subsistences "were purchased by certain civic officials in the name of the town, and then distributed in shares among the merchant burgesses, no one being allowed to buy wares landed in the port unless the municipal authorities refused to purchase them. This seems—he adds—to have been quite a common practice in England, Ireland, Wales, and Scotland."[4] Even in the sixteenth century we find that common purchases of corn were made for the "commoditie and profitt in all things of this. . . . Citie and Chamber of London, and of all the Citizens and Inhabitants of the same as moche as in us lieth"—as the Mayor wrote in 1565. In Venice, the whole of the trade in corn is well known to have been in the hands of the city; the "quarters," on receiving the cereals from the board which ad-

2. When a boat brought a cargo of coal to Würzburg, coal could only be sold in retail during the first eight days, each family being entitled to no more than fifty basketfuls. The remaining cargo could be sold wholesale, but the retailer was allowed to raise a *zittlicher* profit only, the *unzittlicher*, or dishonest profit, being strictly forbidden. Same in London and, in fact, everywhere.
3. It hardly need be added that the tax on bread, and on beer as well, was settled after careful experiments as to the quantity of bread and beer which could be obtained from a given amount of corn.
4. Ch. Gross, *The Guild Merchant*, Ox-ford, 1890, i. 135. His documents prove that this practice existed in Liverpool (ii. 148–150), Waterford in Ireland, Neath in Wales, and Linlithgow and Thurso in Scotland. Mr. Gross's texts also show that the purchases were made for distribution, not only among the merchant burgesses, but "upon all citsains and commynalte" (p. 136, *note*), or, as the Thurso ordinance of the seventeenth century runs, to "make offer to the merchants, craftsmen, *and inhabitants* of the said burgh, that they may have their proportion of the same, according to their necessitys and ability."

ministrated the imports, being bound to send to every citizen's house the quantity allotted to him. In France, the City of Amiens used to purchase salt and to distribute it to all citizens at cost price;[5] and even now one sees in many French towns the *halles* which formerly were municipal *dépôts* for corn and salt. In Russia it was a regular custom in Novgorod and Pskov.

The whole matter relative to the communal purchases for the use of the citizens, and the manner in which they used to be made, seems not to have yet received proper attention from the historians of the period; but there are here and there some very interesting facts which throw a new light upon it. Thus there is, among Mr. Gross's documents, a Kilkenny ordinance of the year 1367, from which we learn how the prices of the goods were established. "The merchants and the sailors," Mr. Gross writes, "were to state on oath the first cost of the goods and the expenses of transportation. Then the mayor of the town and two discreet men were to name the price at which the wares were to be sold." The same rule held good in Thurso for merchandise coming "by sea or land." This way of "naming the price" so well answers to the very conceptions of trade which were current in mediaeval times that it must have been all but universal. To have the price established by a third person was a very old custom; and for all interchange within the city it certainly was a widely-spread habit to leave the establishment of prices to "discreet men"—to a third party—and not to the vendor or the buyer. But this order of things takes us still further back in the history of trade—namely, to a time when trade in staple produce was carried on by the whole city, and the merchants were only the commissioners, the trustees, of the city for selling the goods which it exported. A Waterford ordinance, published also by Mr. Gross, says "that all manere of marchandis *what so ever kynde thei be of* . . . shal be bought by the Maire and balives which bene commene biers [common buyers, for the town] for the time being, and to distribute the same on freemen of the citie (the propre goods of free citisains and inhabitants only excepted)." This ordinance can hardly be explained otherwise than by admitting that all the exterior trade of the town was carried on by its agents. Moreover, we have direct evidence of such having been the case for Novgorod and Pskov. It was the Sovereign Novgorod and the Sovereign Pskov who sent their caravans of merchants to distant lands.

We know also that in nearly all mediaeval cities of Middle and Western Europe, the craft guilds used to buy, as a body, all necessary raw produce, and to sell the produce of their work through

5. In 1485 the city permitted the export to Antwerp of a certain quantity of corn, "the inhabitants of Antwerp being always ready to be agreeable to the merchants and burgesses of Amien."

their officials, and it is hardly possible that the same should not have been done for exterior trade—the more so as it is well known that up to the thirteenth century, not only all merchants of a given city were considered abroad as responsible in a body for debts contracted by any one of them, but the whole city as well was responsible for the debts of each one of its merchants. Only in the twelfth and thirteenth century the towns on the Rhine entered into special treaties abolishing this reponsibility. And finally we have the remarkable Ipswich document published by Mr. Gross, from which document we learn that the merchant guild of this town was constituted by all who had the freedom of the city, and who wished to pay their contribution ("their hanse") to the guild, the whole community discussing all together how better to maintain the merchant guild, and giving it certain privileges. The merchant guild of Ipswich thus appears rather as a body of trustees of the town than as a common private guild.

In short, the more we begin to know the mediaeval city the more we see that it was not simply a political organization for the protection of certain political liberties. It was an attempt at organizing, on a much grander scale than in a village community, a close union for mutual aid and support, for consumption and production, and for social life altogether, without imposing upon men the fetters of the State, but giving full liberty of expression to the creative genius of each separate group of individuals in art, crafts, science, commerce, and political organization. How far this attempt has been successful will be best seen when we have analyzed in the next [section] the organization of labour in the mediaeval city and the relations of the cities with the surrounding peasant population.

II

The mediaeval cities were not organized upon some preconceived plan in obedience to the will of an outside legislator. Each of them was a natural growth in the full sense of the word—an always varying result of struggle between various forces which adjusted and re-adjusted themselves in conformity with their relative energies, the chances of their conflicts, and the support they found in their surroundings. Therefore, there are not two cities whose inner organization and destinies would have been identical. Each one, taken separately, varies from century to century. And yet, when we cast a broad glance upon all the cities of Europe, the local and national unlikenesses disappear, and we are struck to find among all of them a wonderful resemblance, although each has developed for itself, independently from the others, and in different conditions. A small town in the north of Scotland, with its population of coarse labourers and fishermen; a rich city of Flanders, with its world-wide commerce, luxury, love of amusement and animated life; an Italian city enriched by its intercourse with the East, and breeding within its walls a refined artistic taste and civilization; and a poor, chiefly agricultural, city in the marsh and lake district of Russia, seem to have little in common. And nevertheless, the leading lines of their organization, and the spirit which animates them, are imbued with a strong family likeness. Everywhere we see the same federations of small communities and guilds, the same "sub-towns" round the mother city, the same folkmote, and the same insigns of its independence. The *defensor* of the city, under different names and in different accoutrements, represents the same authority and interests; food supplies, labour, and commerce, are organized on closely similar lines; inner and outer struggles are fought with like ambitions; nay, the very formulae used in the struggles, as also in the annals, the ordinances, and the rolls, are identical; and the architectural monuments, whether Gothic, Roman, or Byzantine in style, express the same aspirations and the same ideals; they are conceived and built in the same way. Many dissemblances are mere differences of age, and those disparities between sister cities which are real are repeated in different parts of Europe. The unity of the leading idea and the identity of origin make up for differences of climate, geographical situation, wealth, language, and religion. This is why we can speak of *the* mediaeval city as of a well-defined phase of civilization; and while every research insisting upon local and individual differences is most welcome, we may still indicate the chief lines of development which are common to all cities.

There is no doubt that the protection which used to be accorded to the market-place from the earliest barbarian times has played an important, though not an exclusive, part in the emancipation of the mediaeval city. The early barbarians knew no trade within their village communities; they traded with strangers only, at certain definite spots, on certain determined days. And, in order that the stranger might come to the barter-place without risk of being slain for some feud which might be running between two kins, the market was always placed under the special protection of all kins. It was inviolable, like the place of worship under the shadow of which it was held. With the Kabyles it is still *annaya*, like the footpath along which women carry water from the well; neither must be trodden upon in arms, even during inter-tribal wars. In mediaeval times the market universally enjoyed the same protection.[6] No feud could be prosecuted on the place whereto people came to trade, nor within a certain radius from it; and if a quarrel

6. According to Herodotus, the Argippaeans were considered inviolable, because the trade between the Scythians and the northern tribes took place on their territory. A fugitive was sacred on their territory, and they were often asked to act as arbiters for their neighbours.

arose in the motley crowd of buyers and sellers, it had to be brought before those under whose protection the market stood—the community's tribunal, or the bishop's, the lord's, or the king's judge. A stranger who came to trade was a guest, and he went on under this very name. Even the lord who had no scruples about robbing a merchant on the high road, respected the W*eichbild*, that is, the pole which stood in the market-place and bore either the king's arms, or a glove, or the image of the local saint, or simply a cross, according to whether the market was under the protection of the king, the lord, the local church, or the folkmote—the *vyeche*.

It is easy to understand how the self-jurisdiction of the city could develop out of the special jurisdiction in the market-place, when this last right was conceded, willingly or not, to the city itself. And such an origin of the city's liberties, which can be traced in very many cases, necessarily laid a special stamp upon their subsequent development. It gave a predominance to the trading part of the community. The burghers who possessed a house in the city at the time being, and were co-owners in the town-lands, constituted very often a merchant guild which held in its hands the city's trade; and although at the outset every burgher, rich and poor, could make part of the merchant guild, and the trade itself seems to have been carried on for the entire city by its trustees, the guild gradually became a sort of privileged body. It jealously prevented the outsiders who soon began to flock into the free cities from entering the guild, and kept the advantages resulting from trade for the few "families" which had been burghers at the time of the emancipation. There evidently was a danger of a merchant oligarchy being thus constituted. But already in the tenth, and still more during the two next centuries, the chief crafts, also organized in guilds, were powerful enough to check the oligarchic tendencies of the merchants.

The craft guild was then a common seller of its produce and a common buyer of the raw materials, and its members were merchants and manual workers at the same time. Therefore, the predominance taken by the old craft guilds from the very beginnings of the free city life guaranteed to manual labour the high position which it afterwards occupied in the city. In fact, in a mediaeval city manual labour was no token of inferiority; it bore, on the contrary, traces of the high respect it had been kept in in the village community. Manual labour in a "mystery" was considered as a pious duty towards the citizens: a public function (*Amt*), as honourable as any other. An idea of "justice" to the community, of "right" towards both producer and consumer, which would seem so extravagant now, penetrated production and exchange. The tanner's, the cooper's, or the shoemaker's work must be "just," fair, they wrote in those times. Wood, leather, or thread which are used by the artisan must be "right"; bread must be baked "in justice," and so on. Transport this language into our present life, and it would seem affected and unnatural; but it was natural and unaffected then, because the mediaeval artisan did not produce for an unknown buyer, or to throw his goods into an unknown market. He produced for his guild first; for a brotherhood of men who knew each other, knew the technics of the craft, and, in naming the price of each product, could appreciate the skill displayed in its fabrication or the labour bestowed upon it. Then the guild, not the separate producer, offered the goods for sale in the community, and this last, in its turn, offered to the brotherhood of allied communities those goods which were exported, and assumed responsibility for their quality. With such an organization, it was the ambition of each craft not to offer goods of inferior quality, and technical defects or adulterations became a matter concerning the whole community, because, an ordinance says, "they would destroy public confidence." Production being thus a social duty, placed under the control of the whole *amitas*, manual labour could not fall into the degraded condition which it occupies now, so long as the free city was living.

A difference between master and apprentice, or between master and worker (*compayne, Geselle*), existed in the mediaeval cities from their very beginnings; but this was at the outset a mere difference of age and skill, not of wealth and power. After a seven year apprenticeship, and after having proved his knowledge and capacities by a work of art, the apprentice became a master himself. And only much later, in the sixteenth century, after the royal power had destroyed the city and the craft organization, was it possible to become master in virtue of simple inheritance or wealth. But this was also the time of a general decay in mediaeval industries and art.

There was not much room for hired work in the early flourishing periods of the mediaeval cities, still less for individual hirelings. The work of the weavers, the archers, the smiths, the bakers, and so on, was performed for the craft and the city; and when craftsmen were hired in the building trades, they worked as temporary corporations (as they still do in the Russian *artels*), whose work was paid *en bloc*. Work for a master began to multiply only later on; but even in this case the worker was paid better than he is paid now, even in this country, and very much better than he used to be paid all over Europe in the first half of this century. Thorold Rogers has familiarized English readers with this idea; but the same is true for the Continent as well, as is shown by the researches of Falke and Schönberg, and by many occasional indications. Even in the fifteenth century a mason, a carpenter, or a smith worker would be paid at Amiens four *sols* a day, which corresponded to forty-eight pounds of bread, or to the eighth part of a small ox (*bouvard*). In Saxony, the salary of the *Geselle* in the building trade was such that, to put it in Falke's words, he could buy with his six days wages three sheep and one pair of shoes. The donations of workers (*Geselle*) to cathedrals also bear testimony of their relative well-being, to say nothing of the glorious donations of certain craft guilds nor of what they used to spend in festivities and pageants.[7] In fact, the more we learn about the mediaeval city, the more we are convinced that at no time has labour enjoyed such conditions of prosperity and such respect as when city life stood at its highest.

More than that; not only many aspirations of our modern radicals were already realized in the middle ages, but much of what is described now as Utopian was accepted then as a matter of fact. We are laughed at when we say that work must be pleasant, but— "every one must be pleased with his work," a mediaeval Kuttenberg ordinance says, "and no one shall, while doing nothing (*mit nichts thun*), appropriate for himself what others have produced by application and work, because laws must be a shield for application and work." And amidst all present talk about an eight hour day, it may be well to remember an ordinance of Ferdinand the First relative to the Imperial coal mines, which settled the miner's day at eight hours, "as it used to be of old" (*wie vor Alters herkommen*), and work on Saturday afternoon was prohibited. Longer hours were very rare, we are told by Janssen, while shorter hours were of common occurrence. In this country, in the fifteenth century, Rogers says, "the workmen worked only forty-eight hours a week." The Saturday half-holiday, too, which we consider as a modern conquest, was in reality an old mediaeval institution; it was bathing-time for a great part of the community, while Wednesday afternoon was bathing-time for the *Geselle*.[8] And although school meals did not exist—probably because no children went hungry to school—a distribution of bath-money to the children whose parents found difficulty in providing it was habitual in several places. As to Labour Congresses, they also were a regular feature of the middle ages. In some parts of Germany craftsmen of the same trade,

7. To quote but one example out of many which may be found in Schönberg's and Falke's works, the sixteen shoemaker workers (*Schusterknechte*) of the town Xanten, on the Rhine, gave, for erecting a screen and an altar in the church, 75 guldens of subscriptions, and 12 guldens out of their box, which money was worth, according to the best valuations, ten times its present value.

8. At Paris, the day of labour varied from seven to eight hours in the winter to fourteen hours in summer in certain trades, while in others it was from eight to nine hours in winter, to from ten to twelve in summer. All work was stopped on Saturdays and on about twenty-five other days (*jours de commun de vile foire*) at four o'clock, while on Sundays and thirty other holidays there was no work at all. The general conclusion is, that the mediaeval worker worked *less* hours, all taken, then the present-day worker.

belonging to different communes, used to come together every year
to discuss questions relative to their trade, the years of apprenticeship, the wandering years, the wages, and so on; and in 1572, the
Hanseatic towns formally recognized the right of the crafts to come
together at periodical congresses, and to take any resolutions, so
long as they were not contrary to the cities' rolls, relative to the
quality of goods. Such Labour Congresses, partly international like
the Hansa itself, are known to have been held by bakers, founders,
smiths, tanners, sword-makers, and cask-makers.

The craft organization required, of course, a close supervision of
the craftsmen by the guild, and special jurates were always nominated for that purpose. But it is most remarkable that, so long as
the cities lived their free life, no complaints were heard about the
supervision; while, after the State had stepped in, confiscating the
property of the guilds and destroying their independence in favour
of its own bureaucracy, the complaints became simply countless.
On the other hand, the immensity of progress realized in all arts
under the mediaeval guild system is the best proof that the system
was no hindrance to individual initiative.[9] The fact is, that the
mediaeval guild, like the mediaeval parish, "street," or "quarter,"
was not a body of citizens, placed under the control of State functionaries; it was a union of all men connected with a given trade:
jurate buyers of raw produce, sellers of manufactured goods, and
artisans—masters, "compaynes," and apprentices. For the inner
organization of the trade its assembly was sovereign, so long as it
did not hamper the other guilds, in which case the matter was
brought before the guild of the guilds—the city. But there was in it
something more than that. It had its own self-jurisdiction, its own
military force, its own general assemblies, its own traditions of
struggles, glory, and independence, its own relations with other
guilds of the same trade in other cities: it had, in a word, a full
organic life which could only result from the integrality of the vital
functions. When the town was called to arms, the guild appeared as
a separate company (*Schaar*), armed with its own arms (or its own
guns, lovingly decorated by the guild, at a subsequent epoch),
under its own self-elected commanders. It was, in a word, as independent a unit of the federation as the republic of Uri or Geneva
was fifty years ago in the Swiss Confederation. So that, to compare

9. Adam Smith and his contemporaries knew well what they were condemning when they wrote against the *State* inter-ference in trade and the trade monopolies of *State* creation. Unhappily, their follow-ers, with their hopeless superficiality, flung mediaeval guilds and State inter-ference into the same sack, making no distinction between a Versailles edict and a guild ordinance. It hardly need be said that the economists who have seriously studied the subject, like Schönberg (the editor of the well-known course of *Po-litical Economy*), never fell into such an error. But, till lately, diffuse discussions of the above type went on for econom-ical "science."

it with a modern trade union, divested of all attributes of State sovereignty, and reduced to a couple of functions of secondary importance, is as unreasonable as to compare Florence or Brügge with a French commune vegetating under the Code Napoléon, or with a Russian town placed under Catherine the Second's municipal law. Both have elected mayors, and the latter has also its craft corporations; but the difference is—all the difference that exists between Florence and Fontenay-les-Oies or Tsarevokokshaisk, or between a Venetian doge and a modern mayor who lifts his hat before the *sous-préfet's* clerk.

The mediaeval guides were capable of maintaining their independence; and, later on, especially in the fourteenth century, when, in consequence of several causes which shall presently be indicated, the old municipal life underwent a deep modification, the younger crafts proved strong enough to conquer their due share in the management of the city affairs. The masses, organized in "minor" arts, rose to wrest the power of the hands of a growing oligarchy, and mostly succeeded in this task, opening again a new era of prosperity. True, that in some cities the uprising was crushed in blood, and mass decapitations of workers followed, as was the case in Paris in 1306, and in Cologne in 1371. In such cases the city's liberties rapidly fell into decay, and the city was gradually subdued by the central authority. But the majority of the towns had preserved enough of vitality to come out of the turmoil with a new life and vigour. A new period of rejuvenescence was their reward. New life was infused, and it found its expression in splendid architectural monuments, in a new period of prosperity, in a sudden progress of technics and invention, and in a new intellectual movement leading to the Renaissance and to the Reformation.

The life of a mediaeval city was a succession of hard battles to conquer liberty and to maintain it. True, that a strong and tenacious race of burghers had developed during those fierce contests; true, that love and worship of the mother city had been bred by these struggles, and that the grand things achieved by the mediaeval communes were a direct outcome of that love. But the sacrifices which the communes had to sustain in the battle for freedom were, nevertheless, cruel, and left deep traces of division on their inner life as well. Very few cities had succeeded, under a concurrence of favourable circumstances, in obtaining liberty at one stroke, and these few mostly lost it equally easily; while the great number had to fight fifty or a hundred years in succession, often more, before their rights to free life had been recognized, and another hundred years to found their liberty on a firm basis—the twelfth century charters thus being but one of the stepping-stones to freedom. In reality, the mediaeval city was a fortified oasis amidst a country plunged into feudal submission, and it had to make room for itself by the force of its arms. In consequence of the causes briefly alluded to in the preceding chapter, each village community had gradually fallen under the yoke of some lay or clerical lord. His house had grown to be a castle, and his brothers-in-arms were now the scum of adventurers, always ready to plunder the peasants. In addition to three days a week which the peasants had to work for the lord, they had also to bear all sorts of exactions for the right to sow and to crop, to be gay or sad, to live, to marry, or to die. And, worst of all, they were continually plundered by the armed robbers of some neighbouring lord, who chose to consider them as their master's kin, and to take upon them, and upon their cattle and crops, the revenge for a feud he was fighting against their owner. Every meadow, every field, every river, and road around the city, and every man upon the land was under some lord.

The hatred of the burghers towards the feudal barons has found a most characteristic expression in the wording of the different charters which they compelled them to sign. Heinrich V is made to sign in the charter granted to Speier in 111, that he frees the burghers from "the horrible and execrable law of mortmain, through which the town had been sunk into deepest poverty" (*von dem scheusslichen und nichtswürdigen Gesetze, welches gemein Budel genannt wird*, Kallsen, i. 307). The *coutume* of Bayonne, written about 1273, contains such passages as these: "The people is anterior to the lords. It is the people, more numerous than all others, who, desirous of peace, has made the lords for bridling and knocking down the powerful ones," and so on. . . . A charter submitted for King Robert's signature is equally characteristic. He is made to say in it: "I shall rob no oxen nor other animals. I shall seize no merchants, nor take their moneys, nor impose ransom. From Lady Day to the All Saints' Day I shall seize no horse, nor mare, nor foals, in the meadows. I shall not burn the mills, nor rob the flour. . . . I shall offer no protection to thieves," etc. The charter "granted" by the Besançon Archbishop Hugues, in which he has been compelled to enumerate all the mischiefs due to his mortmain rights, is equally characteristic. And so on.

Freedom could not be maintained in such surroundings, and the cities were compelled to carry on the war outside their walls. The burghers sent out emissaries to lead revolt in the villages; they received villages into their corporations, and they waged direct war against the nobles. In Italy, where the land was thickly sprinkled with feudal castles, the war assumed heroic proportions, and was fought with a stern acrimony on both sides. Florence sustained for seventy-seven years a succession of bloody wars, in order to free its *contado* from the nobles; but when the conquest had been accomplished (in 1181) all had to begin anew. The nobles rallied; they constituted their own leagues in opposition to the leagues of the towns, and, receiving fresh support from either the Emperor or the Pope, they made the war last for another 130 years. The same took place in Rome, in Lombardy, all over Italy.

Prodigies of valour, audacity, and tenaciousness were displayed by the citizens in these wars. But the bows and the hatchets of the arts and crafts had not always the upper hand in their encounters with the armour-clad knights, and many castles withstood the ingenious siege-machinery and the perseverance of the citizens. Some cities, like Florence, Bologna, and many towns in France, Germany, and Bohemia, succeeded in emancipating the surrounding villages, and they were rewarded for their efforts by an extraordinary prosperity and tranquillity. But even here, and still more in the less strong or less impulsive towns, the merchants and artisans, exhausted by war, and misunderstanding their own interests, bargained over the peasants' heads. They compelled the lord to swear allegiance to the city; his country castle was dismantled, and he agreed to build a house and to reside in the city, of which he became a co-burgher (*com-bourgeois, con-cittadino*); but he maintained in return most of his rights upon the peasants, who only won a partial relief from their burdens. The burgher could not understand that equal rights of citizenship might be granted to the peasant upon whose food supplies he had to rely, and a deep rent was traced between town and village. In some cases the peasants simply changed owners, the city buying out the barons' rights and selling them in shares to her own citizens. Serfdom was maintained, and only much later on, towards the end of the thirteenth century, it was the craft revolution which undertook to put an end to it, and abolished personal servitude, but dispossessed at the same time the serfs of the land. It hardly need be added that the fatal results of such policy were soon felt by the cities themselves; the country became the city's enemy.

The war against the castles had another bad effect. It involved the cities in a long succession of mutual wars, which have given origin to the theory, till lately in vogue, namely, that the towns lost their independence through their own jealousies and mutual fights. The imperialist historians have especially supported this theory, which, however, is very much undermined now by modern research. It is certain that in Italy cities fought each other with a stubborn animosity, but nowhere else did such contests attain the same proportions; and in Italy itself the city wars, especially those of the earlier period, had their special causes. They were (as was already shown by Sismondi and Ferrari) a mere continuation of the war against the castles—the free municipal and federative principle unavoidably entering into a fierce contest with feudalism, imperialism, and papacy. Many towns which had but partially shaken off the yoke of the bishop, the lord, or the Emperor, were simply driven against the free cities by the nobles, the Emperor, and Church, whose policy was to divide the cities and to arm them against each other. These special circumstances (partly reflected on to Germany also) explain why the Italian towns, some of which sought support with the Emperor to combat the Pope, while the others sought support from the Church to resist the Emperor, were soon divided into a Gibelin and a Guelf camp, and why the same division appeared in each separate city.

The immense economical progress realized by most Italian cities just at the time when these wars were hottest, and the alliances so easily concluded between towns, still better characterize those struggles and further undermine the above theory. Already in the years 1130–1150 powerful leagues came into existence; and a few years later, when Frederick Barbarossa invaded Italy and, supported by the nobles and some retardatory cities, marched against Milan, popular enthusiasm was roused in many towns by popular preachers. Crema, Piacenza, Brescia, Tortona, etc., went to the rescue; the banners of the guilds of Verona, Padua, Vicenza, and Trevisa floated side by side in the cities' camp against the banners of the Emperor and the nobles. Next year the Lombardian League came into existence, and sixty years later we see it reinforced by many other cities, and forming a lasting organization which had half of its federal war-chest in Genoa and the other half in Venice. In Tuscany, Florence headed another powerful league, to which Lucca, Bologna, Pistoia, etc., belonged, and which played an important part in crushing down the nobles in middle Italy, while smaller leagues were of common occurrence. It is thus certain that although petty jealousies undoubtedly existed, and discord could be easily sown, they did not prevent the towns from uniting together for the common defence of liberty. Only later on, when separate cities became little States, wars broke out between them, as always must be the case when States struggle for supremacy or colonies.

Similar leagues were formed in Germany for the same purpose. When, under the successors of Conrad, the land was the prey of interminable feuds between the nobles, the Westphalian towns concluded a league against the knights, one of the clauses of which was never to lend money to a knight who would continue to conceal stolen goods. When "the knights and the nobles lived on plunder, and murdered whom they chose to murder," as the *Wormser Zorn* complains, the cities on the Rhine (Mainz, Cologne, Speier, Strasburg, and Basel) took the initiative of a league which soon numbered sixty allied towns, repressed the robbers, and maintained peace. Later on, the league of the towns of Suabia, divided into three "peace districts" (Augsburg, Constance, and Ulm), had the same purpose. And even when such leagues were broken,[1] they lived long enough to show that while the supposed peacemakers—the kings, the emperors, and the Church—fomented discord, and were themselves helpless against the robber knights, it was from the cities that the impulse came for re-establishing peace and union. The cities—not the emperors—were the real makers of the national unity.

Similar federations were organized for the same purpose among small villages, and now that attention has been drawn to this subject by Luchaire we may expect soon to learn much more about them. Villages joined into small federations in the *contado* of Florence, so also in the dependencies of Novgorod and Pskov. As to France, there is positive evidence of a federation of seventeen peasant villages which has existed in the Laonnais for nearly a hundred years (till 1256), and has fought hard for its independence. Three more peasant republics, which had sworn charters similar to those of Laon and Soissons, existed in the neighbourhood of Laon, and, their territories being contiguous, they supported each other in their liberation wars. Altogether, Luchaire is of the opinion that many such federations must have come into existence in France in the twelfth and thirteenth centuries, but that documents relative to them are mostly lost. Of course, being unprotected by walls, they could easily be crushed down by the kings and the lords; but in certain favourable circumstances, when they found support in a league of towns and protection in their mountains, such peasant republics became independent units of the Swiss Confederation.

As to unions between cities for peaceful purposes, they were of quite common occurrence. The intercourse which had been established during the period of liberation was not interrupted afterwards. Sometimes, when the *scabini* of a German town, having to pronounce judgment in a new or complicated case, declared that they knew not the sentence (*des Urtheiles nicht weise zu sein*), they sent delegates to another city to get the sentence. The same happened also in France; while Forli and Ravenna are known to have mutually naturalized their citizens and granted them full rights in both cities. To submit a contest arisen between two towns, or within a city, to another commune which was invited to act as arbiter, was also in the spirit of the times. As to commercial treaties between cities, they were quite habitual. Unions for regulating the production and the sizes of casks which were used for the commerce in wine, "herring unions," and so on, were mere precursors

---

1. For Aachen and Cologne we have direct testimony that the bishops of these two cities—one of them bought by the enemy—opened to him the gates.

of the great commercial federations of the Flemish Hansa, and, later on, of the great North German Hansa, the history of which alone might contribute pages and pages to illustrate the federation spirit which permeated men at that time. It hardly need be added, that through the Hanseatic unions the mediaeval cities have contributed more to the development of international intercourse, navigation, and maritime discovery than all the States of the first seventeen centuries of our era.

In a word, federations between small territorial units, as well as among men united by common pursuits within their respective guilds, and federations between cities and groups of cities constituted the very essence of life and thought during that period. The first five of the second decade of centuries of our era may thus be described as an immense attempt at securing mutual aid and support on a grand scale, by means of the principles of federation and association carried on through all manifestations of human life and to all possible degrees. This attempt was attended with success to a very great extent. It united men formerly divided; it secured them a very great deal of freedom, and it tenfolded their forces. At a time when particularism was bred by so many agencies, and the causes of discord and jealousy might have been so numerous, it is gratifying to see that cities scattered over a wide continent had so much in common, and were so ready to confederate for the prosecution of so many common aims. They succumbed in the long run before powerful enemies; not having understood the mutual-aid principle widely enough, they themselves committed fatal faults; but they did not perish through their own jealousies, and their errors were not a want of federation spirit among themselves.

The results of that new move which mankind made in the mediaeval city were immense. At the beginning of the eleventh century the towns of Europe were small clusters of miserable huts, adorned but with low clumsy churches, the builders of which hardly knew how to make an arch; the arts, mostly consisting of some weaving and forging, were in their infancy; learning was found in but a few monasteries. Three hundred and fifty years later, the very face of Europe had been changed. The land was dotted with rich cities, surrounded by immense thick walls which were embellished by towers and gates, each of them a work of art in itself. The cathedrals, conceived in a grand style and profusely decorated, lifted their bell-towers to the skies, displaying a purity of form and a boldness of imagination which we now vainly strive to attain. The crafts and arts had risen to a degree of perfection which we can hardly boast of having superseded in many directions, if the inventive skill of the worker and the superior finish of his work be appreciated higher than rapidity of fabrication. The navies of the free cities furrowed in all directions the Northern and the Southern Mediterranean; one effort more, and they would cross the oceans. Over large tracts of land well-being had taken the place of misery; learning had grown and spread. The methods of science had been elaborated; the basis of natural philosophy had been laid down; and the way had been paved for all the mechanical inventions of which our own times are so proud. Such were the magic changes accomplished in Europe in less than four hundred years. And the losses which Europe sustained through the loss of its free cities can only be understood when we compare the seventeenth century with the fourteenth or the thirteenth. The prosperity which formerly characterized Scotland, Germany, the plains of Italy, was gone. The roads had fallen into an abject state, the cities were depopulated, labour was brought into slavery, art had vanished, commerce itself was decaying.

If the mediaeval cities had bequeathed to us no written documents to testify of their splendour, and left nothing behind but the monuments of building art which we see now all over Europe, from Scotland to Italy, and from Gerona in Spain to Breslau in Slavonian territory, we might yet conclude that the times of independent city life were times of the greatest development of human intellect during the Christian era down to the end of the eighteenth century. On looking, for instance, at a mediaeval picture representing Nuremberg with its scores of towers and lofty spires, each of which bore the stamp of free creative art, we can hardly conceive that three hundred years before the town was but a collection of miserable hovels. And our admiration grows when we go into the details of the architecture and decorations of each of the countless churches, bell-towers, gates, and communal houses which are scattered all over Europe as far east as Bohemia and the now dead towns of Polish Galicia. Not only Italy, that mother of art, but all Europe is full of such monuments. The very fact that of all arts architecture—a social art above all—had attained the highest development, is significant in itself. To be what it was, it must have originated from an eminently social life.

Mediaeval architecture attained its grandeur—not only because it was a natural development of handicraft; not only because each building, each architectural decoration, had been devised by men who knew through the experience of their own hands what artistic effects can be obtained from stone, iron, bronze, or even from simple logs and mortar; not only because each monument was a result of collective experience, accumulated in each "mystery" or craft—it was grand because it was born out of a grand idea. Like Greek art, it sprang out of a conception of brotherhood and unity fostered by the city. It had an audacity which could only be won by audacious struggles and victories; it had that expression of vigour, because vigour permeated all the life of the city. A cathedral or a communal house symbolized the grandeur of an organism of which every mason and stone-cutter was the builder, and a mediaeval building appears—not as a solitary effort to which thousands of slaves would have contributed the share assigned them by one man's imagination; all the city contributed to it. The lofty bell-tower rose upon a structure, grand in itself, in which the life of the city was throbbing—not upon a meaningless scaffold like the Paris iron tower, not as a sham structure in stone intended to conceal the ugliness of an iron frame, as has been done in the Tower Bridge. Like the Acropolis of Athens, the cathedral of a mediaeval city was intended to glorify the grandeur of the victorious city, to symbolize the union of its crafts, to express the glory of each citizen in a city of his own creation. After having achieved its craft revolution, the city often began a new cathedral in order to express the new, wider, and broader union which had been called into life.

The means at hand for these grand undertakings were disproportionately small. Cologne Cathedral was begun with a yearly outlay of but 500 marks; a gift of 100 marks was inscribed as a grand donation; and even when the work approached completion, and gifts poured in in proportion, the yearly outlay in money stood at about 5,000 marks, and never exceeded 14,000. The cathedral of Basel was built with equally small means. But each corporation contributed its part of stone, work, and decorative genius to *their* common monument. Each guild expressed in it its political conceptions, telling in stone or in bronze the history of the city, glorifying the principles of "Liberty, equality, and fraternity,"[2] praising the city's allies, and sending to eternal fire its enemies. And each guild bestowed its *love* upon the communal monument by richly decorating it with stained windows, paintings, "gates, worthy to be the gates of Paradise," as Michel Angelo said, or stone decorations of each minutest corner of the building.[3] Small cities, even small parishes, vied with the big agglomerations in this work, and the cathedrals of Laon and St. Ouen hardly stand behind that of Rheims, or the Communal House of Bremen, or the folkmote's bell-tower of Breslau. "No works must be begun by the commune but such as are conceived in response to the grand heart of the commune, composed of the hearts of all citizens, united in one common

2. The three statues are among the outer decorations of Nôtre Dame de Paris.
3. Mediaeval art, like Greek art, did not know those curiosity-shops which we call a National Gallery or a Museum. A picture was painted, a statue was carved, a bronze decoration was cast to stand in its proper place in a monument of communal art. It lived there, it was part of a whole, and it contributed to give unity to the impressions produced by the whole.

will"—such were the words of the Council of Florence; and this spirit appears in all communal works of common utility, such as the canals, terraces, vineyards, and fruit gardens around Florence, or the irrigation canals which intersected the plains of Lombardy, or the port and aqueduct of Genoa, or, in fact, any works of the kind which were achieved by almost every city.

All arts had progressed in the same way in the mediaeval cities, those of our own days mostly being but a continuation of what had grown at that time. The prosperity of the Flemish cities was based upon the fine woollen cloth they fabricated. Florence, at the beginning of the fourteenth century, before the black death, fabricated from 70,000 to 100,000 *panni* of wollen stuffs, which were valued at 1,200,000 golden florins.[4] The chiselling of precious metals, the art of casting, the fine forging of iron, were creations of the mediaeval "mysteries" which had succeeded in attaining in their own domains all that could be made by the hand, without the use of a powerful prime motor. By the hand and by invention, because, to use Whewell's words:

> Parchment and paper, printing and engraving, improved glass and steel, gunpowder, clocks, telescopes, the mariner's compass, the reformed calendar, the decimal notation; algebra, trigonometry, chemistry, counterpoint (an invention equivalent to a new creation of music); these are all possessions which we inherit from that which has so disparagingly been termed the Stationary Period.

True that no new principle was illustrated by any of these discoveries, as Whewell said; but mediaeval science had done something more than the actual discovery of new principles. It had prepared the discovery of all the new principles which we know at the present time in mechanical sciences: it had accustomed the explorer to observe facts and to reason from them. It was inductive science, even though it had not yet fully grasped the importance and the powers of induction; and it laid the foundations of both mechanics and natural philosophy. Francis Bacon, Galileo, and Copernicus were the direct descendants of a Roger Bacon and a Michael Scot, as the steam engine was a direct product of the researches carried on in the Italian universities on the weight of the atmosphere, and of the mathematical and technical learning which characterized Nuremberg.

But why should one take trouble to insist upon the advance of

---

4. In 1336 it had 8,000 to 10,000 boys and girls in its primary schools, 1,000 to 1,200 boys in its seven middle schools, and from 550 to 600 students in its four universities. The thirty communal hospitals contained over 1,000 beds for a population of 90,000 inhabitants. It has more than once been suggested by authoritative writers that education stood, as a rule, at a much higher level than is generally supposed. Certainly so in democratic Nuremberg.

science and art in the mediaeval city? Is it not enough to point to the cathedrals in the domain of skill, and to the Italian language and the poem of Dante in the domain of thought, to give at once the measure of what the mediaeval city *created* during the four centuries it lived?

The mediaeval cities have undoubtedly rendered an immense service to European civilization. They have prevented it from being drifted into the theocracies and despotical states of old; they have endowed it with the variety, the self-reliance, the force of initiative, and the immense intellectual and material energies it now possesses, which are the best pledge for its being able to resist any new invasion of the East. But why did these centres of civilization, which attempted to answer to deeply-seated needs of human nature, and were so full of life, not live further on? Why were they seized with senile debility in the sixteenth century? and, after having repulsed so many assaults from without, and only borrowed new vigour from their interior struggles, why did they finally succumb to both?

Various causes contributed to this effect, some of them having their roots in the remote past, while others originated in the mistakes committed by the cities themselves. Towards the end of the fifteenth century, mighty States, reconstructed on the old Roman pattern, were already coming into existence. In each country and each region some feudal lord, more cunning, more given to hoarding, and often less scrupulous than his neighbours, had succeeded in appropriating to himself richer personal domains, more peasants on his lands, more knights in his following, more treasures in his chest. He had chosen for his seat a group of happily-situated villages, not yet trained into free municipal life—Paris, Madrid, or Moscow—and with the labour of his serfs he had made of them royal fortified cities, whereto he attracted war companions by a free distribution of villages, and merchants by the protection he offered to trade. The germ of a future State, which began gradually to absorb other similar centres, was thus laid. Lawyers, versed in the study of Roman law, flocked into such centres; a tenacious and ambitious race of men issued from among the burgesses, who equally hated the naughtiness of the lords and what they called the lawlessness of the peasants. The very forms of the village community, unknown to their code, the very principles of federalism were repulsive to them as "barbarian" inheritances. Caesarism, supported by the fiction of popular consent and by the force of arms, was their ideal, and they worked hard for those who promised to realize it.

The Christian Church, once a rebel against Roman law and now its ally, worked in the same direction. The attempt at constituting the theocratic Empire of Europe having proved a failure, the more intelligent and ambitious bishops now yielded support to those whom they reckoned upon for reconstituting the power of the Kings of Israel or of the Emperors of Constantinople. The Church bestowed upon the rising rulers her sanctity, she crowned them as God's representatives on earth, she brought to their service the learning and the statesmanship of her ministers, her blessings and maledictions, her riches, and the sympathies she had retained among the poor. The peasants, whom the cities had failed or refused to free, on seeing the burghers impotent to put an end to the interminable wars between the knights—which wars they had so dearly to pay for—now set their hopes upon the King, the Emperor, or the Great Prince; and while aiding them to crush down the mighty feudal owners, they aided them to constitute the centralized State. And finally, the invasions of the Mongols and the Turks, the holy war against the Maures in Spain, as well as the terrible wars which soon broke out between the growing centres of sovereignty—Ile de France and Burgundy, Scotland and England, England and France, Lithuania and Poland, Moscow and Tver, and so on—contributed to the same end. Mighty States made their appearance; and the cities had now to resist not only loose federations of lords, but strongly-organized centres, which had armies of serfs at their disposal.

The worst was, that the growing autocracies found support in the divisions which had grown within the cities themselves. The fundamental idea of the mediaeval city was grand, but it was not wide enough. Mutual aid and support cannot be limited to a small association; they must spread to its surroundings, or else the surroundings will absorb the association. And in this respect the mediaeval citizen had committed a formidable mistake at the outset. Instead of looking upon the peasants and artisans who gathered under the protection of his walls as upon so many aids who would contribute their part to the making of the city—as they really did—a sharp division was traced between the "families" of old burghers and the new-comers. For the former, all benefits from communal trade and communal lands were reserved, and nothing was left for the latter but the right of freely using the skill of their own hands. The city thus became divided into "the burghers" or "the commonalty," and "the inhabitants." The trade, which was formerly communal, now became the privilege of the merchant and artisan "families," and the next step—that of becoming individual, or the privilege of oppressive trusts—was unavoidable.

The same division took place between the city proper and the surrounding villages. The commune had well tried to free the peasants, but her wars against the lords became, as already mentioned, wars for freeing the city itself from the lords, rather than for freeing the peasants. She left to the lord his rights over the villeins, on condition that he would molest the city no more and would become co-burgher. But the nobles "adopted" by the city, and now residing within its walls, simply carried on the old war within the very precincts of the city. They disliked to submit to a tribunal of simple artisans and merchants, and fought their old feuds in the streets. Each city had now its Colonnas and Orsinis, its Overstolzes and Wises. Drawing large incomes from the estates they had still retained, they surrounded themselves with numerous clients and feudalized the customs and habits of the city itself. And when discontent began to be felt in the artisan classes of the town, they offered their sword and their followers to settle the differences by a free fight, instead of letting the discontent find out the channels which it did not fail to secure itself in olden times.

The greatest and the most fatal error of most cities was to base their wealth upon commerce and industry, to the neglect of agriculture. They thus repeated the error which had once been committed by the cities of antique Greece, and they fell through it into the same crimes.[5] The estrangement of so many cities from the land necessarily drew them into a policy hostile to the land, which became more and more evident in the times of Edward the Third, the French Jacqueries, the Hussite wars, and the Peasant War in Germany. On the other hand, a commercial policy involved them in distant enterprises. Colonies were founded by the Italians in the south-east, by German cities in the east, by Slavonian cities in the far north-east. Mercenary armies began to be kept for colonial wars, and soon for local defence as well. Loans were contracted to such an extent as to totally demoralize the citizens; and internal contests grew worse and worse at each election, during which the colonial politics in the interest of a few families was at stake. The division into rich and poor grew deeper, and in the sixteenth century, in each city, the royal authority found ready allies and support among the poor.

And there is yet another cause of the decay of communal institutions, which stands higher and lies deeper than all the above. The history of the mediaeval cities offers one of the most striking illustrations of the power of *ideas* and *principles* upon the destinies of mankind, and of the quite opposed results which are obtained when a deep modification of leading ideas has taken place. Self-reliance and federalism, the sovereignty of each group, and the construction

---

5. The trade in slaves kidnapped in the East was never discontinued in the Italian republics till the fifteenth century. Feeble traces of it are found also in Germany and elsewhere.

of the political body from the simple to the composite, were the leading ideas in the eleventh century. But since that time the conceptions had entirely changed. The students of Roman law and the prelates of the Church, closely bound together since the time of Innocent the Third, had succeeded in paralyzing the idea—the antique Greek idea—which presided at the foundation of the cities. For two or three hundred years they taught from the pulpit, the University chair, and the judges' bench, that salvation must be sought for in a strongly-centralized State, placed under a semi-divine authority; that *one* man can and must be the saviour of society, and that in the name of public salvation he can commit any violence: burn men and women at the stake, make them perish under indescribable tortures, plunge whole provinces into the most abject misery. Nor did they fail to give object lessons to this effect on a grand scale, and with an unheard-of cruelty, wherever the king's sword and the Church's fire, or both at once, could reach. By these teachings and examples, continually repeated and enforced upon public attention, the very minds of the citizens had been shaped into a new mould. They began to find no authority too extensive, no killing by degrees too cruel, once it was "for public safety." And, with this new direction of mind and this new belief in one man's power, the old federalist principle faded away, and the very creative genius of the masses died out. The Roman idea was victorious, and in such circumstances the centralized State had in the cities a ready prey.

Florence in the fifteenth century is typical of this change. Formerly a popular revolution was the signal of a new departure. Now, when the people, brought to despair, insurged, it had constructive ideas no more; no fresh idea came out of the movement. A thousand representatives were put into the Communal Council instead of 400; 100 men entered the *signoria* instead of 80. But a revolution of figures could be of no avail. The people's discontent was growing up, and new revolts followed. A saviour—the "tyran"—was appealed to; he massacred the rebels, but the disintegration of the communal body continued worse than ever. And when, after a new revolt, the people of Florence appealed to their most popular man, Gieronimo Savonarola, for advice, the monk's answer was:—"Oh, people mine, thou knowest that I cannot go into State affairs. . . . purify thy soul, and if in such a disposition of mind thou reformest thy city, then, people of Florence, thou shalt have inaugurated the reform in all Italy!" Carnival masks and vicious books were burned, a law of charity and another against usurers were passed—and the democracy of Florence remained where it was. The old spirit had gone. By too much trusting to government, they had ceased to trust to themselves; they were unable to open new issues. The State had only to step in and to crush down their last liberties.

And yet, the current of mutual aid and support did not die out in the masses, it continued to flow even after that defeat. It rose up again with a formidable force, in answer to the communist appeals of the first propagandists of the reform, and it continued to exist even after the masses, having failed to realize the life which they hoped to inagurate under the inspiration of a reformed religion, fell under the dominions of an autocratic power. It flows still even now, and it seeks its way to find out a new expression which would not be the State, nor the mediaeval city, nor the village community of the barbarians, nor the savage clan, but would proceed from all of them, and yet be superior to them in its wider and more deeply humane conceptions.

Selections from

The Great French Revolution

The Two Great Currents of the Revolution

Two great currents prepared and made the Great French Revolution. One of them, the current of ideas, concerning the political reorganisation of States, came from the middle classes; the other, the current of action, came from the people, both peasants and workers in towns, who wanted to obtain immediate and definite improvements in their economic condition. And when these two currents met and joined in the endeavour to realise an aim which for some time was common to both, when they had helped each other for a certain time, the result was the Revolution.

The eighteenth-century philosophers had long been sapping the foundations of the law-and-order societies of that period, wherein political power, as well as an immense share of the wealth, belonged to the aristocracy and the clergy, whilst the mass of the people were nothing but beasts of burden to the ruling classes. By proclaiming the sovereignty of reason; by preaching trust in human nature—corrupted, they declared, by the institutions that had reduced man to servitude, but, nevertheless, certain to regain all its qualities when it had reconquered liberty—they had opened up new vistas to mankind. By proclaiming equality among men, without distinction of birth; by demanding from every citizen, whether king or peasant, obedience to the law, supposed to express the will of the nation when it has been made by the representatives of the people; finally, by demanding freedom of contract between free men, and the abolition of feudal taxes and services—by putting forward all these claims, linked together with the system and method characteristic of French thought, the philosophers had undoubtedly prepared, at least in men's minds, the downfall of the old *régime*.

This alone, however, would not have sufficed to cause the outbreak of the Revolution. There was still the stage of passing from theory to action, from the conception of an ideal to putting it into practice. And the most important point in the study of the history of that period is to bring into relief the circumstances that made it possible for the French nation at a given moment to enter on the realisation of the ideal—to attempt this passage from theory to action.

On the other hand, long before 1789, France had already entered upon an insurrectionary period. The accession of Louis XVI to the throne in 1774 was the signal for a whole series of hunger riots. These lasted up to 1783; and then came a period of comparative quiet. But after 1786, and still more after 1788, the peasant insurrections broke out again with renewed vigour. Famine had been the chief source of the earlier disturbances, and the lack of bread always remained one of the principal causes of the risings. But it was chiefly disinclination on the part of the peasants to pay the feudal taxes which now spurred them to revolt. The outbreaks went on increasing in number up to 1789, and in that year they became general in the east, north-east and south-east of France.

In this way the disaggregation of the body social came about. A *jacquerie* is not, however, a revolution, even when it takes such terrible forms as did the rising of the Russian peasants in 1773 under the banner of Pougatchoff. A revolution is infinitely more than a series of insurrections in town and country. It is more than a simple struggle between parties, however sanguinary; more than mere street-fighting, and much more than a mere change of government, such as was made in France in 1830 and 1848. A revolution is a swift overthrow, in a few years, of institutions which have taken centuries to root in the soil, and seem so fixed and immovable that even the most ardent reformers hardly dare to attack them in their writings. It is the fall, the crumbling away in a brief period, of all that up to that time composed the essence of social, religious, political, and economic life in a nation. It means the subversion of acquired ideas and of accepted notions concerning each of the complex institutions and relations of the human herd.

In short, it is the birth of completely new ideas concerning the manifold links in citizenship—conceptions which soon become realties, and then begin to spread among the neighbouring nations, convulsing the world and giving to the succeeding age its watchword, its problems, its science, its lines of economic, political, and moral development.

To arrive at a result of this importance, and for a movement to assume the proportions of a revolution, as happened in England between 1648 and 1688, and in France between 1789 and 1793, it is not enough that a movement of ideas, no matter how profound it may be, should manifest itself among the educated classes; it is not enough that disturbances, however many or great, should take place in the very heart of the people. The revolutionary action coming from the people must coincide with a movement of revolutionary thought coming from the educated classes. There must be a union of the two.

That is why the French Revolution, like the English Revolution of the preceding century, happened at the moment when the middle classes, having drunk deep at the sources of current philosophy, became conscious of their rights, and conceived a new scheme of political organisation. Strong in their knowledge and eager for the task, they felt themselves quite capable of seizing the government by snatching it from a palace aristocracy which, by its incapacity, frivolity, and debauchery, was bringing the kingdom to utter ruin. But the middle and educated classes could not have done anything alone, if, consequent on a complete chain of circumstances, the mass of the peasants had not also been stirred, and, by a series of constant insurrections lasting for four years, given to the dissatisfied among the middle classes the possibility of combating both King and Court, of upsetting old institutions and changing the political constitution of the kingdom.

The history of this double movement remains still to be written. The history of the great French Revolution has been told and retold many times, from the point of view of as many different parties; but up to the present the historians have confined themselves to the political history, the history of the triumph of the middle classes over the Court party and the defenders of the institutions of the old monarchy.

Thus we know very well the principles which dominated the Revolution and were translated into its legislative work. We have been enraptured by the great thoughts it flung to the world, thoughts which civilised countries tried to put into practice during the nineteenth century. The Parliamentary history of the Revolution, its wars, its policy and its diplomacy, has been studied and set forth in all its details. But the *popular* history of the Revolution remains still to be told. The part played by the *people* of the country places and towns in the Revolution has never been studied and narrated in its entirety. Of the two currents which made the Revolution, the current of *thought* is known; but the other, the current of *popular action*, has not even been sketched.

It is for us, the descendants of those called by their contemporaries the "anarchists," to study the popular current, and to try to reconstruct at least its main features.

The Idea

To understand fully the idea which inspired the middle classes in 1789 we must consider it in the light of its results—the modern States.

The structure of the law-and-order States which we see in Europe at present was only outlined at the end of the eighteenth century. The system of the centralised authority, now in full working order, had not then attained either the perfection or uniformity it possesses today. That formidable mechanism, by which an order sent from a certain capital puts in motion all the men of a nation, ready for war, and sends them out to carry devastation through countries, and mourning into families; those territories, overspread with a network of officials whose personality is completely effaced by their bureaucratic apprenticeship, and who obey mechanically the orders emanating from a central will; that passive obedience of citizens to the law; that worship of law, of Parliament, of judges and their assistants, which we see about us today; that mass of hierarchically organised and disciplined functionaries; that system of schools, maintained or directed by the State, where worship of power and passive obedience are taught; that industrial system, which crushes under its wheels the worker whom the State delivers over to its tender mercies; that commerce, which accumulates incredible riches in the hands of those who monopolise the land, the mines, the ways of communication and the riches of *Nature*, upon which the State is nourished; and finally, that science, which liberates thought and immensely increases the productive powers of men, but which at the same time aims at subjecting them to the authority of the strongest and to the State—all this was non-existent before the Revolution.

However, long before the Revolution had by its mutterings given warning of its approach, the French middle classes—the Third Estate—had already developed a conception of the political edifice which should be erected on the ruins of feudal royalty. It is highly probable that the English Revolution had helped the French middle class towards a comprehension of the part they would be called on to play in the government of society. And it is certain that the revolution in America stimulated the energies of the middle-class revolutionaries. Thanks to Hobbes, Hume, Montesquieu, Rousseau, Voltaire, Mably, d'Argenson, and others, ever since the beginning of the eighteenth century the study of Politics and the constitution of organised societies based on elective representation had become popular, and to this Turgot and Adam Smith had just added the study of economic questions and the place of property in the political constitution of a State.

That is why, long before the Revolution broke out, the idea of a State, centralised and well-ordered, governed by the classes holding property in lands or in factories, or by members of the learned professions, was already forecast and described in a great number of books and pamphlets from which the men of action during the Revolution afterwards drew their inspiration and their logical force.

Thus it came to pass that the French middle classes in 1789, at the moment of entering upon the revolutionary period, knew quite well what they wanted. They were certainly not republicans—are they republicans even today? But they no longer wanted the King to have arbitrary powers, they refused to be ruled by the princes or by the Court, and they did not recognise the right of the nobility to seize on all the best places in the Government, though they were only capable of plundering the State as they had plundered their vast properties without adding anything to their value. The middle classes were perhaps republican in sentiment, and desired republican simplicity of manners, as in the growing republic of America; but they desired, above all things, government by the propertied classes.

They inclined to free thought without being Atheists, but they by no means disliked the Catholic form of religion. What they detested most was the Church, with its hierarchy and its bishops, who made common cause with the princes, and its priests who had become the obedient tools of the nobility.

The middle classes of 1789 understood that the moment had arrived in France, as it had arrived one hundred and forty years before in England, when the Third Estate was to seize the power falling from the hands of royalty, and they knew what they meant to do with it.

Their ideal was to give France a constitution modelled upon the English constitution, and to reduce the King to the part of a mere enregistering scribe, with sometimes the power of a casting-vote, but chiefly to act as the symbol of national unity. As to the real authority, that was to be vested in a Parliament, in which an educated middle class, which would represent the active and thinking part of the nation, should predominate.

At the same time, their ideal was to abolish all the local powers which at that time constituted so many autonomous units in the State. They meant to concentrate all governmental power in the hands of a central executive authority, strictly controlled by the Parliament, but also strictly obeyed in the State, and combining every department—taxes, law courts, police, army, schools, civic control, general direction of commerce and industry—everything. By the side of this political concentration, they intended to proclaim complete freedom in commercial transactions, and at the same time to give free rein to industrial enterprise for the exploitation of all sorts of natural wealth, as well as of the workers, who henceforth would be delivered up defenceless to any one who might employ them.

All this was to be kept under the strict control of the State, which would favour the enrichment of the individual and the accumulation of large fortunes—two conditions to which great importance was necessarily attached by the middle classes, seeing that the States General itself had been convoked to ward off the financial ruin of the State.

On economic matters, the men of action belonging to the Third Estate held ideas no less precise. The French middle classes had studied Turgot and Adam Smith, the creators of political economy. They knew that the theories of those writers had already been applied in England, and they envied their middle-class neighbours across the Channel their powerful economic organisation, just as they envied them their political power. They dreamed of an appropriation of the land by the middle classes, both upper and lower, and of the revenue they would draw from the soil, which had hitherto lain unproductive in the hands of the nobility and the clergy. In this they were supported by the lower middle class settled in the country, who had become a power in the villages, even before the Revolution increased their number. They foresaw the rapid development of trade and the production of merchandise on a large scale by the help of machinery; they looked forward to a foreign trade with distant lands, and the exportation of manufactured goods across the seas to markets that would be opened in the East, to huge enterprises and colossal fortunes.

But before all this could be realised they knew the ties that bound the peasant to his village must be broken. It was necessary that he should be free to leave his hut, and even that he should be forced to leave it, so that he might be impelled towards the towns in search of work. Then, in changing masters, he would bring gold to trade, instead of paying to the landlords all sorts of rents, tithes, and taxes, which certainly pressed very heavily upon him, but which after all were not very profitable for the masters. And finally, the finances of the State had to be put in order; taxation would be simplified, and, at the same time, a bigger revenue obtained.

In short, what they wanted was what economists have called freedom of industry and commerce, but which really meant the relieving of industry from the harassing and repressive supervision of the State, and the giving to it full liberty to exploit the worker, who was still to be deprived of his freedom. There were to be no guilds, no trade societies; neither trade wardens nor master craftsmen; nothing which might in any way check the exploitation of the wage-earner. There was no longer to be any State supervision which might hamper the manufacturer. There were to be no duties on home industries, no prohibitive laws. For all the transactions of the employers, there was to be complete freedom, and for the workers a strict prohibition against combinations of any sort. *Laisser faire* for the one; complete denial of the right to combine for the others.

Such was the two-fold scheme devised by the middle classes. Therefore when the time came for its realisation, the middle classes, strengthened by their knowledge, the clearness of their views, and their business habits, without hesitating over their scheme as a whole or at any detail of it, set to work to make it become law. And this they did with a consistent and intelligent energy quite impossible to the masses of the people, because by them no ideal had been planned and elaborated which could have been opposed to the scheme of the gentlemen of the Third Estate.

It would certainly be unjust to say that the middle classes were actuated only by purely selfish motives. If that had been the case they would never have succeeded in their task. In great changes a certain amount of idealism is always necessary to success.

The best representatives of the Third Estate had, indeed, drunk from that sublime fount, the eighteenth-century philosophy, which was the source of all the great ideas that have arisen since. The eminently scientific spirit of this philosophy; its profoundly moral character, moral even when it mocked at conventional morality; its trust in the intelligence, strength, and greatness of the free man when he lives among his equals; its hatred of despotic institutions— were all accepted by the revolutionists of that time. Whence would they have drawn otherwise the powers of conviction and the devotion of which they gave such proofs in the struggle? It must also be owned that even among those who worked hardest to realise the programme of enriching the middle classes, there were some who seriously believed that the enrichment of the individual would be the best means of enriching the nation as a whole. Had not the best economists, with Adam Smith at their head, persuasively preached this view?

But however lofty were the abstract ideas of liberty, equality, and free progress that inspired the sincere men among the middle classes of 1789–1793, it is by their practical programme, by the application of their theories, that we must judge them. Into what deeds shall the abstract idea be translated in actual life? By that alone can we find its true measure.

If, then, it is only fair to admit that the middle classes of 1789 were inspired by ideas of liberty, equality (before the law), and political and religious freedom, we must also admit that these ideas, as soon as they took shape, began to develop exactly on the two lines we have just sketched; liberty to utilise the riches of Nature for personal aggrandisement, as well as liberty to exploit human labour without any safeguard for the victims of such exploitation, and political power organised so as to assure freedom of exploitation to the middle classes. And we shall see presently what terrible struggles were evolved in 1793 when one of the revolutionary parties wished to go further than this programme.

Action

But what of the people? What was their idea?

The people, too, had felt to a certain extent the influence of the current philosophy. By a thousand indirect channels the great principles of liberty and enfranchisement had filtered down to the villages and the suburbs of the large towns. Respect for royalty and aristocracy was passing away. Ideas of equality were penetrating to the very lowest ranks. Gleams of revolt flashed through many minds. The hope of an approaching change throbbed in the hearts of the humblest. "Something was to be done by some great folk for such poor ones"—she did not know who, nor how—"but God send us better," said an old woman, in 1789, to Arthur Young, who travelled through France on the eve of the Revolution. That "something" was bound to bring an alleviation of the people's misery.

The question whether the movement which preceded the Revolution, and the Revolution itself, contained any element of Socialism has been recently discussed. The word "Socialism" was certainly not in either, because it dates only from the middle of the nineteenth century. The idea of the State as Capitalist, to which the Social-Democratic fraction of the great Socialist party is now trying to reduce Socialism, was certainly not so much in evidence as it is today, because the founders of Social-Democratic "Collectivism," Vidal and Pecqueur, did not write until the period between 1840 and 1849. But it is impossible to read the words of the pre-Revolutionary writers without being struck by the fact that they are imbued with ideas which are the very essence of modern Socialism.

Two fundamental ideas—the equal rights of all citizens to the land, and what we know today under the name of communism—found devoted adherents among the more popular writers of that time, Mably, d'Argenson, and others of less importance. Manufacturing production on a large scale was in its infancy, so that land was at that time the main form of capital and the chief instrument for exploiting human labour, while the factory was hardly developed at all. It was natural, therefore, that the thoughts of the philosophers, and later on the thoughts of the revolutionists, should turn towards *communal possession of the land*. Did not Mably, who much more than Rousseau inspired the men of the Revolution, declare about 1768, in his *Doutes sur l'ordre naturel et essentiel des sociétés*, that there should be equal rights to the land for all, and communist possession of it? The rights of the nation to all landed property, and to all natural wealth—forests, rivers, waterfalls, etc.—was not this the dominant idea of the pre-Revolutionary writers, as well as of the left wing of the revolutionary masses during the period of upheaval?

Unfortunately, these communistic aspirations were not formulated clearly and concretely in the minds of those who desired the people's happiness. While among the educated middle classes the ideas of emancipation had taken the form of a complete programme for political and economic organisation, these ideas were presented to the people only in the form of vague aspirations. Often they were mere negations. Those who addressed the people did not try to embody the concrete form in which their *desiderata* could be realised. It is even probable that they avoided being precise. Consciously or not, they seemed to say: "What good is there in speaking to the people of the way in which they will be organised later on? It would only chill their revolutionary ardour. All they want is the strength to attack and to march to the assault of the old institutions. Later on we shall see what can be done for them."

Are there not many Socialists and Anarchists who act still in the same way? In their hurry to push on to the day of revolt they treat as soporific theorising every attempt to throw some light on what ought to be the aim of the Revolution.

It must be said, also, that the ignorance of the writers—city men and bookmen for the most part—counted for much in this. Thus, in the whole of that gathering of learned or experienced business men who composed the National Assembly—lawyers, journalists, tradesmen, and so forth—there were only two or three legal members who had studied the feudal laws, and we know there were among them but very few representatives of the peasants who were familiar by personal experience with the needs of village life.

For these reasons the ideas of the masses were expressed chiefly by simple negations. "Let us burn the registers in which the feudal dues are recorded! Down with the tithes! Down with 'Monsieur Veto'! Hang the aristocrats!" But to whom was the freed land to go? Who were to be the heirs of the guillotined nobles? Who was to grasp the political power when it should fall from the hands of "Monsieur Veto," the power which became in the hands of the middle classes a much more formidable weapon than it had been under the old *régime?*

This want of clearness in the mind of the people as to what they should hope from the Revolution left its imprint on the whole movement. While the middle classes were marching with firm and decided steps towards the establishment of their political power in a State which they were trying to mould, according to their preconceived ideas, the people were hesitating. In the towns, especially, they did not seem to know how to turn to their own advantage the power they had conquered. And later, when ideas concerning agrarian laws and the equalising of incomes began to take definite form, they ran foul of a mass of property prejudices, with which even those sincerely devoted to the cause of the people were imbued.

A similar conflict was evoked by the conceptions of the political organisation of the State. We see it chiefly in the antagonism which arose between the governmental prejudices of the democrats of that time and the ideas that dawned in the hearts of the people as to political decentralisation, and the prominent place which the people wished their municipalities to take both in the division of the large towns and in the village assemblies. This was the starting-point of the whole series of fierce contests which broke out in the Convention. Thence, too, arose the indefiniteness of the results obtained by the Revolution for the great mass of the people in all directions, except in the recovery of part of the land from the lords, lay and clerical, and the freeing of all land from the feudal taxes it formerly had to pay.

But if the people's ideas were confused on constructive lines, they were, on the other hand, extremely clear on certain points in their negations.

First of all, the hatred felt by the poor for the whole of the idle, lazy, perverted aristocracy who ruled them, while black misery reigned in the villages and in the dark lanes of the great towns. Next, hatred towards the clergy, who by sympathy belonged more to the aristocracy than to the people who fed them. Then, hatred of all the institutions under the old *régime*, which made poverty still harder to bear because they denied the rights of humanity to the poor. Hatred for the feudal system and its exactions, which kept the labourer in a state of servitude to the landowners long after personal serfdom had ceased to exist. Lastly, the despair of the peasant who in those years of scarcity saw land lying uncultivated in the hands of the lord, or serving merely as a pleasure-ground for the nobility while famine pressed hard on the villages.

It was all this hatred, coming to a head after long years as the selfishness of the rich became more and more apparent in the course of the eighteenth century. And it was this *need of land*—this *land hunger*, the cry of the starving in revolt against the lord who refused them access to it—that awoke the spirit of revolt ever since 1788. And it was the same hatred, and the same need, mingled with the hope of success, which stimulated the incessant revolts of the peasants in the years 1789–1793, revolts which enabled the middle classes to overthrow the old *régime* and to organise its own power under the new one, that of representative government.

Without those risings, without that disorganisation of authority in the provinces which resulted in never-ceasing *jacqueries*, without that promptitude of the people of Paris and other towns in taking

up arms, and in marching against the strongholds of royalty whenever an appeal to the people was made by the revolutionaries, the
middle classes would certainly not have accomplished anything.
But it is to this true fount and origin of the Revolution—the people's readiness to take up arms—that the historians of the Revolution have not yet done justice—the justice owed to it by the history
of civilisation.

Conclusion

When one sees that terrible and powerful Convention wrecking
itself in 1794–1795, that proud and strong Republic disappearing,
and France, after the demoralising *régime* of the Directory, falling
under the military yoke of a Bonaparte, one is impelled to ask,
"What was the good of the Revolution if the nation had to fall back
again under despotism?" In the course of the nineteenth century,
this question has been constantly put, and the timid and conservative have worn it threadbare as an argument against revolutions in
general.

The preceding pages supply the answer. Those who have seen in
the Revolution only a change in the Government, those who are
ignorant of its economic as well as its educational work, those
alone could put such a question.

The France we see during the last days of the eighteenth century,
at the moment of the *coup d'état* on the 18th Brumaire, is not the
France that existed before 1789. Would it have been possible for
the old France, wretchedly poor and with a third of her population
suffering yearly from dearth, to have maintained the Napoleonic
Wars, coming so soon after the terrible wars of the Republic between 1792 and 1799, when all Europe was attacking her?

The fact is, that a new France had been constituted since
1792–1793. Scarcity still prevailed in many of the departments,
and its full horrors were felt especially after the *coup d'état* of
Thermidor, when the maximum price for all food-stuffs was abolished. There were still some departments which did not produce
enough wheat to feed themselves, and as the war went on, and all
means of transport were requisitioned for its supplies, there was
scarcity in those departments. But everything tends to prove that
France was even then producing much more of the necessaries of
life of every kind than in 1789.

Never was there in France such energetic ploughing, Michelet
tells us, as in 1792, when the peasant was ploughing the lands he
had taken back from the lords, the convents, the churches, and was
goading his oxen to the cry of *"Allons Prusse! Allons Autriche!"*

Never had there been so much clearing of lands—even royalist writers admit this—as during those years of revolution. The first good harvest, in 1794, brought relief to two-thirds of France—at least in the villages, for all this time the towns were threatened with scarcity of food. Not that it was scarce in France as a whole, or that the *sans-culotte* municipalities neglected to take measures to feed those who could not find employment, but from the fact that all beasts of burden not actually used in tillage were requisitioned to carry food and ammunition to the fourteen armies of the Republic. In those days there were no railways, and all but the main roads were in the state they are to this day in Russia—well-nigh impassable.

A new France was born during those four years of revolution. For the first time in centuries the peasant ate his fill, straightened his back, and dared to speak out. Read the detailed reports concerning the return of Louis XVI to Paris, when he was brought back a prisoner from Varennes, in June 1791, by the peasants, and say: "Could such a thing, such an interest in the public welfare, such a devotion to it, and such an independence of judgment and action have been possible before 1789?" A new nation had been born in the meantime, just as we see today a new nation coming into life in Russia and in Turkey.

It was owing to this new birth that France was able to maintain her wars under the Republic and Napoleon, and to carry the principles of the Great Revolution into Switzerland, Italy, Spain, Belgium, Holland, Germany, and even to the borders of Russia. And when, after all those wars, after having mentally followed the French armies as far as Egypt and Moscow, we expect to find France in 1815 reduced to an appalling misery and her lands laid waste, we find, instead, that even in its eastern portions and in the Jura, the country is much more prosperous than it was at the time when Pétion, pointing out to Louis XVI the luxuriant banks of the Marne, asked him if there was anywhere in the world a kingdom more beautiful than the one the King had not wished to keep.

The self-contained energy was such in villages regenerated by the Revolution, that in a few years France became a country of well-to-do peasants, and her enemies soon discovered that in spite of all the blood she had shed and the losses she had sustained, France, in respect of her *productivity*, was the richest country in Europe. Her wealth, indeed, is not drawn from the Indies or from her foreign commerce: it comes from her own soil, from her love of the soil, from her own skill and industry. She is the richest country, because of the subdivision of her wealth, and she is still richer because of the possibilities she offers for the future.

Such was the effect of the Revolution. And if the casual observer sees in Napoleonic France only a love of glory, the historian realises that even the wars France waged at that period were undertaken to secure the fruits of the Revolution—to keep the lands that had been retaken from the lords, the priests, and the rich, and the liberties that had been won from despotism and the Court. If France was willing in those years to bleed herself to death, merely to prevent the Germans, the English, and the Russians from forcing a Louis XVIII upon her, it was because she did not want the return of the emigrant nobles to mean that the *ci-devants* would take back the lands which had been watered already with the peasant's sweat, and the liberties which had been sanctified with the patrons' blood. And France fought so well for twenty-three years, that when she was compelled at last to admit the Bourbons, it was she who imposed conditions on them. The Bourbons might reign, but the lands were to be kept by those who had taken them from the feudal lords, so that even during the White Terror of the Bourbons they dared not touch those lands. The old *régime* could not be re-established.

This is what is gained by making a Revolution.

There are other things to be pointed out. In the history of all nations a time comes when fundamental changes are bound to take place in the whole of the national life. Royal despotism and feudalism were dying in 1789; it was impossible to keep them alive; they had to go.

But then, two ways were opened out before France: reform or revolution.

At such times there is always a moment when reform is still possible; but if advantage has not been taken of that moment, if an obstinate resistance has been opposed to the requirements of the new life, up to the point when blood has flowed in the streets, as it flowed on July 14, 1789, then there must be a Revolution. And once the Revolution has begun, it must necessarily develop to its last conclusions—that is to say, to the highest point it is capable of attaining—were it only temporarily, being given a certain condition of the public mind at this particular moment.

If we represent the slow progress of a period of evolution by a line drawn on paper, we shall see this line gradually though slowly rising. Then there comes a Revolution, and the line makes a sudden leap upwards. In England the line would be represented as rising to the Puritan Republic of Cromwell; in France it rises to the *Sans-culotte* Republic of 1793. However, at this height progress cannot be maintained; all the hostile forces league together against it, and the Republic goes down. Our line, after having reached that height, drops. Reaction follows. For the political life of France the line drops very low indeed, but by degrees it rises again, and when peace is restored in 1815 in France, and in 1688 in England—both countries are found to have attained a level much higher than they were on prior to their Revolutions.

After that, evolution is resumed; our line again begins to rise slowly; but, besides taking place on a very much higher level, the rising of the line will in nearly every case be also much more rapid than before the period of disturbance.

This is a law of human progress, and also a law of individual progress. The more recent history of France confirms this very law by showing how it was necessary to pass through the Commune to arrive at the Third Republic.

The work of the French Revolution is not confined merely to what it obtained and what was retained of it in France. It is to be found also in the principles bequeathed by it to the succeeding century—in the line of direction it marked out for the future.

A reform is always a compromise with the past, but the progress accomplished by revolution is always a promise of future progress. If the Great French Revolution was the summing up of a century's evolution, it also marked out in its turn the programme of evolution to be accomplished in the course of the nineteenth century.

It is a law in the world's history that the period of a hundred or a hundred and thirty years, more or less, which passes between two great revolutions, receives its character from the revolution in which this period began. The nations endeavour to realise in their institutions the inheritance bequeathed to them by the last revolution. All that this last could not yet put into practice, all the great thoughts which were thrown into circulation during the turmoil, and which the revolution either could not or did not know how to apply, all the attempts at sociological reconstruction, which were born during the revolution, will go to make up the substance of evolution during the epoch that follows the revolution, with the addition of those new ideas to which this evolution will give birth, when trying to put into practice the programme marked out by the last upheaval. Then, a new revolution will be brought about in some other nation, and this nation in its turn will set the problems for the following century. Such has hitherto been the trend of history.

Two great conquests, in fact, characterise the century which has passed since 1789–1793. Both owe their origin to the French Revolution, which had carried on the work of the English Revolution while enlarging and invigorating it with all the progress that had been made since the English middle classes beheaded their King and transferred his power to the Parliament. These two great triumphs are: the abolition of serfdom and the abolition of absolutism, by which personal liberties have been conferred upon the individual, undreamt of by the serf of the lord and the subject of the absolute king, while at the same time they have brought about the development of the middle classes and the capitalist *régime*.

These two achievements represent the principal work of the nineteenth century, begun in France in 1789 and slowly spread over Europe in the course of that century.

The work of enfranchisement, begun by the French peasants in 1789, was continued in Spain, Italy, Switzerland, Germany, and Austria by the armies of the *sans-culottes*. Unfortunately, this work hardly penetrated into Poland and did not reach Russia at all.

The abolition of serfdom in Europe would have been already completed in the first half of the nineteenth century if the French *bourgeoisie*, coming into power in 1794 over the dead bodies of Anarchists, Cordeliers, and Jacobins, had not checked the revolutionary impulse, restored monarchy, and handed over France to the imperial juggler, the first Napoleon. This ex-*sans-culotte*, now a general of the *sans-culottes*, speedily began to prop up aristocracy; but the impulsion had been given, the institution of serfdom had already received a mortal blow. It was abolished in Spain and Italy in spite of the temporary triumph of reaction. It was closely pressed in Germany after 1811, and disappeared in that country definitively in 1848. In 1861, Russia was compelled to emancipate her serfs, and the war of 1878 put an end to serfdom in the Balkan peninsula.

The cycle is now complete. The right of the lord over the person of the peasant no longer exists in Europe, even in those countries where the feudal dues have still to be redeemed.

This fact is not sufficiently appreciated by historians. Absorbed as they are in political questions, they do not perceive the importance of the abolition of serfdom, which is, however, the essential feature of the nineteenth century. The rivalries between nations and the wars resulting from them, the policies of the Great Powers which occupy so much of the historian's attention, have all sprung from that one great fact—the abolition of serfdom and the development of the wage-system which has taken its place.

The French peasant, in revolting a hundred and twenty years ago against the lord who made him beat the ponds lest croaking frogs should disturb his master's sleep, has thus freed the peasants of all Europe. In four years, by burning the documents which registered his subjection, by setting fire to the *châteaux*, and by executing the owners of them who refused to recognise his rights as a human being, the French peasant so stirred up all Europe that it is today altogether free from the degradation of serfdom.

On the other hand, the abolition of absolute power has also

taken a little over a hundred years to make the tour of Europe. Attacked in England in 1648, and vanquished in France in 1789, royal authority based on divine right is no longer exercised save in Russia, but there, too, it is at its last gasp. Even the little Balkan States and Turkey have now their representative assemblies, and Russia is entering the same cycle.

In this respect the Revolution of 1789–1793 has also accomplished its work. Equality before the law and representative government have now their place in almost all the codes of Europe. In theory, at least, the law makes no distinction between men, and every one has the right to participate, more or less, in the government.

The absolute monarch—master of his subjects—and the lord—master of the soil and the peasants, by right of birth—have both disappeared. The middle classes now govern Europe.

But at the same time the Great Revolution has bequeathed to us some other principles of an infinitely higher import; the principles of communism. We have seen how all through the Great Revolution the communist idea kept coming to the front, and how after the fall of the Girondins, numerous attempts and sometimes great attempts were made in this direction. Fourierism descends in a direct line from L'Ange on one side and from Chalier on the other. Babeuf is the direct descendant of ideas which stirred the masses to enthusiasm in 1793; he, Buonarotti, and Sylvain Maréchal have only systematised them a little or even merely put them into literary form. But the secret societies organised by Babeuf and Buonarotti were the origin of the *communistes matérialistes* secret societies through which Blanqui and Barbès conspired under the *bourgeois* monarchy of Louis-Philippe. Later on, in 1866, the International Working Men's Association appeared in the direct line of descent from these societies. As to "socialism" we know now that this term came into vogue to avoid the term "communism," which at one time was dangerous because the secret communist societies became societies for action, and were rigorously suppressed by the *bourgeoisie* then in power.

There is, therefore, a direct filiation from the *Enragés* of 1793 and the Babeuf conspiracy of 1795 to the International Working Men's Association of 1866–1878.

There is also a direct descent of ideas. Up till now, modern socialism has added absolutely nothing to the ideas which were circulating among the French people between 1789 and 1794, and which it was tried to put into practice in the Year II of the Republic. Modern socialism has only systematised those ideas and found arguments in their favour, either by turning against the middle-class economists certain of their own definitions, or by generalising certain facts noticed in the development of industrial capitalism, in the course of the nineteenth century.

But I permit myself to maintain also that, however vague it may have been, however little support it endeavoured to draw from arguments dressed in a scientific garb, and however little use it made of the pseudo-scientific slang of the middle-class economists, the popular communism of the first two years of the Republic saw clearer, and went much deeper in its analyses, than modern socialism.

First of all, it was communism in the consumption of the necessaries of life—not in production only; it was the communalisation and the nationalisation of what economists know as consumption—to which the stern republicans of 1793 turned, above all, their attention, when they tried to establish their stores of grain and provisions in every commune, when they set on foot a gigantic inquiry to find and fix the true value of the objects of prime and secondary necessity, and when they inspired Robespierre to declare that *only the superfluity of foodstuffs should become articles of commerce, and that what was necessary belonged to all.*

Born out of the pressing necessities of those troublous years, the communism of 1793, with its affirmation of the right of all to sustenance and to the land for its production, its denial of the right of any one to hold more land than he and his family could cultivate —that is, more than a farm of 120 acres—and its attempt to communalise all trade and industry—this communism went straighter to the heart of things than all the minimum programmes of our own time, or even all the maximum preambles of such programmes.

In any case, what we learn today from the study of the Great Revolution is, that it was the source and origin of all the present communist, anarchist, and socialist conceptions. We have but badly understood our common mother, but now we have found her again in the midst of the *sans-culottes*, and we see what we have to learn from her.

Humanity advances by stages and these stages have been marked for several hundred years by great revolutions. After the Netherlands came England with her revolution in 1648–1657, and then it was the turn of France. Each great revolution has in it, besides, something special and original. England and France both abolished royal absolutism. But in doing so England was chiefly interested in the personal rights of the individual, particularly in matters of religion, as well as the local rights of every parish and every community. As to France, she turned her chief attention to the land question, and in striking a mortal blow at the feudal system she struck also at the great fortunes, and sent forth into the world the idea of nationalising the soil, and of socialising commerce and the chief industries.

Which of the nations will take upon herself the terrible but glorious task of the next great revolution? One may have thought for a time that it would be Russia. But if she should push her revolution further than the mere limitation of the imperial power; if she touches the land question in a revolutionary spirit—how far will she go? Will she know how to avoid the mistake made by the French Assemblies, and will she socialise the land and give it only to those who want to cultivate it with their own hands? We know not: any answer to this question would belong to the domain of prophecy.

The one thing certain is, that whatsoever nation enters on the path of revolution in our own day, it will be heir to all our fore-fathers have done in France. The blood they shed was shed for humanity—the sufferings they endured were borne for the entire human race; their struggles, the ideas they gave to the world, the shock of those ideas, are all included in the heritage of mankind. All have borne fruit and will bear more, still finer, as we advance towards those wide horizons opening out before us, where, like some great beacon to point the way, flame the words—LIBERTY, EQUALITY, FRATERNITY.

Selections from
The Conquest of Bread

Expropriation

It is told of Rothschild that, seeing his fortune threatened by the Revolution of 1848, he hit upon the following stratagem: "I am quite willing to admit," said he, "that my fortune has been accumulated at the expense of others, but if it were divided tomorrow among the millions of Europe, the share of each would only amount to five shillings. Very well, then, I undertake to render to each his five shillings if he asks me for it."

Having given due publicity to his promise, our millionaire proceeded as usual to stroll quietly through the street of Frankfort. Three or four passers-by asked for their five shillings, which he disbursed with a sardonic smile. His stratagem succeeded, and the family of the millionaire is still in possession of its wealth.

It is in much the same fashion that the shrewd heads among the middle classes reason when they say, "Ah, Expropriation! I know what that means. You take all the overcoats and lay them in a heap, and every one is free to help himself and fight for the best."

But such jests are irrelevant as well as flippant. What we want is not a redistribution of overcoats, although it must be said that even in such a case, the shivering folk would see advantage in it. Nor do we want to divide up the wealth of the Rothschilds. What we do want is so to arrange things that every human being born into the world shall be ensured the opportunity in the first instance of learning some useful occupation, and of becoming skilled in it; next, that he shall be free to work at his trade without asking leave of master or owner, and without handing over to landlord or capitalist the lion's share of what he produces. As to the wealth held by the Rothschilds or the Vanderbilts, it will serve us to organize our system of communal production.

The day when the labourer may till the ground without paying away half of what he produces, the day when the machines necessary to prepare the soil for rich harvest are at the free disposal of the cultivators, the day when the worker in the factory produces for

226

the community and not the monopolist—that day will see the workers clothed and fed, and there will be no more Rothschilds or other exploiters.

No one will then have to sell his working power for a wage that only represents a fraction of what he produces.

"So far so good," say our critics, "but you will have Rothschilds coming in from outside. How are you to prevent a person from amassing millions in China and then settling amongst you? How are you going to prevent such a one from surrounding himself with lackeys and wage-slaves—from exploiting them and enriching himself at their expense?

"You cannot bring about a revolution all over the world at the same time. Well, then, are you going to establish custom-houses on your frontiers to search all who enter your country and confiscate the money they bring with them,—Anarchist policemen firing on travellers would be a fine spectacle!"

But at the root of this argument there is a great error. Those who propound it have never paused to inquire whence come the fortunes of the rich. A little thought would, however, suffice to show them that these fortunes have their beginnings in the poverty of the poor. When there are no longer any destitute there will no longer be any rich to exploit them.

Let us glance for a moment at the Middle Ages, when great fortunes began to spring up.

A feudal baron seizes on a fertile valley. But as long as the fertile valley is empty of folk our baron is not rich. His land brings him in nothing; he might as well possess a property in the moon.

What does our baron do to enrich himself? He looks out for peasants—for poor peasants!

If every peasant-farmer had a piece of land, free from rent and taxes, if he had in addition the tools and the stock necessary for farm labour, who would plough the lands of the baron? Everyone would look after his own. But there are thousands of destitute persons ruined by wars, or drought, or pestilence. They have neither horse nor plough. (Iron was costly in the Middle Ages, and a draught-horse still more so.)

All these destitute creatures are trying to better their condition. One day they see on the road at the confines of our baron's estate a notice-board indicating by certain signs adapted to their comprehension that the labourer who is willing to settle on this estate will receive the tools and materials to build his cottage and sow his fields, and a portion of land rent free for a certain number of years. The number of years is represented by so many crosses on the sign-board, and the peasant understands the meaning of these crosses.

So the poor wretches swarm over the baron's lands, making

roads, draining marshes, building villages. In nine years he begins to tax them. Five years later he increases the rent. Then he doubles it. The peasant accepts these new conditions because he cannot find better ones elsewhere; and little by little, with the aid of laws made by the barons, the poverty of the peasant becomes the source of the landlord's wealth. And it is not only the lord of the manor who preys upon him. A whole host of usurers swoop down upon the villages, multiplying as the wretchedness of the peasants increases. That is how things went in the Middle Ages. And today is it not still the same thing? If there were free lands which the peasant could cultivate if he pleases, would he pay £50 to some "shabble of a Duke"[1] for condescending to sell him a scrap? Would he burden himself with a lease which absorbed a third of the produce? Would he—on the *métayer* system—consent to give the half of his harvest to the landowner?

But he has nothing. So he will accept any conditions, if only he can keep body and soul together, while he tills the soil and enriches the landlord.

So in the nineteenth century, just as in the Middle Ages, the poverty of the peasant is a source of wealth to the landed proprietor.

The landlord owes his riches to the poverty of the peasants, and the wealth of the capitalist comes from the same source.

Take the case of a citizen of the middle class, who somehow or other finds himself in possession of £20,000. He could, of course, spend his money at the rate of £2,000 a year, a mere bagatelle in these days of fantastic, senseless luxury. But then he would have nothing left at the end of ten years. So, being a "practical person," he prefers to keep his fortune intact, and win for himself a snug little annual income as well.

This is very easy in our society, for the good reason that the towns and villages swarm with workers who have not the wherewithal to live for a month, or even a fortnight. So our worthy citizen starts a factory. The banks hasten to lend him another £20,000, especially if he has a reputation for "business ability"; and with this round sum he can command the labour of five hundred hands.

If all the men and women in the country-side had their daily bread sure and their daily needs already satisfied, who would work for our capitalist at a wage of half a crown a day, while the commodities one produces in a day sell in the market for a crown or more?

---

1. "Shabble of a Duke" is an expression coined by Carlyle; it is a somewhat free rendering of Kropotkin's "Monsieur le Vicomte," but I think it expresses his meaning.—*Trans.*

Unhappily—we know it all too well—the poor quarters of our towns and the neighbouring villages are full of needy wretches, whose children clamour for bread. So, before the factory is well finished, the workers hasten to offer themselves. Where a hundred are required three hundred besiege the doors, and from the time his mill is started the owner, if he only has average business capacities, will clear £ 40 a year out of each mill-hand he employs.

He is thus able to lay by a snug little fortune; and if he chooses a lucrative trade and has "business talents" he will soon increase his income by doubling the number of the men he exploits.

So he becomes a personage of importance. He can afford to give dinners to other personages—to the local magnates, the civic, legal, and political dignitaries. With his money he can "marry money"; by and by he may pick and choose places for his children, and later on perhaps get something good from the Government—a contract for the army or for the police. His gold breeds gold; till at last a war, or even a rumour of war, or a speculation on the Stock Exchange, gives him his great opportunity.

Nine-tenths of the great fortunes made in the United States are (as Henry George has shown in his "Social Problems") the result of knavery on a large scale, assisted by the State. In Europe, nine-tenths of the fortunes made in our monarchies and republics have the same origin. There are not two ways of becoming a millionaire.

This is the secret of wealth; find the starving and destitute, pay them half a crown, and make them produce five shillings worth in the day, amass a fortune by these means, and then increase it by some lucky hit, made with the help of the State.

Need we go on to speak of small fortunes attributed by the economists to forethought and frugality, when we know that mere saving in itself brings in nothing, so long as the pence saved are not used to exploit the famishing?

Take a shoemaker, for instance. Grant that his work is well paid, that he has plenty of custom, and that by dint of strict frugality he contrives to lay by from eighteen pence to two shillings a day, perhaps two pounds a month.

Grant that our shoemaker is never ill, that he does not half starve himself, in spite of his passion for economy; that he does not marry or that he has no children; that he does not die of consumption; suppose anything and everything you please!

Well, at the age of fifty he will not have scraped together £ 800; and he will not have enough to live on during his old age, when he is past work. Assuredly this is not how great fortunes are made. But suppose our shoemaker, as soon as he has laid by a few pence, thriftily conveys them to the savings bank, and that the savings bank lends them to the capitalist who is just about to "employ labour," *i.e.* to exploit the poor. Then our shoemaker takes an apprentice, the child of some poor wretch, who will think himself lucky if in five years time his son has learned the trade and is able to earn his living.

Meanwhile our shoemaker does not lose by him, and if trade is brisk he soon takes a second, and then a third apprentice. By and by he will take two or three working men—poor wretches, thankful to receive half a crown a day for work that is worth five shillings, and if our shoemaker is "in luck," that is to say, if he is keen enough and mean enough, his working men and apprentices will bring him in nearly one pound a day, over and above the product of his own toil. He can then enlarge his business. He will gradually become rich, and no longer have any need to stint himself in the necessaries of life. He will leave a snug little fortune to his son.

That is what people call "being economical and having frugal, temperate habits." At bottom it is nothing more nor less than grinding the face of the poor.

Commerce seems an exception to this rule. "Such a man," we are told, "buys tea in China, brings it to France, and realizes a profit of thirty per cent on his original outlay. He has exploited nobody."

Nevertheless the case is analogous. If our merchant had carried his bales on his back, well and good! In early mediaeval times that was exactly how foreign trade was conducted, and so no one reached such giddy heights of fortune as in our days. Very few and very hardly earned were the gold coins which the mediaeval merchant gained from a long and dangerous voyage. It was less the love of money than the thirst of travel and adventure that inspired his undertakings.

Nowadays the method is simpler. A merchant who has some capital need not stir from his desk to become wealthy. He telegraphs to an agent telling him to buy a hundred tons of tea; he freights a ship, and in a few weeks, in three months if it is a sailing ship, the vessel brings him his cargo. He does not even take the risks of the voyage, for his tea and his vessel are insured, and if he has expended four thousand pounds he will receive more than five thousand; that is to say, if he has not attempted to speculate in some novel commodities, in which case he runs a chance of either doubling his fortune or losing it altogether.

Now, how could he find men willing to cross the sea, to travel to China and back, to endure hardship and slavish toil and to risk their lives for a miserable pittance? How could he find dock labourers willing to load and unload his ships for "starvation wages"? How? Because they are needy and starving. Go to the seaports, visit the cook-shops and taverns on the quays, and look at these men who have come to hire themselves, crowding round the dock-gates, which they besiege from early dawn, hoping to be allowed to work on the vessels. Look at these sailors, happy to be hired for a long voyage, after weeks and months of waiting. All their lives long they have gone to the sea in ships, and they will sail in others still, until they have perished in the waves.

Enter their homes, look at their wives and children in rags, living one knows not how till the father's return, and you will have the answer to the question. Multiply examples, choose them where you will, consider the origin of all fortunes, large or small, whether arising out of commerce, finance, manufactures, or the land. Everywhere you will find that the wealth of the wealthy springs from the poverty of the poor. This is why an anarchist society need not fear the advent of a Rothschild who would settle in its midst. If every member of the community knows that after a few hours of productive toil he will have a right to all the pleasures that civilization procures, and to those deeper sources of enjoyment which art and science offer to all who seek them, he will not sell his strength for a starvation wage. No one will volunteer to work for the enrichment of your Rothschild. His golden guineas will be only so many pieces of metal—useful for various purposes, but incapable of breeding more.

In answering the above objection we have at the same time indicated the scope of Expropriation. It must apply to everything that enables any man—be he financier, mill-owner, or landlord—to appropriate the product of others' toil. Our formula is simple and comprehensive.

We do not want to rob any one of his coat, but we wish to give to the workers all those things the lack of which makes them fall an easy prey to the exploiter, and we will do our utmost that none shall lack aught, that not a single man shall be forced to sell the strength of his right arm to obtain a bare subsistence for himself and his babes. This is what we mean when we talk of Expropriation; this will be our duty during the Revolution, for whose coming we look, not two hundred years hence, but soon, very soon.

The ideas of Anarchism in general and of Expropriation in particular find much more sympathy than we are apt to imagine among men of independent character, and those for whom idleness is not the supreme ideal. "Still," our friends often warn us, "take care you do not go too far! Humanity cannot be changed in a day, so do not be in too great a hurry with your schemes of Expropriation and Anarchy, or you will be in danger of achieving no permanent result."

Now, what we fear with regard to Expropriation is exactly the contrary. We are afraid of not going far enough, of carrying out Expropriation on too small a scale to be lasting. We would not have the revolutionary impulse arrested in mid-career, to exhaust itself in half measures, which would content no one, and while producing a tremendous confusion in society, and stopping its customary activities, would have no vital power—would merely spread general discontent and inevitably prepare the way for the triumph of reaction.

There are, in fact, in a modern State established relations which it is practically impossible to modify if one attacks them only in detail. There are wheels within wheels in our economic organization—the machinery is so complex and interdependent that no one part can be modified without disturbing the whole. This becomes clear as soon as an attempt is made to expropriate anything.

Let us suppose that in a certain country a limited form of expropriation is effected. For example, that, as it has been suggested more than once, only the property of the great landlords is socialized, whilst the factories are left untouched; or that, in a certain city, house property is taken over by the Commune, but everything else is left in private ownership; or that, in some manufacturing centre, the factories are communalized, but the land is not interfered with.

The same result would follow in each case—a terrible shattering of the industrial system, without the means of reorganizing it on new lines. Industry and finance would be at a deadlock, yet a return to the first principles of justice would not have been achieved, and society would find itself powerless to construct a harmonious whole.

If agriculture could free itself from great landowners, while industry still remained the bond-slave of the capitalist, the merchant, and the banker, nothing would be accomplished. The peasant suffers today not only in having to pay rent to the landlord; he is oppressed on all hands by existing conditions. He is exploited by the tradesman, who makes him pay half a crown for a spade which, measured by the labour spent on it, is not worth more than six-pence. He is taxed by the State, which cannot do without its formidable hierarchy of officials, and finds it necessary to maintain an expensive army, because the traders of all nations are perpetually fighting for the markets, and any day a little quarrel arising from the exploitation of some part of Asia or Africa may result in war.

Then again the peasant suffers from the depopulation of country places: the young people are attracted to the large manufacturing towns by the bait of high wages paid temporarily by the producers of articles of luxury, or by the attractions of a more stirring life. The artificial protection of industry, the industrial exploitation of foreign countries, the prevalence of stock-jobbing, the difficulty of improving the soil and the machinery of production—all these agencies combine nowadays to work against agriculture, which is burdened not only by rent, but by the whole complex of conditions in a society based on exploitation. Thus, even if the expropriation of land were accomplished, and every one were free to till the soil and cultivate it to the best advantage, without paying rent, agriculture, even though it should enjoy—which can by no means be taken for granted—a momentary prosperity, would soon fall back into the slough in which it finds itself today. The whole thing would have to be begun over again, with increased difficulties.

The same holds true of industry. Take the converse case: instead of turning the agricultural labourers into peasant-proprietors, make over the factories to those who work in them. Abolish the master-manufacturers, but leave the landlord his land, the banker his money, the merchant his Exchange, maintain the swarm of idlers who live on the toil of the workmen, the thousand and one middle-men, the State with its numberless officials, and industry would come to a standstill. Finding no purchasers in the mass of peasants who would remain poor; not possessing the raw material, and un-able to export their produce, partly on account of the stoppage of trade, and still more so because industries spread all over the world, the manufacturers would feel unable to struggle, and thousands of workers would be thrown upon the streets. These starving crowds would be ready and willing to submit to the first schemer who came to exploit them; they would even consent to return to the old slavery, if only under promise of work.

Or, finally, suppose you oust the landowners, and hand over the mills and factories to the worker, without interfering with the swarm of middlemen who drain the product of our manufacturers, and speculate in corn and flour, meat and groceries, in our great centres of commerce. Then, as soon as exchange is arrested, the great cities are left without bread, and others find no buyers for their articles of luxury, a terrible counter-revolution will take place—a counter-revolution treading upon the slain, sweeping the towns and villages with shot and shell; there would be proscriptions, panic, flight, and all the terrors of the guillotine, as it was in France in 1815, 1848, and 1871.

All is interdependent in a civilized society; it is impossible to reform any one thing without altering the whole. Therefore, on the day we strike at private property, under any one of its forms, territorial or industrial, we shall be obliged to attack them all. The very success of the Revolution will demand it.

Besides, we could not, if we would, confine ourselves to a partial expropriation. Once the principle of the "Divine Right of Property" is shaken, no amount of theorizing will prevent its overthrow, here by the slaves of the toil, there by the slaves of the machine.

If a great town, Paris for example, were to confine itself to taking possession of the dwelling houses or the factories, it would be forced also to deny the right of the bankers to levy upon the Commune a tax amounting to £ 2,000,000, in the form of interest for former loans. The great city would be obliged to put itself in touch with the rural districts, and its influence would inevitably urge the peasants to free themselves from the landowner. It would be necessary to communalize the railways, that the citizens might get food and work, and lastly, to prevent the waste of supplies, and to guard against the trusts of corn-speculators, like those to whom the Commune of 1793 fell a prey, it would have to place in the hands of the City the work of stocking its warehouses with commodities, and apportioning the produce.

Nevertheless, some Socialists still seek to establish a distinction. "Of course," they say, "the soil, the mines, the mills, and manufactures must be expropriated, these are the instruments of production, and it is right we should consider them public property. But articles of consumption—food, clothes, and dwellings—should remain private property."

Popular common sense has got the better of this subtle distinction. We are not savages who can live in the woods, without other shelter than the branches. The civilized man needs a roof, a room, a hearth, and a bed. It is true that the bed, the room, and the house is a home of idleness for the non-producer. But for the worker, a room, properly heated and lighted, is as much an instrument of production as the tool or the machine. It is the place where the nerves and sinews gather strength for the work of the morrow. The rest of the workman is the daily repairing of the machine.

The same argument applies even more obviously to food. The so-called economists of whom we speak would hardly deny that the coal burnt in a machine is as necessary to production as the raw material itself. How then can food, without which the human machine could do no work, be excluded from the list of things indispensable to the producer? Can this be a relic of religious metaphysics? The rich man's feast is indeed a matter of luxury, but the food of the worker is just as much a part of production as the fuel burnt by the steam-engine.

The same with clothing. If the economists who draw this distinction between articles of production and of consumption dressed themselves in the fashion of New Guinea, we could understand their objection. But men who could not write a word without a shirt on their back are not in a position to draw such a hard and fast line between their shirt and their pen. And though the dainty gowns of their dames must certainly rank as objects of luxury, there is nevertheless a certain quantity of linen, cotton, and woollen stuff which is a necessity of life to the producer. The shirt and shoes in which he goes to his work, his cap and the jacket he slips on after the day's toil is over, these are as necessary to him as the hammer to the anvil.

Whether we like it or not, this is what the people mean by a revolution. As soon as they have made a clean sweep of the Government, they will seek first of all to ensure to themselves decent dwellings and sufficient food and clothes—free of capitalist rent.

And the people will be right. The methods of the people will be much more in accordance with science than those of the economists who draw so many distinctions between instruments of production and articles of consumption. The people understand that this is just the point where the Revolution ought to begin; and they will lay the foundations of the only economic science worthy the name—a science which might be called: *"The Study of the Needs of Humanity, and of the Economic Means to satisfy them."*

Dwellings

Those who have closely watched the growth of certain ideas among the workers must have noticed that on one momentous question—the housing of the people, namely—a definite conclusion is being imperceptibly arrived at. It is a known fact that in the large towns of France, and in many of the smaller ones also, the workers are coming gradually to the conclusion that dwelling-houses are in no sense the property of those whom the State recognizes as their owners.

This idea has evolved naturally in the minds of the people, and nothing will ever convince them again that the "rights of property" ought to extend to houses.

The house was not built by its owner. It was erected, decorated, and furnished by innumerable workers—in the timber yard, the brick field, and the workshop, toiling for dear life at a minimum wage.

The money spent by the owner was not the product of his own toil. It was amassed, like all other riches, by paying the workers two-thirds or only a half of what was their due.

Moreover—and it is here that the enormity of the whole proceeding becomes most glaring—the house owes its actual value to the profit which the owner can make out of it. Now, this profit results from the fact that his house is built in a town possessing bridges, quays, and fine public buildings, and affording to its inhabitants a thousand comforts and conveniences unknown in villages; a town well paved, lighted with gas, in regular communication with other towns, and itself a centre of industry, commerce, science, and art; a town which the work of twenty or thirty generations has gone to render habitable, healthy, and beautiful.

A house in certain parts of Paris may be valued at thousands of pounds sterling, not because thousands of pounds' worth of labour have been expended on that particular house, but because it is in Paris; because for centuries workmen, artists, thinkers, and men of learning and letters have contributed to make Paris what it is today —a centre of industry, commerce, politics, art, and science; because Paris has a past; because, thanks to literature, the names of its streets are household words in foreign countries as well as at home; because it is the fruit of eighteen centuries of toil, the work of fifty generations of the whole French nation.

Who, then, can appropriate to himself the tiniest plot of ground, or the meanest building, without commiting a flagrant injustice? Who, then, has the right to sell to any bidder the smallest portion of the common heritage?

On that point, as we have said, the workers are agreed. The idea of free dwellings showed its existence very plainly during the siege of Paris, when the cry was for an abatement pure and simple of the terms demanded by the landlords. It appeared again during the Commune of 1871, when the Paris workmen expected the Communal Council to decide boldly on the abolition of rent. And when the New Revolution comes, it will be the first question with which the poor will concern themselves.

Whether in time of revolution or in time of peace, the worker must be housed somehow or other; he must have some sort of roof over his head. But, however tumble-down and squalid your dwelling may be, there is always a landlord who can evict you. True, during the Revolution he cannot find bailiffs and police-sergeants to throw your rags and chattels into the street, but who knows what the new Government will do tomorrow? Who can say that it will not call in the aid of force again, and set the police pack upon you to hound you out of your hovels? We have seen the Commune proclaim the remission of rents due up to the first of April only![2] After that rent had to be paid, though Paris was in a state of chaos, and industry at a standstill; so that the revolutionist had absolutely nothing to depend upon but his allowance of fifteen pence a day!

Now the worker must be made to see clearly that in refusing to pay rent to a landlord or owner he is not simply profiting by the disorganization of authority. He must understand that the abolition

2. The decree of the 30 March: by this decree rents due up to the terms of Oc-   tober, 1870, and January and April, 1871, were annulled.

of rent is a recognized principle, sanctioned, so to speak, by popular assent; that to be housed rent-free is a right proclaimed aloud by the people.

Are we going to wait till this measure, which is in harmony with every honest man's sense of justice, is taken up by the few socialists scattered among the middle-class elements, of which the Provisionary Government will be composed? We should have to wait long—till the return of reaction, in fact!

This is why, refusing uniforms and badges—those outward signs of authority and servitude—and remaining people among the people, the earnest revolutionists will work side by side with the masses, that the abolition of rent, the expropriation of houses, may become an accomplished fact. They will prepare the ground and encourage ideas to grow in this direction; and when the fruit of their labours is ripe, the people will proceed to expropriate the houses without giving heed to the theories which will certainly be thrust in their way—theories about paying compensation to landlords, and finding first the necessary funds.

On the day that the expropriation of houses takes place, on that day, the exploited workers will have realized that the new times have come, that Labour will no longer have to bear the yoke of the rich and powerful, that Equality has been openly proclaimed, that this Revolution is a real fact, and not a theatrical make-believe, like so many others preceding it.

If the idea of Expropriation be adopted by the people it will be carried into effect in spite of all the "insurmountable" obstacles with which we are menaced.

Of course, the good folk in new uniforms, seated in the official arm-chairs of the Hôtel de Ville, will be sure to busy themselves in heaping up obstacles. They will talk of giving compensation to the landlords, of preparing statistics, and drawing up long reports. Yes, they would be capable of drawing up reports long enough to outlast the hopes of the people, who, after waiting and starving in enforced idleness, and seeing nothing come of all these official researches, would lose heart and faith in the Revolution and abandon the field to the reactionaries. The new bureaucracy would end by making expropriation hateful in the eyes of all.

Here, indeed, is a rock which might shipwreck our hopes. But if the people turn a deaf ear to the specious arguments used to dazzle them, and realize that new life needs new conditions, and if they undertake the task themselves, then Expropriation can be effected without any great difficulty.

"But how? How can it be done?" you ask us. We shall try to reply to this question, but with a reservation. We have no intention of tracing out the plans of Expropriation in their smallest details. We know beforehand that all that any man, or group of men, could suggest today would be far surpassed by the reality when it comes. Man will accomplish greater things, and accomplish them better and by simpler methods than those dictated to him beforehand. Thus we are content to indicate the manner by which Expropriation *might* be accomplished without the intervention of Government. We do not propose to go out of our way to answer those who declare that the thing is impossible. We confine ourselves to replying that we are not the upholders of any particular method of organization. We are only concerned to demonstrate that Expropriation *could* be effected by popular initiative, and *could not* be effected by any other means whatever.

It seems very likely that, as soon as Expropriation is fairly started, groups of volunteers will spring up in every district, street, and block of houses, and undertake to inquire into the number of flats and houses which are empty and of those which are over-crowded, the unwholesome slums and the houses which are too spacious for their occupants and might well be used to house those who are stifled in swarming tenements. In a few days these volunteers would have drawn up complete lists for the street and the district of all the flats, tenements, family mansions, and villa residences, all the rooms and suites of rooms, healthy and unhealthy, small and large, foetid dens and homes of luxury.

Freely communicating with each other, these volunteers would soon have their statistics complete. False statistics can be manufactured in board rooms and offices, but true and exact statistics must begin with the individual and mount up from the simple to the complex.

Then, without waiting for any one's leave, those citizens will probably go and find their comrades who were living in miserable garrets and hovels and will say to them simply: "It is a real Revolution this time, comrades, and no mistake about it. Come to such a place this evening; all the neighbourhood will be there; we are going to redistribute the dwelling-houses. If you are tired of your slum-garret, come and choose one of the flats of five rooms that are to be disposed of, and when you have once moved in you shall stay, never fear. The people are up in arms, and he who would venture to evict you will have to answer to them."

"But every one will want a fine house or a spacious flat!" we are told. No, you are mistaken. It is not the people's way to clamour for the moon. On the contrary, every time we have seen them set about repairing a wrong we have been struck by the good sense and instinct for justice which animates the masses. Have we ever known them [to] demand the impossible? Have we ever seen the people of

Paris fighting among themselves while waiting for their rations of bread or firewood during the two sieges? The patience and resignation which prevailed among them was constantly held up to admiration by the foreign Press correspondents; and yet these patient waiters knew full well that the last comers would have to pass the day without food or fire.

We do not deny that there are plenty of egotistic instincts in isolated individuals in our societies. We are quite aware of it. But we contend that the very way to revive and nourish these instincts would be to confine such questions as the housing of the people to any board or committee, in fact, to the tender mercies of officialism in any shape or form. Then indeed all the evil passions spring up, and it becomes a case of who is the most influential person on the board. The least inequality causes wranglings and recriminations. If the smallest advantage is given to any one, a tremendous hue and cry is raised—and not without reason.

But if the people themselves, organized by streets, districts, and parishes, undertake to move the inhabitants of the slums into the half-empty dwellings of the middle classes, the trifling inconveniences, the little inequalities will be easily tided over. Rarely has appeal been made to the good instincts of the masses—only as a last resort, to save the sinking ship in times of revolution—but never has such an appeal been made in vain; the heroism, the self-devotion of the toiler has never failed to respond to it. And thus it will be in the coming Revolution.

But, when all is said and done, some inequalities, some inevitable injustices, will remain. There are individuals in our societies whom no great crisis can lift out of the deep ruts of egoism in which they are sunk. The question, however, is not whether there will be injustices or no, but rather how to limit the number of them.

Now all history, all the experience of the human race, and all social psychology, unite in showing that the best and fairest way is to trust the decision to those whom it concerns most nearly. It is they alone who can consider and allow for the hundred and one details which must necessarily be overlooked in any merely official redistribution.

Moreover, it is by no means necessary to make straightway an absolutely equal redistribution of all the dwellings. There will no doubt be some inconveniences at first, but matters will soon be righted in a society which has adopted Expropriation.

When the masons, and carpenters, and all who are concerned in house building, know that their daily bread is secured to them, they will ask nothing better than to work at their old trades a few hours a day. They will adapt the fine houses which absorbed the time of a whole staff of servants, and in a few months homes will have sprung up, infinitely healthier and more conveniently arranged than those of today. And to those who are not yet comfortably housed the anarchist Commune will be able to say: "Patience, comrades! Palaces fairer and finer than any the capitalists built for themselves will spring from the ground of our enfranchised city. They will belong to those who have most need of them. The anarchist Commune does not build with an eye to revenues. These monuments erected to its citizens, products of the collective spirit, will serve as models to all humanity; they will be yours."

If the people of the Revolution expropriate the houses and proclaim free lodgings—the communalizing of houses and the right of each family to a decent dwelling—then the Revolution will have assumed a communistic character from the first, and started on a course from which it will be by no means easy to turn it. It will have struck a fatal blow at individual property.

For the expropriation of dwellings contains in germ the whole social revolution. On the manner of its accomplishment depends the character of all that follows. Either we shall start on a good road leading straight to anarchist communism, or we shall remain sticking in the mud of despotic individualism.

It is easy to see the numerous objections—theoretic on the one hand, practical on the other—with which we are sure to be met. As it will be a question of maintaining iniquity at any price, our opponents will of course protest "in the name of justice." "Is it not a crying shame," they will exclaim, "that the people of Paris should take possession of all these fine houses, while the peasants in the country have only tumble-down huts to live in?" But do not let us make a mistake. These enthusiasts for justice forget, by a lapse of memory to which they are subject, the "crying shame" which they themselves are tacitly defending. They forget that in this same city the worker, with his wife and children, suffocates in a noisome garret, while from his window he sees the rich man's palace. They forget that whole generations perish in crowded slums, starving for air and sunlight, and that to redress this injustice ought to be the first task of the Revolution.

Do not let these disingenuous protests hold us back. We know that any inequality which may exist between town and country in the early days of the Revolution will be transitory and of a nature to right itself from day to day; for the village will not fail to improve its dwellings as soon as the peasant has ceased to be the beast of burden of the farmer, the merchant, the money-lender, and the State. In order to avoid an accidental and transitory inequality, shall we stay our hand from righting an ancient wrong?

The so-called practical objections are not very formidable either.

We are bidden to consider the hard case of some poor fellow who by dint of privation has contrived to buy a house just large enough to hold his family. And we are going to deprive him of his hard-earned happiness, to turn him into the street! Certainly not. If his house is only just large enough for his family, by all means let him stay there. Let him work in his little garden too; our "boys" will not hinder him—nay, they will lend him a helping hand if need be. But suppose he lets lodgings, suppose he has empty rooms in his house; then the people will make the lodger understand that he need not pay his former landlord any more rent. Stay where you are, but rent free. No more duns and collectors; Socialism has abolished all that!

Or again, suppose that the landlord has a score of rooms all to himself, and some poor woman lives near by with five children in one room. In that case the people would see whether, with some alterations, these empty rooms could not be converted into a suit-able home for the poor woman and her five children. Would not that be more just and fair than to leave the mother and her five little ones languishing in a garret, while Sir Gorgeous Midas sat at his ease in an empty mansion? Besides, good Sir Gorgeous would probably hasten to do it of his own accord; his wife will be de-lighted to be freed from half her big, unwieldy house when there is no longer a staff of servants to keep it in order.

"So you are going to turn everything upside down," say the defenders of law and order. "There will be no end to the evictions and removals. Would it not be better to start fresh by turning everybody out of doors and redistributing the houses by lot?" Thus our critics; but we are firmly persuaded that if no Government interferes in the matter, if all the changes are entrusted to those free groups which have sprung up to undertake the work, the evictions and removals will be less numerous than those which take place in one year under the present system, owing to the rapacity of land-lords.

In the first place, there are in all large towns almost enough empty houses and flats to lodge all the inhabitants of the slums. As to the palaces and suites of fine apartments, many working people would not live in them if they could. One could not "keep up" such houses without a large staff of servants. Their occupants would soon find themselves forced to seek less luxurious dwellings. The fine ladies would find that palaces were not well adapted to self-help in the kitchen. Gradually people would shake down. There would be no need to conduct Dives to a garret at the bayonet's point, or install Lazarus in Dives's palace by the help of an armed escort. People would shake down amicably into the available dwell-ings with the least possible friction and disturbance. Have we not

the example of the village communes redistributing fields and disturbing the owners of the allotments so little that one can only
praise the intelligence and good sense of the methods they employ.
Fewer fields change hands under the management of the Russian
Commune than where personal property holds sway, and is for ever
carrying its quarrels into courts of law. And are we to believe that
the inhabitants of a great European city would be less intelligent
and less capable of organization than Russian or Hindoo peasants?

Moreover, we must not blink the fact that every revolution
means a certain disturbance to everyday life, and those who expect
this tremendous lift out of the old grooves to be accomplished
without so much as jarring the dishes on their dinner tables will
find themselves mistaken. It is true that Governments can change
without disturbing worthy citizens at dinner, but the crimes of
society towards those who have nourished and supported it are not
to be redressed by any such political sleight of parties.

Undoubtedly there will be a disturbance, but it must not be of
pure destruction; it must be minimized. And again—it is impossible
to lay too much stress on this maxim—it will be by addressing
ourselves to the interested parties, and not to boards and committees, that we shall best succeed in reducing the sum of inconveniences for everybody.

The people commit blunder on blunder when they have to
choose by ballot some hare-brained candidate who solicits the
honour of representing them, and takes upon himself to know all,
to do all, and to organize all. But when they take upon themselves
to organize what they know, what touches them directly, they do it
better than all the "talking-shops" put together. Is not the Paris
Commune an instance in point? and the great dockers' strike? and
have we not constant evidence of this fact in every village commune?

Selections from
Fields, Factories, and Workshops

The Decentralisation of Industries

Who does not remember the remarkable chapter by which Adam Smith opens his inquiry into the nature and causes of the wealth of nations? Even those of our contemporary economists who seldom revert to the works of the father of political economy, and often forget the ideas which inspired them, know that chapter almost by heart, so often has it been copied and recopied since. It has become an article of faith; and the economical history of the century which has elapsed since Adam Smith wrote has been, so to speak, an actual commentary upon it.

"Division of labour" was its watchword. And the division and subdivision—the permanent subdivision—of functions has been pushed so far as to divide humanity into castes which are almost as firmly established as those of old India. We have, first, the broad division into producers and consumers: little-consuming producers on the one hand, little-producing consumers on the other hand. Then, amidst the former, a series of further subdivisions: the manual worker and the intellectual worker, sharply separated from one another to the detriment of both; the agricultural labourers and the workers in the manufacture; and, amidst the mass of the latter, numberless subdivisions again—so minute, indeed, that the modern ideal of a workman seems to be a man or a woman, or even a girl or a boy, without the knowledge of any handicraft, without any conception whatever of the industry he or she is employed in, who is only capable of making all day long and for a whole life the same infinitesimal part of something, who from the age of thirteen to that of sixty pushes the coal cart at a given spot of the mine or makes the spring of a pen-knife or "the eighteenth part of a pin." Mere servants to some machine of a given description; mere flesh-and-bone parts of some immense machinery; having no idea how and why the machinery performs its rhythmical movements.

Skilled artisanship is being swept away as a survival of a past condemned to disappear. For the artist who formerly found aesthetic enjoyment in the work of his hands is substituted the human slave of an iron slave. Nay, even the agricultural labourer, who formerly used to find a relief from the hardships of his life in the home of his ancestors—the future home of his children—in his love of the field, and in a keen intercourse with nature, even he has been doomed to disappear for the sake of division of labour. He is an anachronism we are told; he must be substituted, in a Bonanza farm, by an occasional servant hired for the summer, and discharged as the autumn comes, a tramp who will never again see the field he has harvested once in his life. "An affair of a few years," the economists say, "to reform agriculture in accordance with the true principles of division of labour and modern industrial organisation."

Dazzled with the results obtained by our century of marvellous inventions, especially in England, our economists and political men went still farther in their dreams of division of labour. They proclaimed the necessity of dividing the whole of humanity into national workshops having each of them its own speciality. We were taught, for instance, that Hungary and Russia are predestined by nature to grow corn in order to feed the manufacturing countries; that Britain had to provide the world-market with cottons, iron goods, and coal; Belgium with woollen cloth; and so on. Nay, within each nation, each region had to have its own speciality. So it has been for some time since; so it ought to remain. Fortunes have been made in this way, and will continue to be made in the same way. It being proclaimed that the wealth of nations is measured by the amount of profits made by the few, and that the largest profits are made by means of a specialisation of labour, the question was not conceived to exist as to whether human beings *would* always submit to such a specialisation; whether nations could be specialised like isolated workmen. The theory was good for today—why should we care for tomorrow? Tomorrow might bring its own theory!

And so it did. The narrow conception of life which consisted in thinking that *profits* are the only leading motive of human society; and the stubborn view which supposes that what has existed yesterday would last for ever, proved in disaccordance with the tendencies of human life; and life took another direction. Nobody will deny the high pitch of production which may be attained by specialisation. But, precisely in proportion as the work required from the individual in modern production becomes simpler and easier to be learned, and, therefore, also more monotonous and wearisome— the requirements of the individual for varying his work, for exercising all his capacities, become more and more prominent. Humanity perceives that there is no advantage for the community in riveting a human being for all his life to a given spot, in a workshop or a mine; no gain in depriving him of such work as would bring him into free intercourse with nature, make of him a conscious part of the grand whole, a partner in the highest enjoyments of science and art, of free work and creation.

Nations, too, refuse to be specialised. Each nation is a compound aggregate of tastes and inclinations, of wants and resources, of capacities and inventive powers. The territory occupied by each nation is again a most varied texture of soils and climates, of hills and valleys, of slopes leading to a still greater variety of territories and races. Variety is the distinctive feature, both of the territory and its inhabitants; and that variety implies a variety of occupations. Agriculture calls manufactures into existence, and manufactures support agriculture. Both are inseparable; and the combination, the integration of both, brings about the grandest results. * * *

When we thus revert from the scholastics or our text-books, and examine human life as a whole, we soon discover that, while all the benefits of a temporary division of labour must be maintained, it is high time to claim those of the *integration of labour*. Political economy has hitherto insisted chiefly upon *division*. We proclaim *integration*; and we maintain that the ideal of society—that is, the state towards which society is already marching—is a society of integrated labour; a society where each individual is a producer of both manual and intellectual work; where each able-bodied human being is a worker, and where each worker works both in the field and the industrial workshop; where each aggregation of individuals, large enough to dispose of a certain variety of natural resources—it may be a nation, or rather a region—produces and itself consumes most of its own agricultural and manufactured produce.

Of course as long as society remains organised so as to permit the owners of the land and capital to appropriate for themselves, under the protection of the State and historical rights, the yearly surplus of human production, no such change can be thoroughly accomplished. But the present industrial system, based upon a permanent specialisation of functions, already bears in itself the germs of its proper ruin. The industrial crises, which grow more acute and protracted, and are rendered still worse and still more acute by the armaments and wars implied by the present system, are rendering its maintenance more and more difficult. Moreover, the workers plainly manifest their intention to support no longer patiently the misery occasioned by each crisis. And each crisis accelerates the day when the present institutions of individual property and production will be shaken to their foundations with such internal struggles as will depend upon the more or less good sense of the now privileged classes.

But we maintain also that any Socialist attempt at remodelling the present relations between Capital and Labour will be a failure, if it does not take into account the above tendencies towards integration. Those tendencies have not yet received, in our opinion, due attention from the different Socialist schools—but they must. A reorganised society will have to abandon the fallacy of nations specialised for the production of either agricultural or manufactured produce. It will have to rely on itself for the production of food and many if not most of the raw materials; it must find the best means of combining agriculture with manufacture—the work in the field with a decentralised industry—and it will have to provide for "integrated education," which education alone, by teaching both science and handicraft from earliest childhood, can give to society the men and women it really needs.

Each nation her own agriculturist and manufacturer; each individual working in the field and in some industrial art; each individual combining scientific knowledge with the knowledge of a handicraft—such is, we affirm, the present tendency of civilised nations.

The prodigious growth of industries in Great Britain, and the simultaneous development of the international traffic which now permits the transport of raw materials and articles of food on a gigantic scale, have created the impression that a few nations of West Europe were destined to become *the* manufacturers of the world. They need only—it was argued—to supply the market with manufactured goods, and they will draw from all over the surface of the earth the food they cannot grow themselves, as well as the raw materials they need for their manufactures. The steadily increasing speed of transoceanic communications and the steadily increasing facilities of shipping have contributed to enforce the above impression. If we take the enthusiastic pictures of international traffic, drawn in such a masterly way by Neumann Spallart —the statistician and almost the poet of the world-trade—we are inclined indeed to fall into ecstasy before the results achieved. "Why shall we grow corn, rear oxen and sheep, and cultivate orchards, go through the painful work of the labourer and the farmer, and anxiously watch the sky in fear of a bad crop, when we can get, with much less pain, mountains of corn from India, America, Hungary, or Russia, meat from New Zealand, vegetables from the Azores, apples from Canada, grapes from Malaga, and so on?" exclaim the West Europeans. "Already now," they say, "our food consists, even in modest households, of produce gathered from all over the globe. Our cloth is made out of fibres grown and wool sheared in all parts of the world. The prairies of America and Australia; the mountains and steppes of Asia; the frozen wildernesses of the Arctic regions; the deserts of Africa and the depths of the oceans; the tropics and the lands of the midnight sun are our tributaries. All races of men contribute their share in supplying us with our staple food and luxuries, with plain clothing and fancy dress, while we are sending them in exchange the produce of our higher intelligence, our technical knowledge, our powerful industrial and commercial organising capacities! Is it not a grand sight, this busy and intricate exchange of produce all over the earth which has suddenly grown up within a few years?"

Grand it may be, but is it not a mere nightmare? Is it necessary? At what cost has it been obtained, and how long will it last?

Let us turn eighty years back. France lay bleeding at the end of the Napoleonic wars. Her young industry, which had begun to grow by the end of the last century, was crushed down. Germany, Italy, were powerless on the industrial field. The armies of the great Republic had struck a mortal blow to serfdom on the Continent; but with the return of reaction efforts were made to revive the decaying institution, and serfdom meant no industry worth speaking of. The terrible wars between France and England, which wars are often explained by merely political causes, had a much deeper meaning—an economical meaning. They were wars for the supremacy on the world market, wars against French commerce and industry—and Britain won the battle. She became supreme on the seas. Bordeaux was no more a rival to London, and the French industries seemed to be killed in the bud. And, favoured by the powerful impulse given to natural sciences and technology by the great era of inventions, finding no serious competitors in Europe, Britain began to develop her manufactures. To produce on a large scale in immense quantities became the watchword. The necessary human forces were at hand in the peasantry, partly driven by force from the land, partly attracted to the cities by high wages. The necessary machinery was created, and the British production of manufactured goods went on at a gigantic pace. In the course of less than seventy years—from 1810 to 1878—the output of coal grew from 10 to 133,000,000 tons; the imports of raw materials rose from 30 to 380,000,000 tons; and the exports of manufactured goods from 46 to 200,000,000 pounds. The tonnage of the commercial fleet was nearly trebled. Fifteen thousand miles of railways were built.

It is useless to repeat at what a cost the above results were achieved. The terrible revelations of the parliamentary commissions of 1840–42 as to the atrocious condition of the manufacturing classes, the tales of "cleared estates" and kidnapped children are still fresh in the memory. They will remain standing monuments for showing by what means the great industry was implanted in this country. But the accumulation of wealth in the hands of the privileged classes was going on at a speed never dreamed of before. The incredible riches which now astonish the foreigner in the private houses of England were accumulated during that period; the exceedingly expensive standard of life which makes a person considered rich on the Continent appear as only of modest means in Britain was introduced during that time. The taxed property alone doubled during the last thirty years of the above period, while during the same years (1810 to 1878) no less than £ 1,112,000,000 —nearly £ 2,000,000,000 by this time—was invested by English capitalists either in foreign industries or in foreign loans.

But the monopoly of industrial production could not remain with England for ever. Neither industrial knowledge nor enterprise could be kept for ever as a privilege of these islands. Necessarily, fatally, they began to cross the Channel and spread over the Continent. The Great Revolution had created in France a numerous class of peasant-proprietors, who enjoyed nearly half a century of a comparative well-being, or, at least, of a guaranteed labour. The ranks of homeless town workers increased slowly. But the middle-class revolution of 1789–1793 had already made a distinction between the peasant householders and the village *prolétaires*, and, by favouring the former to the detriment of the latter, it compelled the labourers who had no household nor land to abandon their villages, and thus to form the first nucleus of working classes given up to the mercy of manufacturers. Moreover, the peasant-proprietors themselves, after having enjoyed a period of undeniable prosperity, began in their turn to feel the pressure of bad times, and were compelled to look for employment in manufactures. Wars and revolution had checked the growth of industry; but it began to grow again during the second half of our century; it developed, it improved; and now, notwithstanding the loss of Alsace, France is no longer the tributary to England for manufactured produce which she was forty years ago. Today her exports of manufactured goods are valued at nearly one-half of those of Great Britain, and two-thirds of them are textiles; while her imports of the same consist chiefly of the finer sorts of cotton and woollen yarn—partly re-exported as stuffs—and a small quantity of woollen goods. For her own consumption France shows a decided tendency towards becoming entirely a self-supporting country, and for the sale of her manufactured goods she is tending to rely, not on her colonies, but especially on her own wealthy home market.

Germany follows the same lines. During the last twenty-five years, and especially since the last war, her industry has undergone a thorough reorganisation. Her machinery has been thoroughly improved, and her new-born manufactures are supplied with a machinery which mostly represents the last word of technical progress; she has plenty of workmen and technologists endowed with a superior technical and scientific education; and in an army of learned chemists, physicists and engineers her industry has a most powerful and intelligent aid. As a whole, Germany offers now the spectacle of a nation in a period of *Aufschwung*, with all the forces of a new start in every domain of life. Thirty years ago she was a customer to England. Now she is already a competitor in the markets of the south and east, and at the present speedy rate of growth of her industries her competition will be soon yet more acute than it is.

The wave of industrial production, after having had its origin in the north-west of Europe, spreads towards the east and south-east, always covering a wider circle. And, in proportion as it advances east, and penetrates into younger countries, it implants there all the improvements due to a century of mechanical and chemical inventions; it borrows from science all the help that science can give to industry; and it finds populations eager to grasp the last results of modern knowledge. The new manufactures of Germany begin where Manchester arrived after a century of experiments and gropings; and Russia begins where Manchester and Saxony have now reached. Russia, in her turn, tries to emancipate herself from her dependency upon Western Europe, and rapidly begins to manufacture all those goods she formerly used to import, either from Britain or from Germany.

* * *

The monopoly of the first comers on the industrial field has ceased to exist. And it will exist no more, whatever may be the spasmodic efforts made to return to a state of things already belonging to the domain of history. New ways, new issues must be looked for: the past *has* lived, and it will live no more.

* * *

. . . Where half a century was required in olden times to develop an industry, a few years are sufficient now. In the year 1864 only 160,000 cwts. of raw cotton were imported into Germany, and only 16,000 cwts. of cotton goods were exported; cotton spinning and weaving were mostly insignificant home industries. Twenty years later the imports of raw cotton were already 3,600,000 cwts., and in another two years they rose to 5,556,000 cwts.; while the exports of cotton stuffs and yarn were valued at £ 3,600,000 in 1883, and £ 7,662,000 in 1893. A great industry was thus created in less than thirty years. . . . One can easily win applause from uninformed auditories by exclaiming with more or less pathos that German produce can *never* equal the English! The fact is that it competes in cheapness, and sometimes also—where it is needed—in an equally good workmanship; and this circumstance is due to many causes.

The "cheap labour" cause, so often alluded to in discussions about "German competition" which take place in this country and in France, must be dismissed by this time, since it has been well proved by so many recent investigations that low wages and long hours do not necessarily mean cheap produce. Cheap labour and protection simply mean the possibility for a number of employers to continue working with obsolete and bad machinery; but in highly developed staple industries, such as the cotton and the iron industries, the cheapest produce is obtained with high wages, short hours and the best machinery. When the number of operatives which is required for each 1,000 spindles can vary from seventeen (in many Russian factories) to three (in England), no reduction of wages can possibly compensate for that immense difference. Consequently, in the best German cotton-mills and iron-works the wages of the worker . . . are not lower than they are in Great Britain. All that can be said is, that the worker in Germany gets more for his wages than he gets in this country—the paradise of the middle-man—a paradise which it will remain so long as it lives chiefly on imported food produce.

The chief reason for the successes of Germany in the industrial field is the same as it is for the United States. Both countries just now enter the industrial phase of their development, and they enter it with all the energy of youth and novelty. Both countries enjoy a widely-spread scientifically-technical—or, at least, concrete scientific—education. In both countries manufactories are built according to the newest and best models which have been worked out elsewhere; and both countries are in a period of awakening in all branches of activity—literature and science, industry and trade. They enter on the same phase in which Great Britain was in the first half of this century, when British workers invented so much of the wonderful modern machinery.

We have simply before us a fact of *the consecutive development of nations*. And instead of decrying or opposing it, it would be much better to see whether the two pioneers of the great industry—Britain and France—cannot take a new initiative and do something new again; whether an issue for the creative genius of these two nations must not be sought for in a new direction—namely, the utilisation of both the land and the industrial powers of man for securing well-being to the whole nation instead of to the few.

* * *

Progress is in . . . producing for home use. The customers for the Lancashire cottons and the Sheffield cutlery, the Lyons silks and the Hungarian flour-mills, are not in India nor in Africa. They are amidst the home producers. No use to send floating shops to New Guinea with German or British millinery when there are plenty of would-be customers for British millinery in these very islands, and for German goods in Germany. And, instead of worrying our brains by schemes for getting customers abroad, it would be better to try to answer the following questions: Why the British worker, whose industrial capacities are so highly praised in political speeches; why the Scotch crofter and the Irish peasant, whose obstinate labours in creating new productive soil out of peat bogs are occasionally so much spoken of, are no customers to the Lancashire weavers, the Sheffield cutlers and the Northumbrian and Welsh pitmen? Why the Lyons weavers not only do not wear silks, but sometimes have no food in their attics? Why the Russian peasants sell their corn, and for four, six, and sometimes eight months every year are compelled to mix bark and auroch grass to a handful of flour for baking their bread? Why famines are so common amidst the growers of wheat and rice in India?

Under the present conditions of division into capitalists and labourers, into property-holders and masses living on uncertain wages, the spreading of industries over new fields is accompanied by the very same horrible facts of pitiless oppression, massacre of children, pauperism, and insecurity of life. The Russian Fabrics Inspector's Reports, the Reports of the Plauen Handelskammer, and the Italian inquests are full of the same revelations as the Reports of the Parliamentary Commissions of 1840 to 1842, or the modern revelations with regard to the "sweating system" at Whitechapel and Glasgow, and London pauperism. The Capital and Labour problem is thus universalised; but, at the same time, it is also simplified. To return to a state of affairs where corn is grown, and manufactured goods are fabricated, for the use of those very people who grow and produce them—such will be, no doubt, the problem to be solved during the next coming years of European history. Each region will become its own producer and its own consumer of manufactured goods. But that unavoidably implies that, at the same time, it will be its own producer and consumer of agricultural produce; and that is precisely what I am going to discuss next.

The Possibilities of Agriculture

. . . We have been taught, both by economists and politicians, that the territories of the West European States are so overcrowded with inhabitants that they cannot grow all the food and raw produce which are neccesary for the maintenance of their steadily

increasing populations. Therefore the necessity of exporting manufactured goods and of importing food. And we are told, moreover,
that even if it were possible to grow in Western Europe all the food
necessary for its inhabitants, there would be no advantage in doing
so as long as the same food can be got cheaper from abroad. Such
are the present teachings and the ideas which are current in society
at large. And yet it is easy to prove that both are totally erroneous:
plenty of food could be grown on the territories of Western Europe
for much more than their present populations, and an immense
benefit would be derived from doing so. These are the two points
which I have now to discuss.

To begin by taking the most disadvantageous case: is it possible
that the soil of Great Britain, which at present yields food for one-
third only of its inhabitants, could provide all the necessary amount
and variety of food for 33,000,000 human beings when it covers
only 56,000,000 acres all told—forests and rocks, marshes and peat
bogs, cities, railways and fields—out of which only 33,000,000
acres are considered as cultivable? The current opinion is, that it by
no means can; and that opinion is so inveterate that we even see
men of science, who are generally cautious when dealing with
current opinions, endorse that opinion without even taking the
trouble of verifying it. It is accepted as an axiom. And yet, as soon
as we try to find out any argument in its favour, we discover that it
has not the slightest foundation, either in facts or in judgment upon
well-known facts.

Let us take, for instance, J. B. Lawes' estimates of crops which
are published every year in *The Times*. In his estimate of the year
1887 he made the remark that during the eight harvest years
1853–1860 "nearly three-fourths of the aggregate amount of wheat
consumed in the United Kingdom was of home growth, and little
more than one-fourth was derived from foreign sources"; but five
and twenty years later the figures were almost reversed, that is,
"during the eight years 1879–1886, little more than one-third has
been provided by home crops and nearly two-thirds by imports."
But neither the increase of population by 8,000,000 nor the increase of consumption of wheat by six-tenths of a bushel per head
could account for the change. In the years 1853–60 the soil of
Britain nourished one inhabitant on every two acres cultivated:
why did it require three acres in order to nourish the same inhabitant in 1887? The answer is plain: merely and simply because
agriculture had fallen into neglect.

In fact, the area under wheat had been reduced since 1853–60
by full 1,590,000 acres, and therefore the average crop of the years
1883–86 was below the average crop of 1853–60 by more than

40,000,000 bushels; and this deficit alone represented the food of more than 7,000,000 *inhabitants*. At the same time the area under barley, oats, beans, and other spring crops had also been reduced by a further 560,000 acres, which, at the low average of thirty bushels per acre, would have represented the cereals necessary to complete the above for the same 7,000,000 inhabitants. And it could be said that if the United Kingdom imported cereals for 17,000,000 inhabitants in 1887, instead of for 10,000,000 in 1860, it was simply because more than 2,000,000 acres had gone out of cultivation. These facts are well known; but usually they are met with the remark that the character of agriculture had been altered; that instead of growing wheat, meat and milk were produced in this country. . . .

Need I say . . . that quite to the contrary of what we are told about the British agriculturists becoming "meat-makers" instead of "wheat-growers" no increase of live stock took place during the last ten years. Where, indeed, could they find their food? Far from devoting the land freed from cereals to "meat-making," the country further reduced its live stock. It had 6,597,964 head of horned cattle in 1885, and 6,354,336 only in 1895; 26,534,600 sheep in 1885 and 25,792,200 sheep in 1895. True, the number of horses was increased; every butcher and greengrocer runs now a horse "to take orders at the gents' doors" (in Sweden and Switzerland, by the way, they do it by telephone); and consequently Great Britain has 1,545,228 horses instead of the 1,408,788 she had in 1885. But the horses are imported, as also the oats and a considerable amount of the hay that is required for feeding them. And if the consumption of meat has really increased in this country, it is due to cheap imported meat, not to the meat that would be produced in these islands. In short, agriculture has not changed its direction, as we are often told; it simply went down in all directions. Land is going out of culture at a perilous rate, while the latest improvements in market-gardening, fruit-growing, and poultry-keeping are but a mere trifle if we compare them with what has been done in the same direction in France, Belgium, and America.

The cause of this general downward movement is self-evident. It is the desertion, the abandonment of the land. Each crop requiring human labour has had its area reduced; and one-third of the agricultural labourers have been sent away since 1861 to reinforce the ranks of the unemployed in the cities, so that far from being over-populated, the fields of Britain are *starved of human labour* as James Caird used to say. The British nation does not work on her soil; she is prevented from doing so; and the would-be economists complain that the soil will not nourish its inhabitants!

I once took a knapsack and went on foot out of London, through Sussex. I had read Léonce de Lavergne's work and expected to find a soil busily cultivated; but neither round London nor still less farther south did I see men in the fields. In the Weald I could walk for twenty miles without crossing anything but heath or woodlands, rented as pheasant-shooting grounds to "London gentlemen," as the labourers said. "Ungrateful soil" was my first thought; but then I would occasionally come to a farm at the crossing of two roads and see the same soil bearing a rich crop; and my next thought was *tel seigneur, telle terre,* as the French peasants say. Later on I saw the rich fields of the midland counties; but even there I was struck by not perceiving the same busy human labour which I was accustomed to admire on the Belgian and French fields. But I ceased to wonder when I learnt that only 1,383,000 men and women in England and Wales work in the fields, while more than 16,000,000 belong to the "professional, domestic, indefinite, and unproductive class," as these pitiless statisticians say. One million and three hundred thousand human beings cannot productively cultivate an area of 33,000,000 acres unless they can resort to the Bonanza farm's methods of culture.

Again, taking Harrow as the centre of my excursions, I could walk five miles towards London, or turning my back upon it, and I could see nothing east or west but meadow land on which they hardly cropped two tons of hay per acre—scarcely enough to keep alive one milch cow on each two acres. Man is conspicuous by his absence from those meadows; he rolls them with a heavy roller in the spring; he spreads some manure every two or three years; then he disappears until the time has come to make hay. And that—within ten miles from Charing Cross, close to a city with 5,000,000 inhabitants, supplied with Flemish and Jersey potatoes, French salads, and Canadian apples. In the hands of the Paris gardeners, each thousand acres situated within the same distance from the city would be cultivated by at least 2000 human beings, who would get vegetables to the value of from £50 to £300 per acre. But here the acres which only need human hands to become an inexhaustible source of golden crops lie idle, and they say to us, "Heavy clay!" without even knowing that in the hands of man there are no unfertile soils; that the most fertile soils are not in the prairies of America, nor in the Russian steppes; that they are in the peat-bogs of Ireland, on the sand downs of the northern sea-coast of France, on the craggy mountains of the Rhine, where they have been made by man's hands.

The most striking fact is, however, that in some undoubtedly fertile parts of the country things are even in a worse condition. My heart simply ached when I saw the state in which land is kept in

South Devon, and when I learned to know what "permanent pasture" means. Field after field is covered with nothing but grass,
three inches high, and thistles in profusion. Twenty, thirty such
fields can be seen at one glance from the top of every hill; and
thousands of acres are in that state, notwithstanding that the grandfathers of the present generation have devoted a formidable amount
of labour to the clearing of that land from the stones, to fencing it,
roughly draining it and the like. In every direction I could see
abandoned cottages and orchards going to ruin. A whole population has disappeared, and even its last vestiges must disappear if
things continue to go on as they have gone. And this takes place in
a part of the country endowed with a most fertile soil and possessed
of a climate which is certainly more congenial than the climate of
Jersey in spring and early summer—a land upon which even the
poorest cottagers occasionally raise potatoes as early as the first
half of May. But how can that land be cultivated when there is
nobody to cultivate it? "We have fields; men go by, but never go
in," an old labourer said to me; and so it is in reality.

It will be said, of course, that the above opinion strangely contrasts with the well-known superiority of British agriculture. Do we
not know, indeed, that British crops average twenty-eight bushels of
wheat per acre, while in France they reach only seventeen bushels?
Does it not stand in all almanacs that Britain gets every year
£180,000,000 sterling worth of animal produce—milk, cheese,
meat, and wool—from her fields? All that is true, and there is no
doubt that in many respects British agriculture is superior to that of
many other nations. As regards obtaining the greatest amount of
produce with the least amount of labour, Britain undoubtedly took
the lead until she was superseded by America. Again, as regards the
fine breeds of cattle, the splendid state of the meadows, and the
results obtained in separate farms, there is much to be learned
from Britain. But a closer acquaintance with British agriculture as
a whole discloses many features of inferiority. However splendid, a
meadow remains a meadow, much inferior in productivity to a
cornfield; and the fine breeds of cattle appear to be poor creatures
as long as each ox requires three acres of land to be fed upon.
Certainly one may indulge in some admiration at the average
twenty-eight bushels grown in this country; but when we learn that
only 1,417,000 acres, out of the cultivable 33,000,000, bear such
crops, we are quite disappointed. Any one could obtain like results
if he were to put all his manure into one-twentieth part of the area
which he possesses. Again, the twenty-eight bushels no longer appear to us so satisfactory when we learn that without any manuring, merely by means of a good culture, they have obtained at

Rothamstead an average of fourteen bushels per acre from the same plot of land for forty consecutive years; while with manuring they obtain thirty-eight bushels instead of twenty-eight, and under the allotment system the crops reach forty bushels. In some farms they occasionally attain even fifty and fifty-seven bushels per acre.

If we intend to have a correct appreciation of British agriculture, we must not base it upon what is obtained on a few selected and well-manured plots; we must inquire what is done with the territory, taken as a whole. Now, out of each 1000 acres of the aggregate territory of England, Wales and Scotland, 418 acres are left under wood, coppice, heath, buildings and so on. We need not find fault with that division, because it depends very much upon natural causes. In France and Belgium one-third of the territory is in like manner also treated as uncultivable, although portions of it are continually reclaimed and brought under culture. But, leaving aside the "uncultivable" portion, let us see what is done with the 582 acres out of 1000 of the "cultivable" part (32,777,000 acres in Great Britain). First of all, it is divided into two almost equal parts, and one of them—295 acres out of 1000—is left under "permanent pasture," that is, in most cases it is entirely uncultivated. Very little hay is obtained from it, and some cattle are grazed upon it. More than one-half of the cultivable area is thus left without cultivation, and the remainder, *i.e.*, 287 acres only out of each 1000 acres, is under culture. Out of these last, 110 acres are under corn crops, twenty-one acres under potatoes, fifty-seven acres under green crops, and eighty-four acres under clover fields and grasses under rotation. And finally, out of the 110 acres given to corn crops, the best twenty-five acres (one-fortieth part of the territory, one-twenty-third of the cultivable area) are picked out and sown with wheat. They are well cultivated, well manured, and upon them an average of twenty-eight bushels to the acre is obtained; and upon these twenty-five acres out of 1000 the world superiority of British agriculture is based.

The net result of all that is, that on nearly 33,000,000 acres of cultivable land the food is grown for one-third part only of the population (two-thirds of the food it consumes is imported), and we may say accordingly that, although nearly two-thirds of the territory is cultivable, British agriculture provides home-grown food for each 125 or 130 inhabitants only per square mile (out of 378). In other words, nearly three acres of the *cultivable area* are required to grow the food for each person. Let us then see what is done with the land in France and Belgium.

Now, if we simply compare the average twenty-eight bushels per acre of wheat in Great Britain with the average seventeen bushels in France, the comparison is all in favour of these islands; but such averages are of little value because the two systems of agriculture are totally different in the two countries. The Frenchman also has his picked and heavily manured "twenty-five acres" in the north of France and in Ile-de-France, and from these picked acres he obtains average crops ranging from thirty-one to thirty-three bushels'. However, he sows with wheat, not only the best picked out acres, but also such fields on the Central Plateau and in Southern France as hardly yield ten, eight, and even six bushels to the acre, without irrigation; and these low crops reduce the average for the whole country. The Frenchman cultivates much that is left here under permanent pasture—and this is what is described as his "inferiority" in agriculture. In fact, although the proportion between what we have named the "cultivable area" and the total territory is very much the same in France as it is in Great Britain (624 acres out of each 1000 acres of the territory), the area under wheat crops is nearly *six times* as great, in proportion, as what it is in Great Britain (146 acres instead of twenty-five, out of each 1000 acres); the corn crops altogether cover more than two-fifths of the cultivable area, and large areas are given besides to green crops, industrial crops, vine, fruit, and vegetables.

Taking everything into consideration, although the Frenchman keeps less cattle, and especially grazes less sheep than the Briton, he nevertheless obtains from his soil nearly all the food that he and his cattle consume. He imports, in an average year, but one-tenth only of what the nation consumes, and he exports to this country considerable quantities of food produce (£ 10,000,000 worth), not only from the south, but also, and especially, from the shores of the Channel (Brittany butter and vegetables; fruit and vegetables from the suburbs of Paris, and so on).

The net result is that, although one-third part of the territory is also treated as "uncultivable," the soil of France yields the food for 170 inhabitants per square mile (out of 188), that is, for forty persons more, per square mile, than this country.

It is thus apparent that the comparison with France is not so much in favour of this country as it is said to be. . . . As to the comparison with Belgium, it is even more striking—the more so as the two systems of culture are similar in both countries. To begin with, in Belgium we also find an average crop of twenty-seven and eight-tenths bushels of wheat to the acre; but the area given to wheat is five times as big as Great Britain, in comparison to the cultivable area, and the cereals cover almost one half of the land available for culture. . . . All taken, they grow in Belgium more than 76,000,000 bushels of cereals, *i.e.*, fifteen and seven-tenths bushels per acre of the cultivable area, while the corresponding figure for Great Britain is only eight and a half bushels; and they keep almost twice as much cattle upon each cultivable acre as is kept in Great Britain. Large portions of the land are given besides to the culture of industrial plants, potatoes for spirit, beet for sugar, and so on.

However, it must not be believed that the soil of Belgium is more fertile than the soil of this country. On the contrary, to use the words of Laveleye, "only one half, or less, of the territory offers natural conditions which are favourable for agriculture"; the other half consists of a gravelly soil, or sands, "the natural sterility of which could be overpowered only by heavy manuring." Man, not nature, has given to the Belgian soil its present productivity. With this soil and labour, Belgium succeeds in supplying nearly all the food of a population which is denser than that of England and Wales, and numbers 544 inhabitants to the square mile. If the exports and imports of agricultural produce from and into Belgium be taken into account, we can say that Laveleye's conclusions are still good, and that only one inhabitant out of each ten to twenty requires imported food. The soil of Belgium supplies with home-grown food no less than 490 *inhabitants per square mile*, and there remains something for export—no less than £1,000,000 worth of agricultural produce being exported every year to Great Britain. Besides, it must not be forgotten that Belgium is a manufacturing country which exports home-made goods to the value of £9 per head of population, . . . while the total exports from the United Kingdom attain only £6 7s. per inhabitant. As to separate parts of the Belgian territory, the small and naturally unfertile province of West Flanders not only grows the food of its 580 inhabitants on the square mile, but exports agricultural produce to the value of 25s. per head of its population. And . . . Flemish agriculture would have realised still better results were it not hampered in its growth by the steady and heavy increase of rent. In the face of the rent being increased each nine years, many farmers have lately abstained from further improvements.

Without going as far as China, I might quote similar examples from elsewhere, especially from Lombardy. But the above will be enough to caution the reader against hasty conclusions as to the impossibility of feeding 39,000,000 people from 78,000,000 acres. They also will enable me to draw the following conclusions: (1) If the soil of the United Kingdom were cultivated only as it *was* thirty-five years ago, 24,000,000 people, instead of 17,000,000 could live on home-grown food; and that culture, while giving occupation to an additional 750,000 men, would give nearly 3,000,000 wealthy home customers to the British manufactures. (2) If the cultivable area of the United Kingdom were cultivated as the soil is cultivated *on the average* in Belgium, the United Kingdom would have food for at least 37,000,000 inhabitants; and it might export agricultural produce without ceasing to manufacture so as freely to supply all the needs of a wealthy population. And finally (3), if the population of this country came to be doubled, all that would be required for producing the food for 80,000,000 inhabitants would be to cultivate the soil as it is cultivated in the best farms of this country, in Lombardy, and in Flanders, and to utilise some meadows, which at present lie almost unproductive, in the same way as the neighbourhoods of the big cities in France are utilised for market-gardening. All these are not fancy dreams, but mere realities; nothing but modest conclusions from what we see round about us, without any allusion to the agriculture of the future.

If we want, however, to know what agriculture *can be*, and what can be grown on a given amount of soil, we must apply for information to such regions as the district of Saffelare in East Flanders, the island of Jersey, or the irrigated meadows of Lombardy. . . . Or else we may apply to the market-gardeners in this country, or in the neighbourhoods of Paris or in Holland, to the "truck farms" in America, and so on.

While science devotes its chief attention to industrial pursuits, a limited number of lovers of nature and a legion of workers whose very names will remain unknown to posterity have created of late a quite new agriculture, as superior to modern farming as modern farming is superior to the old three-fields system of our ancestors. Science seldom guided them, and sometimes misguided—as was the case with Liebig's theories, developed to the extreme by his followers, who induced us to treat plants as glass recipients of chemical drugs, and who forgot that the only science capable of dealing with life and growth is physiology, not chemistry. Science seldom has guided them: they proceeded in the empirical way; but, like the cattle-growers who opened new horizons to biology, they have opened a new field of experimental research for the physiology of plants. They have created a totally new agriculture. They smile when we boast about the rotation system, having permitted us to take from the field one crop every year, or four crops each three years, because their ambition is to have six and nine crops from the very same plot of land during the twelve months. They do not understand our talk about good and bad soils, because they make the soil themselves, and make it in such quantities as to be compelled yearly to sell some of it; otherwise it would raise up the level of their gardens by half an inch every year. They aim at cropping, not five or six tons of grass on the acre, as we do, but from fifty to 100 tons of various vegetables on the same space; not £5 worth of hay but £100 worth of vegetables, of the plainest description, cabbage and carrots. That is where agriculture is going now.

We know that the dearest of all varieties of our staple food is meat; and those who are not vegetarians, either by persuasion or by necessity, consume on the average 225 lb. of meat—that is, roughly speaking, a little less than the third part of an ox—every year. And we have seen that, even in this country and Belgium, two to three acres are wanted for keeping one head of horned cattle; so that a community of, say, 1,000,000 inhabitants would have to reserve somewhere about 3,000,000 acres of land for supplying it with meat. But if we go to the farm of M. Goppart—one of the promoters of *ensilage* in France—we shall see him growing, on a drained and well-manured field, no less than an average of 120,000 lbs. of corn-grass in the acre, which gives 30,000 lbs. of dry hay—that is, the food of one horned beast per acre. The produce is thus trebled. As to beetroot, which is used also for feeding cattle, Mr. Champion at Whitby, succeeds, with the help of sewage, in growing 100,000 lbs. of beet on each acre, and occasionally 150,000 and 200,000 lbs. He thus grows on each acre the food of, at least, two or three head of cattle. And such crops are not isolated facts: thus, M. Gros, at Autun, succeeds in cropping 600,000 lbs. of beet and carrots, which crop would permit him to keep four horned cattle on each acre. As to crops of 100,000 lbs. of beet, they occur in numbers in the French competitions, and the success depends entirely upon good culture and appropriate manuring. It thus appears that while under ordinary high farming we need from 2,000,000 acres to keep 1,000,000 horned cattle, double that amount could be kept on one-half of that area; and if the density of population required it, the amount of cattle could be doubled again, and the area required to keep it might still be one-half, or even one-third of what it is now.

The above examples are striking enough, and yet those afforded by the market-gardening culture are still more striking. I mean the culture carried on in the neighbourhood of big cities, and more especially the *culture maraîchère* round Paris. In that culture each plant is treated according to its age. The seeds germinate and the seedlings develop their first four leaflets in especially favourable conditions of soil and temperature; then the best seedlings are picked out and transplanted into a bed of fine loam, under a frame or in the open air, where they freely develop their rootlets and, gathered on a limited space, receive more than usual care; and only after that preliminary training are they bedded in the open ground, where they grow till ripe. In such a culture the primitive condition of the soil is of little account, because loam is made out of the old forcing beds. The seeds are carefully tried, the seedlings receive proper attention, and there is no fear of drought, because of the variety of crops, the liberal watering with the help of a steam engine, and the stock of plants always kept ready to replace the weakest individuals. Almost each plant is treated individually.

There prevails, however, with regard to market-gardening, a mis-understanding which it would be well to remove. It is generally supposed that what chiefly attracts market-gardening to the great centres of population is the market. It must have been so; and so it may be still, but to some extent only. A great number of the Paris *maraîchers*, even of those who have their gardens within the walls of the city and whose main crop consists of vegetables in season, export the whole of their produce to England. What chiefly attracts the gardener to the great cities is stable manure; and this is not wanted so much for increasing the richness of the soil—one-tenth part of the manure used by the French gardeners would do for that purpose—but for keeping the soil at a certain temperature. Early vegetables pay best, and in order to obtain early produce not only the air but the soil as well must be warmed; and that is done by putting great quantities of properly mixed manure into the soil; its fermentation heats it. But it is evident that with the present de-velopment of industrial skill, the heating of the soil could be ob-tained more economically and more easily by hot-water pipes. Con-sequently, the French gardeners begin more and more to make use of portable pipes, or *thermosiphons*, provisionally established in the cool frames. . . .

As to the different degrees of fertility of the soil—always the stumbling-block of those who write about agriculture—the fact is that in market-gardening the soil is always *made*, whatever it origi-nally may have been. Consequently . . . it is now a usual stipulation of the renting contracts of the Paris *maraîchers* that the gardener may carry away his soil, down to a certain depth, when he quits his tenancy. He himself makes it, and when he moves to another plot he carts his soil away, together with his frames, his water-pipes, and his other belongings.

I could not relate here all the marvels achieved in market-garden-ing; so that I must . . . give only a few illustrations. Let us take, for instance, the orchard—the *marais*—of M. Ponce, the author of a well-known work on the *culture maraîchère*. His orchard covered only two and seven-tenths acres. The outlay for the establishment, including a steam engine for watering purposes, reached £1136. Eight persons, M. Ponce included, cultivated the orchard and car-ried the vegetables to the market, for which purpose one horse was kept; when returning from Paris they brought in manure, for which £100 was spent every year. Another £100 was spent in rent and taxes. But how to enumerate all that was gathered every year on this plot of less than three acres, without filling two pages or more with the most wonderful figures? One must read them in M. Ponce's work, but here are the chief items: more than 20,000 lbs. of carrots; more than 20,000 lbs. of onions, radishes, and other vegetables sold by weight; 6000 heads of cabbage; 3000 of cauliflower; 5000 baskets of tomatoes; 5000 dozen of choice fruit; and 154,000 heads of salad; in short, a total of 250,000 lbs. of vegetables. The soil was made to such an amount out of forcing beds that every year 250 cubic yards of loam had to be sold. Similar examples could be given by the dozen, and the best evidence against any possible exaggeration of the results is the very high rent paid by the gardeners, which reaches in the suburbs of London from £ 10 to £ 15 per acre, and in the suburbs of Paris attains as much as £ 32 per acre. No less than 2125 acres are cultivated round Paris in that way by 5000 persons, and thus not only the 2,000,000 Parisians are supplied with vegetables, but the surplus is also sent to London.

The above results are obtained with the help of warm frames, thousands of glass bells, and so on. But even without such costly things, with only thirty-six yards of frames for seedlings, vegetables are grown *in the open air* to the value of £ 200 per acre. It is obvious, however, that in such cases the high selling prices of the crops are not due to the high prices fetched by early vegetables in winter; they are entirely due to the high crops of the plainest ones. Let me add also that all this wonderful culture is a yesterday's growth. Fifty years ago the *culture maraîchère* was quite primitive. But now the Paris gardener not only defies the soil—he would grow the same crops on an asphalt pavement—he defies climate. His walls, which are built to reflect light and to protect the wall-trees from the northern winds, his wall-tree shades and glass protectors, his frames and *pépinières* have made a real garden, a rich Southern garden, out of the suburbs of Paris. He has given to Paris the "two degrees less of latitude" after which a French scientific writer was longing; he supplies his city with mountains of grapes and fruit at any season; and in the early spring he inundates and perfumes it with flowers. But he does not only grow articles of luxury. The culture of plain vegetables on a large scale is spreading every year; and the results are so good that there are now practical *maraîchers* who venture to maintain that if all the food, animal and vegetable, necessary for 3,500,000 inhabitants of the departments of Seine and Seine-et-Oise had to be grown on their own territory (3250 square miles), it could be grown without resorting to any other methods of culture than those already in use—methods already tested on a large scale and proved to be successful.

And yet the Paris gardener is not our ideal of an agriculturist. In the painful work of civilisation he has shown us the way to follow; but the ideal of modern civilisation is elsewhere. He toils, with but a short interruption, from three in the morning till late in the night. He knows no leisure; he has no time to live the life of a human being; the commonwealth does not exist for him; his world is his garden, more than his family. He cannot be our ideal; neither he nor his system of agriculture. Our ambition is, that he should produce even *more* than he does with *less* labour, and should enjoy all the joys of human life. And this is fully possible.

* * *

. . . The resources of science, both in enlarging the circle of our production and in new discoveries, are inexhaustible. And each new branch of activity calls into existence more and more new branches, which steadily increase the power of man over the forces of nature. If we take all into consideration; if we realise the progress made of late in the gardening culture, and the tendency towards spreading its methods to the open field; if we watch the cultural experiments which are being made now—experiments today and realities tomorrow—and ponder over the resources kept in store by science, we are bound to say that it is utterly impossible to foresee at the present moment the limits as to the *maximum* number of human beings who could draw their means of subsistence from a given area of land, or as to what a variety of produce they could advantageously grow in any latitude. Each day widens former limits, and opens new and wide horizons. All we can say now is, that 600 persons could easily live on a square mile; and that, with cultural methods already used on a large scale, 1000 human beings—not idlers—living on 1000 acres could easily, without any kind of overwork, obtain from that area a luxurious vegetable and animal food, as well as the flax, wool, silk, and hides necessary for their clothing. . . .

We thus see that the over-population fallacy does not stand the very first attempt at submitting it to a closer examination. Those only can be horror-stricken at seeing the population of this country increase by one individual every 1000 seconds who think of a human being as a mere claimant upon the stock of material wealth of mankind, without being at the same time a contributor to that stock. But we, who see in each new-born babe a future *worker* capable of producing much more than his own share of the common stock— we greet his appearance. We know that a crowded population is a necessary condition for permitting man to increase the productive powers of his labour. We know that highly productive labour is impossible so long as men are scattered, few in numbers, over wide territories, and are thus unable to combine together for the higher achievements of civilisation. We know what an amount of labour must be spent to scratch the soil with a primitive plough, to spin and weave by hand; and we know also how much less labour it costs to grow the same amount of food and weave the same cloth with the help of modern machinery. We also see that it is infinitely easier to grow 200,000 lbs. of food on one acre than to grow them on ten acres. It is all very well to imagine that wheat grows by itself on the Russian steppes; but those who have seen how the peasant toils in the "fertile" black-earth region will have one desire: that the increase of population may permit the use of the steam-digger and gardening culture in the steppes; that it may permit those who are now the beasts of burden of humanity to raise their backs and to become at last men.

We must, however, recognise that there are a few economists fully aware of the above truths. They gladly admit that Western Europe could grow much more food than it does; but they see no necessity nor advantage in doing so, as long as there are nations which can supply food in exchange for manufactured goods. Let us then examine how far this view is correct.

It is obvious that if we are satisfied with merely stating that it is cheaper to bring wheat from Riga than to grow it in Lincolnshire, the whole question is settled in a moment. But is it so in reality? Is it really cheaper to have food from abroad? And, supposing it is, are we not yet bound to analyse that compound result which we call price, rather than to accept it as a supreme and blind ruler of our actions? . . .

But if we analyse *price*, and make a distinction between its different elements, the disadvantage becomes still more apparent. If we compare, for instance, the costs of growing wheat in this country and in Russia, we are told that in the United Kingdom the hundred-weight of wheat cannot be grown at less than 8s. 7d.; while in Russia the costs of production of the same hundredweight are estimated at from 3s. 6d. to 4s. 9d. The difference is enormous, and it would still remain very great even if we admit that there is some exaggeration in the former figure. But why this difference? Are the Russian labourers paid so much less for their work? Their money wages surely are much lower, but the difference is equalised as soon as we reckon their wages in produce. The twelve shillings a week of the British agricultural labourer represents the same amount of wheat in Britain as the six shillings a week of the Russian labourer represents in Russia, not to say a word about the cheapness of meat in Russia and the low house rent. The Russian labourer is thus paid the same amount of the produce grown as he is paid here. . . .

. . . But the difference of the land rent in both countries would alone account for the difference of prices. In the wheat belt of Russia, where the average rent stands at about 12s. per acre, and the crop is from fifteen to twenty bushels, the rent amounts to from

3s. 6d. to 5s. 8d. in the costs of production of each quarter of Russian wheat; while in this country, where the rent and taxes are valued . . . at no less than 40s. per each wheat-growing acre, and the crop is taken at thirty bushels, the rent amounts to 10s. in the costs of production of each quarter. . . . The false condition of British rural economy, not the infertility of the soil, is thus the chief cause of the Russian competition. . . .

It is evident that the methods of culture must vary according to different conditions. In the vast prairies of North America, where land could be *bought* from 8s. to 40s. the acre, and where spaces of from 100 to 150 square miles in one block could be given to wheat culture, special methods of culture were applied and the results were excellent. Land was bought—not rented. In the autumn, whole studs of horses were brought, and the tilling and sowing were done with the aid of formidable ploughs and sowing machines. Then the horses were sent to graze in the mountains; the men were dismissed, and one man, occasionally two or three, remained to winter on the farm. In the spring the owners' agents began to beat the inns for hundreds of miles round, and engaged labourers and tramps, both freely supplied by Europe, for the crop. Battalions of men were marched to the wheat fields, and were camped there; the horses were brought from the mountains, and in a week or two the crop was cut, thrashed, winnowed, put in sacks, by specially invented machines, and sent to the next elevator, or directly to the ships which carried it to Europe. Whereupon the men were disbanded again, the horses were sent back to the grazing grounds, or sold, and again only a couple of men remained on the farm.

The crop from each acre was small, but the machinery was so perfected that in this way 300 days of one man's labour produced from 200 to 300 quarters of wheat; in other words—the area of land being of no account—every man produced in one day his yearly bread food (eight and a half bushels of wheat); and taking into account all subsequent labour, it was calculated that the work of 300 men in one single day delivered to the consumer at Chicago the flour that is required for the yearly food of 250 persons. Twelve hours and a half of work are thus required in Chicago to supply one man with his yearly provision of wheat-flour.

Under the special conditions offered in the Far West this certainly was an appropriate method for increasing all of a sudden the wheat supplies of mankind. It answered its purpose when large territories of unoccupied land were opened to enterprise. But it could not answer for ever. Under such a system of culture the soil was soon exhausted, the crop declined, and *intensive* agriculture (which aims at high crops on a limited area) had soon to be resorted to. . . .

In fact, . . . the force of "American competition" is not in its mammoth farms, but in the countless small farms upon which wheat is grown in the same way as it is grown in Europe, *i.e.*, with manuring, but with a better organised production and facilities for sale, and without being compelled to pay to the landlord a toll of one-third part, or more, of the selling price of each quarter of wheat. However, it was only after I had myself made a tour in the prairies of Manitoba that I could realise the full truth of the just-mentioned views. The 15,000,000 to 20,000,000 bushels of wheat, which are exported every year from Manitoba, are grown almost entirely in farms of one or two "quarter-sections," *i.e.*, of 160 and 320 acres. The ploughing is made in the usual way, and in an immense majority of cases the farmers buy the reaping and binding machines (the "binders") by associating in groups of four. The threshing machine is rented by the farmer for one or two days, and the farmer carts his wheat to the elevator with his own horses, either to sell it immediately or to keep it at the elevator if he is in no immediate need of money and hopes to get a higher price in one month or two. In short, in Manitoba one is especially struck with the fact that, even under a system of keen competition, the middle-size farm admirably well competes with the mammoth farm, and that it is not manufacturing wheat on a grand scale which pays best. It is also most interesting to note that thousands and thousands of farmers produce mountains of wheat in the Canadian province of Toronto and in the Eastern States, although the land is not prairie-land at all, and the farms are, as a rule, small.

The force of "American competition" is thus not in the possibility of having hundreds of acres of wheat in one block. It lies in the ownership of the land, in a system of culture which is appropriate to the character of the country, in a widely developed spirit of association, and, finally, in a number of institutions and customs intended to lift the agriculturist and his profession to a high level which is unknown in Europe.

. . . In every American State, and in every distinct region of Canada, there is an experimental farm, and all the work of preliminary experiment upon new varieties of wheat, oats, barley, fodder, and fruit, which the farmer has mostly to make himself in Europe, is made under the best scientific conditions at the experimental farms, on a small scale first and on a large scale next. The results of all these researches and experiments are not merely rendered accessible to the farmer who would like to know them, but they are brought to his knowledge, and, so to speak, are forced upon his attention by every possible means. The "Bulletins" of the experimental stations are distributed in hundreds of thousands of copies; visits to the farms are organised in such a way that thousands of farmers should inspect the stations every year, and be shown by specialists the results obtained, either with new varieties of plants or under various new methods of treatment. Correspondence is carried on with the farmers on such a scale that, for instance, at Ottawa, the experimental farm sends out every year a hundred thousand letters and packets. Every farmer can get, free of charge and postage, three pounds of seed of any variety of cereals, out of which he can get next year the necessary seed for sowing several acres. And, finally, in every small and remote township there are held farmers' meetings, at which special lecturers, who are sent out by the experimental farms or the local agricultural societies, discuss with the farmers in an informal way the results of last year's experiments and discoveries relative to every branch of agriculture, horticulture, cattle-breeding, dairying, and agricultural co-operation.

American agriculture really offers an imposing sight. Not in the wheat fields of the far West, which soon will become a thing of the past, but in the development of rational agriculture and the forces which promote it. Read the description of an agricultural exhibition, "the State's fair," in some small town of Iowa, with its 70,000 farmers camping with their families in tents during the fair's week, studying, learning, buying and selling, and enjoying life. You see a *national* fête, and you feel that you deal with a nation in which agriculture is in respect. . . .

* * *

Few books have exercised so pernicious an influence upon the general development of economic thought as Malthus's *Essay on the Principle of Population* exercised for three consecutive generations. It appeared at the right time, like all books which have had any influence at all, and it summed up ideas already current in the minds of the wealth-possessing minority. It was precisely when the ideas of equality and liberty, awakened by the French and American revolutions, were still permeating the minds of the poor, while the richer classes had become tired of their amateur excursions into the same domains, that Malthus came to assert, in reply to Godwin, that no equality is possible; that the poverty of the many is not due to institutions, but is a natural *law*. Population, he wrote, grows too rapidly and the new-comers find no room at the feast of nature; and that law cannot be altered by any change of institutions. He thus gave to the rich a kind of scientific argument against the ideas of equality; and we know that though all dominion is based upon force, force itself begins to totter as soon as it is no longer supported by a firm belief in its own rightfulness. As to the poorer classes—who always resent the influence of ideas circulating at a given time amid the wealthier classes—it deprived them of the very hope of improvement; it made them sceptical as to the promises of the social reformers; and to this day the most advanced reformers entertain doubts as to the possibility of satisfying the needs of all, in case there should be a claim for their satisfaction, and a temporary welfare of the labourers resulted in a sudden increase of population.

Science, down to the present day, remains permeated with Malthus's teachings. Political economy continues to base its reasoning upon a tacit admission of the impossibility of rapidly increasing the productive powers of a nation, and of thus giving satisfaction to all wants. That postulate stands, undiscussed, in the background of whatever political economy, classical or socialist, has to say about exchange value, wages, sale of labour force, rent, exchange, and consumption. Political economy never rises above the hypothesis of *a limited and insufficient supply of the necessaries of life*; it takes it for granted. And all theories connected with political economy retain the same erroneous principle. Nearly all socialists, too, admit the postulate. Nay, even in biology (so deeply interwoven now with sociology) we have recently seen the theory of variability of species borrowing a quite unexpected support from its having been connected by Darwin and Wallace with Malthus's fundamental idea, that the natural resources must inevitably fail to supply the means of existence for the rapidly multiplying animals and plants. In short, we may say that Malthus's theory, by shaping into a pseudo-scientific form the secret desires of the wealth-possessing classes, became the foundation of a whole system of practical philosophy, which permeates the minds of both the educated and uneducated, and reacts (as practical philosophy always does) upon the theoretical philosophy of our century.

True, the formidable growth of the productive powers of man in the industrial field, since he tamed steam and electricity, has somewhat shaken Malthus's doctrine. Industrial wealth *has* grown at a rate which no possible increase of population could attain, and it *can* grow with still greater speed. But agriculture is still considered a stronghold of the Malthusian pseudo-philosophy. The recent achievements of agriculture and horticulture are not sufficiently well known; and while our gardeners defy climate and latitude, acclimatise sub-tropical plants, raise several crops a year instead of one, and themselves make the soil they want for each special culture, the economists nevertheless continue saying that the surface of the soil is limited, and still more its productive powers; they still maintain that a population which should double each thirty years would soon be confronted by a lack of the necessaries of life!

A few data to illustrate what *can* be obtained from the soil were given in the preceding chapter. But the deeper one goes into the subject the more new and striking data does he discover, and the more Malthus's fears appear groundless.

To begin with an instance taken from culture in the open field—namely, that of wheat—we come upon the following interesting fact. While we are so often told that wheat-growing does not pay, and England consequently reduces from year to year the area of its wheat fields, the French peasants steadily increase the area under wheat, and the greatest increase is due to those peasant families which themselves cultivate the land they own. Since the end of the last century they have nearly doubled both the area under wheat, as well as the returns from each acre, so as to increase almost fourfold the amount of wheat grown in France. At the same time the population has only increased by 41 per cent, so that the ratio of increase of the wheat crop has been six times greater than the ratio of increase of population, although agriculture has been hampered all the time by a series of serious obstacles—taxation, military service, poverty of the peasantry, and even, up to 1884, a severe prohibition of all sorts of association among the peasants. It must also be remarked that during the same hundred years, and even within the last fifty years, market-gardening, fruit-culture and culture for industrial purposes have immensely developed in France, so that there would be no exaggeration in saying that the French obtain now from their soil at least six or seven times more than they obtained a hundred years ago. The "means of existence" drawn from the soil have thus grown about fifteen times quicker than the population.

But the ratio of progress in agriculture is still better seen from the rise of the standard of requirement as regards cultivation of land. Some thirty years ago the French considered a crop quite good when it yielded twenty-two bushels to the acre; but with the same soil the present requirement is at least thirty-three bushels, while in the best soils the crop is good only when it yields from forty-three to forty-eight bushels, and occasionally the product is as much as fifty-five bushels to the acre. There are whole countries—Hesse, for example—which are satisfied only when the *average* crop attains thirty-seven bushels; while the experimental farms of Central France produce from year to year, over large areas, forty-one bushels to the acre, and a number of farms in Northern France regularly yield, year after year, from fifty-five to sixty-eight bushels to the acre.

* * *

The various data which have been brought together on the preceding pages make short work of the over-population fallacy. It is precisely in the most densely populated parts of the world that agriculture has lately made such strides as hardly could have been guessed twenty years ago. A dense population, a high development of industry, and a high development of agriculture and horticulture, go hand in hand: they are inseparable. As to the future, the possibilities of agriculture are such that, in truth, we cannot yet foretell what would be the limit of the population which could live from the produce of a given area. Recent progress, already tested on a great scale, has widened the limits of agricultural production to a quite unforeseen extent; and recent discoveries, now tested on a small scale, promise to widen those limits still farther to a quite unknown degree. . . .

Supposing, then, that each inhabitant of Great Britain were compelled to live on the produce of his own land, all he would have to do would be, first, to consider the land of this country as a common inheritance, which must be disposed of to the best advantage of each and all—this is, evidently, an absolutely necessary condition. And next, he would have to cultivate his soil, not in some extravagant way, but no better than land is already cultivated upon thousands and thousands of acres in Europe and America. He would not be bound to invent some new methods, but could simply generalise and widely apply those which have stood the test of experience. He can do it; and in so doing he would save an immense quantity of the work which is now given for buying his food abroad, and for paying all the intermediaries who live upon this trade. . . . If we take, indeed, the masses of produce which are obtained under rational culture, and compare them with the amount of labour which must be spent for obtaining them under an irrational culture, for collecting them abroad, for transporting them, and for keeping armies of middlemen, we see at once how few days and hours need be given, under proper culture, for growing man's food.

For improving our methods of culture to that extent, we surely need not divide the land into one-acre plots, and attempt to grow what we are in need of by every one's separate individual exertions, on every one's separate plot with no better tools than the spade; under such conditions we inevitably should fail. Those who have been so much struck with the wonderful results obtained in the *petite culture*, that they go about representing the small culture of the French peasant, or *maraîcher*, as an ideal for mankind, are evidently mistaken. They are as much mistaken as those other extremists who would like to turn every country into a small number of huge Bonanza farms, worked by militarily organized "labour battalions." In Bonanza farms human labour is reduced, but the crops taken from the soil are far too small, and the whole system is robbery-culture taking no heed of the exhaustion of the soil; while in the *petite culture*, on isolated small plots, by isolated men or families, too much of human labour is wasted even though the crops are heavy. Real economy, of both space and labour, requires quite different methods, representing a combination of machinery work with hand work.

In agriculture, as in everything else, associated labour is the only reasonable solution. Two hundred families of five persons each, owning five acres per family, having no common ties between the families, and compelled to find their living, each family on its five acres, almost certainly would be an economical failure. Even leaving aside all *personal* difficulties resulting from different education and tastes and from the want of knowledge as to what has to be done with the land, and admitting for the sake of argument that these causes do not interfere, the experiment would end in a failure, merely for *economical*, for *agricultural* reasons. Whatever improvement upon the present conditions such an organisation might be, that improvement would not last; it would have to undergo a further transformation or disappear.

But the same two hundred families, if they consider themselves, say, as tenants of the nation, and treat the thousand acres as a common tenancy—again leaving aside the *personal* conditions—would have, economically speaking, from the point of view of the agriculturist, every chance of succeeding, *if they know what is the best use to make of that land.*

In such case they probably would first of all associate for permanently improving the land which required immediate improvement, and would consider it necessary to improve more of it every year, until they had brought it all into a perfect condition. On an area of 340 acres they could most easily grow all the cereals—wheat, oats etc.—required for both the thousand inhabitants and their live stock—without resorting for that purpose to replanted or planted cereals. They could grow on 400 acres, properly cultivated, and irrigated if necessary and possible, all the green crops and fodder required to keep the thirty to forty milch cows which would supply them with milk and butter, and, let us say, the 300 head of cattle required to supply them with meat. On twenty acres, two of which would be under glass, they would grow more vegetables, fruit, and luxuries than they could consume. And supposing that half an acre of land is attached to each house—for hobbies and amusement (poultry-keeping, or any fancy culture, flowers, and the like)—they would still have some 140 acres for all sorts of purposes: public gardens, squares, manufactures, and so on. The labour that would be required for such an intensive culture would not be the hard labour of the serf or slave. It would be accessible to every one, strong or weak, town bred or country born; it would also have many charms besides. And its total amount would be far smaller than the amount of labour which every thousand persons, taken from this or from any other nation, have now to spend in getting their present food, much smaller in quantity and of worse quality. I mean, of course, the technically necessary labour, without even considering the labour which we now have to give in order to maintain all our middlemen, armies, and the like. The amount of labour required to grow food under a rational culture is so small, indeed, that our hypothetical inhabitants would be led necessarily to employ their leisure in manufacturing, artistic, scientific, and other pursuits.

From the technical point of view there is no obstacle whatever for such an organisation being started tomorrow with full success. The obstacles against it are not in the imperfection of the agricultural art, or in the infertility of the soil, or in climate. They are entirely in our institutions, in our inheritances and survivals from the past—in the "Ghosts" which oppress us. But to some extent they lie also—taking society as a whole—in our phenomenal ignorance. We civilised men and women know everything, we have settled opinions upon everything, we take an interest in everything. We only know nothing about whence the bread comes which we eat—even though we pretend to know something about that subject as well—we do not know how it is grown, what pains it costs to those who grow it, what is being done to reduce their pains, what sort of men those feeders of our grand selves are . . . we are more ignorant than savages in this respect, and we prevent our children from obtaining this sort of knowledge—even those of our children who would prefer it to the heaps of useless stuff with which they are crammed at school.

Brain Work and Manual Work

In olden times men of science, and especially those who have done most to forward the growth of natural philosophy, did not despise manual work and handicraft. Galileo made his telescopes with his own hands. Newton learned in his boyhood the art of managing tools; he exercised his young mind in contriving most ingenious machines, and when he began his researches in optics he was able himself to grind the lenses for his instruments, and himself to make the well-known telescope, which, for its time, was a fine piece of workmanship. Liebnitz was fond of inventing machines:

windmills and carriages to be moved without horses preoccupied his mind as much as mathematical and philosophical speculations. Linnaeus became a botanist while helping his father—a practical gardener—in his daily work. In short, with our great geniuses handicraft was no obstacle to abstract researches—it rather favoured them. On the other hand, if the workers of old found but few opportunities for mastering science, many of them had, at least, their intelligences stimulated by the very variety of work which was performed in the then unspecialised workshops; and some of them had the benefit of familiar intercourse with men of science. Watt and Rennie were friends with Professor Robinson; Brindley, the road-maker, despite his fourteen-pence-a-day wages, enjoyed intercourse with educated men, and thus developed his remarkable engineering faculties; the son of a well-to-do family could "idle" at a wheelwright's shop, so as to become later on a Smeaton or a Stephenson.

We have changed all that. Under the pretext of division of labour, we have sharply separated the brain worker from the manual worker. The masses of the workmen do not receive more scientific education than their grandfathers did; but they have been deprived of the education of even the small workshop, while their boys and girls are driven into a mine or a factory from the age of thirteen, and there they soon forget the little they may have learned at school. As to the men of science, they despise manual labour. How few of them would be able to make a telescope, or even a plainer instrument? Most of them are not capable of even designing a scientific instrument, and when they have given a vague suggestion to the instrument-maker they leave it with him to invent the apparatus they need. Nay, they have raised the contempt of manual labour to the height of a theory. "The man of science," they say, "must discover the laws of nature, the civil engineer must apply them, and the worker must execute in steel or wood, in iron or stone, the patterns devised by the engineer. He must work with machines invented for him, not by him. No matter if he does not understand them and cannot improve them: the scientific man and the scientific engineer will take care of the progress of science and industry."

It may be objected that nevertheless there is a class of men who belong to none of the above three divisions. When young they have been manual workers, and some of them continue to be; but, owing to some happy circumstances, they have succeeded in acquiring some scientific knowledge, and thus they have combined science with handicraft. Surely there are such men; happily enough there is a nucleus of men who have escaped the so-much-advocated specialisation of labour, and it is precisely to them that industry owes its chief recent inventions. But in old Europe at least, they are the exceptions; they are the irregulars—the Cossacks who have broken the ranks and pierced the screens so carefully erected between the classes. And they are so few, in comparison with the ever-growing requirements of industry—and of science as well, as I am about to prove—that all over the world we hear complaints about the scarcity of precisely such men.

What is the meaning, in fact, of the outcry for technical education which has been raised at one and the same time in England, in France, in Germany, in the States, and in Russia, if it does not express a general dissatisfaction with the present division into scientists, scientific engineers, and workers? Listen to those who know industry, and you will see that the substance of their complaints is this: "The worker whose task has been specialised by the permanent division of labour has lost the intellectual interest in his labour, and it is especially so in the great industries; he has lost his inventive powers. Formerly, he invented very much. Manual workers—not men of science nor trained engineers—have invented, or brought to perfection, the prime motors and all that mass of machinery which has revolutionised industry for the last hundred years. But since the great factory has been enthroned, the worker, depressed by the monotony of his work, invents no more. What can a weaver invent who merely supervises four looms, without knowing anything either about their complicated movements or how the machines grew to be what they are? What can a man invent who is condemned for life to bind together the ends of two threads with the greatest celerity, and knows nothing beyond making a knot?

"At the outset of modern industry, three generations of workers *have* invented; now they cease to do so. As to the inventions of the engineers, specially trained for devising machines, they are either devoid of genius or not practical enough. Those 'nearly to nothings,' of which Sir Frederick Bramwell spoke once at Bath, are missing in their inventions—those nothings which can be learned in the workshop only, and which permitted a Murdoch and the Soho workers to make a practical engine of Watt's schemes. None but he who knows the machine—not in its drawings and models only, but in its breathing and throbbings—who unconsciously thinks of it while standing by it, can really improve it. Smeaton and Newcomen surely were excellent engineers; but in their engines a boy had to open the steam valve at each stroke of the piston; and it was one of those boys who once managed to connect the valve with the remainder of the machine, so as to make it open automatically, while he ran away to play with other boys. But in the modern machinery there is no room left for naive improvements of that kind. Scientific education on a wide scale has become necessary for further inventions, and that education is refused to the workers. So that there is no issue out of the difficulty unless scientific education and handicraft are combined together—unless integration of knowledge takes the place of the present divisions." Such is the real substance of the present movement in favour of technical education. . . .

. . . We maintain that in the interests of both science and industry, as well as of society as a whole, every human being, without distinction of birth, ought to receive such an education as would enable him, or her, to combine a thorough knowledge of science with a thorough knowledge of handicraft. We fully recognise the necessity of specialisation of knowledge, but we maintain that specialisation must follow general education, and that general education must be given in science and handicraft alike. To the division of society into brain-workers and manual workers we oppose the combination of both kinds of activities; and instead of "technical education," which means the maintenance of the present division between brain work and manual work, we advocate the *éducation intégrale*, or complete education, which means the disappearance of that pernicious distinction. Plainly stated, the aims of the school under this system ought to be the following: To give such an education that, on leaving school at the age of eighteen or twenty, each boy and each girl should be endowed with a thorough knowledge of science—such a knowledge as might enable them to be useful workers in science—and, at the same time, to give them a general knowledge of what constitutes the bases of technical training, and such a skill in some special trade as would enable each of them to take his or her place in the grand world of the manual production of wealth. I know that many will find that aim too large, or even impossible to attain, but I hope that if they have the patience to read the following pages, they will see that we require nothing beyond what can be easily attained. In fact, *it has been attained*; and what has been done on a small scale could be done on a wider scale, were it not for the economical and social causes which prevent any serious reform from being accomplished in our miserably organised society.

The experiment has been made at the Moscow Technical School for twenty consecutive years with many hundreds of boys; and, according to the testimonies of the most competent judges at the exhibitions of Brussels, Philadelphia, Vienna, and Paris, the experiment has been a success. The Moscow school admits boys not older than fifteen, and it requires from boys of that age nothing but a substantial knowledge of geometry and algebra, together with the usual knowledge of their mother tongue; younger pupils are received in the preparatory classes. The school is divided into two sections—the mechanical and the chemical; but as I personally know better the former, and as it is also the more important with reference to the question before us, so I shall limit my remarks to the education given in the mechanical section. After a five or six years' stay at the school, the students leave it with a thorough knowledge of higher mathematics, physics, mechanics, and connected sciences—so thorough, indeed, that it is not second to that acquired in the best mathematical faculties of the most eminent European universities. When myself a student of the mathematical faculty of the St. Petersburg University, I had the opportunity of comparing the knowledge of the students at the Moscow Technical School with our own. I saw the courses of higher geometry some of them had compiled for the use of their comrades; I admired the facility with which they applied the integral calculus to dynamical problems, and I came to the conclusion that while we, University students, had more knowledge of a general character (for instance, in mathematical astronomy), they, the students of the Technical School, were much more advanced in higher geometry, and especially in the applications of higher mathematics to the most intricate problems of dynamics, the theories of heat and elasticity. But while we, the students of the University, hardly knew the use of our hands, the students of the Technical School fabricated *with their own hands*, and without the help of professional workmen, fine steam-engines, from the heavy boiler to the last finely turned screw, agricultural machinery, and scientific apparatus—all for the trade —and they received the highest awards for the work of their hands at the international exhibitions. They were scientifically educated skilled workers—workers with university education—highly appreciated even by the Russian manufacturers who so much distrust science.

Now, the methods by which these wonderful results were achieved were these: In science, learning from memory was not in honour, while independent research was favoured by all means. Science was taught hand in hand with its applications, and what was learned in the schoolroom was applied in the workshop. Great attention was paid to the highest abstractions of geometry as a means for developing imagination and research. As to the teaching of handicraft, the methods were quite different from those which proved a failure at the Cornell University, and differed, in fact, from those used in most technical schools. The student was not sent to a workshop to learn some special handicraft and to earn his existence as soon as possible, but the teaching of technical skill was prosecuted—according to a scheme elaborated by the founder of the school, M. Dellavos, and now applied also at Chicago and Boston—in the same systematical way as laboratory work is taught in the universities. It is evident that drawing was considered as the first step in technical education. Then the student was brought, first, to the carpenter's workshop, or rather laboratory, and there he was thoroughly taught to execute all kinds of carpentry and joinery. No efforts were spared in order to bring the pupil to a certain perfection in that branch—the real basis of all trades. Later on, he was transferred to the turner's workshop, where he was taught to make in wood the patterns of those things which he would have to make in metal in the following workshops. The foundry followed, and there he was taught to cast those parts of machines which he had prepared in wood; and it was only after he had gone through the first three stages that he was admitted to the smith's and engineering workshops. . . .

In America the same system has been introduced, in its technical part, first, in the Chicago Manual Training School, and later on in the Boston Technical School—the best, I am told, of the sort; and in this country, or rather in Scotland, I found the system applied with full success, for some years, under the direction of Dr. Ogilvie at Gordon's College in Aberdeen. It is the Moscow or Chicago system on a limited scale. While receiving substantial scientific education, the pupils are also trained in the workshops—but not for one special trade, as it unhappily too often is the case. They pass through the carpenter's workshop, the casting in metals, and the engineering workshop; and in each of these they learn the foundations of each of the three trades sufficiently well for supplying the school itself with a number of useful things. Besides, as far as I could ascertain from what I saw in the geographical and physical classes, as also in the chemical laboratory, the system of "through the hand to the brain," and *vice versa*, is in full swing, and it is attended with the best success. The boys *work* with the physical instruments, and they study geography in the field, instruments in hands, as well as in the class-room. Some of their surveys filled my heart, as an old geographer, with joy. It is evident that the Gordon's College industrial department is not a mere copy of any foreign school; on the contrary, I cannot help thinking that if Aberdeen has made that excellent move towards combining science with handicraft, the move was a natural outcome of what has been practised long since, on a smaller scale, in the Aberdeen daily schools.

The Moscow Technical School surely is not an ideal school. It totally neglects the humanitarian education of the young men. But we must recognise that the Moscow experiment—not to speak of hundreds of other partial experiments—has perfectly well proved the possibility of combining a scientific education of a very high standard with the education which is necessary for becoming an excellent skilled labourer. It has proved, moreover, that the best means for producing really good skilled labourers is to seize the bull by the horns, and to grasp the educational problem in its great features, instead of trying to give some special skill in some handicraft, together with a few scraps of knowledge in a certain branch of some science. And it has shown also what can be obtained, without over-pressure, if a rational economy of the scholar's time is always kept in view, and theory goes hand in hand with practice. Viewed in this light, the Moscow results do not seem extraordinary at all, and still better results may be expected if the same principles are applied from the earliest years of education. Waste of time is the leading feature of our present education. Not only are we taught a mass of rubbish, but what is not rubbish is taught so as to make us waste over it as much time as possible. . . .

It is evident that the years of childhood ought not to be spent so uselessly as they are now. German teachers have shown how the very plays of children can be made instrumental in conveying to the childish mind some concrete knowledge in both geometry and mathematics. The children who have made the squares of the theorem of Pythagoras out of pieces of coloured cardboard, will not look at the theorem, when it comes in geometry, as on a mere instrument of torture devised by the teachers; and the less so if they apply it as the carpenters do. Complicated problems of arithmetic, which so much harassed us in our boyhood, are easily solved by children seven and eight years old if they are put in the shape of interesting puzzles. . . . In fact, it is almost impossible to imagine, without having tried it, how many sound notions of nature, habits of classification, and taste for natural sciences can be conveyed to the children's minds; and, if a series of concentric courses adapted to the various phases of development of the human being were generally accepted in education, the first series in all sciences, save sociology, could be taught before the age of ten or twelve, so as to give a general idea of the universe, the earth and its inhabitants, the chief physical, chemical, zoological, and botanical phenomena, leaving the discovery of the *laws* of those phenomena to the next series of deeper and more specialised studies. On the other side, we all know how children like to make toys themselves, how they gladly imitate the work of full-grown people if they see them at work in the workshop or the building-yard. But the parents either stupidly paralyse that passion, or do not know how to utilise it. Most of them despise manual work and prefer sending their children to the study of Roman history, or of Franklin's teachings about saving money, to seeing them at a work which is good for the "lower classes only." They thus do their best to render subsequent learning the more difficult.

And then come the school years, and time is wasted again to an incredible extent. Take, for instance, mathematics, which every one ought to know, because it is the basis of all subsequent education, and which so few really learn in our schools. In geometry, time is foolishly wasted by using a method which merely consists in committing geometry to memory. In most cases, the boy reads again and again the proof of a theorem till his memory has retained the succession of reasonings. Therefore, nine boys out of ten, if asked to prove an elementary theorem two years after having left the school, will be unable to do it, unless mathematics is their specialty. They will forget which auxiliary lines to draw, and they never have been taught to *discover* the proofs by themselves. . . . There is, however, the other method which permits progress, as a whole, at a much speedier rate, and under which he who once has learned geometry will know it all his life long. Under this system, each theorem is put as a problem; its solution is never given beforehand, and the pupil is induced to find it by himself. Thus, if some preliminary exercises with the rule and the compass have been made, there is not one boy or girl, out of twenty or more, who will not be able to find the means of drawing an angle which is equal to a given angle, and to prove their equality, after a few suggestions from the teacher; and if the subsequent problems are given in a systematic succession (there are excellent text-books for the purpose), and the teacher does not press his pupils to go faster than they can go at the beginning, they advance from one problem to the next with an astonishing facility, the only difficulty being to bring the pupil to solve the first problem, and thus to acquire confidence in his own reasoning.

Moreover, each abstract geometrical truth must be impressed on the mind in its concrete form as well. As soon as the pupils have solved a few problems on paper, they must solve them in the playing-ground with a few sticks and a string, and they must apply their knowledge in the workshop. Only then will the geometrical lines acquire a concrete meaning in the children's minds; only then will they see that the teacher is playing no tricks when he asks them to solve problems with the rule and the compass without resorting to the protractor; only then will they *know* geometry. "Through the eyes *and* the hand to the brain"—that is the true principle of economy of time in teaching. I remember as if it were yesterday, how geometry suddenly acquired for me a new meaning, and how this new meaning facilitated all ulterior studies. It was as we were mastering a Montgolfier balloon, and I remarked that the angles at the summits of each of the twenty strips of paper out of which the balloon was going to be made must cover less than the fifth part of a right angle each. I remember, next, how the sinuses and the tangents ceased to be mere cabalistic signs when they permitted us to calculate the length of a stick in a working profile of a fortification; and how geometry in space became plain when we began to make on a small scale a bastion with embrasures and barbettes—an occupation which obviously was soon prohibited on account of the state into which we brought our clothes. "You look like navvies," was the reproach addressed to us by our intelligent educators, while we were proud precisely of being navvies, and of discovering the use of geometry.

By compelling our children to study real things from mere graphical representations, instead of *making* those things themselves, we compel them to waste the most precious time; we uselessly worry their minds; we accustom them to the worst methods of learning; we kill independent thought in the bud; and very seldom we succeed in conveying a real knowledge of what we are teaching. Superficiality, parrot-like repetition, slavishness and inertia of mind are the results of our method of education. We do not teach our children how to learn. . . .

If waste of time is characteristic of our methods of teaching science, it is characteristic as well of the methods used for teaching handicraft. . . . Reuleaux has shown in that delightful book, the *Theoretische Kinematik*, that there is, so to say, a philosophy of all possible machinery. Each machine, however complicated, can be reduced to a few elements—plates, cylinders, discs, cones, and so on—as well as to a few tools—chisels, saws, rollers, hammers, etc.; and, however complicated its movements, they can be decomposed into a few modifications of motion, such as the transformation of circular motion into a rectilinear, and the like, with a number of intermediate links. So also each handicraft can be decomposed into a number of elements. In each trade one must know how to make a plate with parallel surfaces, a cylinder, a disc, a square, and a round hole; how to manage a limited number of tools, all tools being mere modifications of less than a dozen types; and how to transform one kind of motion into another. This is the foundation of all mechanical handicrafts; so that the knowledge of how to make in wood those primary elements, how to manage the chief tools in wood-work, and how to transform various kinds of motion, ought to be considered as the very basis for the subsequent teaching of all possible kinds of mechanical handicraft. The pupil who has acquired that skill already knows one good half of all possible trades. Besides, none can be a good worker in science unless he is in possession of good methods of scientific research; unless he has learned to observe, to describe with exactitude, to discover mutual relations between facts seemingly disconnected, to make hypotheses and to verify them, to reason upon cause and effect, and so on. And none can be a good manual worker unless he has been accustomed to the good methods of handicraft. . . . Be it handicraft, science, or art, the chief aim of the school is not to make a specialist from a beginner, but to teach him the elements of knowledge and the good methods of work, and, above all, to give him that general inspiration which will induce him, later on, to put in whatever he does a sincere longing for truth, to like what is beautiful both as to form and contents, to feel the necessity of being a useful unit amidst other human units, and thus to feel his heart at unison with the rest of humanity.

* * *

It is evident that celerity of work is a most important factor in production. . . . However plain his work, the educated worker makes it better and quicker than the uneducated. Observe, for instance, how a good worker proceeds in cutting anything—say a piece of cardboard—and compare his movements with those of an improperly trained worker. The latter seizes the cardboard, takes the tool as it is, traces a line in a haphazard way, and begins to cut; half-way he is tired, and when he has finished, his work is worth nothing; whereas, the former will examine his tool and improve it if necessary; he will trace the line with exactitude, secure both cardboard and rule, keep the tool in the right way, cut quite easily, and give you a piece of good work. That is the true time-saving celerity, the most appropriate for economising human labour; and the best means for attaining it is an education of the most superior kind. The great masters painted with an astonishing rapidity; but their rapid work was the result of a great development of intelligence and imagination, of a keen sense of beauty, of a fine perception of colours. And that is the kind of rapid work of which humanity is in need.

Much more ought to be said as regards the duties of the school, but I hasten to say a few words more as to the desirability of the kind of education briefly sketched in the preceding pages. Certainly, I do not cherish the illusion that a thorough reform in education, or in any of the issues indicated in the preceding chapters, will be made as long as the civilised nations remain under the present narrowly egotistic system of production and consumption. All we can expect, as long as the present conditions last, is to have some microscopical attempts at reforming here and there on a small scale—attempts which necessarily will prove to be far below the expected results, because of the impossibility of reforming on a small scale when so intimate a connection exists between the manifold functions of a civilised nation. But the energy of the constructive genius of society depends chiefly upon the depths of its conception as to what ought to be done, and how; and the necessity of recasting education is one of those necessities which are most comprehensible to all, and are most appropriate for inspiring society with those ideals, without which stagnation or even decay are unavoidable. So let us suppose that a community—a city, or a territory which has, at least, a few millions of inhabitants—gives the above-sketched education to all its children, without distinction of birth (and we *are* rich enough to permit us the luxury of such an education), without asking anything in return from the children but what they will give when they have become producers of wealth. Suppose such an education is given, and analyse its probable consequences.

I will not insist upon the increase of wealth which would result from having a young army of educated and well-trained producers; nor shall I insist upon the social benefits which would be derived from erasing the present distinction between the brain workers and the manual workers, and from thus reaching the concordance of interest and harmony so much wanted in our times of social struggles. I shall not dwell upon the fulness of life which would result for each separate individual, if he were enabled to enjoy the use of both his mental and bodily powers; nor upon the advantages of raising manual labour to the place of honour it ought to occupy in society, instead of being a stamp of inferiority, as it is now. Nor shall I insist upon the disappearance of the present misery and degradation, with all their consequences—vice, crime, prisons, price of blood, denunciation, and the like—which necessarily would follow. In short, I will not touch now the great social question, upon which so much has been written and so much remains to be written yet. I merely intend to point out in these pages the benefits which science itself would derive from the change.

Some will say, of course, that to reduce men of science to the *rôle* of manual workers would mean the decay of science and genius. But those who will take into account the following considerations probably will agree that the result ought to be the reverse—namely, such a revival of science and art, and such a progress in industry, as we only can faintly foresee from what we know about the times of the Renaissance. It has become a commonplace to speak with emphasis about the progress of science during the nineteenth century; and it is evident that our century, if compared with centuries past, has much to be proud of. But, if we take into account that most of the problems which our century has solved already had been indicated, and their solutions foreseen, a hundred years ago, we must admit that the progress was not so rapid as might have been expected, and that something hampered it. The mechanical theory of heat was very well foreseen in the last century by Rumford and Humphrey Davy, and even in Russia it was advocated by Lomonosoff. However, much more than half a century elapsed before the theory reappeared in science. Lamarck, and even Linnaeus, Geoffroy Saint-Hilaire, Erasmus Darwin, and several others were fully aware of the variability of species; they were opening the way for the construction of biology on the principles of variation; but here, again, half a century was wasted before the variability of species was brought again to the front; and we all remember how Darwin's ideas were carried on and forced on the attention of university people, chiefly by persons who were not professional scientists themselves; and yet in Darwin's hands 'the theory of evolution surely was narrowed, owing to the overwhelming importance given to only one factor of evolution. For many years past astronomy has been needing a careful revision of the Kant and Laplace's hypothesis; but no theory is yet forthcoming which would compel general acceptance. Geology surely has made wonderful progress in the reconstitution of the palaeontological record, but dynamical geology progresses at a despairingly slow rate; while all future progress in the great question as to the laws of distribution of living organisms on the surface of the earth is hampered by the want of knowledge as to the extension of glaciation during the Quaternary epoch. In short, in each branch of science a revision of the current theories as well as new wide generalisations are wanted. And if the revision requires some of that inspiration of genius which moved Galileo and Newton, and which depends in its appearance upon general causes of human development, it requires also an increase in the number of scientific workers. When facts contradictory to current theories become numerous, the theories must be revised (we saw it in Darwin's case), and thousands of simple intelligent workers in science are required to accumulate them.

* * *

However, there is another feature of modern science which speaks more strongly yet in favour of the change we advocate. While industry, especially by the end of the last century and during the first part of the present, has been inventing on such a scale as to revolutionise the very face of the earth, science has been losing its inventive powers. Men of science invent no more, or very little. Is it not striking, indeed, that the steam-engine, even in its leading principles, the railway-engine, the steamboat, the telephone, the phonograph, the weaving-machine, the lace-machine, the lighthouse, the macadamised road, photograph in black and in colours, and thousands of less important things, have *not* been invented by professional men of science, although none of them would have refused to associate his name with any of the above-named inventions? Men who hardly had received any education at school, who had merely picked up the crumbs of knowledge from the tables of the rich, and who made their experiments with the most primitive means—the attorney's clerk Smeaton, the instrument-maker Watt, the brakesman Stephenson, the jewellers' apprentice Fulton, the millwright Rennie, the mason Telford, and hundreds of others whose very names remain unknown, were, as Mr. Smiles justly says, "the real makers of modern civilisation"; while the professional men of science, provided with all means for acquiring knowledge and experimenting, have invented little in the formidable array of implements, machines, and prime-motors, which has shown to humanity how to utilise and to manage the forces of nature. The fact is striking, but its explanation is very simple: those men—the Watts and the Stephensons—knew something which the *savants* do not know—they knew the use of their hands; their surroundings stimulated their inventive powers; they knew machines, their leading principles, and their work; they had breathed the atmosphere of the workshop and the building-yard.

We know how men of science will meet the reproach. They will say, "We discover the laws of nature, let others apply them; it is a simple division of labour." But such a rejoinder would be utterly untrue. The march of progress is quite the reverse, because in a hundred cases against one the mechanical invention comes before the discovery of the scientific law. It was not the dynamical theory of heat which came before the steam-engine—it followed it. When thousands of engines already were transforming heat into motion under the eyes of hundreds of professors, and when they had done so for half a century, or more; when thousands of trains, stopped by powerful brakes, were disengaging heat and spreading sheaves of sparks on the rails at their approach to the stations; when all over the civilised world heavy hammers and perforators were rendering burning hot the masses of iron they were hammering and perforating—then, and then only, a doctor, Mayer, ventured to bring out the mechanical theory of heat with all its consequences: and yet the men of science almost drove him to madness by obstinately clinging to their mysterious caloric fluid, and they described Joule's work on the mechanical equivalent of heat as "unscientific."

When every engine was illustrating the impossibility of utilising all the heat disengaged by a given amount of burnt fuel, then came the law of Clausius. When all over the world industry already was transforming motion into heat, sound, light, and electricity, and each one into each other, then only came Grove's theory of the "correlation of physical forces." It was not the theory of electricity which gave us the telegraph. When the telegraph was invented, all we knew about electricity was but a few facts more or less badly arranged in our books; the theory of electricity is not ready yet; it still waits for its Newton, notwithstanding the brilliant attempts of late years. Even the empirical knowledge of the laws of electrical currents was in its infancy when a few bold men laid a cable at the bottom of the Atlantic Ocean, despite the warnings of the authorised men of science.

The name of "applied science" is quite misleading, because, in the great majority of cases, invention, far from being an application of science, on the contrary creates a new branch of science. The American bridges were no application of the theory of elasticity; they came before the theory, and all we can say in favour of science is, that in this special branch, theory and practice developed in a parallel way, helping one another. It was not the theory of the explosives which led to the discovery of gunpowder; gunpowder was in use for centuries before the action of the gases in a gun was submitted to scientific analysis. And so on. The great processes of metallurgy; the alloys and the properties they acquire from the addition of very small amounts of some metals or metalloids; the recent revival of electric lighting; nay, even the weather forecasts which truly deserved the reproach of being "unscientific" when they were started by an old Jack tar, Fitzroy—all these could be mentioned as instances in point. Of course, we have a number of cases in which the discovery, or the invention, was a mere application of a scientific law (cases like the discovery of the planet Neptune), but in the immense majority of cases the discovery, or the invention, is unscientific to begin with. It belongs much more to the domain of art—art taking the precedence over science, as Helmholtz has so well shown in one of his popular lectures—and only after the invention has been made, science comes to interpret it. It is obvious that each invention avails itself of the previously accumulated knowledge and modes of thought; but in most cases it makes a start in advance upon what is known; it makes a leap in the unknown, and thus opens a quite new series of facts for investigation. This character of invention, which is to make a start in advance of former knowledge, instead of merely applying a law, makes it identical, as to the processes of mind, with discovery; and, therefore, people who are slow in invention are also slow in discovery.

In most cases, the inventor, however inspired by the general state of science at a given moment, starts with a very few settled facts at his disposal. The scientific facts taken into account for inventing the steam-engine, or the telegraph, or the phonograph were strikingly elementary. So that we can affirm that what we presently know is already sufficient for resolving any of the great problems which stand in the order of the day—prime-motors without the use of steam, the storage of energy, the transmission of force, or the flying-machine. If these problems are not yet solved, it is merely because of the want of inventive genius, the scarcity of educated men endowed with it, and the present divorce between science and industry. On the one side, we have men who are endowed with capacities for invention, but have neither the necessary scientific knowledge nor the means for experimenting during long years; and, on the other side, we have men endowed with knowledge and facilities for experimenting, but devoid of inventive genius, owing to their education and to the surroundings they live in—not to speak of the patent system, which divides and scatters the efforts of the inventors instead of combining them.

The flight of genius which has characterised the workers at the outset of modern industry has been missing in our professional men of science. And they will not recover it as long as they remain strangers to the world, amidst their dusty bookshelves; as long as they are not workers themselves, amidst other workers, at the blaze of the iron furnace, at the machine in the factory, at the turning-lathe in the engineering work-shop; sailors amidst sailors on the sea, and fishers in the fishing boat, wood-cutters in the forest, tillers of the soil in the field. Our teachers in art have repeatedly told us of late that we must not expect a revival of art as long as handicraft remains what it is; they have shown how Greek and mediaeval art were daughters of handicraft, how one was feeding the other. The same is true with regard to handicraft and science; their separation is the decay of both. As to the grand inspirations which unhappily have been so much neglected in most of the recent discussions about art—and which are missing in science as well—these can be expected only when humanity, breaking its present bonds, shall make a new start in the higher principles of solidarity, doing away with the present duality of moral sense and philosophy.

It is evident, however, that all men and women cannot equally enjoy the pursuit of scientific work. The variety of inclinations is such that some will find more pleasure in science, some others in art, and others again in some of the numberless branches of the production of wealth. But, whatever the occupations preferred by every one, every one will be the more useful in his own branch if he is in possession of a serious scientific knowledge. And, whosoever he might be—scientist or artist, physicist or surgeon, chemist or sociologist, historian or poet—he would be the gainer if he spent a part of his life in the workshop or the farm (the workshop *and* the farm), if he were in contact with humanity in its daily work, and had the satisfaction of knowing that he himself discharges his duties as an unprivileged producer of wealth. How much better the historian and the sociologist would understand humanity if they knew it, not in books only, not in a few of its representatives, but as a whole, in its daily life, daily work, and daily affairs! How much more medicine would trust to hygiene, and how much less to prescriptions, if the young doctors were the nurses of the sick and the nurses received the education of the doctors of our time! And how much the poet would gain in his feeling of the beauties of nature, how much better would he know the human heart, if he met the rising sun amidst the tillers of the soil, himself a tiller; if he fought against the storm with the sailors on board ship; if he knew the poetry of labour and rest, sorrow and joy, struggle and conquest! *Greift nur hinein in's volle Menschenleben!* Goethe said; *Ein jeder lebt's—nicht vielen ist's bekannt.* But how few poets follow his advice!

The so-called division of labour has grown under a system which condemned the masses to toil all the day long, and all the life long, at the same wearisome kind of labour. But if we take into account how few are the real producers of wealth in our present society, and how squandered is their labour, we must recognize that Franklin was right in saying that to work five hours a day would generally do for supplying each member of a civilised nation with the comfort now accessible for the few only, provided everybody took his due share in production. But we have made some progress since Franklin's times, and some of that progress in the hitherto most backward branch of production has been indicated in the preceding pages. Even in that branch the productivity of labour can be immensely increased, and work itself rendered easy and pleasant. More than one half of the working day would thus remain to every one for the pursuit of art, science, or any hobby he might prefer; and his work in those fields would be the more profitable if he spent the other half of the day in productive work—if art and science were followed from mere inclination, not for mercantile purposes. Moreover, a community organised on the principles of all being workers would be rich enough to conclude that every man and woman, after having reached a certain age—say of forty or more—ought to be relieved from the moral obligation of taking a direct part in the performance of the necessary manual work, so as to be able entirely to devote himself or herself to whatever he or she chooses in the domain of art, or science, or any kind of work. Free pursuit in new branches of art and knowledge, free creation, and free development thus might be fully guaranteed. And such a community would not know misery amidst wealth. It would not know the duality of conscience which permeates our life and stifles every noble effort. It would freely take its flight towards the highest regions of progress compatible with human nature.

Conclusion

Readers who have had the patience to follow the facts accumulated in this book; especially those who have given them a thoughtful attention, will probably feel convinced of the immense powers over the productive forces of Nature that man has acquired within the last half a century. Comparing the achievements indicated in this book with the present state of production, some will, I hope, also ask themselves the question which will be ere long the main object of a scientific political economy: Whether the means now in use for satisfying human needs, under the present system of permanent division of functions and production for profits, are really *economical*; whether they really lead to economy in the expenditure of human forces; or whether they are not mere wasteful survivals from a past that was plunged into darkness, ignorance and oppression, and never took into consideration the economical and social value of the human being?

In the domain of agriculture it may be taken as proved that if a small part only of the time that is now given in each nation or region to field culture was given to well thought out and socially carried out permanent improvements of the soil, the duration of work which would be required afterwards to grow the yearly bread-food for an average family of five would be less than a fortnight every year; and that the work required for that purpose would not be the hard toil of the ancient slave, but work which would be agreeable to the physical forces of every healthy man and woman in the country.

It has been proved that by following the methods of intensive market-gardening—partly under glass—vegetables and fruit can be grown in such quantities that men could be provided with a rich vegetable food and a profusion of fruit, if they simply devoted to the task of growing them the hours which every one willingly devotes to work in the open air, after having spent most of his day in the factory, the mine, or the study. Provided, of course, that the production of food-stuffs should not be the work of the isolated individual, but the planned out and combined action of human groups.

It has also been proved—and those who care to verify it by themselves may easily do so by calculating the real expenditure for labour which was lately made in the building of workmen's houses by both private persons and municipalities—that under a proper combination of labour, twenty to twenty-four months of one man's work would be sufficient to secure forever, for a family of five, an apartment or a house provided with all the comforts which modern hygiene and taste could require.

And it has been demonstrated by actual experiment that, by adopting methods of education, advocated long since and partially applied here and there, it is most easy to convey to children of an average intelligence, before they have reached the age of fourteen or fifteen, a broad general comprehension of Nature, as well as of human societies; to familiarise their minds with sound methods of both scientific research and technical work; and inspire their hearts with a deep feeling of human solidarity and justice. And that it is extremely easy to convey during the next four or five years a reasoned, scientific knowledge of Nature's laws, as well as a knowledge, at once reasoned and practical, of the technical methods of satisfying man's material needs. Far from being inferior to the "specialised" young persons manufactured by our universities, the *complete* human being, trained to use his brain and his hands, excels them, on the contrary, in all respects, especially as an initiator and an inventor in both science and technics.

All this has been proved. It is an acquisition of the times we live in—an acquisition which has been won despite the innumerable obstacles always thrown in the way of every initiative mind. It has been won by the obscure tillers of the soil, from whose hands greedy States, landlords and middlemen snatch the fruit of their labour even before it is ripe; by obscure teachers who only too often fall crushed under the weight of Church, State, commercial competition, inertia of mind and prejudice.

And now, in the presence of all these conquests—what is the reality of things?

Nine-tenths of the whole population of grain-exporting countries like Russia, one-half of it in countries like France which live on home-grown food, work upon the land—most of them in the same way as the slaves of antiquity did, only to obtain a meager crop from a soil, and with a machinery which they cannot improve, because taxation, rent, and usury keep them always as near as possible at the margin of starvation. At the beginning of this century, whole populations plough with the same plough as their mediaeval ancestors, live in the same incertitude of the morrow, and are as carefully denied education; and they have, in claiming their portion of bread, to march with their children and wives against their own son's bayonets, as their grandfathers did a hundred and three hundred years ago.

In industrially developed countries, a couple of months' work, or even much less than that, would be sufficient to produce for a family a rich and varied vegetable and animal food. But the researches of Engel (at Berlin) and his many followers tell us that the workman's family has to spend one full half of its yearly earnings—that is, to give six months of labour, and often more, to provide its food. And what food! Is not bread and dripping the staple food of more than one-half of English children?

One month of work every year would be quite sufficient to provide the worker with a healthy dwelling. But it is from 25 to 40 per cent of his yearly earnings—that is, from three to five months of his working time every year—that he has to spend in order to get a dwelling, in most cases unhealthy and far too small; and this dwelling will never be his own, even though at the age of forty-five or fifty he is sure to be sent away from the factory, because the work that he used to do will by that time be accomplished by a machine and a child.

We all know that the child ought, at least, to be familiarised with the forces of Nature which some day he will have to utilise; that he ought to be prepared to keep pace in his life with the steady progress of science and technics; that he ought to study science and learn a trade. Every one will grant thus much; but what do we do? From the age of ten or even nine we send the child to push a coal-cart in a mine, or to bind, with a little monkey's agility, the two ends of threads broken in a spinning gin. From the age of thirteen we compel the girl—a child yet—to work as a "woman" at the weaving-loom, or to stew in the poisoned, over-heated air of a cotton-dressing factory, or, perhaps, to be poisoned in the death chambers of a Staffordshire pottery. As to those who have the relatively rare luck of receiving some more education, we crush their minds by useless overtime, we consciously deprive them of all possibility of themselves becoming producers; and under an educational system of which the motive is "profits," and the means "specialisation," we simply work to death the women teachers who take their educational duties in earnest. What floods of useless sufferings deluge every so-called civilised land in the world!

When we look back on ages past, and see there the same sufferings, we may say that perhaps then they were unavoidable on account of the ignorance which prevailed. But human genius, stimulated by our modern Renaissance, has already indicated new paths to follow.

For thousands of years in succession to grow one's food was the burden, almost the curse, of mankind. But it need be so no more. If you make yourselves the soil, and partly the temperature and the moisture which each crop requires, you will see that to grow the yearly food for a family, under rational conditions of culture, requires so little labour that it might almost be done as a mere change from other pursuits. If you return to the soil, and cooperate with your neighbours instead of erecting high walls to conceal yourself from their looks; if you utilise what experiment has already taught us, and call to your aid science and technical invention which never fail to answer to the call—look only at what they have done for warfare—you will be astonished at the facility with which you can bring a rich and varied food out of the soil. You will admire the amount of sound knowledge which your children will acquire by your side, the rapid growth of their intelligence, and the facility with which they will grasp the laws of Nature, animate and inanimate.

Have the factory and the workshop at the gates of your fields and gardens, and work in them. Not those large establishments, of course, in which huge masses of metals have to be dealt with and which are better placed at certain spots indicated by Nature, but the countless variety of workshops and factories which are required to satisfy the infinite diversity of tastes among civilised men. Not those factories in which children lose all the appearance of children in the atmosphere of an industrial hell, but those airy and hygienic, and consequently economical, factories in which human life is of more account than machinery and the making of extra profits, of which we already find a few samples here and there; factories and workshops into which men, women, and children will not be driven by hunger, but will be attracted by the desire of finding an activity suited to their tastes, and where, aided by the motor and the machine, they will choose the branch of activity which best suits their inclinations.

Let those factories and workshops be erected, not for making profits by selling shoddy or useless and noxious things to enslaved Africans, but to satisfy the unsatisfied needs of millions of Europeans. And again, you will be struck to see with what facility and in how short a time your needs of dress and of thousands of articles of luxury can be satisfied, when production is carried on for satisfying real needs rather than for satisfying shareholders by high profits or for pouring gold into the pockets of promoters and bogus directors. Very soon you will yourselves feel interested in that work, and you will have occasion to admire in your children their eager desire to become acquainted with Nature and its forces, their inquisitive inquiries as to the powers of machinery, and their rapidly developing inventive genius.

Such is the future—already possible, already realisable; such is the present—already condemned and about to disappear. And what prevents us from turning our backs to this present and from marching towards that future, or, at least, making the first steps towards it, is not the "failure of science," but first of all our crass cupidity—the cupidity of the man who killed the hen that was laying golden eggs—and then our laziness of mind—that mental cowardice so carefully nurtured in the past.

For centuries science and so-called practical wisdom have said to man: "It is good to be rich, to be able to satisfy, at least, your material needs; but the only means to be rich is to so train your mind and capacities as to be able to compel other men—slaves, serfs, or wage-earners—to make these riches for you. You have no choice. Either you must stand in the ranks of the peasants and the artisans who, whatsoever economists and moralists may promise them in the future, are now periodically doomed to starve after each bad crop or during their strikes, and to be shot down by their own sons the moment they lose patience. Or you must train your faculties so as to be a military commander of the masses, or to be accepted as one of the wheels of the governing machinery of the State, or to become a manager of men in commerce or industry." For many centuries there was no other choice, and men followed that advice, without finding in it happiness, either for themselves and their own children, or for those whom they pretended to preserve from worse misfortunes.

But modern knowledge has another issue to offer to thinking men. It tells them that in order to be rich they need not take the bread from the mouths of others; but that the more rational outcome would be a society in which men, with the work of their own hands and intelligence, and by the aid of the machinery already invented and to be invented, should themselves create all imaginable riches. Technics and science will not be lagging behind if production takes such a direction. Guided by observation, analysis, and experiment they will answer all possible demands. They will reduce the time which is necessary for producing wealth to any desired amount, so as to leave to every one as much leisure as he or she may ask for. They surely cannot guarantee happiness, because happiness depends as much, or even more, upon the individual himself as upon his surroundings. But they guarantee, at least, the happiness that can be found in the full and varied exercise of the different capacities of the human being, in work that need not be overwork, and in the consciousness that one is not endeavouring to base his own happiness upon the misery of others.

These are the horizons which the above inquiry opens to the unprejudiced mind.

A Note on the Texts

Many of Kropotkin's writings were first published in the anarchist newspaper *Le Révolté* or, in pamphlet form, by Freedom Press, both of which were founded by him. Translations of his writings have appeared in most European languages, and in Esperanto, Japanese, Chinese, and Hindustani as well. The following bibliographic notes include only those pamphlets, articles, and books represented in this collection.

"The Spirit of Revolt" was first published in *Le Révolté* in 1880. The first English translation appeared in England in *Commonweal* in 1892, and the edited version reprinted here was translated by Arnold Roller for Roger Baldwin's fine collection *Kropotkin's Revolutionary Pamphlets*. New York: Vanguard Press, 1927.

"An Appeal to the Young," one of the best-known and most influential of Kropotkin's pamphlets, was first published in *Le Révolté* in 1880. It was translated into English by H. M. Hyndman and published, in London, by Modern Press in 1885 and Freedom Press in 1899.

"Law and Authority" first appeared in *Le Révolté*, and was first published in English by Freedom Press (London) in 1886.

"Prisons and their Moral Influence on Prisoners," a speech delivered in Paris in 1877, was published in France in pamphlet form. The observations and ideas embodied therein are to be found in an expanded and more discursive form in Kropotkin's *In Russian and French Prisons*. The speech itself, perhaps the clearest, most concise, and radical statement concerning penology made by any writer, first appeared in English in 1927 in *Kropotkin's Revolutionary Pamphlets*.

Modern Science and Anarchism was first published in London in Russian (1901). English translations were published by the Social Science Club (Philadelphia) in 1903 and by Freedom Press in London in 1912. The version reprinted here is an edited one.

The Wage System was published in English by Freedom Press in 1889 and 1920, and a revised version was included in *The Conquest of Bread*.

"Anarchism" was written for the 11th edition of the *Encyclopædia Britannica*, published in 1910.

Memoirs of a Revolutionist was first published, in serial form, in

Atlantic Monthly (1898–1899), under the title "The Autobiography of a Revolutionist." Kropotkin added to the text for its publication in book form by Houghton Mifflin in 1899.

Mutual Aid first appeared as a series of articles in the British periodical *Nineteenth Century*. It was published as a book by Heinemann in London in 1902.

The Great French Revolution appeared in French and English editions in 1909. The publishers of the English translation were G. P. Putnam in New York and Heinemann in London.

The Conquest of Bread was first published in Paris in 1892. The first English edition was published in London by Chapman and Hall, 1906.

Fields, Factories, and Workshops, expanded from a series of articles in *Nineteenth Century* and the *Forum*, was first published by Houghton Mifflin in Boston in 1899. A revised edition was published by G. P. Putnam, New York, in 1913.

Peter Kropotkin was born in Moscow in 1842. A scion of the princes of Kiev, he was chosen by Nicholas I for the Corps of Pages, from which academy he was graduated, first in his class, in 1862. In search of strenuous and useful activity, he turned his back on the brilliant military career awaiting him to join the obscure Amur Cossack regiment in eastern Siberia. While a member of that regiment, he made a number of exploratory trips along the Amur and into unknown parts of Asiatic Russia, mapping the passes into China and developing the skill as an explorer that was to serve him so well in his subsequent activities as a geologist and geographer. Disgusted with the corruption and hopeless inefficiency of governmental, military, and prison administration in Siberia, he resigned his commission to pursue his scientific interests. His early Siberian expeditions as well as later trips to Sweden and Finland led to his speculations on the physical origins of the Urals and the glaciation of northern Europe and secured him the offer, in 1871, of the secretaryship of the Russian Geographic Society. His social conscience awakened, he refused the post in order to throw himself into the revolutionary activity to which he devoted himself until his death in 1921.

Emile Capouya was educated at Columbia College and Oriel College, Oxford. A youth spent in the working class as a seaman, longshoreman, and common laborer gave him the grounds for his quarrel with our present social arrangements, which his subsequent rise into the middle class—first as senior editor in various book publishing houses, and later as literary editor of *The Nation* and professor of English at Baruch College of the City University of New York—has not persuaded him to relinquish. Partly out of family tradition and partly from distaste for the authoritarian modes of political revolution he was led to Godwin, Proudhon, Thoreau, Bakunin, and Kropotkin. He has found that predilection no inconsiderable handicap to survival in a cash economy.

Keitha Tompkins, lexicographer and editor, has served as senior editor and consultant to a number of New York publishing firms. Her naturally anarchist temper she ascribes to her descent from that class of American yeomanry that has been a casualty of the

Industrial Revolution but that has maintained, in poverty and independence, its distrust of government and coercive regulation to the present day. In consequence, she sees in anarchist thought an intrinsically American spirit, for which she finds evidence from the beginnings of the republic down to the present time—and this not just in the persons of great exemplars, such as Thoreau, but in the manifest tendency of the American people. She is preparing an edition of the writings of John Jay Chapman, representing, in two volumes, the political and literary works of that remarkable man.